DIVINE KAIROS

A WINDOW IN TIME

Training Church Leaders in an Area Called Devil Country

by Kathy Tinklenberg

"Divine Kairos" is a Greek phrase meaning a privileged window in time.
See 1 Corinthians 7:26, 2 Corinthians 6:1-2.
Front Cover Background: Traditional lappa cloth worn as a wrap-around skirt and used to construct other clothing.
Cover design by KVB Art and Design

Biblical quotations are from the English Standard Version

ISBN 978-1-7336411-1-1

DIVINE KAIROS
A WINDOW IN TIME

For Laura & Michael, who were too young to remember
and are now old enough to understand

For our parents, who did not know all that happened
but supported us in every way

Let this be written for a future generation,
that a people not yet created may praise the LORD.
Psalm 102:18

Contents

With Appreciation

I am so grateful to our Heavenly Father for His call to go to Liberia, for His safekeeping while we lived there, and for all He has done in my life. I pray He will use this memoir to glorify His Name.

Perry, thank you for your encouragement, patience, and advice through my years of writing, and thank you for sharing your side of the story. I remember how you described the ministry to the Bassa church leaders as a "Divine Kairos", coming from the Greek word meaning a window in time, and that is where the title originated.

I am grateful to my parents, Kenneth and Josephine Plucker, for their comments when I would share segments of the book with them.

My friend Margaret read my first writings and encouraged me to continue what I had started. My parents-in-law, Virgil and Beverly Tinklenberg, Mrs. Etta Tuesink, Rev. John Van Ens, and Mrs. Lu Smith, who are all now in heaven, were other early readers who pressed me to keep writing.

With gratitude I mention my friends who read finished copies and made suggestions: Les Wells, Teresa Luders, Mary Lynn Bussell, Brad and Carol La Vine, Garry Pierce, and Carroll and Ellen Thorson. I also thank Rev. Dr. Abba Karnga, who read a final copy and gave his suggestions and approval.

Theological author Dr. Kent Hughes read an early copy, encouraged a completed book, and provided written comments. Madison McRae gave me much of her time and expertise. Her editing suggested improvements to match today's standards and exposed me to many needed changes. Northwest Christian Writers Conferences were filled with help and advice.

It was a pleasure to work with Kendra Vanden Berg, KVB Art and Design, who created the cover.

Mission Prayer Card

Sent to family, friends and supporting churches.

PERRY AND KATHY TINKLENBERG

Rev. Perry and Kathy Tinklenberg are stationed at the Somah Extension in Grand Bassa County, Liberia. Perry is one of the Theological Education by Extension (TEE) instructors sent by Christian Reformed World Missions to teach church leaders of the many independent Bassa churches. These leaders are often illiterate, so a tape ministry is used to aid the instruction. Each student receives two cassettes weekly at the seminar sessions and they listen to them throughout the week in preparation for the next class discussion.

Perry received a Master of Divinity degree from Calvin Theological Seminary, where he learned of this unique mission work from a missionary on home service. Their interest peaked when Perry and Kathy began a one-year seminary internship in Liberia. During that time Perry acquired the land for the Somah Extension and started one TEE class with 27 church leaders.

Perry and Kathy are excited about their return to Liberia and starting more classes in other areas. They look forward to the unique word and deed ministry among the Bassa people to bring about the Kingdom of God and reclaim the creation in the name of Jesus Christ. It is for this work that they request your prayers.

Maps
Sent to Family

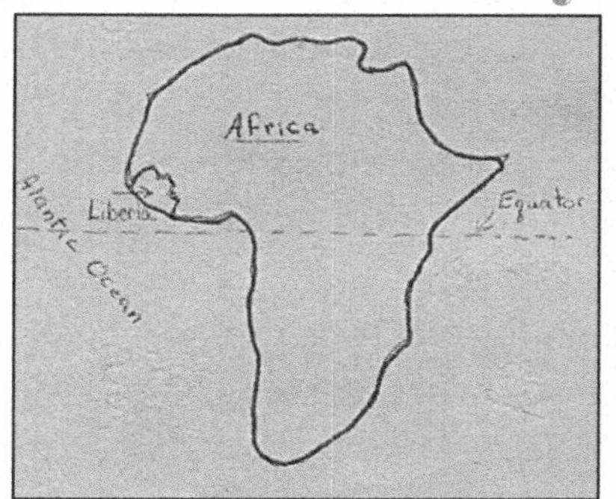

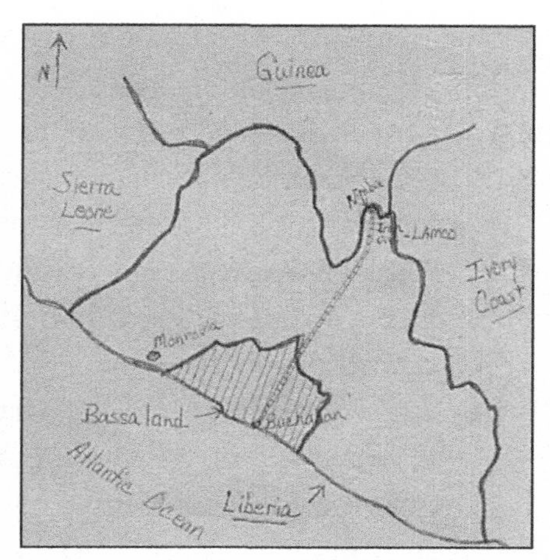

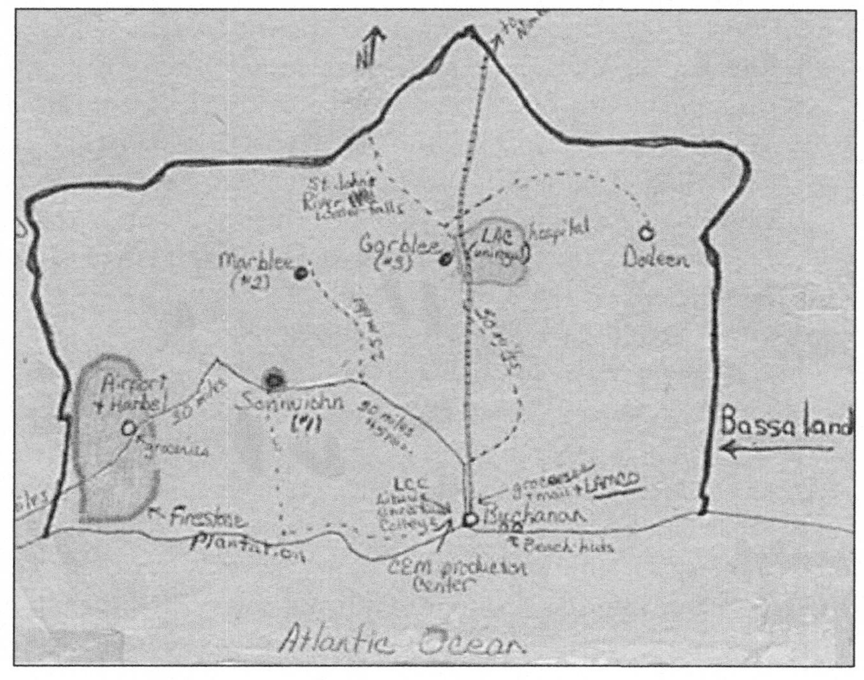

Key

——	Black top highway	●	Mission stations
- - - -	Dirt or Gravel road	o	City or town
▥▥▥	Railroad	▇	Rubber plantations

Abbreviations

AIC African Independent Churches are African initiated churches independently started in Africa by Africans and not by missionaries from another continent. They have their own music and customs.

BBC British Broadcasting Corporation, radio station commonly listened to by missionaries. It had straight forward news of the 3rd world countries.

BMA Bassa Ministerial Association, an organization of Bassa pastors and church leaders, which met in Buchanan for mutual encouragement and for the completion of projects to better the Bassa churches overall.

CEFL Christian Education Foundation of Liberia was founded in 1968. Membership included Bassa church leaders from many different denominations working together to provide Christian education to the Bassa people in the form of Liberia Christian High School, Christian College and TEE. A further goal was a Bassa radio station. Christian Reformed missionaries were seconded to this organization. Rev. Abba Karnga continues to be the head of this foundation.

CEM Christian Extension Ministry, organization of CRWM missionaries and Liberian national Christian leaders offering TEE, Agriculture, Health, Literacy classes, Bible translation and scholarship to the Bassa people.

CHAL Christian Health Association of Liberia, provided resources for Christian health workers and maintained a relationship with Liberia's Health Department.

CRC Christian Reformed Church, we are members of this denomination and Perry is an ordained CRC Minister of the Word.

CRML Christian Reformed Mission in Liberia, combined the Christian Reformed mission endeavors to the Bassa and Via people.

CRWM Christian Reformed World Missions, our sending organization, was in Grand Rapids, MI. Renamed as Resonate Global Missions.

CRWRC Christian Reformed World Relief Committee, for a short time some CRWRC families lived in Monrovia, now World Renew.

ELWA "Eternal Love Winning Africa", a Sudan Interior Mission project centering around their Christian radio station near the capital city of Monrovia which broadcast over the vast, northern region of Africa reaching even the Middle East. A large community of missionaries lived there on a picturesque beach to support the radio station and they operated a small hospital where services were offered to missionaries as well as the public. Our daughter Laura was born there.

IVCF or IV Inter-Varsity Christian Fellowship, an organization based in colleges which features inductive Bible Study, shaping college students for Christian living, Urbana Missionary Convention every three years to name a few. Perry and I met at an IV picnic at the University of South Dakota. Perry was the president of the local chapter for two years and we both led inductive Bible study groups on campus.

LAC Liberia Agricultural Company located near Number 3, Grand Bassa County harvested latex from rubber trees for Uniroyal Rubber Company. Offered hospital care, a grocery store, a golf course and a club with swimming pool and restaurant set upon a high hill.

LAMCO-JV Liberia Agricultural Mining Company Joint Venture run by a Swedish company. A huge operation which mined the world's richest iron ore in the northern mountains of Liberia, transported +it via railroad, and shipped it out of the country through their port in Buchanan. The infra-structure included a hospital where our son Michael was born, a post office where we received mail, a grocery store, a few restaurants, and many homes.

LIM Liberia Inland Mission worked in Liberia for many years. In the early years an airplane was required to reach their mission stations. One station was located near Bassa Government Compound Number 3.

TEE Theological Education by Extension, classes taught by CRC missionaries to Bassa church leaders in different localities, this term was also used by other mission agencies teaching theology

List of Ants

As requested by Laura

Carpenter Ants – red medium sized ants that weave homes in the leaves of trees. Used as a metaphor for Bassa churches to work together, and in CEFL's motto: Except Red Ants come together, they cannot build the nest.

Driver Ants – black medium sized ants that live in large colonies under the ground, often in abandoned termite hills. They travel in columns, build miniature bridges with their own bodies, and forage for food by invading whatever comes in their path, even homes. The African genus is called *Dorylus.*

Red Ants or Fire Ants – small red ants that were transplanted from South America via ships. They first invaded the port of Buchanan and continued to spread up country. They had the nasty habit of biting people causing a strong sting that lingered for some time. If any crumbs of food were left in a car, there was a chance the red ants would invade the vehicle.

Stink Ants – large black ants that are seen meandering around. If they are disturbed, they can send off a strong odor.

Sugar Ants – tiny ants that would seek out sweets or oil in the kitchen, more of a nuisance than anything else and caused a tickling sensation if they crawled on you.

Termites – not actually ants, but ant like. The Bassa called them "bug-a-bug". They lived in termite hills in the bush and were a pest that could eat their way through the supporting structure of buildings. When building a home, the Bassa people broke their hills down, mixed the dirt with water, and then packed the mud around poles to make the sides of houses.

Similar Stories to Ponder

China - One of those who heard Hudson preach at the Bridge Street Chapel was Ni Yongfa, a Ningbo cotton dealer and leader of a reformed Buddhist sect which would have nothing to do with idolatry and was searching for truth. At the end of Hudson's sermon, Ni stood in his place and turned to address the audience.

"I have long searched for the truth as my father did before me. I have traveled far, but I haven't found it. I found no rest in Confucianism, Buddhism or Daoism, but I do find rest in what I have heard tonight. From now on I believe in Jesus."

Ni took Hudson Taylor to a meeting of the sect he had formerly led and was allowed to explain the reasons for his change of faith. Taylor was impressed with the clarity and power with which he spoke. Another member of the group was converted and both he and Ni were baptized.

"How long has the gospel been known in England?" Ni asked Hudson Taylor.

"For several hundred years," replied an embarrassed Hudson Taylor vaguely.

"What!" exclaimed Ni. "And you have only now come to preach it to us? My father sought after the truth for more than twenty years and died without finding it. Why didn't you come sooner?"

It was a difficult question to answer.[1]

~~~

The Mobobowa people are considered to be the oldest inhabitants of The Philippines. They are a nomadic hunting and gathering tribe. They are animists, which means they believe everything is animated by spirits and much of life is consumed with appeasing the spirits and creating favor with the spirits by making blood sacrifices.

They have a belief system that one day a savior will come, and that savior will put an end to their need of making blood sacrifices for atonement for the sins of the people in the community.

When we met this old lady, we had the privilege of telling her the Savior had come. "He's come?" she said, "What's his name?"

"His name is Jesus," we told her.

"Jesus? When did he come?"

We said, "Jesus came 2,000 years ago."

"What?" she said, "What? Do you mean to tell me he came 2,000 years ago and no one bothered to come up the mountain to tell us?"

That question has been reverberating in our minds ever since. Why indeed has no one gone up the mountain or gone to all the other people groups in the world to tell them that the Savior has come?[2]
~~~

Preface

There was only a vague sense of what might lie ahead. We had no concept of the privilege handed to us as missionaries to Liberia. There was no way to understand how vividly the scriptures would come to life as we lived and worked in a third world country. Although we trusted God and knew He would work in wonderful ways, we had no idea how our faith would grow or how it would feel to experience untold wonders. The depths to which our spirits would plummet were equally a mystery to us.

Laura and Michael, this book was started for you. Even though we lived together for 18 years as you were growing up, many of these stories have lain dormant, while some of them you have heard repeatedly. Perhaps they were not shared with you because they happened in a world far away. Our family's return to the States was heart wrenching, so recalling Liberia brought only agony coupled with a longing to return. In some ways, it was better to not look back too often.

Many of these stories have gone untold because we didn't want to emphasize God's work in our lives, but these are our family's stories, and so they are a part of you. Although you did not choose to serve as missionaries, you lived under the blessing of "the call", which your father and I received to serve the Bassa people and help them realize their dreams. You also personally paid a price for our family's great privilege. Thank you for serving so willingly with us in your early childhoods and for your eagerness to always return "home". Here is the long past-due account of our lives in Liberia.

To our parents: You too have not heard some of the things relayed here. When our children left our home and one of them eventually became a missionary, we experienced a glimpse of the sacrifice you made as we followed God's call to Liberia. We always knew you supported us and were proud of us. Thank you for concealing your anxieties, which may have caused us to reconsider going to Africa. We are grateful, because God called us, and Liberia was where we needed to be during the '80's. The sacrifices each of you made by visiting us twice was not only crucial to our wellbeing, but also for your understanding of our lives and work there. Thank you to our mothers, Josephine and Beverly, for keeping most of our letters and other documents. They have been an invaluable resource as I record our experiences. Most of all - thank you to our parents for telling us about Jesus, our Savior, raising us in Christian homes, taking us to church, and nurturing our faith.

Christian Reformed World Missions (CRWM) was eager for Perry and me join the team of young missionaries who had been ministering to the Bassa people for a couple of years. The mission agency even offered us an actual missionary position, instead of a seminary internship while Perry was a student at Calvin Theological Seminary. We clearly understood the mission's objective was to entice us to consider long term missionary service. The appointment would allow for full medical insurance and a higher pay scale than typical seminary interns received. Our seminary colleagues envied the agreement we felt called to make with CRWM. However, it was not by any means the meager employment package that drew us initially to Liberia. It was solely the fact that we could not deny our Lord was calling us to the specific work of training indigenous pastors. We were soon to discover the privilege would present us with serious responsibilities and a certain amount of heartache.

When the staff at CRWM interviewed us for the position in 1980, they asked when we had first considered being missionaries. Perry answered that for him it had been several years prior, during an Inter Varsity Christian Fellowship (IVCF) mission trip to Guatemala. How well I remembered his serious questions to me when he returned to the States. He asked if I would be open to God calling us to possibly work in missions. At the time we were engaged to be married and I was relieved he wasn't telling me something horrible, like we should break our engagement. His question, in my mind, was simple to answer. Of course, I was open to God calling us to do anything for Him, including missionary service. To follow God's calling was my sole desire. How comforting to know that my intended life partner desired to be open to the possibility of missions. If I had answered Perry's questions negatively, saying I could not consider missions, his intention had been to postpone the wedding. That is how serious he was about seeking God's will for our lives.

Rev. Harold DeGroot and Rev. John Van Ens, being veteran missionaries, had whetted our appetites for missions early in our relationship. We were also influenced at the Urbana '76 Missionary Conference sponsored by IVCF, where one of the speakers really sparked our attention. He was Luis Palau, a South American evangelist, who told the audience that the era of missionaries planting churches was nearly over. Instead missionaries should consider educating national church leaders, who would in turn make a huge impact in their communities. I was also touched by the message Dr. Helen Roseveare delivered concerning her experiences in Africa. She built a hospital in the Congo, which was later taken over by rebels who tortured her. (Her book is entitled "Give Me this Mountain".)

The day of our interview at the mission headquarters, I vividly remembered God calling me to missions when I was a three-year-old in

Sunday School. A memory came to me of sitting on a bench at a low table in the basement kitchen of the old Reformed Church in Chancellor, SD. We had just heard a missionary speak, but that is not the part I remembered. It was afterwards when the teacher prayed with us. I remember her asking God to let one of the children in the class become a missionary. As she prayed, I clearly felt God give me the desire to be a missionary, and I was happy and excited, but then selfishness and greed rushed in. I wanted to be the one God called and selfishly hoped it would not be some of the other children. My young conscience had been properly trained; I knew God would not be pleased with my attitude. The sin of pride and selfishness is divisive even in the heart of a three-year-old. At that moment of God's calling, my immature heart harbored the ugliness of sin and clouded the joy that comes from sensing God's will and walking in it. How appropriate that one of my first memories includes that of sin, for sin is part of the human experience; yet God sent Jesus through His gracious kindness to save us from its curse.

The memory of who that teacher might have been haunted me for years. I asked several women in my childhood church if they had been my preschool teacher, but each denied teaching that class. Finally, the mystery was solved when a former pastor's wife, Mrs. Etta Tuesink (Ray), and her family visited our Spokane home. We discovered she had taught that Sunday School class and was delighted to hear my recollections. How thankful I am that my parents faithfully took me to Sunday School. It was through their obedience and the prayer of the Sunday School teacher that God gently created in me a lifelong excitement for missions and anticipation for the call He had prepared for us to do.

As I look back, I can see other ways God prepared me for mission life. Growing up on a farm I learned to exist without friends close by, to prepare live chickens for cooking, and to survive without frequent trips to the grocery store. When our family's well became contaminated and we were without water on the farm, I learned from my mother's water conservation and ingenuity, which I would later have to use. When my father was away, she demonstrated bravery and resourcefulness. These lessons were vitally important for my adaptation to solitary living in remote Africa.

God prepared me for missionary life through many experiences. My pastor was on fire for the Lord and prayed with me asking God to fully heal my heart, diseased with rheumatic fever. God granted his prayer and I was able to live a full life! God also showed me how He would preserve my faith and even cause it to thrive in the hostile environment of high school. Through my church, He developed within me an implicit love for studying God's Word and to a greater extent in college through Inter

Varsity Christian Fellowship. I received important and useful training in health care at the University of South Dakota as I studied health science and majored in dental hygiene.

I hope we are a little wiser and closer to our Savior after our years in Liberia. It would be to our shame to live among the Bassa people as missionaries and not experience a closer walk with Jesus. Many people experience life changing incidents that help mature their faith and walk with the Lord. Our experiences as missionaries in Liberia had that effect on us. Not that we had reached maturity at the conclusion of ten years as missionaries, nor would we claim to have fully reached it now; but our years with the Bassa people were a unique part of the process the Lord brought us through.

The following pages are not a record of what we did, but what the Lord did through us. He called us to go, gave us the desire to serve Him, and worked through us to bless the Bassa people.

We experienced a *Divine Kairos!* A window in time – granted to fulfill the mission God had prepared in advance and called us to do. What an honor and privilege to be called to go on His behalf and what a responsibility to be His ambassadors to the Bassa, a people He had called to Himself.

To God be the Glory,
Kathy Tinklenberg
2018

I

Arrival

As thick, humid air penetrated its way through the airplane, we waited anxiously for our first steps on African soil and our new life as missionaries.

Throughout the flight anticipation rose with a growing awareness that we were entering a much different world than we had left behind. We faced this realization when we arrived at the waiting area in JFK Airport. African women were dressed in brightly colored lappa suits, accented with flamboyantly tied head wraps, and their rapid speech in indiscernible dialects suddenly closed us out.

Awareness we were leaving our homeland symbolically mounted as we gazed out the jet window leaving the Statue of Liberty quickly behind. A sickening feeling welled up in my stomach and questions entered my mind: What have we done? Are we being wise? Had God really called us to go to Africa? Prayer calmed me and I recalled God's strong call for us to go to the Bassa people.

Why had we been given such a strange, strong urge to leave our country and family behind and travel so far from everyone we held dear? What would God require of us in a distant land and what did He intend to teach us? How could we possibly make a difference for a people whose life expectancy was roughly 40 years of age, infant mortality was high, literacy rate was only 20 percent, and the annual per capita income was estimated around $3 a day?

During the long voyage aboard a packed Pan Am flight, I renewed my promise to the Lord to go wherever He called us to go. The popular Maranatha! Music song "Make Me a Servant" played repeatedly in my mind as I gazed out the window at the night sky. I silently sang that song under my breath as we crossed the Atlantic Ocean below the stars, and in the years to come it would play again and again on my mind and often fill my heart.

Make me a servant, humble and meek,
Lord let me lift up those who are weak
And may the prayer of my heart always be:
Make me a servant, Make me a servant,
Make me a servant today.[3]

As we approached Robertsfield International Airport, a vast sea of green became miniature palm trees and dense foliage. No large city was in sight only a building near the runway below. The airplane stopped some distance from the terminal, and we watched as a stairway mounted on a pickup was backed up to our plane's door.

An indescribable wave of humidity and heat struck us squarely as we neared the exit. Wishing those ahead would hurry, I fought off an irresistible urge to rip off my panty hose. Passengers pulled out large suitcases masquerading as carry-ons, and everyone was in a hurry to leave the plane.

Descending the steps to the tarmac, I gripped my stylish straw hat and welcomed a light breeze in the intense heat and humidity. We followed fellow travelers hurriedly walking to a large run-down terminal. Its exterior walls were growing mold and crying out for fresh paint.

People quickly ascended some stairs to a second-floor door, but we were distracted by some white folks waving from the observation balcony and yelling our names. Assuming they were missionaries who had come to pick us up, we went to greet them, but they quickly pointed us toward the same stairs and doorway.

We climbed the steps and entered the immigration room, only to be introduced to an even higher level of smoldering heat. The room appeared to be air-conditioned - it was not, and I do not recall the room was ever cool when we arrived.

Here we met the foreign world of opportunists speaking Liberian

English. A young Liberian man eagerly approached us, and we struggled to understand that he was offering his assistance through customs. It was unclear as to whether this would be to our advantage. But we took the chance and with the aid of our able assistant, we managed to discern the protocol of entry into the country receiving the appropriate stamps in our passports.

A large customs room was next. It was filled with low sturdy tables where our luggage would be checked. The officials opened all our duffel bags and began to rummage through them, searching for any items requiring duty payment.

The head of Christian Reformed Missions in Liberia (CRML), made his way into the noisy area to assist us while our baggage was inspected. Larry had a soft voice and spoke respectfully to the officials, while giving us a warm handshake and welcome. The rigors of the procedure were trying, and we forced ourselves to remain patient and calm.

As we approached customs inspection for the first time, we did not know what to expect. Our wonder and excitement were balanced with the shock of inexperience. I was surprised to witness a female inspector pilfering a package of travel tissues, but it seemed unnecessary to point this out to other officials in the room. In years to come, the stress of going through customs was known to bring veteran missionary wives to tears as every personal item was scrutinized.

As we exited the room, a barrage of young men seemed to be yelling at us. Larry stepped in and hired the eager porters to haul our heavy duffel bags to the car. We then met Larry's wife, Ann and their children, Erica–six, Joel–four, and five-month-old baby Anna. Margaret, the mission health care instructor, was there as well. The ladies were dressed in a strange style of frumpy clothes, and I noted their worn sandals and muddy feet, but their gracious welcomes were inviting.

Stepping outside where the rain had begun to fall, sidewalk vendors selling candies, cigarettes, and magazines in front of the airport called for our attention. Small yellow run-down taxis dashed around honking their horns trying to entice patrons. Confusion surrounded us as we were hustled for business.

We followed the missionaries to the parking lot and a Peugeot station wagon splattered with orange mud. The porters struggled with our heavy duffel bags and quickly loaded them in the back of the car. Meanwhile, other young men attempted to convince us to pay them for services we had neither requested, nor received.

Gazing out the car window as we drove away, I was struck with the realization that we were indeed entering a new realm of God's creation. People walked along the side of the road and there was no shoulder, so our car came dangerously close to them. Some carried loads on their heads, while bicycles dashed between the traffic blowing little horns on the handlebars.

Further up the road I became entranced by the beautiful, lush, overgrown foliage contrasted with the deep orange soil, and I marveled at God's ingenuity with creation. It appeared the jungle was so thick it would be impenetrable. Rainfall had saturated the ground, and palm trees towered above swaying in the breeze and shaking off the heavy August rain.

In the downpour the windshield wipers beat out a frantic rhythm. My new colleagues were eager to get acquainted, while I could hardly keep myself from being distracted with the fascinating countryside passing my window. They asked what my first impression was, and I hastily answered that there was a foul smell in the air, like mildew. This comment drew laughter from the veterans, and I determined to not be so spontaneous with my comments in the future.

Our destination and temporary home for the next two weeks was nearly two hours from the airport. We traveled for some time on a paved stretch of road, passing over an old rusty bridge perched high above a rushing river and swerving to avoid an alarming number of large, deep potholes.

We came to a thin rope stretched across the two-lane road and it brought us to a stop. The missionaries explained it was a police gate. A police officer questioned Larry as to our reason for travel and where we were going.

Perry and I had been briefed and told to not say anything. We were to let Larry and the others do all the talking. After a brief dialog, we traveled on, while the seasoned missionaries gave thanks to God for not being asked to open our bags obviously stowed in the back of the station wagon.

A comment then surfaced that we were driving through Devil Country, known for its activity with the country devils and society business. Perry and I wanted to know more, but the others responded it was a long and complicated subject. Unknown to any of us, this was the area God would assign to Perry and me in the future. We would live nearby for eight years to train church leaders with God's Word.

The rain subsided and we traveled on for some distance with condensation covering the rainy windows and pleasant conversation to get acquainted. Slowing only slightly, Larry turned to the left at mile marker #17. We began to travel north on a dirt, sometimes graveled road. It sported an amazing array of ruts, potholes, twists, and turns. We climbed small steep hills that jolted our stomachs going over the top and drove over culverts with swift flowing streams below. We traveled on for twelve nauseating miles, while the children happily serenaded us.

Along the heavily jungled roadside, people seemed to be walking great distances from houses or villages. I wondered where they were going. The women's skirts were brightly colored fabric wrapped around their waist. They also wore blouses and head ties. Sometimes there was a baby riding on its mother's back, secured with a wide band of fabric. Little feet stuck out the side and the head of a napping baby often bobbed in the back. The men wore trousers or shorts, shirts, and often some type of hat. It seemed a little strange to me that some of them wore stocking hats, and I noted it was not uncommon for people to be without shoes as they walked along the road.

Some were carrying huge loads on their heads. When they turned to look at us, their whole bundle would turn in slow motion, creating a fascinating sight. Some people walking along the roadside would stretch out their arm and wave their fingers in a downward motion. That was the Liberian way of showing they wanted to hitch a ride. The missionaries explained they usually stopped and gave people a lift, but the Peugeot was too full that day.

I noted villages had square homes the color of the ground and they were in close proximity. There were a variety of roof coverings ranging from thatch to corrugated metal, and the homes had small square windows with wooden shutters. Often bright colors were used to paint the shutters with large geometric designs. Some of the homes even had interesting paintings on them, while others were painted completely white or left mud colored.

There were also structures with only roofs supported by four large corner poles, sometimes fires burned under these shelters and people seemed to gather there. We would soon discover these were kitchen areas, the center of Bassa life.

Bouncing over the rough roads while staring out the window brought me to a sickening point, and I fought off nausea. Tired from many hours of travel, little sleep on the night flight, and prone to car sickness, the final leg of our journey began to take its toll. I wanted nothing more than to get out of the packed car with steamed over windows.

2

Adjustments

A small sign announcing, "CR Mission" gave me anticipation of relief from the nauseating trip. Larry swung a left-hand turn and proceeded down a two-lane dirt path. There were only trees and jungle in sight, but at the end of the short driveway was a beautifully cleared area with palm trees hovering over flowering bushes and a green lawn.

Here was the hub of the Christian Reformed work for the Bassa people. On the grounds were two homes built by a short-term volunteer builder. Missionaries had added a guest house and storage shed with an attached car port.

The parcel of land had been loaned to our mission for 99 years by officials at the nearby Government Compound Number 2 in Grand Bassa County. Therefore, the mission station had been appropriately and affectionately named "Number 2". It was also known by its Bassa name, Marblee.

A second mission station, where Don and Marty lived, was located some distance away. Not surprisingly it was called "Number 3", since it was located near the Government Compound Number 3. The Bassa called that area Gorblee.

Grand Bassa County was divided into five legislative districts. Rather than assign tribal names to the areas, which might cause jealousy and tension among the people, the government had given numerical designations. The CR mission followed suit in naming its mission stations.

Both mission residences and the guest house at Number 2 looked like the larger Bassa homes. It was explained they were constructed of the same termite mud. However, the mission's windows were larger than most Bassa had. Living in a tropical area, it was not necessary to have glass in the windows. There were only screens, which a few Bassa homes had. Heavy wooden shutters, typical for both Bassa and missionary homes, could be closed when the houses were vacant or in the case of high winds and rain. The Bassa closed their wooden shutters tight each night, but the missionaries typically left them open for ventilation.

The entrance to these missionary homes was only a simple screen door with a wood frame. It opened into a large screened-in room located in the center of the house, called the "breeze-way". The distinct sound of the screen door drew me back to my childhood home as the spring stretched and reverberated when the door slapped shut. This familiar sound quickly meant "home" to me, and somehow gave me a sense of connection with my past and extended family left behind.

Ann had decorated her home's breezeway, or common receiving area, in an attractive way with ornate African baskets hanging on the walls, and a locally woven hammock in one corner. Uncomfortable chairs from the local market with a type of woven wicker seat were arranged around a large homemade table. Strung across the breezeway were several clotheslines complete with clothes pins. I wondered why Ann would have clotheslines in her house. After a few days of rainy season, I was left with little doubt of their usefulness.

The breezeway joined two sections of the one-story mission house. The kitchen, pantry, and living room were through a door on the right. A door on the left led to three bedrooms and a bathroom.

We were shown to a nice sized bedroom at Larry and Ann's home, which their children, Erica and Joel normally occupied. Their baby, Anna, had a nursery in the third smaller bedroom.

As was the case for all the CR missionary homes in Liberia, the floors and interior walls had a cement finish. The bathroom looked curiously modern with a flush toilet, sink, and shower area. Larry had assembled a clever towel rack with wide, varnished bamboo poles in the hope that the towels would dry in the humid climate.

The living room furniture was obviously homemade, but attractive, serviceable, and comfortable. Beautiful African baskets, curtains, a bookshelf, and desk also graced Ann's living room.

Kitchen cupboards were made from plywood and painted white, but there were no upper cupboards mounted to the wall. This was because bush poles within the wall might not support the weight of hanging cupboards.

A small bottle gas stove stood nearby, and a modest sized kerosene refrigerator answered the questionable scent of fuel my finicky nose was tracking. A stainless-steel sink with an attached drainage board was mounted in the countertop, and just above it was a large window with view of the mission property. Off the kitchen was a large walk-in pantry lined with shelves from floor to ceiling, stacked with supplies in bug and humidity proof containers.

Heavy rain began to make a racket on the aluminum roof, while across the yard a beam of sun shone through. Under an umbrella Mark and Pat, carrying Marie, their ten-month-old baby, quickly crossed the mission grounds and called out, "Bauk, bauk" before entering the house.

I asked why they had said, "Bauk, bauk" wondering if it meant "hello". Everyone laughed saying it meant, "Knock, knock". The Bassa said, "Bauk, bauk" instead of knocking on a door. Since their houses were made from termite mud, there was no sound if you knocked on it. While living there we would have to begin to adapt to the culture and say, "Bauk, bauk", instead of "knock, knock".

Mark and Pat lived a short distance away in the small two-bedroom guest house, a temporary home for them while they did language and culture study. They anticipated moving to Buchanan, the second largest city in Liberia, where a mission station was slated to be built.

Having recently arrived on the field eight months earlier, they were obviously excited to meet us, and easily won us over with their glowing smiles and affable personalities. Not yet understanding the depths of solitude missionaries endure, nor the assumed comradery, I was somewhat taken back by their eager friendliness to people they didn't know.

Equally surprising was their clothing and bare feet. Pat wore a wild tie

Perry inspects the blossom of an immature bunch of bananas on our day of arrival.

dye t-shirt and wrap-around skirt, a lost art I had dismissed to the hippy era. Mark wore a geometrically designed African shirt, which he must have forgotten to tuck in, since at that time men tucked in their shirts. They also wore flip flops and their feet were noticeably tanned and muddied.

Although they appeared somewhat frumpy at first observation, I later realized this was typical attire for missionaries and similar to clothing styles worn by the Bassa people. I soon found myself in similar, serviceable clothing and shoes. Trying to make favorable first impressions, I would later remember to dress in "American" clothes when we went to the airport to get people visiting Liberia for the first-time.

After Mark and Pat returned to their home, I began to feel an unaccustomed tiredness from jet lag. A heavy feeling came over me making me question the wisdom of going to a foreign country to live with people we didn't know - both missionaries and Liberians. Furthermore, the great distance between us and the familiarity of the United States began to weigh on me. While Ann cared for her baby, I found myself alone and noted how oppressive the dank heaviness of the moist air felt.

As I stood in the middle of the breezeway, unsure of what to do, I realized everything around me was different. The songs of the birds, the smells of mold and kerosene, new words, and new personal relationships

- everything was strange and uncertain. My throat began to tighten, and tears stung my eyes with homesickness, not only for home, but even more for my culture, language, and nation.

Feeling the need to be near my husband and seeking some fresh air, I stepped through the squeaky screen door, only to add oppressive heat to my melancholy. Some rays of the sun were managing to beat through the high humidity with an eerie glow, and moisture was visibly rising from the ground. It seemed the heavy liquid air needed to part as I walked.

We had done our research and knew the average temperature would range from 81 to 90 degrees, but I didn't know it would feel so oppressive coupled with high humidity of 90% and above. I felt the need to escape, but took a deep breath and quickly deflected feelings of entrapment.

A whispered prayer formed on my lips for the Lord to calm me as I brushed tears away. I heard a strange noise above me and looking up I noticed two palm trees swaying against the blue sky, while others around them stood still. Their leaves were making a type of swishing noise and I thought they looked as though they were waving to get my attention. They drew my eyes toward the heavens, and I recited, *Where does my help come from? My help comes from the LORD, the maker of heaven and earth,* Psalm 121:2. At that point, I felt God renew the hope of happy, light hearted times ahead, and I resolved to not give way to fear and doubt, but to remember God's definite call leading us there.

Joining the men outside, I grabbed Perry's hand out of habit, but also for comfort. Larry gave us a brief tour of the mission storage shed which housed the cherished generator and contained barrels of gasoline, kerosene, and propane. Since the mission vehicles were heavily used for the teaching programs and gas stations were some distance away it was necessary to stockpile fuel. We were also informed of occasional national shortages of these commodities, and therefore it was wise to have surplus available.

Near the storage shed, Larry had a rabbit project to supplement protein in their diet. He hoped the Bassa people would someday raise their own rabbits. He was proud of the hutches he had built. They were curiously high off the ground and the legs of the cages stood in large cans of oil.

He explained the height was necessary, due to a problem of ants invading the cages. Periodically he had to clear spider webs and leaves from the legs, since the ants would use them as a bridge to reach the rabbits. It seemed he was being overly protective of his little furry friends, but that was before I had experienced the destructiveness of the notorious driver ants.

He pointed out the gorgeously broad-leafed banana plants growing behind the rabbit cages, thriving on rabbit droppings and plant compost. A huge bunch of green bananas hung from a broad stalk with a large cone shaped pink flower at the end.

I asked how the bananas could be harvested, since they were growing so high off the ground. Larry explained that when the green fruit began to ripen the stalk was cut at the base with a cutlass, and the large bunch was harvested all at once. A second person was required to catch the stalk and avoid bruising the bananas. Banana plants are classified in the grass family, so when the main stalk was cut down a secondary shoot would quickly grow to produce another bunch.

There were some Bassa men close by observing us and we had the pleasure of meeting them. They were workers on the mission grounds and were laboriously cutting the grass by swinging "L" shaped metal tools, called "whippers".

I wondered if there wasn't an easier, quicker way to cut the grass. Considering the periodic gas shortages, I thought perhaps the old-style push mower could be utilized and the grass cut much quicker. Little did I know that the men held coveted jobs, which supported their extended families.

They greeted us in Bassa, "Moh way" and Larry tried to help us pronounce our first Bassa words in response, "Aã Moh way". It appeared they were very kind in their acceptance of our replies. They asked a few other questions while Larry translated for us.

Ann was watching from her kitchen window and later explained the men had spoken part of the conversation in Liberian English. I was shocked, but she replied that by listening carefully we would soon understand the dialect. She said it was easy to learn and would be the quickest way for us to begin communicating with most Bassa people.

English is the official language of the country, but Liberian English proved to be a heavily accented dialect that dropped most final consonants of words with bits of British English thrown in. Ann was right too. It was a means for quickly learning to carry on a conversation with most Bassa people.

At first, I was put off by broken grammatical rules, and thought I would never speak English in that manner. However, after a short time, the ease and fun of conversing with people won out over the difficultly of learning the complex Bassa language.

Liberians enjoy a special snap-handshake and our first day in the country was the perfect time to learn it. The mission grounds keepers taught us how. First a firm shake was given in the traditional western manner, but it was finished in an unusual way. Using a fluid motion, the grasp was released while applying pressure on the other person's longest finger resulting in an audible snap-off each other's finger. The louder the snap - the more heartfelt the relationship. At times the snap would not result, perhaps due to clumsiness. In those cases, the handshake was repeated to establish sincere good will.

Tradition said this custom started because it contrasted with the terrible history of slave traders grabbing people while shaking hands. They would pull them into slavery and not let them go. The snap-off symbolized the good will of setting each other free.

I thought I would get to practice the fun handshake after Perry. Instead, I was told that women did not often shake hands with a man, nor did they use the snap-handshake. The ladies instead gave a light touch with an open hand, especially when shaking the hand of a man. Here too the sad history of procuring slaves affected the handshake. The light quick touch would not allow the slave traders to grab hold of the women.

Christians added yet another element to their Liberian snap. After the firm handshake, they would continue through by grasping each other's wrists signifying unity. It was then followed by the release of a friendly snap-off.

I eventually learned the snap that day with the mission workers but was warned of the taboo of a woman shaking hands with a man. It was not often that I had the privilege to use the snap. But in years to come I would enjoy using it at special times with pastors whom my husband taught or with his coworkers.

That first day Ann told us several other essential cultural changes we'd need to make. We had to get used to how to talk to people. She said we must be careful not to look people in the eye when talking to them. It was far too personal and would make some people fearful we were trying to steal their soul.

It took a real conscious effort to get used to this on my part and it felt rude, however we had to do it. Unfortunately, I think it became a permanent habit for me. Returning to the States, I have found myself in the habit of not looking straight on at people. Although I try, it has been difficult to resume my culture's habit of looking people in the eye.

Ann observed me taking my husband's hand and cautioned that holding hands in public was considered obscene. We were told to refrain from any show of intimacy. Later, a Bassa girlfriend told me people might vomit if they saw a man and woman holding hands. However, it was acceptable for a man to tweak his wife's breast in public – shocking in my culture.

On our first day we had already seen it was common for men to hold hands with other men, and women would hold each other's hands. It showed they were close friends, and at that time there was no thought of them being a gay couple.

Another important thing we were told the first day was that there would be little or no twilight. If we were gone from home without a flashlight, we should hurry back since the jungle would quickly become dark. Being located only six degrees north of the equator, when the sun got close to the horizon it would disappear and suddenly be dark.

Later in the day, Margaret invited us to her home for iced tea and freshly made banana bread. She escorted us down a small hill and across the driveway with long, determined strides. Being a registered nurse and mid-wife, her part of the mission was to train Christian health workers and traditional mid-wives.

Number 2 was her permanent home, having lived there for two years. It was impressive how well the health program was going in such a short time. I found her accounts of teaching classes and working with students fascinating and enjoyed talking with her about medical issues.

Her home always seemed so peaceful with a reflective atmosphere and was tidy with everything in its place. It had the same layout as the Vanderaa's house, and I noticed she too had clotheslines strung across her breezeway with clothes pins in a caddy. Her living room chairs were beautiful wicker with a matching coffee table, and I wondered where she had bought them.

A little stream followed through her back yard, and apparently the house was built too far down the hill allowing the ground's water level to seep into the cement floors. They often glistened with moisture and could be slippery.

Since we knew our presence in Ann's house meant Erica and Joel had to give up their bedroom, it occurred to me that perhaps we could stay in Margaret's house for orientation. That arrangement might ease the congestion and the workload for Ann, while providing companionship for Margaret. I decided to hold my comment until I better understood the housing situation.

Later I learned that Margaret had hosted two families for lengthy periods of time after they arrived in country. It was then Ann's turn to host a new family and lighten the burden for Margaret, who kept a full-time schedule with her mission responsibilities.

Mark and Pat's temporary home was the smaller mission guest house with two bedrooms. Lacking the necessary storage area for a family with a baby, it seemed to overflow in a pleasant sort of way.

They invited us to dinner shortly after our arrival and we had a wonderful evening with them filled with all kinds of information, helpful hints, and honest reflection. Perry knew Mark from seminary since Mark was a couple of years ahead of Perry's class, but I had never met them before.

They were eager to work with the local people and dive into the teaching ministry, but I sensed a reluctance on the part of other missionaries to let them do anything, except language and culture study. This caused me to wonder what the relationships among the missionaries were like.

Their honest conversation and confession that they were growing weary in their attempts to communicate in Bassa hit us with the realization that the Bassa language would be difficult to learn. We had arrived fresh out of linguistics school in Toronto and felt rather confident, although we knew we faced a complex, tonal language that had not been fully studied.

They also confessed they especially missed worshipping in their own culture with family. We were anxious to experience this new form of worship ourselves but dreaded the day when we too longed for our church home and family.

As both houseguests at Ann's house and newcomers to a foreign way of life, a few house rules were certainly needed on our first day. With evening approaching the method of lighting the mission houses was explained. In each room were small fluorescent 12-volt lights, used in campers in the States. They were to be used sparingly since they ran off large car-like batteries, which were recharged by the mission generator. The goal was to run the generator only when water needed to be pumped from the well, then the small washing machine could also be used while the batteries charged.

In the evening if we simply went to get something from our bedroom, we were asked to use a flashlight, or better yet a candle since turning on the house lights took a lot of battery energy. Therefore, most evenings were spent together with Larry and Ann in the living room sharing one 12-volt light to save battery power, while allowing for wonderful times of fellowship with Bible study, praise in song, and prayer.

It was also wise to save flashlight batteries for outside use, since there were no streetlights, and the paths were not level. Mark demonstrated the difference between our state-side batteries and those he had recently purchased in the local market. It was amazing how dim his flashlight was compared to ours. (In Liberian-English final consonants were dropped, so flashlight was pronounced "fla'-lie".)

The use of water was another matter which deserved early explanation. Obviously, there was never a shortage of water in rainy season, between June and September. Rainwater was collected in 55-gallon steel barrels as it flowed off the roof and down the eaves. A pipe was hooked to the bottom of the rain barrel, which provided water to the kitchen and bathroom. Clothes were also washed with rainwater.

In the hot season water conservation needed to be strictly practiced. When the rain barrels ran dry, it was necessary to use the generator to pump water from the well to a small water tower, which was plumbed into the house.

Drainage from the kitchen and bathroom sinks emptied through pipes into drywells, which were large holes in the ground filled with rocks. For toilets actual septic tanks with drainage fields had been constructed by the volunteer mission builders.

Shortly after we arrived at their home, Ann approached me and asked if I would like to shower anytime soon. I was surprised by this question and wondered if she was hinting I needed a shower after the long trip. But once I understood the system, I realized she simply needed adequate time to prepare hot water. A kettleful of water needed to be heated on the kitchen propane stove, or often a bucket of water was warmed on an outdoor coal fire. If the water was heated too soon, it could cool before shower time.

When preparing for a shower, hot water was poured into a shower bucket hanging from the ceiling. Cold water was then added by turning a valve in the wall for water to pass through a pipe in the ceiling and fill the suspended bucket. The shower bucket was modified with a pipe protruding from the bottom. Attached to it was a gate valve with a shower head at the end.

The bucket could be raised and lowered with a rope through a pulley attached to the ceiling. Missionary families had knots tied in this rope corresponding to the various heights of the family members. The knot was hooked to the wall, allowing each person to reach the valve at the bottom of the bucket. Now when it was time to shower, the valve was simply turned open and warm refreshing water flowed from it.

It was shocking to learn that Larry and Ann were proud to use only one bucket of water for everyone in their family. Why would they do this, and was it possible for them to get clean with such little water? I was not

impressed. I personally felt one bucket of water was hardly adequate to sufficiently wash and rinse my long hair. I had no choice but to get by on that amount.

Ann went so far as to give me some helpful tips for showering. First get completely wet and quickly turn off the water. Without the water running, soap completely down and shampoo the hair. Finish with a quick cleansing rinse, using as little water as possible. It was surprising to learn how little water it takes to rinse off and get clean. I realized that it was essential to change my view of showering from a refreshing, relaxing time to simply getting clean.

In later years when our generator wasn't working or the well was running low in dry season, Perry and I could easily shower using very little water. There were times when another missionary family was staying overnight, and both our families adequately showered using only ONE bucket of water for us all. Furthermore, when water levels were low, we showered while standing in a metal tub to catch the gray water and use it for flushing the toilet.

As our first day ended, I realized my feelings of home sickness had thankfully diminished from being better acquainted with each of the missionaries. We were excited to have finally arrived in Bassaland, and eager to see everything and learn more about our role in the mission's objectives.

Enclosed that first night in the children's bedroom, I scanned the list of items in our duffle bags to find which one contained a lightweight nightie. I wondered if the supplies we had so carefully accumulated and packed were wise choices after all. What had we missed? America and all its readily available goods now seemed very, very far away.

Upon inspection of the bed, we found two single mattresses were pushed together to make one king-sized bed. These mattresses consisted of thin sheets of foam encased in heavy cloth. They were laid upon plywood held up by a simple legged bed frame. Once in bed, we found the mattresses had little cushion against the hard plywood, making Perry happy even way back then.

It took us a while to adapt to the new scents and feelings. The pillows had a strange musty odor, and the sheets were clammy, nearly moist against our skin. We realized this was unavoidable in such a humid climate. The nighttime temperatures would only dip to 70-75, so only a sheet would be needed.

As we lay in bed countless sounds from the nearby dense jungle consumed our senses. Strangely enough, those foreign sounds had a calming effect and serenaded me to sleep – sounds I often long to hear.

3

Orientation

Mission orientation included many new experiences, and we absorbed every detail we could. The explanation of how Bassa churches started is quite unique. David Shank, a Mennonite missionary, studied the Bassa church phenomena. His research and the information missionaries gleaned from church leaders coincided.

The Bassa were traditionally animists appeasing the dark spirits thought to exist in their environment. In the 1950s and '60s there was a Holy Spirit movement among the Bassa people. Some had spiritually insightful dreams and visions. Miracles in God's name were witnessed, and people began worshipping Him, rather than following their animistic ways.

There had been some influence from early missionary endeavors. Bassa people received the missionaries' message of Christ, but when they also held to some cultural traditions, the missions did not accept the converts. (See Appendix A) They also heard the good news of Christ's salvation through a missionary radio station-ELWA (Eternal Love Winning Africa), which still operates broadcasting to vast West Africa.

As a result of these influences, the Bassa built many churches in local villages to worship God. The churches gravitated together, and denominations were formed. Unfortunately, almost all church leadership had no formal training, in fact many of them were illiterate.

The Bassa churches have been classified with many other rapidly growing gatherings as African Independent Churches (AICs) and defined as:

> [African Independent Churches are churches] formed and existing within a tribe or tribal unit, temporarily or permanently, of any organized religious movement with a distinct name and membership even as a small single organized congregation, which claims the title Christian in that it acknowledges Jesus Christ as Lord, and which has either separated by secession from a mission church or an existing African Independent Church, or has been founded outside the mission churches as a new kind of religious entity under African initiative and leadership.[4]
>
> ...Churches founded by Africans for Africans in the special African situations. They have all African membership as well as all African leadership. Some were founded by Africans in reaction to some feature of the Christianity of missionary societies; most were founded among those people who had known Christianity the longest.[5]

It was in response to a letter from a Bassa pastor that CRWM first heard of the AIC churches. As a faithful listener to the Christian Reformed "Back to God Hour" on ELWA radio, the pastor wrote a letter to the program's stateside headquarters and requested training for uneducated Bassa pastors. His letter was forwarded to the CRWM board. One of the board members had a son, Larry, in Liberia working with the Christian Service Corps, so the connection was simple. (See Appendix B)

Larry took the opportunity to meet with Bassa pastors and in particular with Rev. Dr. Abba Karnga. The church leaders informed Larry of many uneducated pastors, who deeply desired Biblical training. Abba and Larry collaborated to present CRWM with a plan to teach the indigenous leaders through Theological Education by Extension (TEE). This could be accomplished by missionaries living in distant locations and traveling to churches in their area where local pastors would gather for a weekly class.

Larry and Ann followed God's call to return to Liberia as missionaries. They spearheaded the new ministry and did the groundwork of beginning our denomination's history with the Bassa church.

The Christian Reformed World Mission's mandate for the work in Bassaland became: We shall promote the growth of Independent Churches which presently exist, rather than forming a new denomination in Bassaland.

From the beginning, no Christian Reformed Churches existed in Liberia and the mission mandate was to not start any. The mission board understood that the Spirit of God had already done the planting of many churches. Discipling and educating their leaders were to be the missionaries' goals. Therefore, it was somewhat of a surprise to find that this had become a point of contention among the missionaries.

When we arrived, CRWM missionaries worked under the Christian Education Foundation of Liberia (CEFL) and its leader, Rev. Abba Karnga. Slated to become a tribal chief before he became a Christian, he was a visionary leader, respected among the Bassa churches, and endowed with charisma. He was the type of person people sought out for wisdom, and he encouraged believers to work together for the betterment of all. Perry and I enjoyed a personal relationship with him and affectionately called him our boss and even our surrogate father, and I suspect all our missionaries felt the same way about him.

Abba and two other associates had a threefold vision to educate their people for the sake of Christ's Kingdom. The Christian Education Foundation of Liberia had been established to meet the needs of Christ's churches in Bassaland. God graciously fulfilled their three goals, in the following ways:

1. Christian College and Bassa Christian High School – These institutions of learning were already built and had been holding classes for many years before CRWM sent missionaries to Bassaland. The schools had Liberian teachers and American missionary teachers from the Christian Church denomination.
2. Theological Education by Extension - Training for area pastors and church leaders was first offered by CRWM missionaries seconded to the CEFL, yet they worked autonomously operating various training programs. Later Liberian teachers were hired to work with missionaries and an organization called Christian Extension Ministries (CEM) was formed. The CEM oversaw additional

Rev. Dr. Abba Karnga

extension ministries, including training for Village Health Workers (VHW) and Traditional Birth Attendants (TBA), agricultural training, community development, literacy training and literature production, Bible translation, and scholarships.

3. Bassa Christian Radio station – At that time, an unrealized dream.

When we arrived in Bassaland, Larry had been teaching TEE classes to spiritually thirsty Bassa pastors. He was encouraged by the effect it was having on them and their churches.

Initially, the pastors received a cassette player, and at each class two newly recorded tapes were handed out for them to study over the week. When the class met Larry would lecture on the lesson speaking in Liberian English, which was interpreted by a Bassa man repeating the lesson in Bassa, phrase by phrase.

Perry attended some classes with Larry and eagerly anticipated being involved in the ministry. It was the TEE program which had drawn us to Liberia. While Perry was a first-year student at Calvin Theological Seminary, Larry made a presentation to recruit new missionaries. What interested us most was how God had started the churches, and the untrained Bassa church leaders were eager to learn.

Our initial experiences with church leaders in worship services included unusual explanations of the Scripture. It was not difficult to understand that there was a serious felt need among them for in-depth training.

During our orientation to the mission work, I also attended some of the TEE classes. The men were eager, sitting on the edges of their seats. Larry amazed and amused the students with a portable white board and erasable markers. We understood that most of the students were illiterate, although some had Bassa New Testaments and were struggling to read. Others held their Bibles upside down and assumed a reading posture.

Some pastors perched in the windowsill for better lighting, straining with poor eyesight. Some wore eyeglasses, likely purchased in the market from boxes of donated prescription lenses, which made it difficult to meet individual needs.

Larry gave us a little more background on the life of the student pastors. Many of them were polygamists and members of a tribal secret society. I later remarked to Perry that polygamy should be one of the first lessons in the classes, but he explained that the TEE classes were taught book by book of the Bible, so that topic would be covered when they came to it. The Bassa church leaders had to first understand the Bible is God's divine Word, then they would have to decide for themselves how the Bible was calling them to live as a Christian in their culture.

While I attended a class, I became distracted by the loud popping and creaking of the hot tin roof and the entry of a chicken chasing a bug in flight. The class ignored these things. I was therefore surprised when suddenly a student jumped up and began to dash around the church in pursuit of a small fly.

On the way home, Larry explained that a tsetse fly had been spotted. Those pesky insects were known for their transmission of a variety of serious diseases. It was certainly necessary to rid the room of the pest.

Tsetse flies were nasty, tricky flies identified by their wings crossed over their back, as if they had one. They flew low and were sneaky, biting people unaware. They were known for flying up ladies' skirts, so I was advised to occasionally flick my skirt hem to keep them away.

The tsetse flies were fond of catching a person napping and then sucking up as much blood as they could, only to spit it out, and gorge themselves on more. This was not only disgusting but could spread dreaded diseases and leave a temporary dent in the tissue of the unsuspecting victim. When the tsetse flew away with their bellies full, they couldn't get much altitude and made a distinct low buzzing sound which sent me running after them. It was gross to hit one with a fly swatter and a mess to clean up.

Larry further explained that for many TEE students who lived in an interior village, it was necessary to travel great distances on foot to get to class. This certainly indicated the deep commitment the pastors had for education. The missionaries would often give them rides before and after class as far as they could on the road. To get home the pastor might have to walk several hours, or even a day or two, on the jungle trails.

When they were given a ride, the student pastors would regularly stow an interesting array of belongings on board. Anything could be expected from a couple of live chickens to a bunch of ripening bananas, which might be tied to the top of the car. I once sat next to a pastor holding an armadillo curled up in a ball. When it would start to unroll, the pastor stroked it, and it quickly curled up again.

There was no sense of too many students being squeezed into the Peugeot station wagon's three seats. Often it was so tight in the front seat that the driver had difficulty reaching the shift handle on the steering column.

It was always a little comical when a few of the students were dropped off leaving an empty spot, and the remaining passengers would not think to slide over. It was just not part of their culture to spread out and give each other a little more personal space. Sometimes the missionary would have to kindly suggest that they slide over, so he could have more room to drive and shift.

During orientation, we learned that Sunday breakfasts were "take and go", as we rushed out the door to be at church around 7:00 AM. Missionaries rotated through their students' churches on Sundays, so one church did not appear to be favored.

The worship services were always incredibly joyful. Bass and tenor drums called out a catchy rhythmic beat, while worshippers clapped hands or snapped fingers, and rows of people swayed together to the beat of the music. A lone singer would lead the songs, while the congregation antiphonally replied by alternating with the soloist.

At our first worship service, the Lord's supper was served and what a symbolic event it was, thinking of our oneness with the Bassa believers. As I watched the elements being served, I realized it would be to my advantage to sit in the front row and be one of the first to take communion. The juice was served in a tin can and passed from one person to the other. I surmised if I was sitting in the front row, I could determine which part of the cup the people ahead of me had used and rotate the cup to hopefully have a fresh spot.

Someone later told me it was not necessary to take the risk of exposure to disease at communion - I could just fake taking a sip. Of course, it was a personal choice, but it seemed dishonest, and I was aware people closely watched me. I would be uneasy with just bringing the cup to my mouth and giving the false impression of partaking with fellow Christians. Others would realize the missionary did not actually share communion with the church of Christ. It was at these times of drinking the juice that true heartfelt prayer was offered during Lord's Supper.

Most of the church buildings were constructed by the local worshippers. Various materials were used, such as corrugated tin nailed to bush poles or boards imbedded in the ground, mud from termite hills packed around sticks, or concrete brick walls. Bush pole rafters were nearly always visible inside the church, with dirt or thin cement floors.

It was not uncommon for several bamboo poles to serve as pews while praising God. Chairs or benches constructed by local carpenters were often uncomfortable by the end of three hours of worship or TEE class. The people didn't care what they had to sit on, so we politely accepted their hospitality and together focused on worship of the one true God.

Some type of pulpit was generally placed in the front, often with a table just below it for the deacons. The table served for counting money, sometimes done during the worship service. It was their custom for the women to sit on the left side of the church and men on the right. Babies went with the mothers, and weaned boys sat with the fathers. This held true for the TEE classes as well, although there were few women.

The mission had a good problem - there were more pastors and church leaders requesting TEE classes than the missionaries could handle. The mission policy was that the missionaries should complete language and culture acquisition before teaching a class. The normal allotted time was one year, but it was a little difficult for the missionaries to wait that long.

After a show of good effort in learning Bassa and passing the first language proficiency test, the men were usually allowed to hold one class with the aid of a Bassa interpreter. This was a great incentive and opportunity to practice their new language skills, but it was understood diligent language study was to continue.

When we arrived on the field, our mission not only offered classes for the pastors and church leaders, but the existing health program was well established and a proven model for other agencies under the able and wise guidance of Margaret. Further programs were being planned for training in agriculture and literacy. Although Don was teaching TEE, he was also beginning to develop an interest in translation of the Bassa Bible, which had been slowly progressing for some years by another mission group. There was much work to do, and CEM was always seeking qualified Liberian teachers.

A young Bassa man named Henry was recommended as a TEE teacher to help meet the requests for more classes. He returned to Liberia after studying at Moody Bible Institute in Chicago. After an interview with the mission Henry was hired to teach classes for waiting pastors.

His interview was most impressive, and the mission was unanimous in asking him to work alongside us to teach God's Word. After completing his study at Moody college in the States, Henry had returned to his homeland. Immediately he set about preaching and spreading the gospel to interior villages, taking the opportunity to travel and preach in many secluded areas.

At one point he and his companions reached the swollen St. John River in the middle of rainy season, and yet Henry was determined that God was calling them to preach on the other side. He convinced his traveling companions to cross the dangerous river with him in a dug-out canoe. There was a lady who was eager to get across and she asked to join them.

They paddled part way across the turbulent river, but were drawn into a large, dangerous whirlpool. Knowing that the canoe was destined to be overturned and the people lost in the raging river, Henry stood and prayed that God would act on their behalf so they might continue spreading the gospel.

God then did a great thing and slowly the canoe began to move in reverse against the current until it climbed out of the strangling funnel. It was a great display of God's power and might to those in the canoe, and to a group of people watching from the shore!

After they reached the other side, the woman knelt on the ground and acknowledged that she believed Henry's God was the one true God. Henry preached the good news of Jesus and the observers on the shore heard the message of Christ. They too responded in faith and cut down their sacred grove, the center piece of idolatrous ancestral worship and the location of a secret bush school.

One request to start new classes came while we were eating lunch with Larry and Ann in their breezeway. A group of strangers approached the house and Larry invited them inside. They introduced themselves as pastors and church leaders coming from Devil Country at Number 1 and produced an envelope containing a petition to the CR Mission.

The petition requested TEE classes be started in their area, so they could be taught more about Jesus and the Bible. The head of the delegation was a fiery older lady named Pastor Mondamaa Beegar, and she wasn't afraid to speak out.

The delegation was invited to attend the next missionary field council to formally present their petition, and the missionaries thankfully received their request. Larry and Perry honored the delegation by taking them home which was about an hour away.

Number 1 had been the mission's first goal when setting up mission stations. Larry and Ann had offered TEE classes there, but tribal leaders had rejected the proposal saying, "We don't want a mission here - Number 1 is 'Devil Country'". By the time we had arrived, the churches in the area had apparently banded together to sign the petition inviting a TEE program to come. God's Spirit had been at work, so it was exciting news.

Ann casually mentioned to me there was a possibility that Perry and I would be asked to fulfill the request at Number 1. This would most likely happen if we would return to work among the Bassa people after Perry's final two semesters at seminary. I felt a cold chill at her news, the thought of living in Devil Country was alarming.

4

Surprises

Our first year in Liberia two things happened to me which I would have never thought a possibility. Both could have easily swayed me to never return to Liberia.

The first of them was part of being an expatriate while living in Liberia. A trip to the capital city of Monrovia was required to get a resident visa and driver's license. Larry helped us begin this process shortly after we arrived. A few weeks later Perry and I returned alone to complete the paperwork and begin to purchase supplies for our eventual relocation to a house of our own at Number 3. We took the Peugeot station wagon into Monrovia and enjoyed our freedom after living in close quarters for some time.

We reserved a luxuriously air-conditioned room at ELWA mission for one night. However, by that time our bodies had adjusted to the heat, so the AC felt rather cold, especially to me. Our rented room was on a beautiful palm lined beach, where we could hear the ocean waves rolling in. But most of all, we relished the hot running water and a nice long shower.

In the city shops, we gathered a few supplies and successfully completed the legal paperwork. When we started our journey back to Grand Bassa County the sun was fading, and it was necessary to travel through several official checkpoints on the road.

The first check point was located a short distance outside Monrovia at Camp Schiefflin Army Post. It was around dusk and raining lightly when we pulled up to the gate, which was two long metal poles across the road. We were confident as we approached the officers at the gatehouse. Larry had tutored us to be patient and courteous allowing the Liberian military to complete their job. We also understood that it wouldn't hurt to hint we were missionaries, if we sensed they were stalling for a bribe.

To our shock, a young solider ran to my window and knocked on it with the barrel of his Uzi gun, aggressively yelling, "Roll the window down, roll the window down!" I fearfully and slowly cranked it down. "Don't you know the speed limit is one mile per hour?" he asked with slurred speech and bulging eyes fierce with anger. He seemed either intoxicated or stoned.

We did not argue, although we had been approaching the gate at an extremely slow pace and had customarily reduced the headlights to parking lights. Perry politely answered, "Please excuse - never mind." ("Never mind" means "sorry" in Liberian English.)

Suddenly he pointed his gun to my head - pressing the cold metal just above my ear. I felt drenched and weakened with fear. With his gun he pushed my head to an angle and yelled that we should move the car to the commander's office. I dared not breath lest the slightest movement would activate his trigger finger.

Not only was the position of his gun a grave concern to me, but the demanding young soldier had instructed us to go where Larry told us to never go - on the grounds of the post. Within its boundary anything could happen and rumors abounded especially after the recent coup.

Our silent prayers were rapid and fervent. They were partly answered when Perry started to inch the car forward and the soldier moved the position of his gun.

Then our salvation appeared suddenly in the form of the soldier's commanding officer, who yelled at our captor asking what he was doing. He was informed that under no circumstances was he to ever let foreigners go on the post. He told Perry to drive away.

As we slowly took our leave, the commander was consumed with berating the young soldier in his care. I was shocked by what had just happened. We realized God's protective hand in our potentially serious experience and cried out our praise to Him on the way home.

This rude awakening reminded us we were no longer in the USA, where people are truly free to travel without being questioned every few miles. The realization that we were indeed inexperienced newcomers began to replace our earlier confident attitude, and we wished we had been traveling in the daylight instead of the early evening.

The second thing which happened to me was just as dramatic as having a gun pointed to my head, and it personally devastated me. It all began with our first outing to the Atlantic beach near Buchanan, a seemingly necessary and exciting part of orientation. We had seen pictures and were anxious for a chance to have some fun there. To our surprise the missionaries had what they called a "beach hut". They had spoken of how wonderful it was, so I was excited to see it and relax in all its amenities.

A simply gorgeous setting awaited us at Silver Beach, with tall coconut palms bending slightly toward the ocean and pure white sand stretching as far as the eye could see. The beach hut turned out to be little more than a rusty picnic table embedded in the sand under a primitive thatch roof. The missionary ladies giggled when they saw they had successfully fooled me into thinking it was more than that. The hut was simply a place to get out of the sun or rain.

The pleasure of occasionally occupying the beach cost the missionaries $40.00 a year and later it jumped to $100, which was divided equally among five families. This included the services of a local older man to build the structure and take care of necessary thatch upkeep. Other huts located there were leased by European employees of the nearby Liberia Agricultural Mining Company (LAMCO).

People in the States of course always thought it sounded rather luxurious, and perhaps a bit extravagant, for missionaries to have a beach hut, so I tried to remember to call it a "picnic area" and that did describe it best.

It held one of the few opportunities missionaries had to refresh themselves and cool off in the ocean. Of course, it was a pure delight to go there and relax or explore away from the watchful culture of the people we served. New missionaries often joked that they were willing to do language study in the Bassa village nearby. And I asked, "What would be wrong with that?"

This location proved to be an ideal place to do some body surfing. There was a huge rock island several hundred feet from the beach, which usually interrupted the undertow making it safe for swimmers. The waves were just right for riding the first time we arrived at Silver Beach, and everyone encouraged us to give it a try. I was somewhat anxious, not being a strong swimmer, but wanting to join in the fun I waded out where the waves could catch us and carry us in. After a little coaching, I too experienced the thrill of riding a wave to the shoreline.

As I jumped up to exclaim how exciting the ride had been, everyone around me suddenly froze in place, and Perry kept trying to sputter something to me. Suddenly, Ann screamed, "Your top!" I looked down and wondered where my bathing suit had gone? Horrified, I sank beneath the water to cover up and move the twisted suit back in place.

Completely humiliated, Perry and I strolled down the beach, while I cried and told him I wanted to get on an airplane, go home, and never see any of those people again in my lifetime. This was one of the most humiliating things to ever happen to me.

Later I learned that most of my colleagues had experienced similar problems, however they hid beneath the waves accessing their situation before standing up. Nevertheless, I was never again so enthusiastic about riding the waves and was extra careful before getting out of the water - funny how that could be.

On the mission was the cutest pygmy goat family with twin kids that jumped and frolicked around the yard. They were clever little babies and had figured they might as well use the cat door to come in the house at will. We thought it was so cute to see them enjoying themselves in the breezeway. The mother goat was too large to enter the opening and would stand outside calling to them through the screen wall.

I wondered if a snake might enter the house through the cat hole but was told to not worry about it since that had never happened. Later we were to question this theory after a dangerous experience.

Erica and Joel also enjoyed picking fruit from their trees and brought it home as a treat to share with the family. Ann and I were a little surprised at all the "paw-paw" (papaya) her children apparently ate at the breeze-way table. There seemed to always be paw-paw seeds spilled on the table, but it wasn't a big deal. We just brushed the seeds off with our hands and cleaned the table that way before meals.

Until... one day I noticed the cute pygmy baby goats had jumped up on the table and were depositing their "paw-paw seeds" right there! Ann and I were sufficiently grossed out at the thought. Soon the small cat door was narrowed to an even smaller size and the cute baby goats were banished to outdoor life.

Ann's steward was a Bassa man and his job was to help Ann in the house with cleaning, cooking, and doing the laundry. He was a local church pastor and TEE student, who spoke a little Liberian English.

It appeared he was slow in his work, and I concluded Ann didn't worry about his work habits since there was an apparent reason. It was immediately obvious upon meeting him that he suffered with a physical handicap, and I surmised he had a greatly enlarged inguinal hernia. The mass was so large that he had difficulty walking and had to have special pants made by a tailor.

I had seen an inguinal hernia in a medical missionary's home slide show. The doctor had held the slide on the screen for a long time and made me guess what it was. I was a little embarrassed to look at the picture, and unable to decipher what he had photographed. It appeared to be a mass that could have been a third, middle leg of equal thickness, cut off a short distance above the knee.

The doctor explained the surgery was simple and the recovery rate was excellent. The indigenous patients however were often reluctant to have it repaired, since they feared not being able to father children post-operatively.

Individuals with this problem are to be pitied and in remote areas of the world it is difficult to have the corrective surgery. The condition not only hampers someone's lifestyle, but the intestine within the hernia can become dangerously strangled and even cause death.

Larry and Ann had inquired at the ELWA mission hospital and found the corrective surgery was relatively inexpensive, around $200. They offered to pay for the hernia repair, however it was another matter to convince the pastor to submit to it.

Sometime later, he came to a point of trusting Larry. He agreed to set a date for the procedure assured a Christian doctor would remove only the herniated mass. The hernia was easily corrected, and we were all surprised by his active lifestyle afterwards, not to mention a new baby in his family about a year later.

As part of our orientation it was important to meet the other missionaries, so we traveled with everyone to a field council meeting at Number 3. I became car sick sitting crowded in the third-row seat. The road seemed unending with bumpy washboard, deep potholes filled with water, curves dipping into valleys, and hill tops that gave our stomachs a jolt.

As we bounced down the roads, the tenor's solo in Handels' Messiah came to mind, *Every valley shall be exalted, and every mountain and hill made low, the crooked straight, and the rough places plain,* from Isaiah 40:4.

It had never occurred to me before what that passage might mean. After all, I was accustomed to traveling on perfectly smooth roads in the USA. How wonderful to think the rough, winding roads would be prepared for the coming of Christ.

Here began my practice of what I personally called "zoning out". When the road conditions were so terrible and I felt carsick, I would fall half-asleep to ignore the endless swaying of the car and lurching of the stomach.

All missionaries attended our first field council meeting. Don and Marty had just welcomed their second son, Ben, and everyone celebrated his safe arrival. They hosted the meeting in their home, and I found the interpersonal relationships to be very interesting. Some of the conversations seemed strained. The men appeared tense, including an uncomfortable conversation concerning who would build a table for the guest house, our future home.

During the meeting differences of opinion concerning mission strategy became apparent and heated. This was quite a shock for Perry and me. Hadn't everyone agreed to the mission mandate of teaching existing pastors before arriving in Liberia? One of the women left the meeting in tears. I asked what the problem was, but people were reluctant to explain.

After the meeting we toured the guest house which had been recently built but was not quite ready to move into. We set out to travel back to Number 2, and I again suffered with car sickness. Our dinner consisted of peanut butter sandwiches made with Lebanese flat bread, which we ate in the car. We arrived after dark exhausted from the long trip and activities of the day.

Perry and I had many questions and uncertainties on our minds. How could our colleagues be divided in the goals of the mission work and how would it affect us and the strategy of the ministry?

5

Trekking

We stayed a little longer at Number 2 than originally planned for Perry to go on his first trek to visit interior villages. He was invited to accompany Larry and they would be trekking a great distance. They would make a wide arch through the area north of the mission, while staying in Bassa homes along the way. No roads existed in the area, so they would walk the jungle paths. There would be no form of communication from them for about a week, since cell phones had not been invented, and they planned return by taxi coming down the road from the north.

It would have been exciting to accompany them, but it was to be a man's trek. If I had gone with them, it would mean imposing on a village for two overnight rooms, and I realized it was best for Perry to travel with Larry alone. I stayed with Ann and the kids, but it was exciting to see the men walk off the mission grounds with only light back packs.

The purpose of the trek was multifaceted. Not only did it increase the population's awareness of the mission's presence and work in the area, but it also gave the missionaries an idea of the villages and more importantly a chance to record the churches that existed.

As they visited with church pastors and leaders, they would inform them of available classes. Another reason of visiting these areas was to observe the culture and be immersed in the Bassa language. Since this was Perry's first trek, Larry also introduced him to the etiquette of spending the night in Bassa villages.

A TEE student, Saturday Paagee, acted as Perry and Larry's guide and introduced his companions as missionary teachers to pastors living in the interior. He walked the jungle paths barefoot as assuredly as if he wore steel-toed boots. Slung across his back were his shoes, which he would stop to put on when they neared a village in order to make an impressive entrance.

In the end, this trek was deemed successful since many churches and worshipping fellowships were discovered in the area. Pastors and church leaders were interested in attending a new class, which would be held in a church on the road north of the mission. These pastors would walk to the class location each week and after class walk back home.

When the men returned from the trek, Perry told me of his adventures. They had traversed through great high, virgin jungles which kept the paths below amazingly cool. Streams and rivers were crossed by balancing on logs or by wading through the waters, while dug-out canoes were required to cross the wider rivers. The farther they trekked into the interior, the larger the villages were, and the more thatched roofs they saw in place of corrugated metal.

He saw enormous up-land rice fields tended by lone farmers. There were also large cassava fields, which was another common crop, planted like a potato, and ready to be dug up a year later. After crossing these farms in the hot sun, it was a welcome relief to step into the coolness of the jungle shade.

With disappointment he explained the farm areas were left fallow after a single year of crop growth, and not used again until seven years later. The slash and burn type of agriculture could decimate the rain forest, putting the natural foliage at risk, and depleting topsoil easily washed away in the tropical rainstorms.

While trekking, the men discussed the need of developing new farming methods to save the jungle and all it holds for mankind. In the future our group of missionaries would include an agronomist who prepared a demonstration rice paddy and taught people how to farm using the preferred, new method.

Larry showed Perry places where people had made simple sacrifices of eggs or rice to their ancestors. The Bassa traditionalist believed in a creator God, but they were traditional animists believing that everything was infused with a spirit.

The people felt they needed to appease God to have a relationship with Him, so sacrifices were made to Bassa family members who had recently died. It was thought they would readily remember what it was like to live on earth and would act as intermediaries to keep the living protected from evil spirits. Occasionally these simple sacrifices could be seen in the jungle and are undoubtedly still made in some areas today.

The men also came upon adolescents on the paths who were obviously in the secretive bush school. Dressed in traditional garb, their bodies were covered with white chalk. The trail which led to the bush school was barred from entrance in no uncertain manner.

We had been warned that it was forbidden to enter these hidden areas for adolescent training. Once the son of a missionary rode a motorcycle into a bush school as a prank, and the society men harassed the family and mission until they were forced to leave the country.

As Perry and Larry trekked, they both carried a cutlass in defense of snakes or to clear the jungle from the path. In these interior areas they came upon villages where children had never seen a white person before. The young ones sometimes screamed and ran at the sight of the men's astonishing white skin.

Unfortunately, parents would at times threaten their children by saying something like, "You'd better behave, or the white people will come and get you." Larry carried small pieces of wrapped hard candy for the sole purpose of convincing the children they should not be frightened.

Naturally the Bassa were curious about white people when they first saw them. They not only looked strange but had different customs and mannerisms. While the men were on trek and talking with village people around the kitchen fires, some would venture close enough to examine the hair on the missionaries' legs and arms. Coming from an African culture, the Bassa's definition of personal space was different from our own. They were unhindered by thoughts of intruding into personal space as defined by the western culture.

Perry told me he was apprehensive to enter one village deep in the jungle. It was almost dark, and the path was eerily lined with skulls mounted on poles. With inexperience he wondered if they could have stumbled upon a remote headhunters' village. It was a great relief, but also unfortunate, to find out the skulls were the remains of chimpanzees. Apparently, the residents were merely advertising their hunting skills.

The most interior village they reached on the trek was the home of their guide, Saturday Paagee. It was impressive to learn it took him two days to walk to the TEE class Larry taught, and two days to walk home again. So, four days out of every week were spent commuting on foot to class.

Another interesting fact about this man was that he boasted he had two rows of teeth. Being a dental hygienist, this greatly intrigued me. I later had the opportunity to look in his mouth and it appeared that he simply had not lost his deciduous teeth as a child. His permanent teeth erupted buccally, outside the baby teeth, creating an unusual second row, although most of the baby teeth were worn down the gum with use.

Overall, Perry's first trek was inspiring and gave us great excitement and vision for the training of church leaders. These leaders were literally crying out for someone to assist them with biblical and theological education. We caught the vision and were excited and humbled to be involved in such a strategy that equipped the local God ordained leaders.

6

Guest House

We felt a bit trapped when it came time for us to move to the guest house at Number 3. With the end of rainy season, the monsoon rains deposited countless inches of rain. The one road out of the Number 2 area developed impassable stretches, unfortunately leaving area residents and motorists stranded. Without the use of heavy road equipment, residents tried various methods to repair the deep, muddy ruts, and bottomless potholes, but the poor road conditions kept forcing our departure date further and further back.

Liberia is in a tropical zone so there are two distinct seasons. Dry/Hot season was from November to April, including Harmattan around January with heavy dust laden winds from the Sahara Desert. There was also wet/rainy season from May to October, which brought almost 200 inches of intense monsoon rain, meaning it could literally pour rain for days in a row. This was coupled with intense lightening, which could be incredibly loud and seem alarmingly close.

In August there was often a reprieve from the heavy rains called the mid-dry, but after that heavy torrents would fall from the sky and water would stand on the saturated ground. We were trying to move during the late rains, and water overflowed everywhere.

One morning it appeared our travel plans would be indefinitely postponed. A river halfway down the road had swollen causing an irreparable cut 20 feet wide. Some local men built a foot bridge with logs, which wouldn't hold the weight of a vehicle. That evening the river's water rose again making a 30-40 foot gap, washing the temporary bridge out.

Perry went with Larry to investigate and returned saying a large culvert had washed out, although the flow of the river had apparently reduced from its destructive state. Even though we faced the disappointment of not moving, more importantly Mark and Pat needed to get to the airport to pick up his parents coming for a visit from Michigan. And most important of all, if an emergency should arise there was no way to travel out for medical care.

At the lunch table that day, a plan for our departure was formed requiring quick action and all hands. We had just heard through the mission workers that the river had reduced to just a trickle and a taxi had driven across. In fact, several taxis had gone down the ditch and across the riverbed to get to the other side. If we hurried before the water level rose, we might be able to get across as well.

I hastily packed our belongings but jumped back when I felt a furry thing in the bedroom closet. What kind of animal might be hiding there? I had no idea. Since it didn't move, I looked closely and found it was green and in the shape of my straw hat. Due to high humidity, the hat had apparently grown moldy fur. How utterly gross. I naturally threw it away, but the missionary ladies said I could have scrubbed it with bleach or vinegar, and it would be like new.

When we got to the cut in the road, we found the water flow was ankle deep. People were walking across the river with loads on their heads. Then they climbed up the ditch on the opposite side to the waiting taxis and continued down the road to their destinations.

Our plan was similar. We wanted to get the mission pickup and one of the two mission station wagons across the riverbed. First brush was cleared from the ditch with cutlasses and then rocks in the riverbed were rearranged to create a hard surface beneath the water.

Larry slowly drove down the cleared ditch and across the riverbed, then up the steep ditch on the other side. In the end we got the pickup and a station wagon across the washout. The station wagon was left there for missionaries to use in the case of an emergency, to get supplies, or to make the airport run. We had no idea when the road would be repaired. It appeared it might be a long time, so leaving the car there was a good safety measure.

Our belongings were carried on the heads of Bassa friends across the river and loaded into the pickup. I felt a sense of embarrassment as I watched people carrying our duffel bags full of things we had accumulated. Yet on the other hand, I knew I had only gathered what was necessary. This tug of war in my mind became a frequent and never resolved conflict during our years in Liberia. My perceived necessities often felt like extravagance compared to the people living around me.

With a sense of excitement Perry and I set out in the old pickup on the three-hour journey to Number 3. We did not start out alone, since many local people were seeking a ride. Even though the taxi drivers protested, we invited travelers to crowd into the pickup or ride in the back, and we set off down the muddy Number 2 road.

Turning left at the paved road, we made our way to the city of Buchanan. There we stopped to purchase additional supplies, check for mail, and become better acquainted with the city. Leaving Buchanan, we turned north off the paved road near Hotel Louisa and traveled for one hour or 30 miles up the Number 3 road. Passing the entrance to the rubber plantation owned by Liberia Agricultural Company (LAC), we turned left at the government clinic. The mission was located a short distance at the road's end.

The cost of traveling from one mission to the other was $50.00 for gas, so trips between them were not often made. The Number 3 road had more gravel and was wider than the Number 2 road. Since LAC, a division of the Uniroyal Rubber Company, was located up the road, it was in the company's best interest to keep it maintained. Still we had to maneuver ruts, potholes and miles upon miles of washboard conditions on the endlessly winding road that usually made me carsick.

Don and Marty and their two young sons had lived at the Number 3 Christian Reformed mission for a year and a half. Jonathan or "Jay-Jay" was two years old and Benjamin was a newborn when we arrived. Their mission compound had a distinctively different look than the Number 2 station. It was a smaller plot of land and most of the jungle had been cleared away revealing a beautiful view.

The mission house at Number 3 was constructed with 2x4 studs connected with chicken wire and plastered with cement, unlike the first mission homes at Number 2, which were built with traditional stick and termite mud. It was hoped the cement over the wire would avoid termite invasion and increase the longevity of the building. The result was walls that were squared off nicely and pleasing to our western eyes. However, they were hollow - allowing a haven for mice that could make a terrible commotion in the evening. A house cat solved this problem nicely. Completing the distinctive look of the mission station, the exterior of the home and the bottom reaches of the palm trees were whitewashed.

As was the case in all our mission homes, ceilings were tightly secured to the walls allowing missionaries to live nearly bug and rodent free. Screens covered the window spaces, and mats could be unrolled to keep rain and wind out, whereas Number 2 had wooden shutters.

Expanded metal was added to the windows at Number 3 for protection from thieves, which was a controversial issue among the missionaries, since it prevented escape in an emergency. It was thought to be wise to install more of a barrier in these homes due to a higher population in the area and their exposure to LAC rubber plantation.

Since the guest house was completely furnished, all we had to do was move our personal things in and begin our assignment of language and culture study. Our new home was situated with a beautiful view of two ranges of hills and valleys covered with lush tropical jungle. In harmony with the larger mission house, it was whitewashed on the outside and had expanded metal in the windows, a fact I would soon appreciate.

As was the case with all the mission houses, the roof was covered with corrugated aluminum, which accentuated each falling raindrop. Marty had decorated the guest house and furnished it with bright African fabric, which I loved. We thought the little house was adorable and comfortable, by missionary standards. I was excited to have bamboo living room furniture, a kitchen table and chairs, as well as bedroom furniture.

The main room consisted of a living room and dining room with the kitchen along one wall. Its plywood cupboards were painted white and a

Cleaning furniture of mildew at the guest house.

small stainless-steel sink was mounted in a thin white laminate countertop. Attached to the sink was a stainless-steel drain-board, which annoyingly drained in the wrong direction.

Next to the cupboards stood a small European bottle gas stove with three burners and kerosene refrigerator, which required no small amount of care. It was necessary to keep a circular, blue flame burning for proper refrigeration, but this unit had been dropped and damaged, therefore it was purchased at a lower price.

Due to the inevitable invasion of termites, the guest house wood was treated with creosote, which is evidently distasteful to insects. However, Perry and I found the odor from the treated wood offensive. It seemed to give us constant headaches, and a dry cough. Thankfully the large windows afforded good air movement and some relief from the smell of the deterrent. We questioned whether it was safe to breathe these fumes all the time, but we had little choice in the matter.

Our new Bassa neighbors came to greet us and wanted to know our names. Perry had received a Bassa name earlier. The pastors in Larry's TEE class were impressed with his ability to run fast enough to catch Larry as he was driving away in the car. So, they started calling him "Fleé", which is the Bassa name for a bird that darts around and isn't idle. But that was more of a nickname, therefore the pastors changed it to "Ga-dee-ay", spelled Gardeah, meaning "new man". This was a suitable name since he not only was the new man on the mission station, but also a new man in Christ.

I had not yet been given a Bassa name and needed one because my English name was not easy for Bassa people to pronounce. It was suggested by David, a mission grounds worker, that I take the name "Gre-kpoh-kpé" (Gray-kpaa-kpay). This was difficult for me to say, so we asked if it was a good name. The people responded favorably encouraging me to adopt it and it did prove to be a wonderful name!

My new name meant "God has the ultimate power and authority". When the Bassa people asked me, "Wheh ne nyin chuwa", [what is your name] my reply was, "M' nyinny ma Gde Kpau Kpe." My name reminded them that there is a God who is in complete control. This was wonderful news to them since they believed intermediary spirits of their ancestors lurked in the water, dark jungle, or other objects of God's creation.

For the Bassa people, one of the most awesome qualities of God was that He is "God Almighty" or in Hebrew *El Shaddai. The LORD appeared to Abram and said to him, "I am God Almighty…"*, Genesis 17:1. What a relief it was for the Bassa to put their faith in the One True God, who has universal dominion over all things, including all spirits and evilness of the world. As Christians they knew they were protected and secure, a realization that would comfort us as well in a few short months.

Just up the road north of the Number 3 mission was the Liberia Inland Mission (LIM), which had been successfully evangelizing the area for many years. Two single ladies, Wilma and Betty, had lived there a long time and managed a clinic, Bible school, and church. Don and Marty enjoyed their company and occasionally attended their church. The first Sunday we worshipped at their mission compound, I was impressed by the size of the congregation, the work the mission was doing, and the impact they were having on the community.

While I enjoyed worshipping with believers at the mission, it was immediately apparent to me that there were two distinct differences between the mission churches and the African Independent Churches our mission was serving. I noticed the Bassa women and girls at the mission did not cover their heads for worship, whereas women in the other churches did. Women commonly wore head ties in public and for everyday living, so why weren't they wearing them in church?

It was surprising to see the ladies immediately put their head tie back on as they exited the church, presumedly to shield their heads from hot sun. Were they not covering their heads in church because they were following the example of the missionary ladies - worshipping without scarves? It was difficult to know for sure.

As I sat in church, it was interesting to observe the beautifully designed cornrows in the ladies' hair. Obviously, they had prepared themselves to look their best for worship, and that was right and good. Still, in that culture, it seemed only right to wear a head tie for worship. It does clearly say in the Bible that women should cover their heads in worship. *Every wife who prays or prophesies with her head uncovered dishonors her head – it is same as if her head were shaved*, 1 Corinthians 11:5.

I became convinced that when we got to the point of working with church leaders, I didn't want to be the cause of women changing the tradition of covering their heads. Why would we want to change a custom so ingrained in the culture, which was obviously supported by scripture? I decided it would be important to wear a head tie to church, and not impose my culture upon them.

As the years went by, I always wore head ties to church. I must say I did not enjoy it. They were hot and uncomfortable, and it seemed they were always slipping out of place. At church women would come up to me shaking their heads and try to adjust my scarf, but there were also comments that I was looking "fine" that day.

I came to find there was a real advantage, too. Under a scarf tied at the back of the neck, there was no need to worry about hair styling early Sunday mornings. I could simply get up, comb through my hair, and put on a head tie before going out the door.

A second difference noted at the mission church, was that people did not kneel in prayer. Perry was disturbed by this when he also saw kneeling was no longer practiced in some independent churches nearby. Could the influence of missionaries have changed that established practice?

True, it was uncomfortable to kneel on the dirt or cement floors. It seemed a rock or something would usually dig into the knees, and the kneeling position could become painful during long prayers. We decided to always join in kneeling when we visited Bassa churches and came to enjoy this position of worshipping in prayer.

Marty thoughtfully suggested two young people from the mission church for our language informants. Perry interviewed a young man named David and enlisted his help. It was no surprise he progressed quickly with David's guidance, since he was accustomed to learning different languages. In college and seminary, he had studied seven languages: Spanish, German, Latin, Lakota, Greek, Hebrew, and hieroglyphics. He had also dabbled in Dutch and French.

I was introduced to Janet, who was probably in her late teens and I liked her immediately. Although she was quiet and somewhat serious, I enjoyed her company and tutelage for only a matter of months. She then abruptly announced she was getting married and moved to LAC rubber plantation, where her new husband was employed and housed.

From our informants we began to get a feel for the difficulty of the Bassa language. At my first session I found myself in the situation of being told I was a rude person. Naturally shocked and blinking back tears, I tried to discover what I might be doing to bring such a blunt comment. It turned out that my voice was too soft, making it difficult for people to hear me.

I had noticed the Bassa talked quite loudly, but was I required to do so as well? It seemed to me I was talking loudly enough. Must I shout to please the general population? The volume that Janet coached me to use was nearly too loud for my ears. I felt like I was yelling at people, nearly at an impolite level. I had no choice but to get used to speaking with increased volume, however I'm not sure I always remembered to turn it up.

Janet told me it was not acceptable to exclude people by speaking softly. Therefore, one should speak loudly enough for everyone to hear, even from a distance. This concept played out in other areas of life as well. For instance, it was considered selfish to have your radio on, but not play it loud enough for others to hear.

At my second language session with Janet, I proudly counted to ten in Bassa - with a loud voice, but she frowned and said something was wrong. I was sorely disappointed. She simply said she couldn't "hear" me. Thinking I wasn't loud enough, I repeated the numbers in a louder voice; still she frowned and was unable to explain what I was doing wrong.

I listened carefully to her count again for me. Yes, I was sure I had the words correct, but she refused to grant that I was saying the numbers correctly. What could be wrong? She left our language session early, frustrated that she couldn't help me, and I was equally perplexed.

I should have known what was wrong from my linguistic training in Toronto. Perry came to the rescue asking if I had said the tones correctly, and therein was the key. Janet couldn't understand me because I had failed to incorporate the tones in my words. I had been merely repeating the sounds of the letters without using the appropriate tones. This was not something that Janet was probably aware of, and she couldn't explain it either.

The Bassa language has five different tones and several tonal glides, which are combined with the sounds of the letters. There is the high tone, low tone, mid tone, slanting tone, and double tone, which are placed on seven vowels. Different words can sound the same, but the meaning changes when a different tone is applied to it.

There is also a distinction between implosive and explosive. If a word is said with the air going in, it is implosive. Pronouncing the same word while the air is going out is called explosive, but it will mean something completely different.

One of our favorite illustrations of language learning was with the sound "bo":

bòò – long "O" in a lower tone held out means banana

bo – leg

Ɓo – implosive (said with the air going in) means okra

One day I asked Janet, "What do Bassa people talk about?" She explained that when they meet on the path, they ask each other, "Where are you going, and where are you coming from?" So those were some of the essential phrases I first learned. They also inquired if their body was cold, meaning do you have a fever, or the common greeting, "How are you?"

After that they would question each other to see if they had eaten anything that day by saying, "Did you chew or swallow your food?" This question would decipher what they had eaten. As Americans we don't think to ask people if they have found anything to eat, but around much of the world this is a normal topic of conversation.

When I mentioned to her one morning, "It sure did rain hard last night." She frowned at me and turned away. I was curious about her reaction. The other missionaries told me they had found the Bassa never talked about the weather, even though they are dependent upon it for their crops. Apparently when you live in an area where the rainfall could exceed 200 inches a year, you take rain for granted, and dismiss it entirely from the list of conversation topics.

Day to day domestic chores took much more time on primitive mission stations than they do in the States. While we were getting settled in the guest house, I asked if I could use Marty's small washing machine. Although she was most gracious and accommodating, I soon realized it required interrupting a household with two small children. In addition, the washing machine was something they had personally shipped out from the States, what if I broke it?

The washing machine also required running the expensive gas generator just to wash a couple loads of clothes. Therefore, I took our clothes to the nearby creek where the Bassa ladies congregated at the large rocks to wash their clothes. I figured I could do some language and culture study while I washed clothes with my neighbors and reasoned - it wouldn't be so bad.

I thought I would enjoy washing clothes at the waterside, but I had no clue how to hand wash. The Bassa had a rhythm to their washing and used a great many suds. I watched out of the corner of my eye and gave it a go. People laughed out loud as I washed my clothes, since I was embarrassingly clumsy. What must they have thought of someone who didn't even know how to wash her clothes? One lady commented it looked like it was my first-time washing clothes, indeed.

I came to the point of watching for people to leave the waterside and then I would take my turn down at the little stream. There I would hurriedly try to improve my technique of clothes washing.

Of course, dirty clothes began to pile up to unmanageable amounts for hand washing. Furthermore, we did not follow the Bassa rule of everyone, except young children, having to wash their own clothes. Janet saw her opportunity and asked if she could do the laundry for us. This was not only a relief for me, but also an additional source of income for her.

The Bassa washed their clothes, dishes and bodies with an all-purpose bar of soap that was locally made and available in the markets in lengths of about 20 inches. Sections of the soap were cut off as needed. When Janet washed our clothes, we always knew which ones they were, since they retained the scent of the market soap. It wasn't the perfect solution, however since the urgency of getting our clothes washed sometimes took the place of language lessons.

Our Bassa neighbors dried their clothes on the ground, including even the road, or laid them over bushes. I did try this method at first but found it unsatisfactory since my clean clothes would retain stones, sticks, leaves, and so on. The Bassa neighbors just shook these things off, but I felt it would be far better to use a clothesline. Perry constructed one like the other missionaries had out of bush poles and wire. I was glad I had clothes pins along, from the list of prescribed things to bring from the States.

In the dry season, the laundry dried so quickly that the first clothes up were often dry before I could finish getting them all on the line. If left on the clothesline overnight, the clothes could become wet all over again from the heavy tropical dew. During rainy season it took much longer to dry the clothes, even days. We hung them inside the house or under the ample eves. When we were not home, we also hung the clothes inside to avoid tempting those passing by.

The guest house quickly became our new home. We noted the turn of the seasons as the rains lessened. The heat of the dry season would soon be upon us. As the rain clouds began to clear away, we were often presented with a view of the beautiful rolling hills in the distance – God's beautiful creation!

7
Nutrition

Before we departed for Africa I wondered, and others often asked me, what we would eat. I really wasn't sure, but veteran missionaries told us to not worry about it. They said, "Everything will fall into place."

Orientation at the Vanderaa's helped in that regard, and we followed their lifestyle. Sometimes we ate Liberian food and sometimes we had common American food. Western style food was available in grocery stores in the cities and at commissaries at the iron-ore and rubber companies. Although their prices were a little high, we were able to enjoy food from our homeland.

It was not uncommon to go for a month or two without going to a grocery store. That took some getting used to, but I found that growing up on a farm had prepared me to live without grocery stores nearby.

If Perry had a meeting in town, he would stop at the store to pick up things we needed. There was also the chance of borrowing from missionary neighbors. When members of our mission team were passing by a teammate's home, we would always be helpful and deliver a few needed supplies for the other family, but those times were rare.

Since we went for long periods of time without shopping in the cities, staples were purchased in large amounts and put in our storage pantries. We could get flour and rice in 100-pound bags, which was a little much, so we often split it between families. The grain would become bug infested if left too long, and all flour had to sifted with a very fine net. We joked there was extra protein in the flour, and at least we knew the flour wasn't full of pesticides.

Everything had to be stored in tightly sealed containers to keep bugs and humidity out. I was shown plastic containers which had been used to store flour. The wheat weevils had actually drilled miniscule holes in the plastic sides, so large tin cans which originally contained powered milk were the best for storing flour.

Food preparation became a necessary part of my day and it was important to not become overwhelmed with it. What I found was that almost all cooking started from scratch, although there were some exceptions such as pasta. Cooking was often an adventure and substitutions were frequently made when we didn't have the ingredients commonly used in a recipe.

We tried to live off the land, harvesting from our gardens or fields. We also bought local foods from neighbors or at the weekly market in our area. Any of the basics for Bassa meal preparation were available there - such as rice, squash, legumes, oil, salt, greens, peppers, etc.

Chicken eggs could also be found in the market; however, they were usually boiled due to lack of refrigeration. When an egg was sold it was customary to distinguish what type of egg it was. After all, other birds such as ducks, and even snakes lay eggs.

Fresh or smoked meat could be purchased at the local market, and you never knew what you'd find for sale. There could be fish, jungle deer, or meat from any jungle animal, as well as domesticated sheep and goat. It was always a bit of a shock to see a monkey carcass hanging from a vendor's stall. They looked so human-like and eerily resembled a baby. Hunters would sell them in the market, and they were considered typical food.

Suddenly in 1982, the whole world changed with the identification of AIDS (Acquired Immune Deficiency Syndrome) originating from the primates.[6,7] In the African markets, the purchase of monkey meat was eventually considered dangerous. I never ate monkey, although for Perry it was certainly possible while on trek or while visiting people's homes.

Every week I made a large batch of bread from scratch. From it would come cinnamon rolls, pizza dough, buns, and bread. It was rewarding to pull a pan of cinnamon rolls from the oven, and there is nothing better than fresh bread. We often made sandwiches for a quick meal.

Bottle gas for our small European stove had to be used sparingly, because it could only be purchased in the capital city, and sometimes it was not available. Missionaries often cooked outside on a "coal pot", a small free-standing metal grill which burned locally made coal. I had a difficult time adjusting to this type of cooking and often took the chance of using the bottle gas, knowing at any time my supply could run out.

A small, collapsible camping oven was used over the coal pot to bake a single loaf of bread or an 8x8 sized pan. The insufferable fragile oven brought much frustration. It could easily collapse and had to be tended the entire time to keep the desired baking temperature regulated.

Preparing drinking water was a major task as well. It needed to be properly decontaminated and stored. Each mission family had developed their own process of treating water, so we tried several methods. At first, we added a chemical to purify it. It seemed wise to avoid ingesting the chemicals, so we filtered and/or boiled our drinking water. This seemed the best thing to do. Years later we devised a large container to filter the water and that was most convenient method.

Our first year, it seemed to be somewhat of an inconvenience to bring drinking water to the bathroom to brush our teeth. Eventually, we became careless and felt we if could swish and spit without swallowing any water, we were safe, since it came straight from the water tower, which was covered.

The missionary men assured the ladies the water tower had a filter, which we learned later was merely an athletic sock! Since all the water was either from our underground well or just rainwater captured from our roofs, it couldn't get contaminated - could it?

All that changed when a strange thing happened convincing us otherwise. Marty had mentioned there were plumbing problems in their bathroom with intermittent water supply from the faucet. One day when the tap was opened a mother snake exited the spout followed by several babies. It was at this point that inconvenience was no longer felt, and everyone saw to it that a pitcher of purified drinking water was available in the bathroom for brushing teeth.

One food item we longed for was a nice juicy tomato. We could buy a type of hard cherry tomato in the market, but they weren't the same as we had back in the States. Don did everything he could to grow beautiful tomato plants on our mission compound, but they were not fruitful. They grew quickly in the Liberian heat and displayed many yellow flowers, but it was a mystery as to why no fruit ever developed.

Several different varieties were tried, but none would set fruit. Don even sterilized dirt by heating it in a big metal barrel and kept it unpolluted in a screened planter box up off the ground. Again, the tomato seeds grew into beautiful plants, but even when the flowers were hand pollinated no tomatoes developed.

Not only did water need to be purified, but caution in eating local food needed to be practiced. The basic rule we followed was:

Boil it, Cook it, Peel it, or Leave it!

It took some time to get used to Liberian "chop", as their food is called in general. My main objection was to the hot pepper, a common ingredient in most Bassa foods. I tried to get used to it by slowly increasing the amount we used in our home, but it was always difficult for me to handle. (Years later, I was told I have a medical condition which cannot tolerate pepper.)

The Liberian peppers were unusually hot. They used a shriveled-up type of pepper called a ghost pepper and it is one of the hottest in the world. We have not been able to find it in the States. In fact, most people order it from Liberia, if they want to prepare authentic dishes.

Contact with it could literally burn the skin and it was advisable to wear rubber gloves. Some parents used it on their children as an admonishment. I personally felt this was quite harsh, and defiant children suffered for days afterwards.

No wonder the inside of my mouth often peeled after a simple meal enhanced with this pepper, but most missionaries liked it. From the beginning Perry always enjoyed the hot pepper. He could eat with the Bassa men who would playfully add more and more to the common bowl.

The traditional dishes were sauces called "soups", which were served over the main staple of rice. Probably the most common dish we ate in Liberia was sweet potato greens finely cut by hand and fried in burnt palm oil. Water, meat, onions, salt, hot pepper, and a seasoning cube were added to the greens, and then all boiled together. Collard greens were also similarly prepared using vegetable oil.

There were a couple different varieties of squash, which were used to prepare "pumpkin" soup. The squash was peeled and diced, then fried in oil with onion. Water was then added to the mixture, and the squash mashed down to a sauce. Pieces of fried fish were stirred into the squash for a surprisingly delicious dish.

Peanuts, which they called "ground pea", were also made into a sauce and eaten over rice. They would boil the peanuts, then beat them in a large mortar with a pestle, resulting in peanut butter. After cooking it with a few other ingredients and adding meat, a delightful soup was ready to be served over rice. (See Appendix C for my Liberian recipes.)

On my first trip to the local market I noticed that a lot of ladies were selling rice, but it all appeared the same to me. It didn't take too long to recognize the many varieties of rice, and eventually I became quite choosy when making my purchases. In the States, it is impossible to match the rice we purchased from the local markets and so enjoyed.

Bassa families often took pride in growing a distinct strain of rice they had developed through the years. Our favorite was a red rice grown by Corpu, a future neighbor, and his family. Their meticulously cultivated rice was carefully beaten to remove just the right amount of outer bran resulting in a delicious nutty taste. This is one thing we often crave but are unable to get in the States.

The Bassa people also made a totally different type of food called "dumboy" and "fufu". It was made from the tubular, very starchy root plant called cassava, which had the appearance of a long, narrow sweet potato. An advantage of growing cassava was that it could be harvested anytime of the year, thereby serving as a vital food source during the hungry times when the rice supply was depleted, normally the months of May and June.

To prepare cassava for dumboy, it had to be dug up in the field, then peeled, and sliced. The pieces were boiled, then pounded in a large wooden mortar with a pestle until a gelatinous, starchy mass was formed, resembling a mound of bread dough set aside to rise. Since the mass was so sticky, it was necessary for the pestle to be dipped in a bucket of water. In the village setting, this would be water brought straight from a nearby stream or river. Since the dumboy was not cooked, the use of river water allowed exposure to a whole realm of health problems.

The women often worked together to "beat" the cassava in turn, creating a beautiful rhythmic cadence, which could be heard in the distance. My attempts to join the pounding only slowed the process down considerably and resulted in laughter.

Fufu was made in a similar fashion but was a fermented variety of dumboy. A friend described the lengthy preparation. Peel the cassava and put it in water for several days, until there is a fermented smell and it gets a little soft. This will take 2-3 days. Put the cassava in a mortar and pound it, then put it in a rice bag (plastic woven bags that 100 lbs. of rice were sold in). Set the bag behind the house, with a large flat rock on top of it, and put another rock on top of that.

After some time drain the water off. Beat it again and take the strings out. Sift the cassava then put water in it and squeeze it until it dissolves, drain any extra water off. Cook the fufu over the fire, mashing it with a big wooden spoon while it boils. Sprinkle a little water on it if it gets dry and cook until bottom of pan turns brown. Cool it in an open pan, cut, and form into serving pieces.

Both dumboy and fufu were rounded and put into bowls in either single servings or larger amounts to be shared in rotation. A water-based soup with hot pepper was then poured over the beaten cassava. The soup often contained bitterball, a vegetable I never came to appreciate.

I found it difficult to eat both dumboy and fufu and never developed an appreciation for the soup. I preferred dumboy over fufu, since I could never get past the fermented scent and taste. If chewed, both cassava dishes would stick to the teeth like old gum to a finger. Such a predicament would be a source of amusement for those eating with you. Therefore, dumboy and fufu were simply swallowed.

The first time I ate it, David, Perry's language informant, carefully explained the procedure. It was necessary to first wet the spoon with the soup. If eating in the traditional manner, the fingers would be dipped in the soup. Using the edge of the spoon or the fingertips, a portion of dumboy was cut off no larger than you could swallow. Once again, the spoon and the dumboy were carefully coated with soup. Meanwhile, it was important to take a drink getting all your teeth sufficiently moist. A bite size piece was then simply placed in the mouth and swallowed without chewing or allowing it to touch the teeth.

Thus, when referring to this type of meal, the people would remark that they had "swallowed" their food, as opposed to having chewed something else. That way everyone would know they had swallowed dumboy or fufu.

In my experience, the first three spoonfuls went down reasonably well. After that, it was no longer possible to gracefully swallow without initiating the gagging reflex, which is difficult to hide and quite embarrassing. I found it worked well to eat a few bites, and then engage in conversation until the throat felt rested enough to resume the meal.

Perry's experience was more positive, and he felt quite comfortable sharing a bowl of dumboy or fufu with the Bassa men. When a meal is shared, a large bowl of food is placed in the center of a circle. One person would start eating, and it was considered polite to note the size taken. Each person would take an equal bite and they ate in rotation around the circle. Occasionally someone would add pepper or salt and it would be stirred into the whole pot of food for everyone to enjoy.

Traditionally the Bassa men would eat with spoons, and they ate before their dependents. The women and children ate whatever the men left for them, using a special cupped hand technique. Because of this style of family eating, the Bassa had the saying that a husband shows love for his wife and family by leaving enough meat for them.

When we were guests for a meal, it would have been unkind to eat all the food served to us. It was best to leave a nice portion for the children and the cook. Possibly, they might not have anything else to eat. If we cleaned our plate it would be insulting to our hostess, meaning we felt we had not been served enough, and had to eat it all.

8

Disease & Malaria

Although we frequently saw people with unfortunate diseases around us, we felt somewhat immune to tropical infirmities. We were of the common assumption that those things would not happen to us. However, even before we left Number 2, I developed some weird blisters and open sores on my face that were uncomfortable. I ended up seeing the doctor at LAC, where we learned I had impetigo, a highly contagious bacterial skin infection treated with antibiotic ointment.

We were also exposed to more serious conditions. Once while strolling down a path, we met two women and stopped to customarily converse with them in Bassa. I reached out and shook their hands, then noticed one of the ladies had several fingers missing and she had lost her nasal cartilage, both sure signs of leprosy. This was my first encounter with the disease and now I had exposed myself to it as well. I knew that leprosy is not easily contracted and requires lengthy repeated exposure to become infected. Still, it did cause some concern as I considered this introduction to an exotic disease and ran home to thoroughly wash my hands.

Several days later, I approached a roadside food stand concentrating on practicing a Bassa lesson to say I wanted to buy bananas. As I spoke, a very short lady turned to face me, and she had the most grotesque growth on her face I had ever seen. This would certainly not be the last time we witnessed something of that magnitude since medical care was not readily available to everyone. Unbeknown to us, we would soon endure a frightening ailment acquired from the infamous Anopheles mosquito.

Joe Fleming became a regular visitor as he worked around the mission doing carpenter jobs. He claimed to be a Christian, yet he was deceived by the "Never Die Church" and their unusual interpretation of the Bible. This church taught that if you truly believe in God you will never get sick and you will never die. There were many sad stories of his church abandoning their own members as they neared timely deaths. The church members said, "If they die, they never believed in the first place." Perry argued long and hard with Joe, but to our knowledge he was never persuaded.

Joe was also a victim of the dreaded guinea worm, although at the time we didn't know what it was. He showed us how he could press an open sore and a long stringy worm jutted out. Not only that, but it spit a flying string of sputum containing larvae. Shocked, I jumped back. How horrible to be host to a parasite like that!

Guinea worms are terribly painful and can reach 3 feet in length, being 1-2mm wide. The worm is contracted when villagers consumed water containing fleas that harbor guinea worm larvae. The larvae grow to maturity inside the body and emerge after a year as a fully grown two to three-foot-long worm that often exits through the leg or foot, but they can be anywhere under the skin. To alleviate the pain individuals often immerse the limb in water to cool the burning sensation, allowing the worm to eject its larvae in the water which starts the cycle all over again.

Guinea worm was once a problem affecting millions of people. Its eradication began in 1986 and it is nearly complete in a large part due to the efforts of the Jimmy Carter Center. The solution has been to simply filter water using a piece of ordinary cloth. When the program began, there were an estimated 3.5 million infected with Guinea worm in 21 countries, by 2016 only 25 cases were reported.[8]

Joe Fleming also suffered with Filaria, sometimes called lymphatic filariasis or elephantiasis. Exposure to this disease came through the bite of a mosquito or small fly. Another similar disease was onchocerciasis/ River Blindness. In the case of river blindness, a small humpbacked fly transported a parasitic worm from one person to another. The fly lived near fast flowing streams, such as were close to our guest house. After the worm was transferred it would produce micro-filaria, which could reside in the lymph glands and eyes - possibly causing swollen legs and even blindness.[9]

This disease was hyper-endemic in each area where we lived. We saw many people with swollen legs, and pastors in Perry's classes often complained of poor eyesight. He used our simple otoscope to confirm the worms in his students' eyes and would send them for treatment.

Several missionary families were particularly plagued with this disease. It seemed they were always searching out the best and latest medication. At that time diethylcarbamazine (DEC) was used, but it only killed immature parasites and resulted in severe itching caused by decomposing filaria material within the body.[10] The remedy was so miserable causing intense itching for lengthy periods of time, that people often decided to forego the treatment.

As if that wasn't enough, sometimes a mature filaria worm would attach itself to the tail bone and produce more worms. One of our missionaries had to go to the doctor in the States and have a mature worm literally chipped off the tail bone. The doctors were quite shocked to treat such an ailment. Perry and I had a positive filaria test but were fortunate to not experience any further symptoms of the disease.

After we left Liberia, Ivermectin (Mectizan) and albendazole were introduced. The medications quickly destroy the parasites without causing intense itching. It has been provided free of charge by Merck Pharmaceuticals as long as needed.[11]

On one of our visits to a nearby village, the young children screamed and ran away from us. Apparently, they had never seen white people before. The people of the village were friendly and eager to speak with us and we returned often.

Perry and I had learned at linguistics school that it would be advantageous to live in a village and become immersed in the culture and language. We felt segregated living on the mission station, although villages were quite close. It seemed that the village we had been visiting would be an ideal location in which to live part time.

We arranged to rent a room in a house that was being built and I began to make some simple curtains for privacy. We ordered a bed to be constructed by a local carpenter and were waiting for doors and shutters to be made when our plans suddenly changed.

The African night is a wonder to behold. Without the competition of artificial lights, God's starry display is there in its complete splendor. It was while living at Number 3 that the clouds cleared, and we first saw the Southern Cross and Big Dipper in the same sky. It seemed the Big Dipper was one of our few links with home, and the Southern Cross was a reminder of God's protection and sovereignty in a foreign world.

Perhaps we gazed at the starry wonder too long allowing another of God's creation, the mosquito, to work its wonder on our physical bodies. It wasn't long afterwards that Perry complained of headache, fever, and stomachache. Later that day, he became violently ill with vomiting and diarrhea. The next day he felt better although incredibly tired, and he complained of a terrible backache. We assumed he had a virus, especially when I developed the same symptoms.

We then experienced the more violent second wave of illness, followed by a short reprieve, and before long Perry was very ill again. We laid on the bathroom floor after vomiting and diarrhea, too exhausted to leave. Being rookies was taking its toll, any experienced missionary would have recognized malaria!

We were too sick for language study and apparently our language informants told the nurse at the LIM mission. She sent word that she suspected we had malaria, and we should start a course of chloroquine treatment immediately.

We took the initial four pills, but by that time Perry was too sick to keep any tablets down. His temperature rose above 104° F, he became delirious, and I could not get his fever under control with sponge baths.

I became seriously concerned when he showed signs of confusion. Since he couldn't keep anything down, it became clear to me that he hadn't gotten enough chloroquine and acetaminophen into his system. I hurried across the mission station to report to Marty that Perry was in a serious state. We agreed Perry needed to get to the LAC hospital as soon as possible to see a doctor.

I was surprised when Perry could not rise from the bed and was unable to walk. Marty and I each looped our arms around an arm pit and dragged him out to the car, leaving two trails in the rocks with his heels.

As Marty raced the car down the road to the LAC plantation, Perry lay across my lap in the back seat. We opened all the windows and I threw water on him, trying to get his fever to break. We were finally successful, and he stirred from his stupor, asking where we were going.

Arriving at the hospital, Marty ran into the office and returned with Dr. Williams, a British doctor employed by the rubber company. He came and grabbed Perry out of the car. Getting him into a wheelchair he exclaimed, "My God, he's burning up". The doctor hurried away, pushing Perry in front of him.

As I followed them into a hospital room, the doctor barked out orders for a malarial smear and other blood tests. He then quickly gave Perry two shots of chloroquine. One was injected in the backside and the other directly into the liver, which caused him to awaken from his delirium with a scream. Intravenous feeding was then started to replenish his fluids.

The doctor wondered how he had gotten to such a state, so I explained we thought we had a virus. Realizing I too most likely had malaria, he gave me a packet of chloroquine tablets to complete my treatment and told me to go home with Marty.

Thinking Perry was in serious condition, I refused to leave the hospital. But the doctor assured me repeatedly that Perry had a positive malaria smear and with the chloroquine injections he would soon be feeling better.

I remember the British doctor saying, "Cerebral Malaria is always serious, and you almost waited too long, but since we've treated him, you won't recognize him in the morning. He'll be greatly improved."

Throughout the night when Perry would stir from his sleep, he found the doctor sitting near his bedside. And, Dr. Williams had told the truth. In the morning when I wearily returned to the hospital driving the difficult stick-shift pickup, I was shocked to see him up and ready to go home.

Don and Marty had left early that morning for a Bible translation checking conference in River Cess, so we were alone on the mission station to rest and recover. Experiencing overwhelming weakness, Perry and I slept the day away. As our bodies recovered from the effects of the disease, at times we still argued over who would use the bathroom first.

Exhausted and weak from the illness, we barely managed to feed ourselves and prepare water to drink. Even taking a much-needed shower was surprisingly fatiguing. Afterwards I lay on the bathroom floor for some time trying to regain my strength to get up.

9

Protection

Perry's first night home from the hospital, we fell into a deep sleep, but I awoke suddenly in the middle of the night. There was a strange feeling on my neck and chest, and I was scratching incessantly. Then I had a God-like call to get out of bed and write a letter to Perry's Grandma Tink'. She had told us she would be our prayer warrior and I wanted to ask her to pray for us.

Fidgety and unable to sleep, I decided to follow my "calling". I stepped out of bed, only to realize the bedroom floor needed to be better swept. It seemed there were large pieces of sand everywhere. Strange, I hadn't remembered the floor being so dirty when we went to bed.

As I bent over to light the kerosene lamp, the flickering flame exposed ants crawling up and down my long hair and nightgown. Wildly shaking my hair and brushing my body, it became apparent that the "sand" on the floor was a multitude of ants - black driver ants! Now as I panicked the ants began to bite and I frantically pulled them off.

I found the flashlight and soon discovered the extent of the invasion. There were ants everywhere invading half of our home. They were even on the bed where Perry lay sleeping. I curiously noted there were no ants on him yet, but I reasoned it was only a matter of time before they got to him.

Being in a panic and not wanting him to startle awake from ant bites, I took a running leap to jump over the ants on the bedroom floor - landing on the bed. He of course then awoke in shock from a screaming wife saying something about "ants…ants".

To this day, Perry thinks the Lord was protecting him from the insects and maintains that I could have let him sleep instead of waking him. We have also thought that perhaps his still fevered body naturally repelled the bothersome creatures. Or perhaps, after taking high doses of chloroquine, it was escaping from his pores and repelling the ants.

Knowing that kerosene was used to turn the pests away, Perry wearily went to the storage shed to get some. He then went back to bed in the second bedroom where there were no ants.

Meanwhile, I poured a thin barrier of kerosene on the floor to hold the ants back and kept watch through the remaining hours of the night, vowing they would not enter the remainder of the house. The ants were somewhat stubborn trying to cross the line of kerosene, but in retrospect it appears this was because I had caged them in, leaving no point of escape.

Driver ants traveled in columns foraging for food by invading whole areas, trees, and even houses. Their bite did not sting, but with large pinchers they were able to pull out hunks of flesh. Before modern medicine was available, their pinchers could be used as sutures. The largest soldier ants were used, and one pincher was offered to each side of a wound. The ant would close its pinchers pulling the skin together, then the body of the ant could be sectioned off, and the wound would heal in place.

Being rookie missionaries had its draw backs. We hadn't recognized when we got malaria and didn't know how to handle driver ants, but we also didn't realize the depths of God's care. As I watched the hours of the night pass, I began to surmise that my all-knowing, all-powerful God had fallen short on His watchfulness.

My prayers became accusations. I reminded God that we had gone to Africa to do His work, so He should be taking better care of us. I could handle getting malaria, perhaps that was to be expected, and I was extremely grateful He had brought Perry back from cerebral malaria, but the additional ant invasion in the middle of the night put me over the edge!

Couldn't God have set up a little roadblock or something in the jungle to turn the ants away from our house, especially on the night Perry had gotten home from the hospital? I knew God could have done all this, I guessed He just didn't want to. Although I knew better, that was the state I worked myself into and I reasoned that I was only being honest with God.

As I witnessed the dawn of a new day and beautiful light began to fill the sky, I was reminded of God's faithfulness to his creation. Begrudgedly,

I began to read some Psalms, coming to concentrate on 102:1-2 and 103:1-5.

Hear my prayer, O Lord;
let my cry for help come to you.
Do not hide your face from me
in the day of my distress!
Bless the LORD, O my soul;
and all that is within me,
Bless his holy name.
Bless the LORD, O my soul,
and forget not all his benefits.
Who forgives all your iniquity,
Who heals all your diseases,
Who redeems your life from the pit,
Who crowns you with steadfast love and mercy,
Who satisfies you with good
So that your youth is renewed like the eagle's.

After accusing God of forgetting us, I was brought to the point of thanking Him for His provisions. My cherished husband had been nearly stripped away the day before. Yet, our Heavenly Father had redeemed our lives from the depths of malaria, just as He had redeemed us from the oppression of our sin. How could I doubt His steadfast love for us?

As the sun rose further in the sky, He drew me back to Himself through His Word and I praised Him. But God was not nearly finished with two young people who claimed they wanted to only focus on God's call for their lives. A couple of eye-opening events would soon thoroughly shake us up.

Under instructions to daily inform the missionaries at Number 2 of our condition, we made our way across the yard to Don and Marty's vacant house to use the mission radio. We reported the ant invasion, dwindling drinking water supply, and general weakness. Even though there were lots of ants to sweep up, everyone agreed that rest was what we needed.

The following day we made an unscheduled transmission to Margaret seeking a medical consult. We were thankful our mission FM radios were never shut off because we needed advice. Perry had developed the additional problem of heavy blood in the stool, making us anxious. Margaret suggested we make an emergency run back to Dr. Williams at LAC, even though it was 10:00 on Saturday night. The doctor was concerned that Perry may have gotten an ameba or something else, but the tests he ran that night turned out negative.

We returned home with a diagnosis of a tired and distressed digestive system. The next morning at our scheduled transmission we were not given an option by our field leader. Larry and family left Number 2 shortly thereafter to take us back with them for recuperation at their home. We were to remain there until the next mission meeting.

That evening we nestled down at Larry and Ann's home in the familiar children's bedroom, anticipating a much-desired night of sleep. In the middle of the night we were awakened – supposedly - by the aftereffects of malaria, and together rushed off to the bathroom in the dark.

Later Perry waited in the doorway turning on the bedroom light to help me find my way. Crawling into bed, I caught movement out of the corner of my eye.

I froze realizing a snake's tail had just slipped from under the covers. My eye followed its long body across the nearby bookshelf and onto a desk. Perry noted the head of the creature approximately 6-7 feet away, and we simultaneously whispered, "Snake".

It is interesting what people do in such a situation. I dashed over the footboard and out the doorway, while Perry attempted to grab a pair of pants hanging over a chair near the watchful eyes of the snake.

Without much thought, I burst into the bedroom where Larry, Ann, Erica and Joel were sleeping and yelled, "Snake, there's a snake in our bedroom!"

After the cutlass was retrieved from behind the refrigerator and Larry had grabbed a shovel, the men noisily searched the bedroom throwing furniture aside. They did not find the snake but discovered a hole in the window screen.

Assuming the reptile had escaped through the opening, they went outside and were amazed to witness its ability move straight up in the air, make a right angle, carry on horizontally, then after another right angle attach to a tree branch, before quickly disappearing. We later identified the snake as a Blanding's Tree snake, which is a rear-fanged venomous snake, mildly poisonous to humans.

The women and children safely assembled in the distant living room, while the men bravely searched for the reptile. I shuttered and Ann offered me a sweater thinking I was chilled. I took the sweater explaining that I was not cold but had felt a chill as I considered my earlier accusations against God. I had actually charged Him with not protecting us.

Since we had seen a snake leaving our bed, perhaps God was clearly demonstrating to me that He *will neither slumber nor sleep*, Psalm 121:3. I was getting the message loud and clear. God was totally in charge and certainly protecting us from serious harm.

While recuperating at Number 2, the effects of malaria began to wear off. However, the typical lingering tiredness from the disease and harsh medication hung on with a sense of depression and disappointment. These haunting feelings gave us cause to reassess our call to Liberia.

One day we took a short walk to the government compound to regain our strength. It was a hot day and as we walked, we wondered how we would know if we should go back to Liberia after Perry's final year in seminary. Perry said he wished we could have some type of sign from God. After walking only a few steps further, we noticed something lying in the road that looked like a gold coin.

Picking it up and turning it over, we were shocked to see it was a key ring medallion and on it was written "PERRY'S". And even more surprising, was the imprint of a large capital "T" as though it stood for "Tinklenberg". Was this the sign we had talked about and not even had the chance to pray for?

We have no idea how the medallion got there in the middle of the orange gravel road. It wasn't something Perry had lost, we had never seen anything like it before, and the whole time we were in Liberia we never met another person named Perry.

But there it was - an overwhelming response for two bewildered kids from South Dakota in the middle of the African jungle. The whole incident was shocking, and we didn't really discuss its implications that day. The medallion became a favorite possession always reminding us of God's careful attention to each detail in our lives. (Unfortunately, it was stolen from our Stateside home with many other things.)

After we returned home to Compound 3, we accepted the invitation of two Lebanese brothers. They ran a store and sold supplies of all kinds to the general population. They often invited us to have a cold coke, and we became friends with them finding it interesting to converse with them in English.

They had living quarters behind the store and Liberian wives and families. The men were Muslims, so we tried to tell them about Jesus, but they were firmly rooted in their religion.

Unfortunately, one of the brothers made me increasingly uncomfortable with his overt friendliness. One evening we sat with them on their back porch and enjoyed a demitasse cup of their strong, thick coffee, while an odorous mosquito coil burned nearby. Perry was only feet away talking to one of the brothers, when the other unashamedly told me his goal was to see Perry and I divorce!

I didn't think I had heard him correctly, but he went on to say he would then marry me, and I would take him to the States. After he gained US citizenship and had a son, he would divorce me, and move his entire family to the States. What an outrageous and alarming thing to hear! I gasped, "That will never happen!"

Shocked, I grabbed Perry by the hand, and we left while the brothers were asking why we were leaving. I said, "I think you know why!" From then on, I kept my distance and refused to stop at their store though they called as I walked by.

Often dangerous reptiles and insects grabbed our interest and attention.

One night a huge scorpion appeared a few feet from the front door to emphasize the importance of using a flashlight and wearing shoes. It was the first one we had seen, and it was about 8-10 inches long, had huge pinchers, and a 6″ tail with a sharp needle at the end.

Something even more dangerous lived in our immediate area. Don and Marty had laying hens in a pen behind the storage shed. Fresh eggs were a real treat and important source of protein. Several chickens died of unknown cause. After no apparent problems, one chicken at a time would end up dead in the morning.

With the flock slowly diminishing in size, the mystery was finally solved when a black cobra was sighted in a palm tree near the chicken coop. The mission ground keepers were able to chase the predator out of the tree and kill it. They explained the snake was smart enough to realize that if it swallowed the chicken whole, it would be unable to pass through the chicken wire. So, it simply sucked the blood out of the bird leaving the carcass behind.

Thinking we were invincible with mosquitoes, we did some star gazing and sure enough contracted malaria again. We took the medication immediately, and even though the disease did not progress, we experienced significant weakness. This was probably since we had not fully recovered from our first bout with malaria. Perry was especially weakened by the return attack, and the gravity of having malaria twice weighed heavily upon us. We began to feel the Bassa mission project was not for us.

Sensing our despair, Larry invited Perry on a five-day trek to the Margibi area north of his mission. He promised to postpone it until Perry had fully regained his strength from having malaria a second time.

The purpose of the trek would be to survey a new area, chart churches, and meet pastors who had expressed their desire for a TEE class. The trek would take them through 'Gibi area and they would walk home to Number 2 mission station. Ann and I drove the guys to Firestone Rubber plantation, where they chartered a taxi to take them to Kakata.

Traveling alone in the back seat of a chartered taxi, they noticed the road was visible between the sides of the car and its floor. Perry wondered if the body was attached to the chassis and pushed up on the roof of the car causing the body to lift slightly from the floor.

The driver yelled to stop lifting the roof and destroying his car. It was a curious thing and they wondered if the car was loose, so Perry and Larry locked elbows and pushed on the side of it lifting the back of the vehicle. At this point the driver threatened to kick them out and leave them in the middle of the road, so they promised to stop fooling around.

During the trek they unfortunately found the church leaders were fighting amongst themselves and were not united. Larry informed the pastors that the mission would not be able to open classes in this area for some time, possibly two years.

They walked 35 miles on this trek, entering three remote villages unannounced, and found lodging in Bassa homes. They again passed through areas of virgin jungle covered with tree top canopies. Of course, Perry hoped to see some exciting wildlife, but he only saw two parrots.

The men were disturbed one night when two adolescent girls appeared at their bedroom door, dressed in the traditional fashion with only a lappa skirt and well-oiled bodies. They giggled shyly and the men had the sense that the girls were forced to come to their room. They spoke to the girls briefly, but they did not allow them to enter the open doorway before asking them to leave. The girls seemed relieved and ran away.

They experienced rats one night in their room, and Larry had trouble with bed bugs the first night of their journey. Strangely enough Perry did not experience them, even though he slept in the same bed.

This immersion into Bassa culture was exactly what Perry needed after enduring two bouts of malaria. We were thankful God had brought healing and Perry had recovered sufficiently to go on the trek, because it gave him renewed excitement and vision for the mission work before us.

A Christian Reformed builder from Iowa named Hank arrived in Liberia to build a home for Mark and Pat's family in the city of Buchanan. He was a great guy and we enjoyed his company. Quiet by nature and an experienced elder, he was perceptive of the relationships between missionaries and the struggle our team was going through concerning the goals of the ministry.

Since it would benefit him as a builder to have a pickup, the mission purchased a new Peugeot station wagon, identical to all the others. Don and Marty drove the new vehicle, and we then received their car as a hand-me-down. It seemed a luxury to have a car after contending with the old pickup.

Shortly before Hank arrived and we still had the pickup, I found myself in a dangerous situation and used it as a get-away vehicle. Perry had taken our "new" station wagon to Buchanan for a meeting with Bassa church leaders and the pickup was parked near our home.

I remained in the guest house, alone on the mission station since the other family was gone as well. Shortly after Perry left, David B. came to the mission compound. He was the young man who had been employed as a mission grounds keeper and had given me a good Bassa name.

Within only a few months, unfortunate circumstances in David B.'s life had caused village elders to attach a chain and heavy log to his ankle. This was used as a punishment, to restrict his movements, and to keep track of him. The rumor was that he had "blown his brains out" on drugs and was often violent.

He had been an excellent football player and had a chance to make it on the national football team. (Soccer is called football in Liberia.) When he went to Monrovia for the team try outs, he unfortunately took some "country medicine," which was supposed to enhance his performance. Instead, it permanently damaged his brain and he was left marginalized to live a difficult life. When he came back home, I hardly recognized him.

Although we took pity on David B, we were warned his behavior was erratic and we should stay away from him. Still, we were accustomed to seeing him wander about the mission, so I was not overly alarmed by his appearance on the driveway that day.

I ignored him, thinking he was only passing through on his way to the nearby stream. Eventually, he dragged his log to my doorway, asking to see Perry. I responded, "Perry can't talk to you right now." I didn't want David B. to know I was home alone.

I told him I was doing housework, so I didn't have time to talk and asked him to go home. He remained near my doorway for a couple hours. I worked steadily in the house under his fixed gaze and continual verbiage. It seemed best to keep occupied and I had lots of nervous energy as my uninvited companion continued his banter through the flimsy screen door.

Listening to what he said, but not conversing with him, I became fearful. On the table near the door I set the tape recorder to record his tauntings and placed a note next to it. It said, "Listen to this recording of David B. if anything happens to me." I eerily thought that it would be evidence of the circumstances, and it afforded me the luxury of mentally shielding my ears from his threats.

As darkness began to fall, I commented to David B. several times that he should return to his town before dark, which he refused to do. I began to feel quite vulnerable, and startled when he rattled the door saying he was coming in. Most worrisome was the front door's fragile lock was only a shallow hook and eye, which I knew would not hold under pressure. It was of some comfort that the house windows were secure with the expanded metal coverings, but they too prevented me from escape.

After a while, I locked myself in the bathroom and remained quiet praying fervently he would go away. I attempted to devise a get-away plan. My main problems were no back door for escape, and I hadn't located the pickup keys where they were supposed to be in the bedroom.

The bathroom door and lock were more secure than the front door, so I figured I'd be safer in there, and if I was out of sight maybe David B. would go home. I didn't want to consider what he could do to the bathroom door by throwing his log and his jeering became increasingly frightening.

Frantic in the bathroom behind the locked door, I considered further options like going through the attic access in the bathroom ceiling, but I remembered the roof was sealed off and possible dangers awaited me there in the form of insects and snakes.

Another consideration was escaping out the shower window, although it too had the expanded metal preventing my escape. I would need a screwdriver and hammer to remove it, and it was above shoulder height making it an impossible to get out.

Then came the answer to my anxious prayers when I noticed the pickup key under something on the counter. David B. was at the front door between me and the pickup. I wondered if I gave the impression that I was removing the bathroom window covering, would he come around to the backside of the house allowing me to get out the front door?

I ran the keys across the expanded metal in the window, and sure enough he made his way around to the back of the house and stood under the bathroom window with his hands on the screen. From that vantage point he continued to taunt me banging on the window.

Knowing my chance had come, I grabbed the key, darted out the front door, padlocked it shut, and ran for the pickup on the other side of the house. David B. heard me securing the door and began yelling loudly. When he saw me at the pickup, he picked up his log, and began to run towards me. My hands were shaking so much that I fumbled with the key to unlock the door.

There was the option of returning to the house or perhaps fleeing to the nearby village, but I was not sure my shaking knees would get me that far. I knew he was a strong young man and he would probably catch up to me. Finally, the pickup door opened, I jumped inside and locked the door.

By then David B. had made it to the passenger window, where he pounded until I was afraid the glass would break. All he had to do was throw his log through the window and my escape would be foiled.

I turned the key in the ignition, but panic gripped me, and I flooded the finicky engine. I cried out, "Please Lord, please." Holding the accelerator to the floor, the engine finally came to a full roar, I shifted to reverse, carefully let out the clutch, and began my escape.

While I was backing up, David B. attempted to jump on the hood, but I got the vehicle out of the way. He picked up his log and came lunging at the driver's side, so I backed further out of his reach.

Full of emotion and a fresh rush of adrenaline, I shifted from reverse and decided to skip first gear and speed ahead in second gear. The clutch was tricky and there in the middle of the mission grounds, the engine stalled.

Panic washed over me as I watched David B. in the side mirror. He was still pursuing me and had nearly reached the pickup again. I realized he could possibly jump in the back and renewed my fight with the difficult clutch.

Fortunately, my grandfather had taught me how to drive stiff stick shifts as a teenager back on the farm. I concentrated and confidently regained control of the motor. Patiently I shifted through each gear, and was quickly on my way. In the rear-view mirror David B. stood shaking his raised fists at me.

I passed the village at a high speed where people on the road stopped and looked quizzically at me. I sped by not knowing where I was going, but I headed towards Buchanan where Perry was, and colleagues lived. As I drove, all my composure from the last hours melted in consideration of the danger I had faced.

About five miles down the road I was unaware when I met Perry in the dark. He was on his way home from Buchanan and recognized the vehicle, including his pale wife staring past him. When I didn't slow down, he blew the horn and flashed his lights, I continued my numb journey.

Perhaps he spun the car in a 180° turn on the gravel road, because he quickly caught up to me honking loudly. I pulled over and tried to explain what had happened, but I felt so bad. Later Perry listened to the recording and commented I had escaped none too soon.

It took me a few days to recover from the fright, and for some time we did not see David B. around the mission or in the village. We thought perhaps they had moved him to another location deeper in the jungle. We later learned the village elders had done the only thing they knew to do, and that was to inflict him with corporal punishment.

This event was quite sobering for me. I lamented the fact that he was beaten so badly, but I could not have changed the reprimand he received. The next trip to town I went along, not wanting to stay home alone. The first thing on the shopping list was a better locking system with a slide bolt on the inside and big, long screws.

Our experiences with illness and danger made the nearness of God and His protection tangible in our lives. To experience His constant defense on our behalf and feel His presence in our lives were intimate blessings from God, giving us peace amid the difficulties of life so far from home.

10

Travels

With the memory of our first solo trip to Monrovia fresh on our minds, Perry and I traveled back to the capital city and successfully completed our resident visa applications. On the way home we were relieved to be cleared for travel past the check point at the dreaded army base.

The evening was hot and humid, and we enjoyed the rush of air from the open windows. As we traveled down the jungle lined roads, it seemed we had avoided any problems, but the evening still held some adventure.

Our conversation turned to wondering about something that had happened to a fellow missionary. While driving alone with the windows down in the dark of night, a long snake in the middle of the road was driven over. It was not an uncommon experience in Liberia, since snakes often laid in the road absorbing warmth. But there was always an eeriness about it, and that evening the "bump" in the road was followed by something tossing around in the back seat. It gave the impression that the snake had somehow flipped up and into the backseat window, possibly as a result of being hit by the car.

In this frightening situation, the vehicle was abandoned. In the morning when the car was retrieved, there was no evidence of a snake having been in the car. Everyone wondered could the snake have been in the car and exited later in the night through an open car windows?

Speculating on the probability of this occurrence, we were stunned when something jumped out of the jungled ditch and our car hit it.

Coming to a stop, Perry ran back to see what was lying in the road. He returned carrying an animal. It looked quite strange with both spots and stripes and a patch over its eyes. I didn't know what it was, but Perry was attuned to the wildlife in our rain forest and knew right away it was a civet cat. He was excited to see one up close. He wrapped it in a plastic gunny sack and threw it in the back of the station wagon.

We drove on with our first scare of the evening lying behind us. I wondered if it wouldn't stink like a skunk, but it did not, and I questioned Perry as to whether it might be still alive. I thought it would be frightening if it suddenly woke up and started running around in the car, but he assured me it was definitely dead.

Our next thought was what we would do with the animal. We had lived in Liberia long enough to know that whomever we gave it to would be grateful to have "fresh meat" for their family. They might even have a special feast and invite friends, so we were pleased to not only see a rare animal, but also to provide food for some family.

A couple miles up the road we came to the police gate at Number 1. Coming to a stop, three officers quietly circled our car shining flashlights in the vehicle. I noted they had not customarily greeted us and held their guns ready. We had been in a similar situation before, and it put us on high alert.

As they shone their flashlights around the interior of the car, one officer went to the driver's side and told us they were looking for suspicious people. He asked if we had given anyone a ride or if we had seen anything strange. We responded we had not. The officers went around to the front, where they all looked at something closely. We could not hear what they were saying.

In the car we quietly considered perhaps they saw blood on our bumper. We would have to tell them what happened and to prove it expose the fresh meat. The officials might feel it was their right and our obligation to "gift" the meat to them, but we were hoping to give it to friends. We waited patiently, hoping they were only memorizing our car license number.

They returned to sternly ask us again if we had given anyone a ride and if we had seen any strange people along the road. We assured them we had been alone, but we were not sure what they meant by "strange people". They asked where we were going and where we had been, common questions.

The officer told us there were strange people out that night, and added, "You know this is Devil Country, and bad things happen here. Let us know if you see someone suspicious and up to no good on the road. Do not stop on your way, even if you get a flat tire." An unnerving feeling passed through us.

They opened the single bar gate, allowing us to pass through. Whenever we were invited to travel beyond the check point, it was always with a sigh of relief, and that time was no exception.

On high alert, I thought it best to roll up the back windows and lock the car doors, but noted there was no one on the road that night. Strangely there were no fires burning in the kitchens. The whole community was apparently afraid and in their houses.

We wondered what was going on. Perry said, "It almost feels like a murderer is on the loose." Little did we know how accurate he was. We drove straight home and made it safely without seeing anything strange.

The next morning Perry gave David, his language informant, quite a surprise when he presented him with the civet cat. He was thrilled and

David, Perry's language informant and recipient of the civet cat, our home is in the background

tutoring was cancelled for the day, since he needed to take it home for meal preparation.

At the time we didn't realize how tasty its meat would be. Several years later, Perry and I along with our children visited one of his TEE students. We found him on his expansive rice farm and he proudly invited us for an impromptu meal. We were served an exceptionally delicious meat with rice and greens as we ate while squatting on a bamboo pole bench in a simple thatch kitchen.

I was curious as to what the meat was. Perry's student answered my question proudly saying it was civet cat. The thought of eating any type of cat nearly repulsed me. Perry said, "Just remember how much you liked it before you knew what it was."

Shortly after Perry's hospitalization with his first bout of malaria, we received word that his parents intended to travel to Liberia and would arrive four days before Christmas. It seemed strange they were coming at Christmas time and not spending the holiday with his two younger brothers.

When we watched his parents disembark from the plane and go into the customs office, we waited closely observing each passenger. And sure enough - his younger brothers tried to sneak past!

They arrived after a layover in Dakar, Senegal where they witnessed several unusual things. In the airport terminal the men's restroom had one toilet – simply a long trough with water running through it. They also saw one of their pieces of luggage leaving the plane on a cart. That suitcase should have stayed on the plane and did not arrive in Liberia until five months later.

We suggested Perry's family make a visit to the restroom before leaving the airport and heading "up country". We explained we had a long four-hour drive ahead of us. They felt sure it was not necessary, so we departed on the journey to our home. Naturally, halfway there Perry's family began to mention the need for a bathroom stop.

In true African custom, Perry pulled the car over to the side of the road and our guests questioned us as to where the restrooms were. "There are many here," was our smirking answer. "The men's is always on the left side of the road and the women's is on the right."

Bev and I picked our way through the grass in the ditch and sought privacy within the jungle. We soon realized the dreaded fire ants had claimed the area and went charging back to the car. Bev's panty hose was tossed aside, since it had been invaded by the stinging ants.

It was fun to introduce Perry's family to our new lifestyle. We felt experienced, having lived there for four months, but we had just begun to understand our host culture.

Perry made a Christmas tree with palm branches stuck into a wooden pole. It looked close enough to the real thing, and we even decorated it with lights his parents had brought out. What a joy it was to celebrate Christmas together in the African jungle.

On January 2, Larry and Ann treated our family with a guided trek to the waterfalls on the St. John River. We drove one hour north of our home, then walked for two hours in the jungle to view a magnificent sight. Even though the river water was quite low, the waterfall was spectacular. We enjoyed cooling off in the water before starting the trek back to the cars.

It was a long hard walk and some in our group became exhausted. We decided the weary ones should be the first in line to follow the Bassa guide, otherwise they lagged behind, felt tired, and were discouraged. After that hike, this became a guideline we followed whenever necessary.

Our first Christmas season we took Perry's parents and brothers to LAC for swimming at the country club and to purchase supplies at the company store. Amenities for expatriate employees included a small country club situated atop a high hill surrounded by a rough nine-hole golf course. The club also had a swimming pool and a short order grill which served hamburgers and hot dogs. The plantation hospital was where we had taken Perry when he had malaria.

One hot day found us drawn to a cooling swim in the pool, where some young Bassa boys approached me asking if I'd like to buy a baby owl. It was the cutest thing, just a ball of down. They sensed I was drawn to the bird, but I told them I wasn't interested.

After a while they came back offering to give me the baby owl.

Knowing it would perish if not well cared for, we took it home with us and were constantly entertained by its growth and development.

In choosing a name we decided on "Poky" after the Bassa word for owl - "pooh-coon". We fed it table scraps of meat, but as it grew its appetite became insatiable and the neighborhood children would often bring lizards to supplement its diet.

One day we arrived home and realized Poky had started to fly when we found it perched on a chair back. Perry's father constructed a cage for it from chicken wire and 2x2 boards. The bird grew quickly and became quite large. The Bassa neighbors were afraid of it, often teasing it, and causing it to hiss at them.

Later Joe Fleming kept Poky for us when we went home to the States. The bird was always tame preferring to live around people and enjoying flights in the jungle. While we were gone, it was unfortunately shot when a soldier mistook it for an evil spirit, a common misconception.

We took our family members to the capital city, where Perry's parents and we purchased wicker chairs. Our chairs were well-made, and we used them for ten years in Liberia. I sometimes wish I still had them.

Since his family was flying home the next day, we wrapped their chairs and baskets in large rice bags to be shipped on the airplane. Transporting the cumbersome chairs on the airlines went surprisingly well, as did passing through customs. The difficult part came in New York when they had to tie them on the outside of the vehicle for a snowy drive to South Dakota - halfway across the U.S.

After Perry's family left, our plan was to start living in our rented village bedroom, where we would settle in for language and culture study. Perry and David checked on the room and found that in our absence the bed, doors, and windows had unfortunately not been completed. The carpenter needed money first for building supplies. We were disappointed since it looked like it would be some time until we could stay there.

David then led Perry into the jungle for a day of hard work harvesting palm nuts from tall trees for his mother. Perry learned that day to climb a single bamboo pole used as a ladder to reach the clusters of red nuts. Later we would join David's family to learn the laborious task of making palm oil used for cooking.

Perry and David took only a few breaks to eat a couple pineapples. Dehydration began to set in while the highly acidic pineapple ate a hole in Perry's stomach lining. He became seriously ill, so they made their way out of the jungle, and David rushed Perry by taxi to the LAC hospital once again. At the hospital, Dr. Williams scolded Perry and told him as his doctor he could not allow him to live in the village. Perry was dehydrated, so after another infusion a lengthy recovery was unfortunately required.

This setback in health caused us to again wonder if God would desire our future service in Liberia. In a state of confusion, I would wander out our front door and down the little hill along a jungle path to the nearby stream. It was one of the most idyllic spots I have ever seen, with numerous water lilies blooming above the lazily flowing water. God had caused the trees to reach out and offer shaded seclusion. Some flat rocks upstream provided a haven on which to ponder many Psalms without the worry of crawling insects or reptiles.

I earnestly sought God's will as to whether we should return to Liberia and asked Him to make His will be mine. My prayer became, "What is Your desire? Not my will, but yours Almighty God!"

Practically speaking, this hideaway was also the popular place for our Bassa neighbors to wash their clothes, bathe, or collect water. My moments of solitude and prayer would quickly vanish when people appeared for their daily chores. Perched on my meditation rock at the stream, Bassa neighbors would question me and ask what I was doing.

At times I longed for privacy that seemed lost when we left the States. We also had to get used to people peeking in our windows. They would ask what we were doing, what we were eating, or if they could have something they saw in my house.

As time passed, I became accustomed to sharing my life with my neighbors. I was less lonely that way, and maybe they were just curious as to how we lived. Strangely enough, I felt isolated when we returned to the States and no one looked in my window, nor cared enough to ask me what I was doing in my house.

As I viewed my homeland through my new African-tinted glasses, I had to wonder why Americans didn't care about each other, and why they wanted to be secluded. How could they leave each other so isolated, tucked away in their houses?

In Liberia whenever we met someone on the path, they would ask where we were going and where we were coming from. We were obligated to tell them and inquire the same of them. To do anything less would simply have been rude. At first, I felt this was somewhat intrusive into my personal life, however as I became accustomed to the rhythms of Bassa life, I found value in learning people's whereabouts and sharing my life with them.

About a half hour drive from our home there was road access to the wide and strong St. John River. One hot afternoon when our mission well had been dry for nearly two weeks, we found a spot on the water's edge.

The original plan was to tackle the laundry which had been piling up and to cool off with a swim in the river. If I thought this would be a family activity, my plans were dashed when Perry brought his fishing pole along. His idea was to learn the secrets of fishing the St. John, and he had invited David along as a fishing guide.

At the riverside, I wandered off to find a suitable place to wash clothes. As I struggled with a large bar of soap and a mound of clothes, some Bassa ladies wandered past and stopped to observe my clumsy washing method. Eager to put an end to my unmanageable task and help the local economy, I hired them to wash our clothes.

Later with the basket of clean clothes in the car, I sought out a place where I could easily wash my hair. I found a wonderful clear pool surrounded by numerous huge boulders sticking out of the river. Thinking it was a spot of privacy I made a quick decision to bathe in the cool refreshing water. There was even a convenient ledge to hold my soap and shampoo.

Soon I found myself the object of amusement for ladies passing by with enormous loads of firewood on their heads. I replied to their Bassa greetings being quite relieved that my observers were ladies, and that the water came to my neck. In that culture of practicality, we occasionally witnessed people bathing in streams along the roadside or in our nearby stream, however mixed company was not considered appropriate. Feeling vulnerable, I hurriedly finished bathing and found my way back to Perry, who proudly presented a stringer of fish.

Recalling our adventure with Perry's family to see the falls, the next month we made a return trip leading a group of anthropology students taking an interim class from Calvin College. In fact, we made a total of five trips to the falls during our years in Liberia. The journeys were always quite adventurous and bonding experiences for each group that went.

Some of the Calvin students, overcome with heat and humidity, found it an arduous trek and lagged behind. We put those struggling in the front of the line, and as experienced before, their pace quickened when they no longer felt they were struggling to keep up.

Some young men were eager to set a faster pace and move ahead with the guide, but we had to insist everyone stay together. We felt responsible for the students and didn't want the group separated.

Even though everyone was told to take enough water for a four-hour trek, there were always those who for some reason did not carry enough. This often made for interesting group dynamics when people felt compelled to share water they worried was not enough for themselves.

A few times those who did not bring an adequate amount ended up getting dehydrated and feeling faint when they didn't ask for help. It was always a welcome relief to return to the vehicle where extra drinking water and food awaited us.

The trail to the falls was challenging - offering steep muddy hills to climb, narrow log bridges over streams, passage through remote villages with shocked children, and the delightful coolness of a bamboo grove. At times we had to literally crawl through areas of sword grass, which seemed to grab those passing by. Its victim would need to suddenly stop to avoid a painful serrated cut. Sometimes others would have to peel a blade of grass off an area that could not be reached.

Passing through thick jungle, there was always the risk of coming upon dangers like a snake. We warned everyone to be observant and some of the men carried cutlasses. Once an entire string of Calvin students, including our Bassa guide, Perry, and the professor, passed unaware within inches of a snakeskin. It was still moist and held its shape, so it had just been shed. I was at the end of the line and called everyone back to the site. They all marveled at how unobservant they had been in a potentially dangerous area and how God was protecting them.

Further up the trail, one of the log bridges crossed a deep narrow stream. When we got there the water was swollen and covered the log. I assumed we would have to turn back. However, Perry pulled a vine from the jungle and tied it to a nearby tree. Using a stick ahead of him to feel the crooked log, he crossed over and tied the other end of the vine to another tree for a handrail. It was a real stretch of courage for some to make it across, but everyone in the group managed.

One girl did slip off the log bridge and could have been swept away in the swift current, but Perry was providentially standing close by. He quickly grabbed her and pulled her to shore. Who knows what would have happened, since she would have been carried downstream, undoubtedly for some distance.

Years later during a dry season trek, I shuttered to see just how deep that ravine was. We were surprised too by several crocodiles resting in the mud near the log crossing, but God always kept us safe.

There was often a rush of adrenaline before we even reached the falls, when everyone first became aware of the roar of water. The trekkers would quicken their pace with eager anticipation, but it was surprising how far we had yet to go.

Finally, the trail would allow a glimpse of the fall's extraordinary display of God's creation. What a true blessing it always was to witness such raw beauty and might. Some of the college men enjoyed a cooling dip in the water, but the girls became hesitant when some noted small fish nibbled their feet.

One journey to the falls was most enjoyable. It was a missionary only trek in dry season, and everyone was accustomed to the climate and in good hiking shape. We knew the route and trekked without a guide, making good time, and enjoying each other's company.

We found the river was very low and were able to get closer to the falls than ever before. Previously hidden natural water slides in the river's rock bed were discovered. Perry and others enjoyed sliding down them, but not everyone was so brave. There were also pools of refreshing, bubbling water that were simply delightful, caressing our tired muscles, and refreshing not only the body, but also the soul.

11

Bassa Lifestyle

★*The first five paragraphs of this chapter may not be suitable for children.*

The sereneness of our mission station was sometimes interrupted by loud volatile voices, and we were alarmed as we sensed a mob passing invisibly behind our home. Large, noisy groups were using a path a mere 50 yards away, and I was glad for a heavily jungled area providing a barricade. It led to a large village some distance away on the St. John River, which was renowned for devil worship and bush school activities.

As long as we lived there, we did not explore this nearby avenue, having been warned it would not be wise to stroll even a short distance down the shaded trail. Later while searching down the pesky driver ant hill, I broke through thick jungle brush onto the surprisingly wide and well-worn path in the orange soil.

I could not have imagined what evil took place at the end of that trail. Our Bassa mentors told us much later of a shocking custom the people practiced there. Apparently when an area chief would die, it was their tradition, because of ancestral worship, to bury four young virgins alive at each of the four corners of his grave.

While we resided in the guest house, a major area chief in the distant village was near death for some time and later died. No doubt the boisterous, drunken mourners passing near our home were pumped up for the murderous deeds which awaited them during the extended time of mourning and revelry after his death.

Years later, Perry trekked through the area. Although he was not permitted in the large village, he did walk the path circumventing it to get to the canoes crossing the St. John River. Nearby he saw the infamous grave of the paramount chief. It was well decorated and had four cement corner posts, memorials of the girls buried there.

Country Devil

We had an intriguing experience when a "country devil" came to a neighboring village. The parents of a boy in the village were sending him to a secretive, cultural school deep in the jungle. His family needed money to send him, so they came to our door asking for donations. They were disappointed we did not contribute.

They said the "devil" was in their town, so we went to see it. It was an unusual appearance, and the only time I saw a country devil, although Perry saw several others. The devils were part of the Secret Society and they went to the villages to "carry" or take adolescents willingly to secluded bush schools.

The devil we saw that day was dressed in a costume with a thick grass skirt. A country cloth gathered above his head draped down and covered his torso. He wove wearily around the town, possibly drunk or stoned, while men on either side guided him with sticks. Several times he lay down seeming to be unable to maneuver. They hit him with sticks and insulted him, not a glamorous position it seemed to me.

Parents wanted their children to go through bush school so they would be accepted in the general society. It was commonly thought it would be an embarrassment to give your son or daughter in marriage if they had not been through the school.

The schools were also called Devil Bush or Sacred Groves. The entrance to the grounds was always clearly marked as a forbidden path, so there was no excuse for going there - except to be an annoyance.

The parents paid fees and provided 100 pounds of rice to enroll their child. The country devil then went to their town on a preplanned day. The children would be outside and available to be "swallowed" by the devil - thereby taken off to bush school. This was the beginning of a young person's enrollment in the indigenous school and lifelong cultural membership in the Secret Society.

The girls' school was called the Sande school and the boys went to the Poro school. Unfortunately, health concerns could take a serious nature in the bush schools. If the tragedy of death occurred, it was announced by leaving the child's empty rice bowl at the family's door.

While the young people attended bush school, they painted themselves white to show they had been "swallowed" by the devil. It was thought the stomach acids would naturally turn their skin white. The boys and girls could occasionally, be seen in public on a break from the school. Their skin would be painted with white chalk, and the girls often wore a grass skirt with a tortoise shell belted on their back. Upon graduation they no longer wore the white chalk, however there was often scarring on the back and chest to look like teeth marks from the country devil swallowing them.

Although most of what goes on at the bush school is a secret, it seemed the youngsters learned a vocation there, like iron working or basket weaving. They also learned to respect their elders and observe customs. They were taught good working attitudes, and the history of their people. (see Appendix D)

In the Sande School girls learned about marriage and how to care for their husbands and children. After graduation the girls were often quickly wed in an arranged marriage, which traditionally consisted of the man and woman publicly jumping over a stick.

Members of the Secret Society were sworn to secrecy. The penalty for leaking secrets was high. If they disclosed anything, the society threatened its members with execution, punishment of their family members, or induced sicknesses until death. In addition, those digging around for society secrets would pay for it.

★*Next paragraph may not be suitable for children.*

Initiation was a huge issue since it included male circumcision and female genital mutilation, FGM. The author Mae Azango created an uproar in 2012 and was forced into hiding after she exposed the serious disadvantages of FGM.[12] Liberia's former President Ellen Johnson Sirleaf banned FGM in 2018 on her last day in office, but the law expired about a year later.[13]

In 2012, Liberia's government banned all Sande schools indefinitely. The law makers recognized the fact that young girls were taken out of formal education to attend bush schools. Often upon graduation, dowries for young girls were paid, and they were quickly married off. This was very unfortunate since it left further education nearly impossible.[14]

The secret society most likely had some evil aspects. TEE pastors in Larry's class publicly denounced their standing and membership in the organization. Their resignations told us that policies and practices in the society did not coincide with the Biblical principles they were learning in TEE classes. It was exciting to realize the pastors were whole heartedly adopting God's lifechanging truth from His inspired Word. *If we say we have fellowship with Him while we walk in darkness, we lie and do not practice the truth,* 1 John 1:6.

It seemed their resignations could have placed them in personal danger, since leaving the society was not an option. We later learned that when they announced they were leaving; the pastors boldly defended the gospel. The church leaders were then granted a broad type of amnesty, which was offered for a short time.

Apparently, the leaders of the society understood their practices were not in agreement with Christian truths. Retaining believing Christians in their organization could have been a constant impediment to their activities.

Some of our Bassa ministry staff lamented the loss of cultural training in bush schools. Since more and more Christians were abandoning bush schools, it was suggested a Christian retreat center could train the youth in the good practices lost. It is interesting that God in His providence guided societies, who did not know Him in basic truths of recognizing authority, honoring marriages, and good stewardship of creation. These truths were instilled in the Bassa leadership before they knew Him.

★*Next paragraph may not be suitable for children.*

Some of the highest atrocities committed within the secret society came from offshoots called the Leopard Society and Crocodile Society, which "needed to feed" on human body parts. They also used specific body parts to make "juju", a powerful medicine against people. Apparently, the night we were driving home from Monrovia something like that was taking place. In the future we would live where this division practiced their evil art - it was known as Devil Country.

The Bassa homes were used for shelter from the elements, a family's sleeping quarters, and a safe place to store possessions, but the majority of Bassa life was lived in the open-air kitchens. Food was prepared over an open fire and eaten there. Hanging above the cooking fire was often a basket holding meat preserved by the smoke. The kitchen area was also where visitors were received, lively conversation was exchanged, numerous projects were pursued, and babies were nourished and napped.

The kitchens were constructed with four large poles anchored in the ground to support a roof overhead. An attic area was often enclosed and locked, being the storehouse for rice and the next year's seeds. Smoke from the cooking fire below acted as an insect deterrent and preserved the rice.

Polygamy was often practiced especially in the older generations. I was told polygamous families ideally worked their farms together in a harmonious manner. They all lived together under one roof sharing what they had. Each wife had a bedroom and the husband had his own room. Babies slept with their mother, but later the young child would join other children in a separate bedroom. Families of more means might even provide a separate house for each wife.

In the farming season, it was typical for the wives to go to the rice fields to work for the day, while one family member, such as a grandmother, wife, or older child would be responsible for the children in the village.

Sometimes I would ask a Bassa woman if a child was hers, and it would seem she would have to stop and think before answering. Curious about this, I asked a trusted Bassa neighbor lady why the mothers sometimes hesitated before answering. She replied that they would have to remember if they bore that child or not. Children in their homes were not always the biological offspring of the adults living there. She said all children living with the family were treated as the adults actual children and often lived for extended periods of time with relatives or friends.

There were several reasons for children not living with their parents. Often a child may have been taken to the home of family or friends in order to receive an education. In addition, my friend explained, "How else would my niece and nephew know that I love them, unless they live in my home and receive not only my food, but also discipline from me?" It was remarkable to me that children would sometimes be away from their birth parents for years.

★*The next five paragraphs may not be suitable for children.*

It is true that the Bassa women occasionally went topless, and it was acceptable in their culture. However, they normally wore tops in public or when engaged in normal daily activities.

People arriving from the States were often curious about this and wondered how they would react if they witnessed someone topless. Most were surprised that it ended up not being a big deal. In the African setting it seemed quite natural considering the extreme heat and amount of work performed. Typically, they would only go topless if working hard or engaged in something like carrying water where they might get their clothes soiled or wet.

Many of the ladies were aware of differences in cultural norms and would cover up with their outer lappa when they realized white people were around or sensed it made someone uncomfortable. The Bassa people would say going topless was not the "civilized" thing to do.

In general, the Bassa ladies said it was considered obscene to expose anything between the waist and the knees. We also understood they would not respect someone who came to them from another culture and threw their traditional norms of decency to the side.

We heard stories of American women with other missions who thought they would dress, or perhaps I should say undress, more like their African sisters. Not only did the CR mission agency tell us before we went to Africa that this would not be tolerated, but we knew Liberians understood enough of western culture to realize Americans do not go without tops.

Ladies typically wrapped two yards of brightly colored cotton African cloth, called lappas, around their waist and secured it by tucking in at the top. It was a very comfortable article of clothing, which I enjoyed wearing. Usually two lappas were worn, with the bottom one securely fastened. The two lappas did not have to match, but often they did.

The top lappa came in handy when a baby needed to be wrapped on the back or an overflowing load secured. A neighbor friend told me no self-respecting woman would go out with only one lappa on. At that time Bassa ladies wore lappas or skirts and hardly ever pants, so we missionary women always wore dresses, skirts or lappas, too. I understand pants are acceptable attire now.

For special occasions Bassa ladies wore beautiful, custom made lappa suits. They consisted of a tailored top with unique features, a double lappa, and head-tie all from the same fabric. They were made by tailors in little sewing shops on the perimeters of the market. It was fun to go there and see what styles the tailors were making. Often people would choose a favorite tailor and go to him for their sewing needs.

The African cloth was usually cotton and sold in bundles of six yards. There were various grades of fabric, starting with the expensive Dutch wax prints. One of my favorite things became browsing through shops to look at the beautiful African cloth designs.

A Bassa home in the interior could be built quite inexpensively using natural resources from the rain forest. Our neighbor began to prepare a site to build a traditional house, giving us the chance to observe construction step by step.

First the ground was leveled, then strong, straight bush poles were cut from the jungle, and toted on their heads to the house site. The poles were sunk in the ground forming the exterior and interior walls. Cut 2x4 boards were helpful, but not necessary, to horizontally hold the bush poles together at the top. To add collective strength, vines were securely woven around the bush poles, or bamboo slats were diagonally nailed to them.

Roof construction took place next. From the jungle they harvested long poles for the rafters and batten. Either a zinc or thatch roof was then placed over the top. The big thatch leaves were readily available in the jungle, but it took a lot of layers to produce a rainproof roof.

It seemed the tin roofs were preferred and a type of status symbol, although they rusted in a few years. The wealthier the homeowner, the more expensive and durable the roofing material was. Aluminum sheets were the top of the line since they didn't rust.

It was always a village affair when the sides of a house were mudded. Termite hills were broken down with pickaxes and mixed with water by a lot of foot stomping. The termite mud was used like cement and daubed or packed into the sides of the house covering all the bush poles from the ground up, while leaving space for framed in windows and doors. The process took some time to get the termite mud packed tightly.

After it dried several layers of nice smooth mud mixed with dung were rubbed on the walls to fill in the cracks. The finished product was a home with sturdy walls, which would last many years despite tropical rainstorms.

Mud blocks could also be locally fabricated for economical home construction. Termite hills were broken down and mixed with straw and water. The mud mixture was packed into wooden brick-sized forms and tipped out to dry in the hot sun. When they were thoroughly baked, the mud blocks were surprisingly hard and durable for the walls of a house.

The homes were further secured with wooden shutters and doors which were often painted with decorative designs in geometric shapes or soles of shoes, leaves and even handprints dipped in paint to create a unique look.

Beautifully woven mats made of rattan stripped from palms in the jungle were used for ceilings. They were imbedded in the mud walls to keep the homes rodent free but were not entirely bug proof.

The Bassa were essentially subsistence farmers, growing their own food and surviving on it. Each February another area of forest, sometimes virgin jungle, would be cut down for the next year's farm. This laborious task was done by the men with only a cutlass or small axe. The fallen foliage and trees were dried in the hot sun for kindling, burned with a good hot fire, and the ashes spread around as the crop's only fertilizer.

When rainy season began, the rice seeds were broadcast by the women. With straight legs, they bent over at the waist, and scratched the seeds into the earth using a short-handled hoe, often with a baby tied on their back. As the rice grew through rainy season, the family protected it against deer, bush cow, and other animals, which could destroy their crop and livelihood.

Usually the men would build a fence of sticks around the entire rice farm. Inventive traps were often set in the fence line to stop animal predators, and possibly gain some meat for the next meal. There were also the infamous rice birds which could ravage a field. Boys in the family were excellent shots with an ancient styled sling shot and could down a small bird in flight.

If all went well the rice would be harvested starting in late July. Harvest was painstaking, cutting each stalk of rice one at a time with a small utility knife and bundled by the handful.

The rice hull was not removed until just before it was cooked, otherwise it did not keep well. When it was threshed, they used a large mortar and pestle to beat the husk off the grain. Using a winnowing basket, they would throw the rice in the air to remove the chaff.

As part of language and culture study, David thought we should visit a big traditional Bassa town. "You will really like it and we'll even get to ride in a 'kay-new'," he told us excitedly. We weren't sure what a kay-new might be. So off we went on a drive, ending up behind LAC rubber plantation where the road ended at a river.

We didn't see any big traditional village, but David motioned us to the water's edge where a man was standing in a rather long narrow canoe.

David told us, "We have to get in this 'kay-new' and you have to pay the man." Now we knew what had been lost in translation – It was a round bottomed, dugout canoe made by carefully burning and chipping out the center of a large, long log.

We climbed aboard and the vessel rocked uncomfortably. I noted it sank in the water under our weight. The canoe was wide enough for only one person to sit in the bottom, and David instructed us to pull our legs up. That way the people in front of us could lean their backs on our legs, and we in turn leaned on the person behind us.

We waited and other people came to cross the river. It was surprising for them to see two white people, so David explained we were missionaries and he was showing us a large Bassa town. They loaded their bundles and themselves in the little boat, making me sure it would capsize. I held tight to the edge, while David was asking the owner if they'd seen any river crocodiles lately. "Yes, there is a big one that lives over there," he said pointing just upriver. The whole situation made me rather fearful.

As our little canoe ferry set off to the other side, I noted the water level was only a couple inches from the top. With each stroke of the oar, the vessel leaned precariously from one side to the other. I thought our fellow passengers would sit perfectly still, but the lady sitting against my legs freely moved around to look for something in her bundle, and someone began to swat at an apparent tsetse fly.

Thankfully, we safely reached the other side, but I was none too happy to think of the return trip across the swiftly flowing river with a crocodile waiting nearby. We climbed up the steep bank and a large town came into view.

It was clearly market day and many people had brought their wares for sale, displaying them on ground cloths or market stalls. The vendors called for us to buy their goods as we strolled down the aisles of rice, fruit, palm oil and a huge variety of goods for sale. Nearby, customers loudly bartered with other merchants.

Beyond the market was the village. There were many houses, all constructed of termite mud with their roofed kitchens nearby. Thick thatch was used for the roofs and wooden doors and shutters held customary designs. Only a few houses boasted tin roofs and some of them were already rusty and perhaps not waterproof.

The ground was swept clean and hardened with use. Small buildings for bathing and separate latrines were scattered around the village's perimeter. Banana and papaya trees grew there with the full jungle hovering behind.

Many excited children were scampering around having fun, babies were carried on mother's backs, and people were carrying loads balanced on their heads. Some children, wearing only baggy underpants and others with none, came laughing and carrying water from the river. With one arm reaching up to steady the buckets on their heads, water splashed over the sides, and glistened their dark skin.

Women in their kitchens were sitting on little chairs only a few inches high, stirring their cooking pots on open fires. Some pots bubbled over with rice boiling for the family's next meal, while other pans holding red palm oil smoked as they burned off the impurities. The ladies quickly readjusted and wrapped their outer lappas higher when they saw white people were in the village.

Some older men were gathered on wicker chairs on a little house porch. The smell of a tobacco pipe was in the air and a checkerboard rested between them. They were engaged in serious conversation, while younger men and boys were close by gaining wisdom from their elders. Chickens and dogs wandered at will through the village, looking for a scrap of food to eat.

The smells of food cooking and smoke from the wood fires lingered in the air. Occasionally our nostrils stung from the thick smoke of palm oil being burnt and fish being smoked in woven baskets. Babies cried, people conversed in loud voices, chickens crowed, dogs barked, and the sounds of the jungle blended them all together.

We were visitors, so it was customary for us to be introduced to the village chief. In typical fashion he asked, "What did you bring me?" Coached by David before we left home, Perry gave him a hat from my father's farm. The chief was impressed and asked if my father had a big rice farm. We explained that my parents could not grow rice in their area, because there was not enough rain, but my father and brothers planted so-so corn (so-so means "a lot" in Liberian English), and the hat happened to advertise a seed corn company.

The chief was fascinated to learn my father fed the corn to pigs and cows, or he sold it by the truckload in the market. We further explained he also sold the pigs and cows in a big cattle market, and the money from that was used to buy food and clothing for his family or to purchase corn seed. The chief asked if we liked to eat the corn and we replied we liked to eat sweet corn.

The conversation continued and we told him we had left our home to help train Bassa pastors. Perry explained the good news we have in Christ to the chief and those around him. The chief said he had a church in his town, but since he was so-so busy he didn't go there much. Perry encouraged him to go to church and we took our leave.

What an idyllic, peaceful place, but what a difficult lifestyle to live as subsistent farmers and gatherers in the harsh and dangerous jungle. There were no modern medical facilities, only traditional witch doctors using concoctions of their own design. Without modern plumbing, water needed to be carried every day from a river or nearby water source. Children usually carried it on their heads for cooking purposes or for baths. There were virtually no modern amenities, and yet that was their life - it was their home.

Although we had gone to Liberia to help the people, it seemed there was little we could do to bring change or help make their lives better. And yet, our team of missionaries brought something of more value than material goods or modern conveniences. We were entrusted with the most important thing in the world. We brought the good news of eternal life and salvation in Jesus Christ by training the pastors and church leaders in the TEE classes.

We realized the Kingdom of God and the light of His Salvation must be reflected in other ways than just training pastors. Just as Christ met the needs of people, we the church must be concerned and involved in helping our fellow man. If the Church of Christ would help others in His name and learn to help develop their community, exciting changes could be brought about. Felt needs and difficulties in life could be addressed. The rate of infant mortality could be brought down, health needs could be met, and people could learn to read.

The CR mission had developed programs aiming to minister to people's needs in Christ's name. Our health program sought to train someone in each church to do simple health care, make medicine available, and deliver babies safely in sanitary conditions. The future agriculture program would teach improved farming methods and plans were being made to produce literature to read.

As we returned across the river, I prayed for God's blessings on our team's efforts, and that the chief of the village would consider the good news of Jesus coming to be his Savior.

12
My Trek

I had commented that I would like to make a short trek and experience some of the things Perry had talked about when he stayed in the villages. So, David invited us to visit his extended family in a remote village, which was estimated to be an easy two hour walk from the car road. We anticipated spending a night or two there.

On our way out of town David stopped at a food stand and purchased a one-pound bag of salt for ten cents. It would be a gift to his aunt for hosting us. Perhaps a sack of salt sounds like a strange gift, but to the Africans living in the interior salt was a much-desired staple often lacking in their diet. A century earlier, wars were even fought over salt in that part of the world.

We drove some distance and stopped at a town where we talked to the chief about leaving our car in his village. Then, adjusting our light backpacks and water canteens, we set out for a leisurely walk to David's uncle and aunt's village. In our backpacks we carried a small sized bath towel, a flat twin sized sheet, mosquito coil, matches, flashlight, snacks, water treatment tablets, a bar of soap, travel size shampoo, toothpaste, toothbrush, deodorant, small roll of TP, and one change of clothes.

This was to be my first overnight in a village, and I was excited anticipating the unknown. We set out walking through immense rice fields, where there was no shade from the hot sun. Immature upland rice was still green and hanging heavily on the stalks.

The path led to a steep, muddy incline. We had to grab branches and vines to get up the hill. It was so steep my skirt dragged in the mud behind me. In addition, it was hard to get traction since my muddy feet kept sliding from side to side in hiking sandals.

It seemed unlikely we were on a major path in such difficult terrain. I was sure people could not take that route if they were carrying a load on their head. David commented that he didn't remember climbing a hill like that when he last visited his relatives, and he thought by that time we should have arrived at their village.

After we had walked for several hours, I began to get tired. We stopped to take a drink of water and rest, then moved on with the heat of the sun upon us. We crossed old fields used years before, where the jungle was only beginning to grow back. After being used only one year to grow rice, those barren areas could lay fallow for an indefinite time. The virgin jungle was being destroyed to plant annual crops - little wonder our mission was anxious to introduce improved rice farming methods.

What a treat when the path led us to the cool sanctuary of the virgin jungle. I marveled at immense tree trunks displaying supporting buttresses taller than myself. Their heaven-bound canopies serenely shaded the heated travelers. Undergrowth took on a life of its own with minimal vegetation due to the lack of sunshine. Vines swooped picturesquely from unknown sources creating tranquility.

We reached an area where sword grass had overtaken the trail, making it again apparent this path was one less traveled. The men were carrying cutlasses and used them to clear the nasty grass away sometimes reaching over our heads.

I called for a second rest and dashed behind some bushes for privacy. Perry told me my face was bright red. Perhaps I hadn't been drinking enough, so I drank some more. I tried to focus on the grandeur of God's creation and enjoy the deep shade, but I was surprisingly tired, and my legs felt weak. While I ate some nutritious snacks, Perry made me some walking sticks, and we set off once again.

Several villages we passed through were much larger than anything I had seen before, and occasionally children ran away screaming at the sight of our white skin. Perry had remembered to bring a few candies to share with the children. When they saw it, their fear suddenly disappeared, and they reached out to accept a treat.

The villages themselves were impressively neat with the traditional mud-stick, square houses, and thatch roofs. There were even a few homes with corrugated metal roofs. Evidently, someone had carried all those sheets of tin on the narrow paths of the jungle.

The residents in one village were involved in a heated African-style palaver with soldiers whose guns were strapped on their backs. We successfully passed along the perimeter of the village unobserved.

For some time, David seemed unsure of where we were going. Each person we met was questioned for directions, but they only pointed us further up the road. What was to be an easy two-hour walk had turned into a taxing six-hour obstacle course, and we apparently had further to go. We continued on.

As the sun was setting, we became weary and new fears began to enter our minds. What possible dangers might we encounter in the night? When I asked how long the flashlight batteries would last, David and Perry encouraged me to reserve my batteries and not use them. They said our eyes would become accustomed and use light from the moon.

David was honest and said he had no idea how much further we needed to go. It seemed we would not find the elusive village before darkness fell. Would we spend the night wandering in the jungle, or would we find someplace to lay down on the jungle floor?

I remember being thankful for the cooler temperatures of the evening after a hot day in the sun, and we were quite happy when the full moon ascended to illuminate the night. For the most part we could see where we were going without a flashlight, even though the trees were shading the way.

Our pace necessarily slowed. I kept close behind Perry, and David walked ahead of us hitting the pathway with a branch to chase away any snakes – a comforting thought. We came to a stop and David explained he had come to a fork in the road. The men decided to take the one most traveled, noting we could come back to try the other option later, if needed. We encouraged each other to pray as we walked.

We stumbled through the dark jungle for some time, not knowing if we were on the right path. Then a hint of smoke in the air finally gave us hope of a village close by. As we drew nearer, the smoke was unusually strong. Perhaps this should have alarmed us, but to see the glowing fires of the outdoor kitchens was most inviting to three weary travelers.

As we entered the village, David suddenly let out a yell when he realized we had arrived at his aunt and uncle's town. He ran and heartily greeted them. His uncle wondered why we had come from the north, when we should have entered the village from the south. David explained we had been wandering around all day and were happy to have finally found them. He presented them with the bag of salt, and the ladies of the village were so delighted they did a happy dance in appreciation.

Surveying the village, there were about eight traditional mud and thatch houses with one tin roof and open-air kitchens were nearby. We were startled to see the smoldering remains of four homes, which accounted for the thick smoke in the air. We learned the houses had been lost in a fire the day before.

This unfortunate disaster occurred when a mentally handicapped girl in a fit of rage took a burning stick from the fire and put it to some thatched roofs. Without a fire department or river close by, two other structures had unfortunately caught fire. We were glad to hear no one was hurt other than burns. It was certainly a tragedy - to rebuild the homes and replace belongings would be most difficult.

Relieved and thankful to have finally reach our destination, we were ushered to seats around the fire, while our hosts loudly discussed our need of shelter for the night. In fact, it seemed they were having a palaver. I grew uncomfortable and suspected we were imposing. David listened in on the conversations and assured us this was not the case.

Since many residents of the village were without homes, it became necessary for everyone who had a house, to offer sleeping quarters for their unfortunate neighbors. The fact was that all beds in the village were occupied for the night. Now with the startling arrival of David and two white people, our hosts were again shuffling sleeping arrangements.

During the last leg of our trek, I had experienced stomach problems and several times found it necessary to run behind a distant bush. I recalled from my physiology course that heat exhaustion causes the body to push out all hot liquid, in hopes of being refreshed with something cooler. As we waited in the kitchen by the fire pit, the uncontrollable effects of dehydration and exhaustion once again presented themselves. I was embarrassed and hurriedly asked David to show me where the latrine was.

Perry and David accompanied me to make sure I could find it on the further side of the village, but to my great dismay the latrine door was padlocked. David explained this was done to keep the children out and he rushed off in search of the key, while I pleaded with him to be quick about it. Soon enough he returned.

Since every latrine had its own unique design, it was necessary to scope out the thatch building with the flashlight. This one was fashioned with a low ceiling. I would have to bend over while walking or bump my head on the ceiling and risk acquiring insects or something worse in my hair. David suggested he go in first with a branch to scare any snakes or rodents away. "Great," I thought, "another delay in my miserable state." I asked him to please hurry and he finally left me to have some privacy.

To avoid tripping over my skirt, I hoisted it up a little, and bent low to enter the short door. The floor was a layer of logs covering an apparent pit below. Using the flashlight, I could see where the two center logs had notches cut in them forming a hole to squat over. I made my way hunched over toward the hole and the logs began to role, making the final task rather precarious.

Fortunately, my condition improved. It would seem this might be due to the fear of returning to the unstable latrine in the dark, when in fact I had my hostesses to thank.

Upon our arrival, the ladies of the village set about cooking. They were pleased that a duiker or small jungle deer had been recently killed by village hunters giving them meat to offer their rare guests. The cooks proudly presented us with liver soup. Being sick to my stomach, I was not thrilled to hear what was featured on the menu.

Using traditional posture, David squatted in front of me and quietly encouraged me to try some broth, saying the soup was good for people who were sick. Perry too pressed me to at least try a spoonful in consideration of David's aunt and the cooks, who were watching from a distance.

Not wanting to appear rude, I took a sip and much to my surprise, one spoonful was enough to prove its excellence. The telltale smiles of the cooks told me they knew I would appreciate it. Apparently, the broth and liver were exactly the components my body needed. I finished the soup, leaving a polite amount in the bowl, and soon felt much better.

We were shown to a room and I was impressed with its neat and tidy appearance. Obviously, it was a children's bedroom with small sized clothes hanging on wooden pegs embedded in the mud wall. The hardened dirt floor was neatly swept, and a bed spread of striped country cloth was carefully laid over the bed. A clothesline tied to the rafters stretched from one wall to the other.

Obviously, we could not fit on the short, narrow bed together, but Perry assured me he had an idea to make it longer. I thought we might slide the little bed out a bit from the wall to give us more room but was surprised to find the legs of the bed embedded in the dirt floor.

Curious about the bed's construction, I looked underneath only to come eyeball to eyeball with a creature. Jumping back in fright, I was greeted with a small "cluck" and found it was merely a setting hen. Having grown up on a farm and accustomed to setting hens, her presence only added to the fun of spending the night in the village.

So, it was that we met our first roommate for the evening, but she would only be performing the task of sitting on her eggs. It wouldn't be too long before other creatures joined us.

We noted it was quite warm in our bedroom, probably since our hostess had lit a candle which was creating a lot of heat. We blew it out, opened the window, and went outside to the cooler outdoor kitchen.

Our hosts asked for our towels, which were customary to carry in overnight bags, and mentioned that our baths would soon be ready. Perry, being the experienced trekker, told me they would probably place my towel in a bucket of hot water. He had found the best thing to do was to take the towel out of the bucket and hold it over the body relaxing sore muscles as well as freshening up.

Towels in the western world are normally used to dry off, but in that tropical climate, evaporation from the skin happened quickly, even in the evening air. The lightweight, small sized bath towels also quickly dried on trek and would be dry for the backpack in the morning.

David's cousin informed me my bath was ready. I was taken to a small open-air structure reserved exclusively for bathing, while the latrine served its own function and was down the hill some distance away.

I entered through a swinging door held by thick leather hinges and I wondered if they were made from elephant hide. The walls were bamboo poles embedded in the ground in a circular shape and woven together with two jungle vines. There was no roof, only the twinkling stars above. It occurred to me that people might take an all-natural shower when the rain was heavy.

Much to my dismay I noted there were gaping holes where the bamboo did not meet. Although the bath house was set back on the perimeter of the village, it did not appear to offer the privacy I felt necessary with people nearby, but there was no alternative.

It did have a pleasant luxury - the bath floor was several layers of pebbles which allowed bath water to drain and keep the feet clean. There was also a bamboo bench to one side, where I put by soap, shampoo and clean clothes. On the shower floor was a bucket of steaming hot water. Using my flashlight, I could see my towel was in it, but I shut off the light realizing it would expose me.

Looking through the bamboo wall, I could easily see ongoing activity in the village. It was a relief to realize no one seemed to care I was about to bathe, and without a light behind me it was doubtful I was visible. As their guest, I assumed the privacy they offered was adequate and accepted their sincere hospitality.

Sure enough, after the liver soup and refreshing bath time, I felt surprisingly rejuvenated from the draining midday hike. I stepped out of the bathhouse with a content smile on my face, but the residents of the village stopped everything, stared at me, and laughed. A quick check noted all my clothing was in place.

I asked David if people were laughing at me. "Oh, yes," he said unable to holdback a snicker. Then he explained that people were laughing because my long-wet hair was now flat to my head. They also noted it made me look "dry" not fat like they would expect.

I wondered out loud, "Why would they think I would be fat?" David replied it was because they assumed I had plenty to eat, and rightly so. Keeping that in mind, I later understood when people told me with a twinkle in their eye, "O, I know when you come back from your home [in the States] you will be 'so-so' fat."

We returned to our room, but found it was very warm, since the candle had been re-lit, presumably by our hosts. In addition, the window shutter was again closed making the room hot and stuffy. Desiring the cool evening air for sleeping, we again blew out the candle, opened the shutters, and left the hot room to cool down in the outdoor kitchen.

Our ever-watchful hosts returned to light the candle and close the shutter for a second time, making their desire known to us. We wondered if they had closed the shutter to try to keep out the mosquitoes, since there was no screen. Or, since the Bassa generally considered cold night air detrimental to one's health, perhaps they thought we would not want our room to cool down for sleeping.

As for the candle again burning, didn't they realize we had a flashlight with us, so we wouldn't need to use their candle? There was however a more important purpose, which we would soon discover.

When we decided to retire for the evening, Perry told me to casually carry a selected chair to our bedroom while he did the same. He explained that on his former treks with Larry, the beds were also much shorter than we are accustomed to. In fact, they were so short that the men would have had to sleep with the knees tightly curled up causing trek weary legs to cramp. Larry, a tall man, had devised a plan to sleep with the shoulders and hips on the bed, while extending the legs off the side and onto a chair. That was what Perry planned for us to do, and I must say it worked quite well.

You never know what will happen in an African village in the quiet of the night, what creatures might share the space with you, or if you'll be able to sleep, but we were confident – and naïve. Before wrapping my flat sheet around me for the night, I checked the chicken under the bed and she responded with a little "cluck", as if to say, "Good night".

With a mosquito coil lit, the hostess' candle out, and the shutter once again open for the night; we lay our torsos on the crinkly straw mattress covered with a thick cloth. Our legs and feet extended off the bed and rested on the borrowed chairs.

Commenting that we were somewhat comfortable, we began to relax by lying as still as possible to allow our bodies to cool down in the hot room. We felt the evening air drift through the window and knew it would cool the room down. It seemed it would be a comfortable night.

Soon however, with the aid of moonlight from the window, we noticed some movement above us and lay frozen as two rats walked the clothesline stretched above us. They were rather big rats, flicking their tails from side to side for balance as they walked the tightrope. With careful slow steps and their clawed toes spread wide, their legs shook with the movement of the clothesline. We shook as well, fearing they would fall on us. It seemed best to not startle them.

Perry had told me of a similar problem with rats he and Larry had on trek. The men had simply gotten their spray cans of deodorant and sprayed it through a lighted match. A torch resulted and caused the rats to shriek and hopefully discouraged them from returning.

The woven ceiling above us was low with loose fraying strings hanging down, so we were cautious of starting a fire from torching the rats. That village had already lost too many houses by flame.

The rats managed to cross the room and disappeared into a hole in the ceiling. In the darkness of the room, we began to figure things out. We recalled hearing that Bassa people prefer to sleep with a small lantern glowing in their rooms. That would apparently discourage the rodents from entering for fear of being seen.

Our hosts offered us candles to use through the night; but we thought we knew better and extinguished the flame. The darkness only encouraged the rats' visit. Perry got up, closed the shutter, and lit the candle for the night as our hosts desired.

An astonishing part of the rat stories we had heard, and did not want to experience, was that given the opportunity rats would actually chew off the heavy skin on the bottoms of people's feet as they slept. Why they did this and what they did with the skin, I cannot imagine. I once talked with a missionary from Southeast Asia and it seemed that problem was common knowledge there as well.

How the rat's victim could sleep while the soles of his feet were being chewed and peeled away, was a mystery. Many Bassa people assured us it was true, claiming the rats would blow on the feet as they nibbled, that way the person couldn't feel what was happening. In the morning the person would awaken to find the thick padding on his feet no longer there and be unable to walk for a couple of weeks without pain.

Of course, spending two extra weeks in the village was more culture study than we had planned for that trip, so we double checked to make sure our sheets were snuggly tucked around our feet and tried to settle down for the night. Sleep came easily as we were exhausted from the activities of the day.

The next day we spent an interesting morning in the village. Perry was invited by the men to accompany them on a hunt with traditional bows and arrows made of bamboo, and he still has the set he used that day. I enjoyed helping the ladies prepare food and listening to their chatter as they worked in their kitchens.

David had instructed his aunt to let me have a go at women's work. I was given a little ground-down knife and was shown how to slice sweet potato greens while holding them in my hand. Looking at the large pan of greens set before me, it seemed I was expected to cut all the morning's pickings, so I got to work. People found my awkward food prep entertaining. The ladies came to watch my progress and laughed good naturedly with me. One lady finally took pity and assisted me. On the open fire we cooked a wonderful meal of country rice and potato greens mixed with pieces of fresh meat from the duiker harvested the day before.

As we watched the pot boil, the ladies huddled around me, touching my skin and feeling my hair. I asked if someone would braid my hair and a couple younger ladies eagerly attempted the task, but they were dismayed by the fact that the braids quickly fell out. I had only one elastic ponytail holder along, so we opted for corn rows leading to one ponytail and the ladies approved of that style.

The men returned after seeing some monkeys in the treetops, but they had not been able to shoot them. They were served the meal we had prepared, and I ate with Perry and David in the piazza of a house. Later the women and children ate what we had left for them.

Before starting our journey back to the car, we presented our hosts with gifts of bars of soap and a couple of small Tupperware containers which intrigued them. It was our intention to stay longer, perhaps several nights, but the village was overwhelmed due to the tragic house fires, so we thanked them kindly, and took our leave.

David had obtained new directions to get back to the car and carefully memorized the route. It took us a mere hour and 45 minutes to walk out, compared to our eight-hour meanderings the day and night before, and the direct route was deeply shaded the entire way with no steep hills.

Perry and I felt refreshed and ready for the walk back to the car, however our companion was tired and grumpy. It was little wonder since he had spent the night hardly sleeping in the outdoor kitchen for lack of room in the village.

It had been a terrible night for him. He complained there was no sleeping mat and no place to lie down, so he spent the night cold and teetering on a narrow bench anchored in the kitchen floor. He had hoped to widen the space and balance himself by placing chairs next to the bench but complained that the chairs had disappeared.

We felt awful he had slept outside and told him we were the ones who had snuck the chairs into our bedroom to stretch out. David was a young gentleman, and he had a good-natured laugh, saying we all had the same idea. He politely added it was not that bad and he was happy to do it for us.

On the way home, we kindly refrained from picking up any hitchhikers, allowing David a much-deserved sleep stretched out on the back seat.

13

TEE Conference

Our car was packed tight with happy church leaders as we set off for the first annual TEE conference. It had been wisely decided that a conference would be held each year for instructors and teachers with the purpose of worship, fellowship, and additional teaching.

The theme the first year was simply: "The Church". Through the years the annual conferences always proved to be invaluable retreats for both students and teachers, and certainly memorable highlights of our missionary years.

Different areas hosted the conferences each year, and everyone enjoyed traveling to the interior areas for a return to remote areas and lifestyle. For the first conference, we traveled several hours north of Number 3 to a village called Dodain, which had a large church to accommodate a conference.

Although none of the other missionary women went to the conference, I felt privileged to attend with Perry. Our car was loaded with students who were exceptionally joyful as Perry drove along. We had strapped the luggage on top and opened the third row of seating to accommodate as many as possible. The students talked excitedly among themselves and burst into song. It was a luxury to travel in a private car, and everyone was dressed in their finest with the scent of heavy colognes and perfumes filling the air.

Suddenly the mood was altered when a huge black hooded cobra sprang up in the road. It turned and faced the car with its mouth wide open and fangs thrust defiantly at the car. The car simply plowed into the fearless reptile with a THUD, and everyone yelled in astonishment. As an afterthought, the windows were quickly rolled up although the danger was long past.

Heavy dust from the dirt road shielded the rearview and the possibility of the black snake lying dead in the road. There was no reason to stop and make sure it was killed. No one wanted to take a chance with the deadly snake.

Many jokes were made on the snake's behalf. Maybe the snake thought, "Now, there's a tough-skinned elephant", "Wow - I have a terrible headache," or "Mama told me not to play in the road." When we arrived at the conference more than one of us checked the front of the car to see if the cobra's fangs were embedded or had made a dent, but none were found.

I had assumed Perry and I would be given a room together. However, I was shown to a large dormitory with other Bassa women attending the conference, while Perry was housed with the men. What fun it was to witness "girl talk" among them. Since most of the ladies spoke in Liberian English, I was privy to their conversations.

They lay on each other's beds talking and plaiting one another's hair. Dressing was a fun affair with layers of traditional clothing to assemble and head ties to get just right. They traded earrings and shoes, and I shared my lotion and scented powder.

Their conversations ranged from clothing and food to the ever-popular topics of courtships, husbands, childbirths, and family planning. Some of them had experienced the failure of country medicine for family planning. I innocently asked how it worked and was told they paid money to a reputable country doctor, who placed the correct herbs and charms in a leather packet to wear around the waist.

They also debated if it was best to be pregnant in the rainy season or the dry season. I was amused by how strongly the women held to their opinions. Later I would think of their comments during my pregnancy with Michael in the hot/dry season. I firmly concluded I would not want to be pregnant again in the extreme heat and humidity.

The TEE conference featured the book of Esther. It had recently been translated by a group of Baptist missionaries, and the Bassa people were anxious to hear the story. While the pastors learned how to prepare sermons from the new book, I was given the privilege of presenting the book of Esther to the women and children.

At each session I read a chapter in English and a translator would repeat it in Bassa phrase by phrase. The women and children reacted emotionally to the story with tears, laughter, and boisterous cheering as was common for their uninhibited culture.

At the end of the conference, the women's group asked me to sing a song in English. Although I refused, they encouraged me, so I sang "Great is Thy Faithfulness". Although it does not have a peppy tune, the Bassa ladies snapped their fingers to the beat of the song. God's faithfulness was something I had experienced during our first year in Liberia. The song was often on my heart realizing all God had brought us through, and I still claim its promises.

Conference food was prepared by a group of hard-working ladies, who always worried if they had enough - sometimes the world is the same over. They cooked in a couple of small, thatched, "A" framed, makeshift kitchens constructed with bush poles. With few exceptions, everything was made from scratch in large heavy pots cooked over fires of chopped wood.

For breakfast they prepared roasted plantain, boiled cassava or fried plantain. There was rice with the traditional green sauces for other meals. At first the meat at the conference was tasty, but as the days passed with no refrigeration, the meat began to smell and I had to push it to the side of my bowl, knowing it would not go to waste. The children waiting in the wings would enjoy it later.

Everyone was silent while eating. For Americans this makes us feel uncomfortable, so I tried to make conversation, but the Bassa people only gave short answers or simply nodded. I happened to catch some food in my throat and coughed a little, and suddenly those around us broke into spontaneous laughter.

I felt insulted. Why would everyone laugh at my dilemma? David came to my rescue again and explained that the Bassa are taught to not talk while eating, because they might choke. When I coughed, they laughed because they had been waiting for me to choke in support of their custom .

Elephant Tail School

All the while we were at Dodain Perry kept a keen eye out for an elephant herd that was rumored to be foraging in the area. The residents said it was not uncommon to see elephants in the town. He had the opportunity to go out with other men a couple of times during breaks in the conference to find the herd, but never saw them.

There was an image of an elephant painted on the school, and it was named Elephant Tail School, because it was always a happy day when a hunter returned to his town with an elephant tail in hand. Perhaps school would be dismissed for the day as the whole village rushed out to the "fresh meat" and prepared to carry it home.

We of course hoped to see a real one for ourselves, but we also hoped none would be killed. As we drove away, Perry lamented the fact that we hadn't seen any elephants. The students agreed, since they had been anxious to eat elephant meat at the conference.

We learned later that an hour after we left, a herd of elephants passed right through the village, and one was killed for food. How we wish we would have stayed a little longer.

A note about endangered animals:

The duiker we ate, the crocodiles and hippos we saw, and the African bush elephant Perry would encounter years later are only a few of the endangered species in Liberia. The fate of these creatures hangs in the balance as deforestation progresses, and traditional communities exist solely by hunting and gathering.

14

Opening a New Mission

Our stay at the Number 3 guest house was much shorter than the missionaries' field council had anticipated. There were several reasons for this. After the pastors from the Number 1 area presented their petition requesting TEE classes, Larry spent a considerable amount of time traveling there to foster relations in addition to his normal responsibilities. It seemed he was ready to let someone else carry on the initial contacts. Secondly, perhaps the field leader also sensed our discouragement, and thought it was time we get a taste of working in our own area, even though we would be leaving Liberia in four months.

Everyone on the field council agreed we would be stationed in the Number 1 area, if we returned to Liberia after Perry's graduation from seminary. It would therefore be an advantage for us to live there and make ourselves known to local pastors, village chiefs, and government officials. We would also be responsible for finding land and planning for a mission compound to be built.

Before moving, we made several scouting trips to become acquainted with our new area, make contacts, and look for a suitable house to rent. We rented a large older, but secure, house with many rooms. It was close to the paved road which led from Monrovia to Buchanan. It had been part of the country estate of Mr. Summerville, Liberia's former assistant ambassador to Côte d'Ivoire (Ivory Coast).

He was buried in the front yard, about 50 feet from the road, under a large cement enclosed grave, which the neighbors hung their clothes on to dry. We rented the house from Josephine, the ambassador's sister, who lived with other family members in a tin sided house next door. She spoke with a nervous tick, was generally helpful in giving advice, and introduced us to people in the area.

The Summerville house, as we called it, was in good to fair condition, although it had not been lived in for some time. We painted and cleaned, deciding to live in only the back portion of the expansive house. I delighted in sewing curtains and fixing up the place.

The home was not equipped with a kitchen as we have in America, since the original dwellers had undoubtedly cooked their meals in the small cooking shed behind the main house. We made our kitchen in another enclosed back porch area by installing screens over the open lattice cement blocks. Simple cupboards with doors were made of plywood and painted white.

The well on the property only had mud on the bottom, so we put the word out that we needed to find a well digger. Most people were frightened to shimmy down the dark deep hole for fear of snakes and other creatures like scorpions. We were all surprised when a mission worker from Number 2 agreed to descend the well and dig it out to reach an adequate water level.

Shortly after moving in, we realized a small mouse resided in the hollow of our bathroom door. At first, we tried to get rid of it, but then we noticed how innocent and cute it was. It never got in our food or disturbed us as a larger rodent might, so we decided to co-exist and it became a type of little pet.

At the time we were in the habit of enjoying a bowl of popcorn each evening and the friendly mouse would appear for a single piece, then retire to his chamber. One evening he arrived before the popcorn was ready and ran right into Perry's foot as he stood at the stove.

The mouse seemed perplexed that his normal route was blocked and comically backed up repeatedly to get over the new obstacle. After a moment Perry let him pass to his normal waiting spot on the floor at the corner of the cupboard. He sat up on his back legs to assume a begging position. Once fed his quota piece, he retired to his hole in the door.

Shortly after moving in, the cooler temperatures of the dusty harmattan gave way to the dry season with its higher temperatures coupled with high humidity. In the early evening we would often mount the stairs just outside our kitchen door and sit on the flat roof above the kitchen and bedroom.

The African sky was beautiful, and we were struck anew by the wonder of God's handiwork above. Up on the roof the night air would cool and refresh us, but beneath our feet was a shockingly hot flat roof made of concrete. It was often hot enough that we wouldn't place our bare feet on it.

Little wonder then that our bedroom below was uncomfortably hot. In the middle of the night we often awoke in a sweat. Even taking a shower did little to cool us off since the water in the shower bucket was also warm. We would turn over our foam mattress, remake the bed and try to go back to sleep, but the hot air made it impossible to sleep well.

Since we did not have electricity, the luxury of running a fan or air conditioner was not possible. For extra hot nights we would hook up a battery run fan; but blowing the hot air did little good, was quite noisy, and quickly exhausted the batteries. It must have been during one of those sleepless nights that we came upon the idea of bringing a waterbed back – if God called us to return.

The opportunity to live at Number 1 allowed us to sample missionary life lived independently. We thoroughly enjoyed living in the little village setting and pursuing meaningful assignments. Since contacts with the pastors were going well, we began to catch a glimpse of working and ministering to the people there. In fact, we began to feel more like returning to this new area after Perry completed seminary.

Once while out driving, some young men walking along the road waved us down. We stopped to meet them and thought they would request a ride. They skipped the customary greeting and got straight to the point. "What are you 'white people' doing in this area?"

Perry responded, "We are missionaries and will start teaching centers for pastors and church leaders."

They seemed to want to intimidate us by forcefully responding, "We don't want God business here - Don't you know this is Devil Country?" An involuntary chill went up my spine as they described our new area!

Their comments could have been intimidating however we were confident the Lord God Almighty had his claim on the area and He would do great things through the existing churches. God's Spirit gave us confidence and peace! We looked forward to representing His might and authority and felt He had called us to live in that place at that time.

We began to identify with the area and realize there was a certain privilege in being called to live where the devil had a strong hold. What God intended for the area, only He knew, but we knew He had called us there for at least the first four months and we would do our best to represent our Lord and God there.

Perry was assigned the responsibility of obtaining a lease for mission property, so the necessary meetings with Commissioner J. Tah Wah Freeman were arranged. He was a consummate politician and was somewhat proud that we had chosen to reside in his area at Compound 1.

The Commissioner introduced us to the area's Paramount Chief, an aged man named Old Man Somah. ("Old Man" was used as a term of respect and endearment.) The parcel of land the commissioner suggested the mission lease was under Old Man Somah's domain, therefore negotiations with him needed to be made.

The Paramount Chief had a happy, likeable personality and I was aware of the respect due him. I accompanied Perry to the meeting with the commissioner and the tribal leader when the mission boundary lines were drawn on a map.

During the meeting there was a young boy who closely tailed Old Man Somah. He carried a switch made of long, thin sticks. While the men were conversing, the young boy stood nearby and appeared ready to strike his Paramount Chief at any given moment.

Several times I cringed thinking the boy was going to hit him, but the thin sticks would narrowly miss, and smartly smack together near his elder's weathered face. Conversely, Paramount Chief Somah did not seem

Perry and Paramount Chief, Old Man Somah

alarmed and in fact ignored the child completely, as did everyone in the room including Perry.

I was amazed this young boy would act in such a disrespectful manner, and no one seemed to notice except me. I tried to determine whether the child was mentally impaired, but that did not seem to be the case. I could only wait for the time when he would smack his elder's face and all attention in the room would be averted to this child's actions, but the calamity never occurred.

Several people came up to us as we were getting in the car. Some were just curious as to who we were and what we were doing there. Several people requested a ride, in addition to officials who had already loaded in our car.

Before we drove away, a man who had been at the meeting approached us with the boy who had nearly switched the Paramount Chief. The man greeted us and offered to give the boy to us. I thought I must have heard wrong, but in Liberian English he explained that the boy could live with us doing chores, if we in return would see to it that he was educated. We tried to refuse the request politely and the two of them turned and sadly walked away. I was not accustomed to this type of arrangement, but the guests in our car appeared not surprised.

Later Perry and I reasoned that it would be like family members sending their children to live with relatives who could afford to pay for their education. In the past, one the main functions of missions was to provide boarding and educational opportunities for children who came from the interior areas. This man was merely seeking an opportunity to provide an education for his grandson.

I mentioned to Perry I was surprised and upset over this boy's behavior during the meeting, nearly hitting the Paramount Chief with his sticks. Perry was amused with my assessment of the situation. He had witnessed this before on one of his treks and explained that the boy's responsibility was to keep flies off his elder. So, that was the reason for the apparent switching. It had never occurred to me.

Living in another culture, we were sometimes obtuse to what was happening around us. Things are not always as they appear, especially in a foreign culture - but it is also true in one's own culture as well.

Perry set out to explore the land the commissioner proposed to lease to our mission. The commissioner and Paramount Chief Old Man Somah had offered 15 acres on a 99-year lease. We were anxious to see where it was and what type of terrain it had. Situated just off the tar road with a long driveway, it was northeast of the actual government compound. There was a slight slope to the acreage and as Perry cleared a little brush away, it became apparent there was a beautiful view of the rolling hills in the distance.

A plan was devised for the long driveway to wind up the hill to the mission property. The commissioner did not want us to live permanently in a village, explaining we had different cultural habits. Although the village would be nearby, we would have some privacy, which he rightly felt we westerners are more accustomed to. We were not opposed to this plan. After living on both mission compounds and on the edge of a village, we realized that living in a village long term would be difficult with a lack of privacy, constant noise, and interruptions.

When the paperwork was completed to acquire the property, Paramount Chief Somah asked what the name of the mission would be. Perry said, "Maybe we will name it after you, since you have given us the land." He was pleased, and so "Somah Extension" was posted on a sign by our driveway. (While we were gone to the States, other missionaries who didn't know the history of the name changed it to 'Soniwiohn" after the nearby village.)

Perry hired a surveyor and several men to clear a survey line in the jungle, planting the customary soap trees along the boundary lines. This was a hot exhausting task, and Perry was not one to stand in the shade of the trees while there was work to do. As the cutlasses chopped the jungle growth away, a frightening thing happened.

The men up the line yelled, "Snake! Snake!" and they literally dove into the bush to escape the advancing reptile. Perry saw the head of a green snake which seemed to float above the foliage, and he realized it was a deadly green mamba. God created the mambas to move swiftly with their heads held high, casting looks from side to side.

In no time at all it was dangerously close to him. Feeling the time had come to defend his life there was little left to do, he raised his cutlass and "God blessed him" (a common expression in Liberia). Before he had the chance to take a swing, the snake caught his movement, turned, and escaped into the dense foliage.

The news of Perry, the white man, fighting the green mamba snake spread through the area. There were several times when we later entered a village, introduced ourselves, and the people would say they had heard of Perry, the brave white man and his reputation for fighting deadly snakes.

The CR mission board informed us that a young couple from Grand Rapids, Mike and Sue would be arriving as volunteer builders to oversee the construction of two houses at Number 1. Our field council plan called for one house to be ours and the other would be for the mission's agricultural advisor.

Since we would live so close to the highway, the field council decided the one approved plan for mission houses should be changed to something more secure. The vulnerable breezeway in the middle of the home with only screening for walls should be eliminated, security doors would be used, and rogue bars should be embedded in the windows, instead of expanded metal.

We were invited to draw up plans for our house. Missionaries who would live in the other home would design their own floorplan. The mission station was laid out to include a warehouse with an adjacent water tower, and two adjoining offices would be built further down the hill.

The new mission station would join the Christians and their churches already in the area and be a presence of God's work in Devil Country.

15

Acquaintances

Pastor Mondamaa Beegar and the other pastors were encouraged that the initial petition they had "carried" to Number 2 was being taken seriously after only a couple of months. She frequently visited our home to check on Perry's language acquisition. He needed to pass a preliminary language exam, which the mission council required before starting a TEE class for pastors.

He succeeded in passing the exam and I attended the introductory meeting with potential students. They met on a hot day in a tin sided church with the bush poles visible from the inside. Twenty-seven church leaders came to register for TEE classes. The men sat on benches on the right side of the church, while a few ladies sat on the left side. Some brought Bibles and one man went to a window for better lighting to read, possibly suffering from one of the local eye diseases.

The new students were thrilled to receive a free cassette player, and Perry explained how to use them. The first couple of years while they were learning to read, the lessons were recorded on cassettes and handed out each week. Batteries could be purchased from the teacher.

Perry asked them as pastors what they considered important to learn. Those assembled were unaccustomed to conversing with a missionary, so there was hesitation and indirect answers were given. I became restless, feeling the heat of the day, and the tin structure popped and moaned as the metal expanded under the rays of the sun.

"Why can't we just get this over with," I wondered impatiently, frequently looking at the time. "I'm sure Perry knows the best courses to teach. Why doesn't he just announce what he will teach?" But Perry knew the importance of having them grapple with the questions and wanted to extract their heartfelt needs in order to better serve them.

The questions he asked of the church leaders took some time and thought to answer, and it allowed us to learn a lot about them. Though I was hot and tired of waiting, I regretted I was not more patient on such an important and exciting day.

The class discussion led them to request a course on the books of Samuel. This may seem a surprising place to start, but they had heard 1 & 2 Samuel had been recently translated into Bassa and were eager to study it. Perry was pleased, saying they would find the books interesting, since they covered a family and nation story line leading to the arrival of Jesus our Savior.

The spiritual depth of the pastors was impressive, though they were uneducated. They clearly adored their Savior and sat on the edges of their seats eager to learn. There would be much to teach them starting with the basics of reading, progressing on to read the Bible, and finally learning to prepare a sermon.

Perry encouraged the pastors with Acts 4:13, *Now when they saw their boldness and perceived that they were uneducated, common men, they were astonished. And they recognized that they had been with Jesus*. Though the student pastors had not had the opportunity of an education, they had experienced Jesus as their Savior, and God was using them to encourage Christians in their churches.

I was also surprised by the apparent poverty of these men and that they were willing to take a day or maybe two days a week to attend the TEE Bible class. They found their education and training so helpful that they spent a great amount of time studying their lessons together and repeatedly listening to the weekly cassette tapes.

Perry and I tried to visit most of the students in their home villages. We would often have to take the foot trails to reach them, since many of the villages were not located on a car road. Each Sunday we would visit a different student's church and the pastor would always ask his teacher to preach. At first Perry let them know we would be worshipping with them, but then they would have a feast after the worship service. We didn't want to impose, so most of the time we would just show up unannounced on Sunday morning.

Occasionally we visited a student during the week and would find the pastor on his farm tending his rice field or engaged in some other activity. These visits also gave us the chance to meet the family members and see their villages. Sometimes we were served food, but we were always careful to leave some as was proper Bassa etiquette.

It was not uncommon for the pastor to give us a chicken as a take-home gift. Sometimes it appeared it was the last chicken in the village, but it was impolite to refuse a gift. It upset us a great deal to walk away with their last chicken, because we had an abundance of food at home. Not only that, but as we walked away, we were taking their future eggs, chicks, and potential flock.

We let the chickens forage for food around our home. Since they were range chickens, they were very tough and needed to be cooked in a pressure cooker to be edible. Often there were opportunities to favor our guests with the gift of a chicken and we knew it was a real treat.

One of Perry's students in his first class stood out and became a dear friend of ours. His name was Pastor Alexander. He and Perry decided to go on a trek to explore another section of the mysterious Margibi area north of Number 1, also called Number 1B. It was still virgin forest, isolated with no car roads, and reportedly only a few churches in the area.

They planned to meet up with another student of Perry's and trek for about a week, stay in villages as guests, and spread the gospel. They hoped to find Christian churches with pastors who might be interested in TEE classes. While they were trekking, I was invited to stay at the closest mission station, Number 2, so I wouldn't be alone.

By now Perry was accustomed to the wonders of the virgin natural rain forest with its high overhead canopy shading the trails below. One day as they walked along the jungle path, it suddenly appeared as though the sky was moving. Something strange was happening like a swaying gigantic 3D picture.

Perry's eyes suddenly refocused and an elephant came into view - only 20 yards off! They stopped for a while and watched it, then there was only one thing to do and that was to keep moving down the path. What a thrill it was to see a wild elephant at such close range.

When they arrived at a prearranged village where another student, Pastor John F., was to meet them, he was not there. He typically walked one and a half days each week to class, and another one and a half days home. With John's help they planned to hold a mini conference for believers they found living in the isolated area.

Alexander and Perry decided to venture on, asking people in each village they came to where John F. lived. They were told which path John took out of the village on his way home, and the men continued their search.

When they reached John's village, they were told someone had died making it necessary for him to stay with the grieving family. Since everyone was preoccupied with "dead body business", there would be no chance to hold a conference. Instead they met as many people as possible, explaining the gospel and spreading the news that a class for pastors was being held.

Several neighbors near our rented home became endeared to us and would work for us in future years. One man who would be part of our lives was Old Man Pau. He lived in the village between the tar road and the new mission land. Everyone simply called him "Old Man" in respect. He was a bachelor and his mud and stick one-bedroom house had an unusual small porch.

One day from inside his home, he watched us walk around the village. From his window he called us over. This was the first time we met him. We visited with him through his bedroom window, giving us a rare chance to see a private dwelling. Everything in the room was neat and tidy, with the bed covers neatly pulled up and a small wooden table in the corner. As was customary, the interior mud walls had been plastered with any type of paper he could find using rice water paste.

While we talked with him, Perry suddenly asked, "Hey, where did you get my picture?" How bizarre to come upon a house in the African jungle and see your picture plastered on the wall! We looked closer and not only did we see Perry's face, but several of his classmates were also adorning the wall of the small home. We realized somehow Old Man had gotten a copy of the Banner, our denominational magazine, where pictures were published of everyone in Perry's seminary class.

It took us some time to figure out how Old Man Pau had gotten the magazine; but it turned out that Margaret was in the habit of giving people her used periodicals. When she passed through the new area making contacts for future health classes, she had made a few friends by giving them a magazine. Sometimes it is a small world even in the jungle of Africa.

During our conversation with Old Man Pau, he exited his house and we had another surprise when we saw he had suffered a leg amputation. Through the years he would never tell us what happened to his leg, but he liked people to think it was injured during a hunting accident.

Others told us he was part of the original road crew that laid the tar road between Firestone Rubber Plantation and Buchanan. While on the job he suffered an accident and gangrene set in. The leg had to be amputated at LAMCO hospital in Buchanan.

He told me while he was lying in his hospital bed, he looked out the window and saw a person sitting high on the back of a strong animal with long legs and a long-haired tail. It seemed the person could make the animal go where he wanted to go by pulling ropes in the animal's mouth. He didn't remember what it was called. Old Man's eyes got huge when I substantiated his story saying I had ridden a horse before, and we

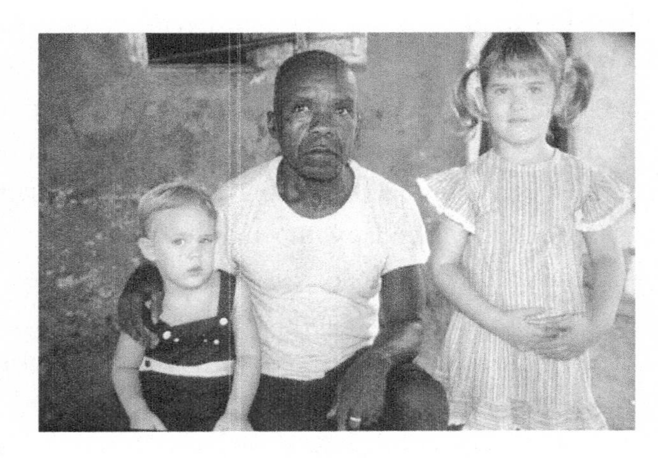

Michael, Old Man Pau, Laura

even had some on my father's farm when I was a child. He said, "Hmm, most people don't believe me."

In years to come Old Man became almost part of our family spending each night with us on the mission grounds as the watchman. Our children loved him and even though he liked to display a rather gruff temperament, he would crack a smile when they ran up and threw their arms around him.

Corpu was a lively middle-aged man with a constant smile and many children. His family also lived in the village nearby. Being a dental hygienist, I noted his darkly stained teeth and reasoned his love of chewing nuts from the kola trees was undoubtedly the reason.

His elderly, frail mother lived with him as a member of the extended family. To our surprise she was the local midwife. Her name was "Dabo", which simply meant "Old Woman". I was intrigued that she was missing one of her great toes, and she couldn't remember what happened to it. When I asked her why her toe was missing, she joked with me, and appeared startled that it was gone.

Her appearance was quite memorable as she would come to my door with bare feet while chewing tobacco or smoking a corncob pipe. Often her face and arms were painted with white streaks of country medicine to cure some unknown illness or perhaps the white concoction was meant to help her smell nice. She was a thin, wisp of a woman, whom Corpu always claimed was 100 years old and she did seem ancient.

Taa was a man who lived on the other side of the driveway with his family. They seemed to be long time acquaintances of the Summerville family, who rented us the big former ambassador's house. Taa would eventually be hired by the mission to cut the grass on its expansive grounds. I say expansive because several acres of jungle were cleared around our houses creating an open area. The grass was kept down by swinging a whipper hour after hour, so considering the task before them, the area was indeed expansive.

Since Taa and his family lived next door to us, we had the chance to observe their daily lives. He seemed to be a misfit and we wondered if it was due to the skinny muscle in one leg causing him to walk with a pronounced limp. I surmised Taa had suffered with polio.

Taa had a pretty, happy little girl named Soma who would sit on the steps of our house waiting for us to come out. Soma became the victim of a set of difficult circumstances. She developed an eye infection, which was probably only a simple case of conjunctivitis, commonly called pink eye. Regrettably, her family sought out and paid for country medicine, which looked to us like some mixture of mud that was forced into her eye.

As missionaries in a foreign culture it was difficult at times to know when to intervene in people's lives if they do not request help. In this situation we wished we had intruded sooner. When we saw the mud impacted eye, we told them to wash out the muddy remedy and gave them antibiotic eye ointment to clear up the infection.

It was disheartening the next day to see they were continuing to use their country medicine. We eventually took her to the doctors at ELWA and later to JFK Hospital in Monrovia. It looked like she was improving, but when the family continued their own treatment, the infection returned.

The awful conclusion of several appointments and various treatments was the removal of her eye. The family was distraught over her appearance, and we watched Soma's general health fail for unknown reasons. Living close by, we wondered if the family was feeding her properly and offered her food. We talked to Taa's family trying to encourage them by explaining Soma would live a normal life, have a family, and be happy. Still her weakness progressed.

One day Perry was restless while we ate lunch. From his spot at the table, he could see she was lying on the ground and struggling in their outside kitchen. He got up from the table and went to the little girl. She was wrapped in a dirty cloth, and seeing she was very ill, he picked her up and prayed for her. While he tenderly held the child in his arms and sang "Jesus Loves Me" to her, she died.

It was heartbreaking. We were shocked at the progression of events over a simple case of pink eye. Margaret told of a similar case where cradle cap on a baby's head became infected and led to death.

This senseless tragedy in our first year affected us greatly and we learned how serious simple health issues can become in the tropics.

16

Politics

When Palm Sunday and Liberia's newly formed National Redemption Day fell on the same day, Grand Bassa County was visited by President Samuel Kanyon Doe. He traveled the tar road just outside our rental home, and it became an eye-opening experience for us paralleling Christ's entrance into Jerusalem.

The day had become a Liberian holiday marking the one-year anniversary of Liberia's first military coup d'état carrying President Doe to power. The occasion was marked with celebration and pomp, and the village people around us were crazy with excitement.

All along the paved road from Monrovia to Buchanan the Bassa people placed arches made of braided palm branches decorated with flowers. This was their traditional way to welcome important guests.

The Bassa side of the boundary river was decorated with an extraordinary palm arch, which went from one side of the road to the other, allowing vehicles and even trucks to pass underneath. Arches along the roadside continued for nearly 60 miles to the city of Buchanan.

Palm trees were stripped of their branches to construct the arches and every flower that could be found was used to decorate them. Since we lived so close to the road, the excitement was unavoidable. After all, the president was coming.

The Bassa people were excited to think President Doe would celebrate the first Redemption Day in their county. They stood along the side of the road waving palm branches as the presidential motorcade passed by. It contained many cars and trucks with armed soldiers, but when Doe's compact baby blue Chevette passed by, the people became euphoric. They cheered and called out waving long palm branches as the entourage passed. Some even dropped to the ground with the honor of being so close to their deliverer.

On that first Redemption Day, it seemed at times we were experiencing the ecstasy of the crowds when Jesus rode into Jerusalem on Palm Sunday. Our minds played the many parallels of this experience, and we suddenly gained new understanding of the eagerness of the people welcoming their deliverer Jesus, whom they supposed would be their political liberator from the Romans. Just as the Liberians had suffered under the hand of the Americo-Liberians, Israel had been under the oppression of Rome, Herod the King, and the governor Pilot. We could envision the waving palms, the expectations, and the cheering of the underprivileged in Jesus' day.

Living in a third world country often helped us gain a better understanding of Biblical times. We soon understood how it must have felt to walk everywhere and how it would be so wonderful for the rough places to be made smooth and every valley to be lifted up for the coming of the Lord.

The lack of readily available medical care helped us understand the desperate situation the sick in Jesus' day experienced, and how wonderful it would be to meet the Great Physician who healed all. When we watched the Bassa carry their water from a stream every day, "He is the living water" became much more meaningful, and the gravity of daily finding food to eat brought new light to the phrase "Jesus is the bread of life".

In 1820 the American Colonization Society sent 86 freed slaves back to Africa and they eventually founded the nation of Liberia. Thousands of former slaves later joined them, some even arriving from other parts of the world. This unique group of people became known as Americo-Liberians, and they established the country of Liberia in 1847.

Since then they have comprised only five percent of the population but held nearly every seat in government. For the past 170 years, the Bassa and other tribal peoples of Liberia have ironically felt enslaved to descendants of freed American slaves.

In 1979, the year before we arrived in Liberia, President William R. Tolbert, an Americo-Liberian and a Baptist minister, spent over $100 million, a third of the national budget, to build a conference center for the Organization of African Unity (OAU). This caused the government to raise the price of rice, the nation's staple.[15] The people revolted and there were deadly rice riots in the capital city.[16]

Spurred by national unrest, a tribal man, Master Sergeant Samuel Kanyon Doe, and his entourage of eighteen enlisted men staged a coup d'état. They had been trained by American soldiers to guard President Tolbert, but they left their president laying in a pool of blood in his mansion.[17]

They simply killed the president they were trained to guard. Many civilians lost their lives as the military took over, and thirteen prominent members of the former government were infamously executed by firing squad on the beach.[18]

When Samuel Kanyon Doe claimed the presidency, he was a 28-year-old, tribal man, who had enlisted in the army, dropped out of school in the 11th grade,[19] and was rumored to be illiterate. It was on the heels of this coup' that we entered the country, and army personnel were still confident, yet tense after gaining power.

At first Doe was their hero, driving his unpretentious little car and leading the indigenous people to opportunities denied them in the past. Unfortunately, in later years the power and money of the office corrupted him, and he met with a worse demise than he and his fellow soldiers gave President Tolbert.

Mission politics also became a part of our new lifestyle. Not only were there differences of opinion among missionaries about mission strategy, but we had to contend with our sending board. They were always asking for the number of new conversions we had. How could they forget? We were not evangelizing. Instead, they had sent us to train church pastors and train indigenous leaders to take our place.

We were glad when three mission board members traveled to Liberia to see the new mission strategy in operation. We hoped if they saw the church leaders being trained, they would identify with our unconventional mission work and speak up for us at board meetings.

Since we lived only an hour from the airport, we were naturally asked to pick them up. We had taken a break to the northern area of Yekepa and not been home the week prior to their arrival, so we were unaware that something had happened in our house.

We entered the kitchen through the back door, and I asked the board members to please find their way down the hallway to the living room, which we had nicknamed "the gym", due to its size. I followed them shortly thereafter with a tray of cold lemonade and was dumb-founded to find a large termite hill had developed in the center of the room!

There it sat - a big mound of wet glistening dirt about hip high. I was naturally shocked and unnecessarily embarrassed about this unique invasion. Although, it certainly had no reflection on my level of housekeeping, as termites often pass through the smallest of cracks to enter buildings, I made no mention of it and neither did anyone else. Everyone seemed to simply ignore the monstrosity in the room!

I guess I had planned to be the perfect hostess and wasn't going to let something like termites ruin my cover. However, it is often the abnormalities of daily living that make life interesting and fun, especially in Africa. But the evening oddities were not quite over.

After dinner I washed the dishes, while the men strolled outside to enjoy the coolness of the evening. We had mentioned being able to see the Southern Cross constellation and they hoped to view it as well. Perry advised them to not walk in a certain area of the yard explaining the dreaded driver ants had been busy making trails there. Our guests ignored his advice, and after a while began to feel the ants crawling up their pants and biting their legs.

Unaware I stepped out of the house to enjoy the cool night air, but Perry hastily told me to go back inside. I pouted a little, thinking I too would like to cool off after washing dishes in the hot water.

Later after our guests had gone to bed, I expressed my thoughts about being shooed back in the house. Perry laughed and told me the men had found it necessary to peel off their pants to hastily remove the nasty ants. When I stepped out of the house, our guests were - shall I say - not properly attired. We found it rather amusing and tried to restrain our giggles, hoping they couldn't hear on the other side of the house.

The next morning when Perry drove the board members to Number 2 mission, I walked in the living room to look at the annoying termite hill. In frustration I gave it a swift kick. To my shock the mound was hard as cement, and I thought I might have broken my toe in my frustration. Funny thing was I had carried a shovel with me thinking I would pitch it out the door since it had the appearance of wet mud. In the end, I hired Taa and some other men with pickaxes to chop it out bit, by bit. They put it in a wheelbarrow and wheeled it home to patch their house.

Before the arrival of the mission board members, our field council had unanimously agreed to pass a motion proposing we all get new cars (paid for by the mission) when the odometers reached 30,000 miles! Imagine that!

When the board members arrived, we were informed that the mission board in Grand Rapids decided we had been rather generous to ourselves and they would require at least three times that many miles, adding most of them drove cars well over the 100,000 mile mark.

The way we were informed of their decision caused us to feel a little ashamed of ourselves. Surely the board members had read our field council minutes where we dutifully explained the grounds for purchasing new cars:

1. Extreme road conditions caused the vehicles considerable wear, to the point of being unsafe.
2. Mission vehicles were breaking down at an alarming rate, putting our families in danger while driving.
3. The model of Peugeot car shipped to third world countries was of lesser quality than the European variety, causing it to wear down prematurely.
4. Repairs by mechanics and parts were depleting the mission budget.
5. The many hours of vehicle upkeep and repair necessary by missionaries were interfering with productivity.

Later during the board members' visit they were scheduled to travel from one mission station to another to conduct a visit with other missionaries. Naturally, they were given use of a mission car, which like all the others had acquired over 30,000 miles.

They set off with directions, but before they got very far, a tire and rim broke off at the axel, and they were shocked to see it precede them rolling down a steep hill. The board members fortunately were not hurt, as the car cruised down the hill, and came to a lopsided stop.

After waiting on the side of the road for a taxi to happen along, they crammed in an over loaded vehicle, and rode back to the mission station. Suddenly, they were quite concerned with the overall condition of our mission vehicles and inspected them. After they returned to the States, an announcement was sent to the field that the board would no longer block new car purchases!

The condition of the mission cars was really that bad. Thus, while we were in Liberia, we had the privilege to drive two brand new mission vehicles, something we had not experienced before, nor since.

I was home alone one day when a large army truck filled with soldiers pulled onto our yard. Since Perry was gone with the car, it appeared we were not home. Standing in the shadows and peering through the lattice work brick wall, I was able to see the soldiers look at our house and then go to our nearby Bassa neighbors. As they were talking, they pointed their guns at my house.

Feeling quite vulnerable, I decided to stay out of sight and sat in the bathroom, our safe inner room sanctuary without a window. I was afraid to handle the situation while home alone. Some soldiers walked over and knocked loudly on my kitchen door. My heart pounded and I stayed motionless in my hiding place. I could hear others were still in the truck.

When no one answered, they pounded loudly and yelled, "Open the door". I was thankful for a thick sturdy door and lock. Some soldiers could even be heard walking on the flat roof above. My stomach lurched within and I worried if I got physically sick, they would hear me. It seemed to me I should follow through with my plan to stay hidden away and control myself to not make any noise for fear of giving my presence away.

My fear resulted from the recent political situation in Liberia and rumors of soldiers' brutality. Normally we had no interaction with soldiers since we lived in the interior. I didn't know if I should pray for Perry to come home and save me or not, that would put him in jeopardy as well, so I just prayed they would leave.

My ears became keen and I heard the soldiers jumping out of the truck and many voices getting closer to my house. Was the situation only going to get worse, would they break down my door, should I run out the front door and down the jungle path? No, it was best to stay in my safe room. Fear mounted exponentially within me and I prayed for God's protection.

Their voices trailed away, but still they were talking and laughing loudly. I dared to creep out the bathroom door and down a windowless hallway in the shadows for a distant peek through the lattice work. I saw they had climbed the guava tree about ten feet from the kitchen, where they were enjoying the ripe fruit and telling loud entertaining stories. Apparently one of the soldiers knew of the tree and since it was guava season, they had stopped for a mid-day snack.

I could also see their machine guns were perched on the branches and pointed in my direction. I silently crawled back to my inner room and waited until they reloaded the truck and drove away. In the end it seemed the soldiers merely wanted to ask permission to pick fruit, but still it was best for me to play it safe.

One day during a visit to our friends in Somah town, we were exposed to yet another new thing. What I witnessed seemed to be cruelty to a chicken. Someone decided to add chicken to the cooking pot that day. Naturally, a chicken roaming around the yard was caught. While we were talking, the cook began sawing across the chicken's neck with a dull knife.

The chicken was squawking, gasping for air, and trying to escape the whole while. At times the cook stopped to insert a lengthy story in the conversation, during which the chicken began to hope for survival, only to be choked, and cut with a dull knife again. This went on for a short time and it was difficult to watch, still the chicken had not been put out of its misery.

I finally asked her, "Would you like me to show you how my grandmother taught me to kill a chicken? It is the 'quick-service' method." Everyone thought they would like to see that, so I took the gasping chicken to the side of the jungle and searched for a sturdy stick. Holding the bird by its feet, I laid its neck on the ground, and positioned the stick evenly over it. With both ends of the stick held down by my feet, I swiftly pulled the chicken up by its feet, which severed the head from the body. A little group of people had gathered around me and they seemed to approve, while I explained that the chicken was no longer suffering.

Sometime later Chief Somah told us people in neighboring villages had started using the quick service method to kill their chickens. He commented it was "fine-o" and the chickens were no longer suffering.

We found it surprising my method had circulated the area, but one of our fellow missionaries was not impressed. The objection was that I shouldn't be changing the culture like that. Perry stood up for me saying, "We are here to improve Bassa lifestyle spiritually and in any other way we can. The culture of the people, and even the chickens, will naturally benefit."

We received word of my Grandpa Andersen's diagnosis of advanced colon cancer, so we were always eager to hear of his condition. We thought we would see him again when we returned to the States, but mail service was slow and letters from family could take anywhere from a week to a month to arrive. I didn't find out he had died until a month after the fact.

It made we wonder what God had done with the prayers I said before I knew he had died. For quite some time I had been praying, while in reality he was already in heaven.** Perhaps the Lord knew what my requests would be and answered them in advance.

At the next meeting of the mission council, some missionaries still did

---

**I was sure Grandpa went to heaven because he was a Christian man of prayer, committed to the Church of Christ, and always wanted to do the right thing. I remember vividly as a child watching him pray on his knees before he went to bed. I saw him through the open doorway in the living room, which led to my grandparents' bedroom. He was accustomed to praying out loud and knelt on the floor beside his bed in his red woolen long-johns. He would pray out loud for some time with his hands folded in front of his face. Scenes of my grandfather praying and other encounters with grandparents have been life changing for me. It is important for young children to witness such acts of devotion. I was also influenced greatly by my Great-Grandma Jurgens and a time of prayer I shared with her. We were also blessed by the prayer life of Perry's Grandma Tinklenberg. Her letters to us in Africa were a spiritual blessing and we referred to her our prayer warrior.

not agree with the mission's strategy. They desired to focus on primary evangelism and plant churches. There was perhaps pressure from their supporting churches in the States to start new churches, and missionaries in other organizations were influential suggesting we not give time and energy to teaching the Bassa African Independent Churches.

Even in the short time we had been there, it was obvious Grand Bassa County was saturated with indigenous churches and the leaders needed education and help. From the beginning it had been the mission's goal to assist those congregations and pastors and equip them for the role God had already given them. If the missionaries were to focus on starting churches, we would be limited to serving only a fraction of our potential and deny training for existing church leaders.

The field council meeting was unpleasant. It grew heavy, and arguments were heated. A motion came to the floor to change the mission strategy from training existing church pastors to planting Christian Reformed Churches. One couple announced they would abstain from voting. It was clear which side everyone else was on. Our privilege to vote as full-time missionaries was crucial as the tiebreaker. Missionaries from both sides of the issue lobbied their interests with us over lunch.

We felt a heavy burden to discern and follow God's will. With a clear conscience we voted to continue the vision of TEE classes. This defeated the motion. The Christian Reformed mission would continue the strategy of teaching and training established church pastors and leaders who craved God's Word and instruction. As we saw it, there was no need to start more churches, but training existing church leaders would meet an important need in Bassaland and they would evangelize their own people.

I was glad when we finally moved on to the next item on the agenda, but it too was difficult. Larry and Ann said they had something to say. They presented a letter to the field council, saying they felt God calling them to reach the Muslim people in northern Africa (where they served as missionaries for 36 more years). And so, it was that Larry and Ann resigned from the Bassa mission. They would leave at the end of their term roughly a year away. Perry and I were crushed, feeling they were the stalwarts of the program, possessing the vision, experience, and leadership the young team of missionaries needed.

As we prepared to leave Liberia and return to the States for Perry's final semesters at Calvin Seminary, we did not make a firm decision to return to the Bassa mission. Our Bassa mentor, Abba Karnga and our fellow missionaries encouraged us to resume what we had begun at Compound Number 1 and join the team being assembled. Perry had once confided to Abba that we were homesick for our families and culture, but Abba replied, "Heaven is your home. And life is a life of service." He also quoted Philippians 3:20, *But our citizenship is in heaven*. This made a lasting impression on us.

It was an exciting time in the mission since an amiable agreement had been made with CEFL for co-ministry to local existing churches. Larry's TEE students were demonstrating fruit after being instructed in the Bible. Their spiritual maturity became evident when they resigned their membership and positions in the Secret Society. The health program was also making great strides with classes producing capable Village Health Care workers and trained Traditional Birth Attendants. The need was great, and it appeared the approach to ministry was producing spiritual fruit.

Probably most importantly, Perry had tasted the joy of teaching church leaders firsthand. His newly formed class in the Number 1 area had drawn 27 church leaders from nine different denominations. Their ecumenical unity was tangible as they came together to study, grow, and learn. They often spoke of being one in the Lord, and yet kept their own theological perspectives. (See Appendix E)

Overall, nearly 200 Bassa church leaders were enrolled in TEE classes offered by CR missionaries. There were another 50-100 who were turned down because of lack of personnel to teach classes.[20] It was evident God's Spirit was active in Bassaland and in the Christian Reformed mission. Were we to join this endeavor? Was God calling us to return?

On our final night in Liberia the missionaries assembled for a sit-down dinner, followed by a time of worship and prayer. It was during this time together that I realized what a privilege it was to be part of this vital program for our Bassa brothers and sisters in Christ. At that time the incentive to return was not as strong for Perry. After suffering several major illnesses and finding how uncomfortable he felt in the extreme heat and humidity, the decision to return was a struggle for him.

We had always held that if one of us did not feel "the call", we would not go. For that reason, I did not say much during the time of his indecisiveness. I had enjoyed being a dental hygienist while Perry was furthering his training and could have easily insisted that he become a pastor in the States, so I could pursue my own career.

We had decided to discern and follow the Lord's calling together. It was not clear what type of ministry God would entrust to us, but we desired to follow His will and waited for His call.

Missionaries at our farewell dinner:
Perry & Kathy, Larry & Ann, their children Joel & Erica, Mike & Sue, Mark & Pat, with baby Marie, Don & Marty. Not pictured: Margaret who was babysitting, Anna, J.J. and Ben.

17

Return

Culture shock hit us squarely between the eyes when we returned to our home in Grand Rapids, Michigan. Leaving Africa, we had first flown to South Dakota to visit our families, and everything seemed normal. They were living in the same houses and doing the things they had always done, so nothing appeared out of the ordinary.

When we entered our house in Grand Rapids however, we were immediately struck with our materialism in contrast to the life of barrenness we had lived in Liberia. Although we were living as "poor" seminary students with secondhand furniture, old clothes, and a late model car, it was surprising to remember we had desired even more.

Was all we had accumulated necessary? Why hadn't we been able to give more to missions and needy people in our neighborhood? I now felt my set of china, among other things, was extremely frivolous and was sorely tempted to give it away.

Our seminary friends who were also back from foreign internships expressed similar thoughts. Together we discussed our change of lifestyles and the role of God's call in our lives. Why had we been so blessed with wealth and freedom as Americans, but more importantly how was it that God had placed us in Christian homes to hear of God's love while we were still young - while others around the world struggled to merely survive and had no access to the gospel?

After doing some soul searching, it appeared to us that for some unknown reason God had granted us life with our families and placed us in the country in which we lived. He had done so for a reason. Furthermore, our meager possessions were granted by Him alone, and we had carefully and thoughtfully furnished our home, which was not excessive in our culture.

We came to believe that all we had should be used for God's honor and glory. So, we invited friends over nearly every weekend and used the fancy china dishes, realizing that fellowship with God's people brought honor and glory to Him.

A deeper sense of thankfulness for our Christian families and training also emerged. What an absolute blessing to love Jesus and understand His grace all our lives! Certainly, privileges granted to us were given, so that we might share God's goodness and grace with others both close to home and far away.

Together with seminary friends who had been on cross cultural internships, we felt blessed to experience God at work in another area of His world. Some were considering further ministry overseas, while others had decided to not return to foreign soil. One of Perry's closest friends was flown home on a stretcher and had lost a frightening amount of weight. Another couple was eagerly anticipating the adoption of children from their host country.

Not only did it take some time to recover from culture shock, there were also physical ailments which we hoped would vanish. Upon our return from Africa, it was apparent to our families that both of us had lost a considerable amount of weight. Perry's family doctor admitted him to the hospital for treatment and tests due to prolonged diarrhea.

The mission board felt Perry had suffered an unusual amount of illness, so they sent us to Mt. Sinai's tropical disease lab in Chicago. They took many samples from us, and we both tested positive for filaria, which causes River Blindness. At the time we had no symptoms, so the physician opted for no treatment hoping the disease would simply self-eradicate without further exposure. Fortunately, this parasitic disease never progressed any further for either of us.

Much of Perry's final year at seminary was spent searching for God's will concerning the future. Was Perry to go into traditional pastoral work in a stateside church, or was the Lord calling us to return to Devil Country in Liberia?

Conversations were held at the CRWM head office where we were pressed and encouraged to continue educating the church leaders. After some time, Perry regained his health and prayerfully reassessed the mission strategy. He decided he could recommit to the Bassa mission field and asked if I was ready to go back - I said that I was. I believe that I knew all along we would return to Number 1 and make that area of the world our home, but I had no idea we would live there for the next eight years. This fact would have been too overwhelming to face in the beginning.

While Perry completed his final year of seminary, I was fortunate enough to return to my former employer as a dental hygienist. That year we suffered the trauma of an early miscarriage, followed by a full house robbery. The thieves were thorough, yet we were surprised to learn our insurance company would pay us replacement value for the missing items. With a hefty insurance settlement, God provided money to cover future expenses of outfitting as missionaries.

When Perry graduated from Calvin Theological Seminary, we added to the celebration an announcement that we were expecting a baby in January. Over the summer we sold many of our remaining possessions, received an offer on our house, and in late August drove a U-Haul truck to our parents' homes in South Dakota.

Preparations for missionary life began in earnest. Perry's home church, First CRC in Sioux Falls, agreed to be his "calling church". An oral examination for ordination was conducted by the Iakota Classis. The Classis examiner fired off questions based on the Belgic Confession and Berkhof's Summary of Doctrine. I wrote down every question. It was a thorough exam, and his parents and I were very proud of his in-depth answers.

On September 30, 1982 Perry was ordained into the Ministry of Word and Sacraments by area pastors and elders at his parent's church. As he knelt for ordination, those who placed their hands on him included his father, Elder Virgil Tinklenberg, local pastor and former missionary to Nigeria, Rev. Harold De Groot, and the CRWM director for Africa whom we respected and admired, Rev. Bill Van Tol. At our request, he had traveled from Grand Rapids to preach at the commissioning service.

We were privileged to attend several ordinations of seminary friends and collectively realized the thrill and enormity to which God had called us. Furthermore, Perry and I gravely understood that soon we would be on our own in a distant country, facing a distinct ministry to a foreign people.

From a list we had formed while still in Liberia, future supplies were purchased and assembled. Our first year there we had used mission guest house furnishings, but when we went back, we would have to provide the essentials of a home ourselves. In addition, it was exciting to shop for little baby clothes and dream of starting our family.

The mission board had informed us we would be required to use a mosquito net over our bed each night, due to our history with malaria. I was not familiar with mosquito nets, but Mrs. De Groot, the pastor's wife, came to our aid. Since they had lived in Nigeria where missionaries used netting, she carefully sketched a picture for me.

After a lengthy search for the proper mosquito netting, my mother and I began the process of assembling netting large enough to encase a king size waterbed. I purchased extra yardage to sew a similar enclosure for the baby's crib. (In my lifetime, I have made a total of 14 mosquito nets!)

All other essential items for the mission field were stored in the Tinklenberg family's basement and one day our parents, grandparents, and the De Groots joined us in packing barrels to be shipped to Liberia. Records show we shipped seven 55-gallon steel barrels and one wooden crate, which held a small Hoover washing machine and section of carpet.

We paid $867.88 for these containers to be shipped from Sioux Falls, SD to the Freeport of Monrovia, Liberia. The shipment left New Orleans in October of 1982 and arrived in Liberia the middle of February. We paid $285.23 for duties, customs, and fees to the port and consular.

When we left for Liberia in October, I was seven months pregnant. During our discussions with the mission board, they presented the option of returning to Liberia after our baby was born, and we prayerfully considered it. However, I felt it would be too difficult to return to Africa with a new baby, and we were eager and impatient to get started in the ministry.

The difficulty I foresaw was the emotional tearing away from a sheltered environment surrounded by family, friends, and modern conveniences. It seemed the all-powerful nesting instinct had set in and we desired to get "home" and be ready for our baby's arrival. Also, we knew it could take months to get the baby's passport, travel documents, and proper immunizations for Africa delaying our return. Several missionaries had given birth in Liberia, so that was not a concern for me.

Human reasoning set aside, probably the major reason we returned when we did was that the Lord gave us a real peace and excitement about going back to Liberia. I recall our parents expressed their concern with having a baby in a third world country, and I often saw a heaviness in our mothers' loving eyes. However, after our initial conversations with them, they somehow restrained themselves from further comments, and little was said to reveal any reticence they must have felt.

Leaving the airport for Africa was a difficult thing as we gazed into the years ahead without close family contact. There were always lingering hugs, eyes filled with tears, and hearts aching when we said our good-byes. It is amazing how clearly we felt God's calling to leave. He gave us the confidence to leave family members we dearly loved and remove ourselves from the comforts of the American culture and lifestyle.

We hoped for a final glimpse of loved ones through the airplane window and blew kisses not knowing if our family could see us. As the plane taxied past the home terminal, we were touched to see the lone silhouette of Perry's father as he stood at the end of the concourse waving farewell.

There was a real sense that God was with us. We understood it was a privilege to be called to go, and knew He had a certain job for us to do in His kingdom. There was the feeling that God had a prepared a particular ministry for us to do, and only a certain amount of time to do it. Later Perry would call it a "divine kairos" or a window of time God granted us to minister to His Bassa people.

Upon our return to Liberia, we were taken to our newly constructed mission station at Number 1. We were eager to see how the new buildings and grounds looked, and we were not disappointed. As we drove up the winding driveway, a beautiful picture unfolded. Where the driveway broke free from the jungle at the bottom of the hill, there was a small two room office. Beyond it the mission site had a sense of being well established with over one-hundred tall palm trees gracing the grounds and providing spots of shade.

Two white-washed mission houses stood on either side of the driveway with a warehouse and a small water tower between them. The house on the right was already occupied by our mission station companions, Rick and Kathy, and we would live in the house on the left. It was simply amazing to see the homes standing where once there had been dense jungle. The mission builder, Mike and his wife Sue, had done a great job building a beautiful mission compound and we felt like we were finally home!

Rick and Kathy had already been living in their house roughly six months when we returned. They had designed their home's floor plan, watched the building phase come to completion, and shouldered the initial settling of the mission station. When we arrived back in Liberia, they were in Nigeria taking a course on West African agriculture in preparation for Rick's job of teaching improved farming methods. In their absence we were invited to live in their home until we were ready to move into our own house.

Their home was situated at the highest point and offered an impressive survey of the rolling hills and jungle in the distance. While staying there, I began to covet the view wishing our house had that luxury as well. It was Perry who had laid out the plan for the mission grounds,

Our home for seven years near
Compound Number 1 in Grand Bassa County

so I complained to him. He pointed out it would have been selfish for us to choose the best for ourselves and a possible point of contention, so it was best to bless our coworkers. It was a lovely spot to build a home, but we did have a bit of a view from our spot as well, so I resolved to be content with that decision.

Near our house site we were excited to see a huge, stately tree had survived the building process and stood just outside our front porch door. It provided shade from the African sun, and there seemed to be a breeze which traveled up the driveway and passed through our windows.

The exterior of our new home looked beautiful! Both the outside and interior walls had been plastered with cement and were pleasantly straight and squared to the western eye. Windows were secure from insects and thieves, and the ceiling and roof were rain proof tight.

It seemed everything was built to specifications. The front porch or piazza would be inviting for our guests, and the roof overhang was generous to accommodate several rows of clothesline in the rainy season. We were excited to move into our new house, but it gave the false impression of being ready to occupy.

The structure had been sitting empty for some time allowing the high humidity of Liberia to work its wonder. Notorious black mold grew in patterns up the walls in many places, and the unfinished woodwork and doors had grown several layers of mold. Cupboards for the kitchen and bathroom had to be constructed, and we would have to make or find furniture.

When the main water valve was turned on, there were water leaks everywhere. It seemed the pipes leading from the little water tower had not been glued together. It was therefore necessary to install a completely new plumbing system. Likewise, we found we needed to rewire our home's solar system and 12-volt light wiring. As we made our home ready, we were grateful we could retire just up the hill when darkness fell.

Being pregnant, it was not wise for me to be around molds, paint, and varnish fumes, so we hired Bassa neighbors to help us. This gave us a chance to get to know them again, but they had no experience with the meticulous work and had to be completely trained and monitored.

The walls were raw cement and needed many coats of paint. Since it was low quality, within a year after moving in, the color began to drain down the walls, but there was no other option available in the hardware stores. Our neighbors were also hired to do the required woodwork sanding, and a coat of varnish revealed beautiful locally cut red mahogany wood. Little by little we made progress, but it felt painfully slow and we were glad we were doing the work before our baby arrived.

It was good to see familiar faces again and our Bassa neighbors welcomed us back, saying with a twinkle in their eye, "I knew you would be fat when you came again from your home." Being pregnant I had indeed gained some weight and Perry was heavier after a year of recovery in the States.

They thought it was beautiful to be fat, as it was an indicator of affluence and enough money to splurge on food. In particular, they liked heavy legs, big feet, and a diastema or gap between the front teeth, which they called "open teeth". All strange marks of beauty and unattractive in our culture, but they had the correct assumption that our homeland had an abundance of food to eat.

Perry became reacquainted with his former student, Pastor Alexander, who was also a local carpenter. His face held one of the widest grins. He once told me his joy came from being a believer of Christ, and

I'm sure it was evident to all he met. He was soon put to work building kitchen and bathroom cupboards for our new home, and later he and Perry made essential furniture.

After a prenatal checkup with my doctor near Monrovia, I enjoyed searching through the many fabric stores in the capital's Riverside market, which offered bargain prices. I happily fashioned curtains for every window of the house, and made cushion covers for our living room furniture as well. I had to borrow a hand cranked sewing machine from Margaret. We wanted to purchase our own sewing machine, but they were simply out of stock in the country.

The windows on our new home had several coverings. Screens were framed into the window space making it bug proof, and further secured with rod iron rogue bars buried in the cement walls to prevent thieves. Although there was no glass, wind and rain were kept out by mats attached to the outside of the building. They could be rolled down as needed.

The "as needed" part would prove to be a delicate decision for us to make as a couple, especially in the middle of the night when the monsoon winds began to howl, and my babies were essentially sleeping in the elements. After a little persuasion, my husband usually took my advice to heart and would go outside in the middle of the night to lower the mats and keep his family safe, dry, and yes - happy.

Perry and Pastor Alexander put together a bed frame using beautiful red mahogany, harvested from the Liberian forests, and sold in the local lumber yards. It was then time to fill our king-sized waterbed. We had to enlist the help of people from our village to bring water from a local stream, since the mission well was running a little low in dry season.

In the customary African manner, they carried buckets and tubs of water on their heads to our house. These containers were handed to a man on a ladder, who poured the water into a large funnel attached to a garden hose. The hose passed through the bedroom window and emptied into the bladder of our large bed. This was indeed a curious thing for our Bassa neighbors. They were sure we were joking when we explained that the water was filling our bed. I'm sure they figured something was "lost in translation".

I was thoroughly embarrassed to use so much water in the dry season just for our bed, and the long line of water handlers began to tire of being helpful. We halted the water gathering for the day asking much to their shock that they return the next day to carry more water.

Eventually when the bed was sufficiently full, our helpful neighbors were invited into our home and bedroom to see the bed and try it out. But I don't think anyone was brave enough to climb onto the unbelievable piece of furniture. A few traditional laughing fits were thrown as they touched the bouncy, wavy surface, and people openly remarked how crazy the white people were. Our neighbors were shocked when Perry hopped on the bed to demonstrate and laid down while waves of water moved the mattress from side to side.

Our lives would indeed be interesting as they observed our day to day living. I had worried over the impression we were giving our neighbors by hoarding water even though the rivers were not dry, and our mission well was not seriously low. Eventually, the first night of sleep on our new, cool bed erased all my embarrassment, and confirmed our hopes for a comfortable and refreshing night of sleep. In the end, all the laughter and humiliation were well worth it.

Our mission colleagues were not so easily convinced, and they did their share of teasing. There was speculation that without electricity to heat the water it would be too cold. We, on the other hand, lost no opportunity to advertise how refreshed we felt after a good night's sleep on our cool waterbed. No heater was necessary. We even let it be known when we would be gone, giving opportunity for our co-workers to stay overnight and try out the new bed. Ultimately, each family found a way to get a waterbed bladder shipped from the States and provide them for their older children as well.

18

Baby Laura's Arrival

During our first prenatal visit at ELWA hospital, the doctor frightened us by saying my pregnancy was considered "high risk", and we should have stayed in the states! We were shocked and second guessed our decision to deliver the baby in Liberia. Medical care in the States certainly would have been better. But God put our hearts at ease with the realization that He had led us back to Liberia, and He would be with each member of our family.

I was at high risk since my blood is Rh-negative. When a mother is Rh-negative there is a chance her immune system will attack and destroy the baby's blood cells, if it has Rh-positive blood. Perry's mother came to the rescue by contacting my former doctor, so she could send us the medication RhoGAM to prevent RH incompatibility for my baby.

The nesting instinct was strong, and I worried we would not have the house livable in time for our baby's arrival. Hours in the middle of the night were often heavy for me. I would awake, bright eyed with jet lag, then fright would grip me, and I would weep with home sickness and the fear of delivering my baby in a foreign land. One night I woke Perry from peaceful sleep to tell him my fears and ask him to pray with me.

Even when God's will and call are so evident, it is not always easy to follow Him. However, it is probably more difficult to find oneself not walking with Him. This has always been my chief fear.

When Rick and Kathy came home from their training in Nigeria, they

Lobster was $1 each – 7 months pregnant with Laura

helped us finish the painting and varnishing and we moved into our new home. After we moved in our new home, Perry designed a couch and other furniture. He used red mahogany, and we purchased foam to make cushions. I covered the cushions with loosely woven African country cloth colored with blue, black and white stripes. I thought the new cushions nicely matched our window draperies of lappa cloth.

Before we knew it, late December was upon us and we invited all fellow missionaries to Compound #1 for an overnight Christmas celebration. I was only one and a half weeks away from my due date and preferred to not travel rough roads to the other mission stations. A trip "up country" would only have taken me and our unborn baby further from the ELWA missionary hospital near Monrovia.

The group of missionaries joyfully celebrated Christ's birth by exchanging small gifts, singing, praying, and sharing meals. Viewing the arrival of all our colleagues, our Bassa neighbors later remarked that they couldn't tell the missionaries apart, since white people all look alike. The whole affair must have provided lively speculation around the village fires at night.

By this time most of the members of our team were living at their respective mission sites. Perry and I resided at the Number 1 location with Rick and Kathy, who would eventually have a son. Rick was the mission agriculturalist and Kathy worked with community development.

At the Number 2 mission station, Margaret continued to live in her house and led the health education program teaching Village Health Care Workers and Traditional Birth Attendants. Joseph and Mary had joined the missionary team, replacing Larry and Ann, at the Number 2 mission compound. They would have two children, both born in Liberia. Joe was involved in teaching TEE, while Mary was a registered nurse who occasionally helped Margaret.

Don and Marty and their two sons still lived at the mission station at Number 3. During our first year in Liberia, we had lived several months in their guest house. Don had moved his focus to translating the Bible into Bassa, and they would later move to the city of Buchanan. (The translation of the entire Bible was completed and presented to the Bassa people on Pentecost Sunday, 2005.)

Tim and Dianne, whose company we had enjoyed while living in Grand Rapids, would join our CR team in the future and live at Number 3. They had a son, and two daughters would later be born in country.

Mark and Pat lived in Buchanan in a new mission house, with a newly constructed guest house nearby. They would eventually have three children. Mark was a TEE instructor for church leaders and a liaison for missionaries to CEFL leaders. Another CR couple, Mark and Theresa, were also located in Buchanan. They joined our team for several years, teaching at Liberia Christian High School and welcomed a daughter while living there.

Ron and Shirley from the Christian Church mission lived in Buchanan with their three daughters. They were also seconded to the CEFL, so we frequently fellowshipped with them. Ron was the principal of Liberia Christian High School in Buchanan. Two other couples from the Christian Church mission were in Liberia for periods of time, Ken and Carolyn with four children, and Wayne and Greta to teach at the Christian High School.

Many of these families stayed overnight at our homes at Number 1 on Christmas night. Our bedrooms were packed to the limit and some had to find sleeping space on the floors, but we had great fun staying together. The plan was to go to the beach in the Number 1 area the following day, which was about an hour away.

Perry and I woke early the day after Christmas to prepare a huge breakfast for our house guests. I was surprised with pre-labor signs and knew we would need to head for the hospital soon. We quickly flipped a mountain of pancakes on the stove top griddle. Then, while people were lingering around the breakfast table, we threw our clothes and baby supplies into a suitcase.

With no explanation made, we enlisted help in moving furniture away from the windows. This was routinely done when leaving home for an extended period to avoid getting soaked cushions from blowing rain. While we were putting our luggage in the car, we explained that we were heading to Monrovia to be closer to the hospital instead of going to the beach. They encouraged us to accompany them for a fun day together, noting the due date was nearly eleven days away. I was positive we needed to get ourselves near the hospital, so we turned them down and waved goodbye as they drove away.

After we hastily took a last picture of just the "two" of us with the timed exposure, we were on our way in the opposite direction to Monrovia. I was anxious to get to the guest house we had reserved at ELWA, but Perry asked if we could make a detour down a gravel road. It was his responsibility to check out a beach hotel at the end of the road to see if it was suitable for a future missionary conference. I reluctantly consented, knowing it was better to go at that time, instead of after the baby was born.

We then set off down the road, and it was the most uncomfortable ride I have ever had. We came to a shockingly modern hotel in the middle of nowhere. It was picturesquely set on the edge of a lagoon near the ocean. The drive was fruitful for two reasons. The hotel was later used for a joint conference with missionaries from Sierra Leone, and I am positive it hurried the beginning of labor along.

Arriving at the ELWA mission compound later that day, we were shocked to learn that the mission host had given our reserved apartment to other missionaries. We had been told that maternity bookings could not be canceled. However, ours was - and without apology. We were left with nothing else to do but find some other lodging.

With Christmas and the birth of Christ fresh on our minds, we suddenly knew how Joseph and Mary must have felt to find there was no room at the inn. There were no cell phones, so we had to drive around Monrovia inquiring about a place to stay. It seemed many missionaries were in the capital city for the holidays renting the usual places. We finally spoke to a seasoned missionary couple, who accommodated us in their efficiency guest apartment.

At midnight I startled awake with labor pains and an hour later we left for the hospital, only to be stopped by gruff soldiers at a military barricade. They had guns and questioned us for our reason of traveling after midnight. Perry responded in fine Liberian English, "My wife is coming to have a baby."

At this the soldiers pushed open the barrels blocking the road and yelled, "Go man, go!" At the hospital, Dr. Steven Befus, only a few years older than myself, assured us the baby would be born before 4:00 AM. However, at 4:00 AM it was clear it was not the allotted time of birth.

Perry stayed by my side throughout the labor. We were left alone in a clean but worn hospital room with two beds. Since no one assisted us, we were thankful to have taken labor and delivery classes in the States. I endured mostly back labor without any medication throughout the long night. The progress was slow. At times I made no headway according to medical measurements, but eventually at 8:30 AM the glad news was announced that we should head to the delivery room. Remaining on my hospital bed, I was wheeled outside into the morning air and down the sidewalk - feeling each crack in the concrete.

The door to the surgery room, also used for deliveries, opened simply into the outside corridor of the hospital. While we were in there, people would occasionally stand with the door open and visit with the medical staff. They explained they were stopping by to see if it was true that a white woman was delivering a baby. This was far from the private environment I had assumed, but there was little that could be done. Esther George, a Liberian midwife, assisted Dr. Befus, and my baby was delivered at 10:35 AM.

Our healthy baby girl arrived weighing 7lbs 1oz and we named her Laura Joy. My first glimpse of her was to see the midwife carry her across the room to be cleaned up. Due to a complex delivery, my precious baby had scratches on her face, but still she was absolutely beautiful. As I held her in my arms, I thought I had no idea God created such beautiful babies - and she was mine!

When we were ready to leave the delivery room, Laura and I were simply rolled out the door to the outside world, back down the sidewalk, and into my room across the way.

That evening after sending a cable home to the new grandparents in South Dakota, Perry was able to secure a telephone connection to them with the help of an ELWA ham radio operator. In order to get me to the phone, Perry rolled my bed back outside to the nearby nurses' station where the phone was passed through the doorway. "Hi Mom," I said from my bed sitting outside, "I had a baby girl." It was exhilarating to be able to talk to family members so soon after Laura's arrival.

I settled in for some much-needed sleep and Perry went back to the mission guest room for the night. We understood I would have a private room, so I anticipated a quiet night with my baby cared for in the maternity nursery, but that was not to be the case.

A short time later an African mother in critical condition was brought to the second bed in my room. She had lost a lot of blood due to placenta previa, but her baby had survived the serious condition thanks to an emergency Caesarian delivery. The Nurses were constantly by her bedside watching their patient, while I drifted in and out of sleep. Suddenly, a nurse rushed in, saying they were too busy to watch my baby in the nursery.

Even though our hospital room was very busy that night, it was my time to bond with my precious baby. I counted her fingers and toes, because I had heard that is what good mothers do. Yes, they were all there. Her big dark eyes were alert and, as I held her close she was content to

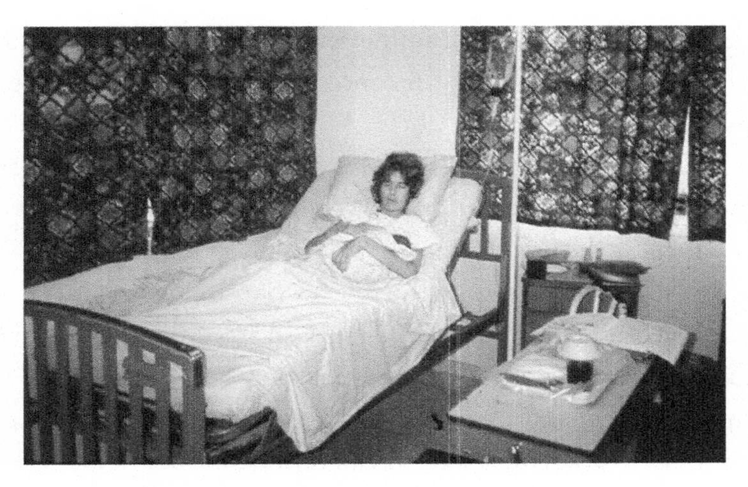

My hospital room at ELWA hospital where Laura was born

listen to my voice and the sounds of my heart. I cherished holding her quietly in my arms, so happy to be a mother! I couldn't believe how beautiful she was, and I prayed that she would know the love of God throughout her life. I told her we had a Savior named Jesus and softly sang "Jesus Loves Me" to baby Laura, hoping to calm us both, while the medical staff rushed in and out of our room ministering to my roommate.

As the night unfolded, nurses and doctors worked franticly to save the woman's life. When the nurses suddenly left the room and began to wail in the corridor, I realized the other mother's life had ended. Tears were shed as I considered her dreams had been shattered and how fragile life can be.

I wondered if she had been a Christian, and who was going to care for the baby. Nurses said she had never been conscious and family was there caring for the baby. The mother was a country woman from the bush and her family had waited too long to bring her to the hospital. Her body remained in the room for some time with the sheet pulled tightly over her head.

The next morning when Perry returned to the hospital, the woman and her bed had been removed. Naturally he was shocked to learn what had taken place, and I asked Perry to please not leave me alone in the hospital again.

A young lab technician, Barb, who was Dr. Befus' niece and a short-term missionary, came to visit bringing a delicious cake she had baked for us. She felt a celebration was in order and I have always been very grateful for her visit.

Two wives from CRWRC living in Monrovia, Trudy and Jan, also visited us in the hospital. Their guidance was extremely helpful to me as a new mother. I'm not sure what I would have done without Trudy's reassurance and practical help in the fine art of nursing.

At the end of the day, we were dismissed from the hospital paying a $394.50 hospital and delivery fee, and we took baby Laura to the small mission guest room. There amid the noises of the African city, a deep sense of loneliness and heartache set in upon me. In the face of caring for a new baby without the guidance of my mothers, family, or friends I felt anxious. I tried to see beyond our situation and relish the first days of caring for our infant, but I longed for visitors and helpful advice, and could not control my emotions.

Perry went to get a few supplies and bartered for a wicker rocking chair, which I loved and used throughout our years in Liberia. Laura slept in a beautiful wicker infant bed we had purchased earlier from a roadside vender. I had fitted it with a little mosquito net to go over the basket. The apartment was literally infested with tiny sugar ants. Every hour we moved the baby's basket so they would not bother our newborn. I was quite paranoid about this, knowing it would not be good for her to be covered with ants.

A return visit to the doctor confirmed our suspicions that Laura had contracted impetigo, most likely in the hospital nursery. It was easily taken care of with an antibiotic ointment.

We were very happy when a missionary couple stopped to see us, since we were anxious to show off our baby. But we were in for a shock because all they did was complain about each other and argue. They didn't even look at our beautiful baby. Feeling worn out, I commented I needed to lie down, and they left.

Many missionaries had stayed for a month in the capital city after delivery, so we were looking forward to maternity leave and sometime in the city. However, the hot noisy apartment was neither relaxing, nor uplifting. We decided to return to our home in the bush ten days later.

Upon our arrival back at the mission station, the neighbor ladies came to see my baby and greeted me with the comment, "I thank God you and the baby didn't die!" We don't think of the risk of birth too much with our modern facilities, but those who live in third world nations certainly do, as the experience with my roommate had proven. This was one thing our mission was trying to change by training traditional birth attendants.

Another reaction we received was shock from our village neighbors. It was difficult to decipher their fits of laughter and why they were so surprised. We thought it was possibly because they had not seen a white baby before, which was certainly the case, but there was another reason which surprised us.

Our uneducated friends reasoned I would have a black baby, since she was born on African soil. We did not discover their reasoning until much later. When Perry heard their thoughts, his private remark was, "It better not be a black baby!" It was a good laugh for us, but we were careful to not insult anyone. After all, these people were adults without the opportunity of higher education and respect was due them.

We frequently had guests from the village who came to see baby Laura. As a first-time mother with an infant, I was naturally concerned about germs and cleanliness. I took care to practice their custom of wrapping newborns tightly in a blanket hoping it would shield her.

Often people would stop by our home after working on their farms all day. I had noted in the villages there was a less than desirable standard of caring for babies. I did not want to offend anyone, but it was important for me to not let people put their fingers in her mouth.

One of my favorite callers was Peéa, a friend and neighbor from the local village. There are some people in the world who possess an air of humble nobility, and she was one of them. Her gracious spirit and quiet, dignified manner drew me to her.

She came shortly after our return home and I was not yet feeling well. She spent a good long time at my side holding my precious Laura. I was able to sleep contently while she sang gentle Bassa songs and rocked my baby in her arms.

Everyone naturally wanted to know our baby's name, and we found

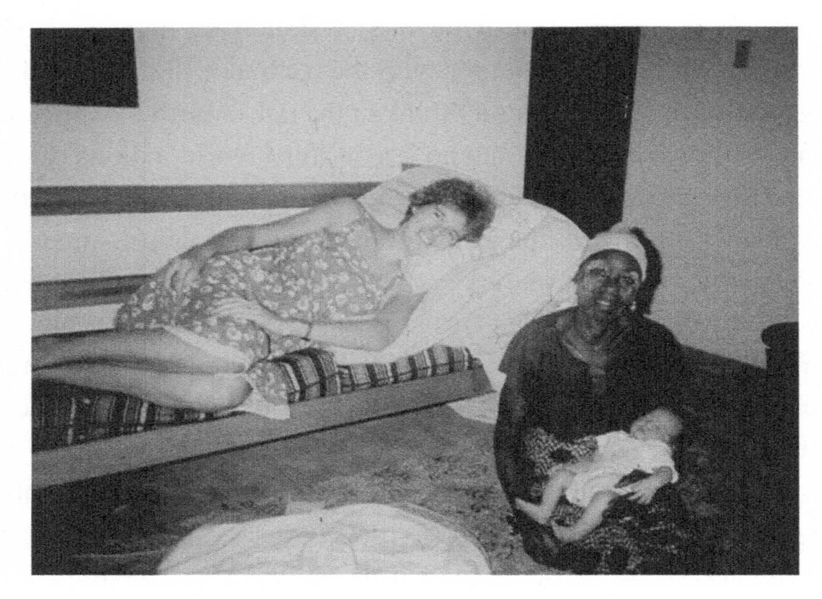

Peéa, a neighbor lady, who came to visit new baby Laura.
Notice white chalking on her face, either perfume or medicine

that Laura was difficult for the Bassa tongue to say. They all thought we would certainly name her "Sunday-ma" since she was born on Sunday, a great joy. In their tradition there were certain days of the week that they enjoyed using for the baby's names. They reasoned with us that it was very special that she was born on Sunday, since that was church day, and her "Pa" was a preacher.

We consulted with church leaders and they interviewed us as to the situation of her birth and our lives. After sorting through everyone's suggestions, we chose the Bassa name "Gre-poh Jon-ja", pronounced something like "Gray-paw John-Jay", which means God's gift, and everyone just called her "John-jay" for short.

We had wanted to have a baby for some time, it seemed only right to think of her as a true gift from God and we acknowledged that in her name. Any Bassa person who heard her name immediately knew she was a special gift from God. Laura has always had a certain loveliness and has truly been a gift from God. She enjoyed using her Bassa name and even incorporated it into one of her email addresses.

While Laura was a new infant, it seemed to me that the Bassa women's comments were particularly sharp, as they took it upon themselves to correct age old practices I had brought from my culture and family. For instance, I felt quite confident when holding and burping my baby. The neighbor ladies did not approve, suggesting I was beating her or that I would choke her, and she would die.

They also informed me she would starve to death, pointing out the fact that there would apparently not be enough milk due to my lack of natural endowment - compared to theirs. Furthermore, they told me it was wasteful to dress her in newborn sized clothes, everyone knew it made sense to dress babies in larger clothing. Not only would I have saved money, since the larger clothes could be worn longer, but it would give the indication that I believed the baby would survive and grow into the larger sizes.

As far as my neighbor ladies were concerned there was a good chance my baby might not live, and they were instinctively helping prepare me for that fact. Unfortunately, these things were true for the people who lived around me. They suffered with very high infant mortality rates and had learned coping measures to not become too attached to their young babies, including not even naming them for a while.

My reaction to their comments was to smile politely and appear to thoughtfully take their advice. However, later in the privacy of my bedroom, I would shed many tears of senseless worry and frustration. God would turn the situation around, but it would be in His timing.

Being a new mother changed a lot of things for me. Gone were the long enjoyable days Perry and I spent in the villages meeting people and learning things together. With the period of maternity leave over, Perry and the other missionaries living at our compound were frequently gone all day doing mission work.

I was often left alone in our jungle home with no means of transportation or communication. This was a time of transition for me from career to motherhood, and the adjustment had to be done on my own without the help of extended family members and friends.

19

Mission Work and Life

Perry resumed language study in earnest, and he could think of no one better to act as his Bassa language tutor and companion than Pastor Alexander. He was not only the pastor at the local St. John's Methodist Episcopal Reformed Church, but he had also been our able carpenter and Perry's TEE student. It was as though they reversed rolls, with the student becoming the language teacher, and the teacher reverting to a student.

They met together four times a week for language study, spending two days at the mission station and two days at Alexander's town. His village was six miles away by jungle path, so Perry traveled there by motorcycle. As fellow pastors, they also shared a great camaraderie and often spoke together of ministry matters.

It was understood we would share the mission owned station wagon with our colleagues living in the other house. This arrangement further complicated busy schedules and close relationships. Work trips and going to town for supplies had to be scheduled in advance and coordinated, leading to a lack of freedom and spontaneity. To alleviate vehicle scheduling, the mission purchased a motorcycle to be used locally for mission business. Later we also purchased a personal motorcycle, which we enjoyed riding.

I attempted to continue studying the Bassa language after my baby arrived, but it was difficult to find the time and my progress was painfully slow. My personal struggle with language learning allowed me to only

Perry teaching TEE class. Notice the woven mat ceiling.

converse in selected topics on an elementary level. I would readily switch over to the much easier national language of "Liberian English", which most people knew.

After Perry passed the next language proficiency test, he resumed teaching his TEE class. It was exciting, since that was the reason for our ministry in Liberia.

I attended some TEE classes and was amazed at his ability to phonetically read the assignments on the black board to his class. He found he could teach the students to read in their own language, since Bassa was written just as it sounds. Still it was necessary for Alexander to translate during the lecture segment of the class.

Health concerns were a part of life. With the high rate of malaria in our area, we were glad for our mosquito nets and it was important to consistently take our weekly anti-malarial treatments. This we did religiously each Sunday before church and included our little baby in the routine from the time she was born.

The prescribed chloroquine was bitter, so Laura quickly learned what was coming and did her best to spit it out. It was a challenge and important to make sure she got an adequate dosage. While taking anti-malarials, it was still possible to get malaria, so we prayed we wouldn't get it like we had before.

At first, I did not relate our weekly anti-malarial treatment with a strange problem I had in church. As the worship service progressed, I would begin to feel dizzy and lightheaded. My heart would occasionally race, and later at home there would be a raging headache sending me to bed.

Then I began to have trouble with hallucinations in church. The first time I saw cartoon like characters parading across the church wall, I turned around to see who was running a projector without electricity. I was surprised to find nothing was there. It was strange too, because they didn't have any religious significance and no one else was distracted by the animations on the wall. I thought surely the Bassa people would have been curious about it as well. Then it was as though they ran out of figures and the side show stopped. I was used to unusual things happening, but that was indeed strange.

On the way home I asked Perry why the cartoon figures were shown during church, he asked if I was going crazy or something. I explained they bounced across the wall behind him, so he couldn't see what was going on, and let it go at that. However, I privately wondered if I was cracking up or perhaps having a strange aversion to worship.

Several weeks later at a different church, it was quite troubling when the animations bounced back again rudely interrupting any sense of worship. I promptly jumped up and took my baby outside for a while.

Alarmed and afraid I was losing touch with reality; I sought the confidence and advice of Margaret. She suggested it might be from the weekly anti-malarial medication taken just before we left for church. One of the first side effects listed was vision problems, including seeing objects.[21] Perry and I were taking the same dosage, but I weighed less and perhaps needed a reduced amount. I pinched a little off my tablet each week and was relieved when the Sunday ordeal with bouncy figures disappeared forever.

When Laura was a baby, four Christian Reformed missionaries were teaching TEE classes, and had over 200 church leaders enrolled in ten different teaching centers. They were all studying the book of Acts and the course was three months long. Perry's class in our area had 28 students and met at 10:00 on Saturday mornings, the same day as market day. Three years later our mission had twelve teaching centers ministering to church leaders from 57 different denominations.

The missionaries would prepare the curriculum, then a team of Bassa men translated the lessons into Bassa and mass recorded them on cassette tapes. At class time each student would receive two cassette tapes, and since they were reading enough, the lessons were also handed out in written form.

The class periods consisted mainly of Biblical teaching, but integrated into the program was an atmosphere of collegiality among the pastors from different churches. By God's grace, many of these study groups still meet for mutual support and enhancement!

Our CEM plan called for Margaret and her health care staff to train certain members of the churches to recognize and treat diseases and infirmities in their communities. Usually those accepted for training the prayer warriors in the church. They were the natural choice because they were accustomed to visiting the sick, practiced the gift of mercy, and had a real desire to help.

Margaret trained them to recognize common diseases and administer appropriate medications. After their course work and passing an exam, they graduated and became Village Health Workers. They visited the sick or people came to see them for diagnosis and medications.

I was asked to sell pharmaceutical supplies from our home for the Village Health Workers in our immediate area. They would come to the house to replenish their medicine bags and I always took them into the privacy of our dining room for the transaction. They could purchase aspirin (4 pills for 5 cents), chloroquine for treatment of Malaria (2 pills for 5 cents), antacid, iron tablets, anti-seizure pills, penicillin, vitamins, eye ointment, bandages, cough syrup, piperazine for worm treatment and benzyl benzoate for lice and scabies infestations.

All medications were available at greatly discounted prices through CHAL, the Christian Health Association of Liberia, which purchased in bulk on the worldwide market. Our Village Health Workers were part of a national program which sold medication to patients for a small profit, retaining enough funds to restock their medical bag.

Being a midwife herself, Margaret also trained Traditional Birth Attendants. One of the main objectives was to provide a clean environment and sanitary razor to avoid tetanus. This proved to be difficult since the families' heirloom knife was used to cut the babies' umbilical cord. Margaret suspected the high rate of tetanus in newborns had to do with reusing the same knife. A compromise was found to have the knives present during the births, but use a new razor blade each time.

It was also customary to give birth on the dirt floor of the home, however that exposed the baby again to tetanus. The problem was solved by putting a clean cloth on the ground for a safe birth, and afterwards spilling the birthing fluids on the floor. These were difficult changes to make but resulted in lowering the infant mortality rate.

Perry and Alexander made plans for their second trek north of our mission compound. Their main goal was to search out church leaders who might be interested in taking classes. Being an experienced evangelist with a gregarious personality, Alexander was the perfect companion for this trip. They planned to be gone at least five days, but due to the uncertainty of foot travel and weather, it could be longer.

We needed to learn more about our area, it was the season for trekking, and I understood the importance for the trek. But, having a colicky baby, I could not deny that I was concerned about being home alone so long.

Laura was several months old and had the habit of crying uncontrollably starting around 7:15 in the evening, and lasting until she became exhausted enough to finally fall asleep around 10:00 or 11:00 PM. The night watchman was frustrated that we let our baby cry so long, but we tried everything every night and nothing pacified her. It was of course

Alexander and Perry leaving for trek, our front yard

exhausting for everyone concerned, and emotional for me. I worried something was wrong with her. The doctor at ELWA assured us she was fine - just colicky in the evening.

In considering Perry's trekking plans we reasoned I would not be alone. Rick and Kathy said they would be nearby and kindly offered to come and help me if they heard Laura cry for long. As I watched Perry walk off the yard with his lightweight backpack and disappear down the jungle path, I felt a deep sense of loneliness and could not restrain some tears of frustration.

At first it seemed the Lord simply took pity on me, because before nightfall I noticed Perry walking up the driveway. Even though his shoulders were slumped as if to carry a heavy load, I cannot deny that my weepy heart rejoiced. I hoped he had not returned home because he thought I couldn't handle things alone for a few days. Unfortunately, my joy was short lived as Perry explained what had happened.

At Dezon, a village north of us, they encountered a tragic disaster. Twenty-six village children had just died in an outbreak of the measles. Many of the children in the village apparently had not been vaccinated, however other parents were surprised to lose children claiming they had taken them to be immunized for measles. In those cases, we suspected that the vaccine had not been properly cooled. The entire village was understandably in deep sorrow. Among the tragedies was one mother who had lost five children.

It is always frightening for me to hear of parents who deliberately avoid vaccinating their children. It has been a couple generations since people died from measles and other serious infectious diseases, so the population has lost sight of the importance of immunizations. When vaccines became available, people were ecstatic. It meant their children were no longer susceptible to those viruses and even death.

Our world is only one short step away from epidemics spreading and bringing disaster. We are not immune from what happened to the families in Dezon, in fact we are setting ourselves up for it by ignoring warnings from the medical field and denying our children and fellow community members safety from devasting diseases.

When Alexander and Perry walked into the village and everyone was weeping, they could travel no further. They saw the need to minister to the people of Dezon, and indeed grieve themselves. It appeared God had brought them to that village and those people in their time of need and mourning.

The next day Alexander and Perry returned to the village. Alexander asked Perry what he should do as a pastor to minister to them. Perry told him to gather the people together and give them a chance to express their grief and tell their stories. This was done for three nights, then finally they were brought to the point of talking about God. Perry and Alexander explained how God cared about us and loved us so much that he sent his son Jesus to suffer for us all. They continued to visit the village often talking with the people and teaching them about a loving God.

As a result, five people decided to put their trust in God and desired to build a church. Later others came to a saving faith. Up to that point the village elders had not allowed any talk of Christianity in their town, saying they were in Devil Country. Now, in the face of a disaster they came face to face with the God who is not to be denied, and they came to the point of believing in Him.

We attended the first joyful worship service held in the new church with 127 people attending. It was amazing to think that only recently they had been mourning for their children and were now praising God in song and worship. Perry wrote more about the experience on August 11 to Rev. Bill Van Tol, the CRWM African director:

I spoke on Romans chapter 6 focusing on baptism as a public mark of God's action uniting us in Christ. I tried to speak to the new believers, now up to 8 people, in such a way as to challenge others in the audience as well. Then as Alexander was saying thank you to me for speaking, one man stood up, stopped him, and asked if he could be baptized too. Alexander asked him some questions and talked with him for some time. In short, the man said that he believed in Jesus Christ as his Savior and with help he would like Him to be his Master! So, they agreed to baptize him. After that two other people stood up and confessed their sin and dependence upon God for his forgiveness and they too asked to be baptized…

…I returned to the church the next morning at 6:30. I could hardly contain my tears as I saw eleven people, three men, four women and four young adults receive the mark of the trinity. I could hardly believe that the death of some children, the prodding of an ignorant expatriate, the zeal of a national evangelist and the pain of a community could all add up to the rejoicing in heaven of eleven lost sheep brought back home. I guess it really does not add up at all, does it? The thing that adds up is that God was there, is there, and promised to continue to be there.

The people of the new church decided they would like to name their church after our mission and become part of our denomination, since Perry had ministered to them. Much to their surprise Perry said he could not allow them to assume our denominational name, since our mission was not starting new churches.

If the church had used the Christian Reformed name, it could have caused jealousy among the other church leaders in the area. Everyone would assume we were monetarily supporting the new church. Feelings of resentment could destroy church relations in the area and leaders might avoid the theological classes intended for all churches regardless of denominational affiliation.

Our return to Liberia was accompanied with renewed exposure to tropical diseases and germs. Perry was the first to contract the dreaded "rīsen" (pronounced in Liberian English with a long "i"), medically known as furuncles, or as my childhood family called them – boils. They were huge, deep, pimple-type infections which festered under the skin with increasing pain each day.

There was always a strong urge to try to pop the infection out, but that was the worst thing you could do. Applying pressure to the boil too early would force the infectious mass deeper still into the tissue and cause an even greater infection in the surrounding area.

The rīsen eventually became so sore that it needed to be soaked in hot water several times a day, pain relievers were needed, and bed rest was not uncommon. After 7-14 days it would finally come to a point where it could be safely lanced, and an unbelievable green core would turn and spiral itself out with just a little pressure.

The relief from pain was immediate, but often a deep pitted scar was left behind as a type of battle wound. Our little baby Laura suffered through a rīsen just below her nose and we had to take her to the hospital to have it lanced. Just the thought of having a boil can bring shivers to the experienced victim.

I would occasionally see a group of ladies coming up the driveway – all dressed up and sauntering along arm in arm. They were visitors and coming to my door would call out "Bauk, Bauk". While I was honored to have guests come, I will be honest - at that time it was a challenge for me to be hospitable, because they often stayed for hours on end. It seemed they would come to see the local curiosity – my little white baby. They would ask to hold her and sometimes would laugh at her features, which were unusual to them.

I genuinely enjoyed visitors and would kindly visit with them for a while, but as time went on, I felt the need to get a couple things done and retreat inside my house. My guests would continue to just sit there for hours on end and apparently enjoy themselves while watching me and enjoying a cup of tea. I was frustrated and at a loss as to how to handle those who had overstayed their welcome.

I decided to do a little culture study on this issue, so one day I packed a few baby supplies and went to the village. As usual, people were thrilled to have me visit them, and then I proceeded to stay as long as I could, like for hours. I wanted to observe what they did when a visitor overstayed her welcome. At first, they visited with me and doted on the baby, but later they got up and started cooking a meal or washing clothes, and I was left to sit by myself observing village life. After a while, I took my leave, satisfied knowing I had handled the situation appropriately at my home.

Bassa guests to our home did another perplexing thing which placed me in a troubling quandary. They would passively ask for articles of clothing I was wearing or for something hanging on the clothesline by saying they liked it. Peering in the windows of my house, they would ask to have pieces of furniture or anything they saw. I knew it was their tradition that when someone openly admired something or asked for it, the other person would give it to them. Incidentally, this is also true in many other parts of the world, and I personally experienced it in Russia.

One day I looked around my home and realized that every item had been requested, including our bed, refrigerator, and bottle gas stove. What was I supposed to do? I couldn't be giving away everything. After all, generosity like that could become big news and we'd have a never-ending line at the "give me" window.

Yet Luke 6:30-31 resounded in my head, *Give to everyone who asks you, and if anyone takes what belongs to you, do not demand it back. Do to others as you would have them do to you.*

And, what of 1 John 3:17-18? *If anyone has material possessions and sees his brother in need but has no pity on him, how can the love of God be in him? Dear children, let us not love with words or tongue but with actions and in truth.* Was I really required by scripture to give everything away to those who simply asked for it?

I inquired further of Bassa friends and neighbors. How did they handle specific requests within their culture? Were there those in the community who took advantage of this custom? Perry and I agreed early on that requests for food should certainly be granted, but was it necessary to give to each person who admired my things?

I asked those questions of my Bassa friends, and their response was: "Of course, if someone asks you for something, you should give it to them." But I wondered how I could possibly do that. It was such a foreign concept to me.

Discussing this one day with a Bassa friend, I asked what she would do if I asked for the blouse she had on. "Oh, you want this blouse?" she beamed and started to unbutton it. I explained it was only an example, but she was confused and saddened that I didn't really want it. I felt humiliated when she added, "Of course I would give you whatever you think you need. And that is how I feel about anyone in my town." I realized I needed to understand that a request meant - they really needed it.

I wondered then if it was embarrassing for her to ask for things. "O yes, it gives me shame, but I think you will want to help me - you have so much." And indeed, we did have so much - ridiculously so. *To whom much is given, much is required,* Luke 12:48.

In the end, I compromised. Certainly, I was not required to give away everything, otherwise we wouldn't be able to live there. But when a request for an item was made, I gladly considered it and would sometimes give what they wanted. It became truly a blessing and great joy to give others what they needed. If a request seemed unreasonable, I would give them a smaller item, so they didn't go home insulted. People seemed pleased with that and it soothed my material laden conscience as well.

One Sunday we did not go far from home to worship but paid a surprise visit to the local church. As I looked around, I was surprised to note that a lot of people and their children were wearing hand-me-downs from my home. Apparently, everyone felt that what I had given them was worthy of their best attire and came to church in clothes from us. I felt honored to bless my neighbors. Indeed, *it is more blessed to give than to receive,* Acts 20:35. And, *blessed are you who are poor, for yours is the kingdom of God,* Luke 6:20.

Sundays became the worst day of the week for us. They were difficult and lonely as we experienced the great distance from our families and worship in the States. Bassa worship services started early in the morning around 7:00 and lasted a couple hours. After that we would arrive home around 10:00 with nothing to do the rest of the day.

Our house felt empty and lonely as the day of rest expanded before us, and we thought of how we might take baby Laura to visit family if we were home. We attempted to have picnics on the way home from church, but stopping on the roadside didn't work in that culture. People walking by would seek an explanation as to what we were doing and hang around to watch.

A solution was found when it was decided to have a palaver hut constructed near the office building on our compound. It was an open-air affair with only a thatched roof, a half wall, and a picnic table underneath. This became our Sunday picnic spot. We often went there for Sunday lunch and hung around playing games or writing letters on the day set aside for the Lord.

The main reason for building the hut was to offer a place to learn to read. The word was put out that everyone was welcome to go to the reading hut and borrow literature from the missionaries. If they had a question, they could easily ask a missionary in their nearby offices for help. It took some time for the concept to catch on, but eventually it was used. I would sometimes look out my kitchen window and see people sitting there with their heads bent over a book, undoubtedly reading slowly out loud as new readers tend to do.

When Perry received an invitation from one of his TEE students to speak at his denomination's church conference, he accepted the invitation and viewed it as a privilege and responsibility. He was asked to give a message on: "How to Preach at the Dedication of a New Church". He was a little frustrated with the topic handed to him, but spent time preparing his message. After the presentation, he came home in a bit of a shock saying it went surprisingly well. Thirteen people had stood saying they wanted to give their lives to Christ.

Another surprising response happened while Perry was teaching a TEE class. His students suddenly jumped to their feet, cheering, and applauding. Earlier another missionary had reported the same reaction when he taught the same lesson.

The lesson bringing such a reaction covered the covenant God made with Abraham. The church leaders in the class were ecstatic to learn the promises of the covenant God. They explained, "We don't have to wait for our children to find God themselves. He calls them to the family of believers and promises to be their God!" It was a huge relief to hear God works in family units and not just with individuals.

One of the biggest regrets of my life happened on a Sunday morning when I decided to not go to church. Rev. Louis Taminga, a mission board member, was at our house for a routine visit. He accompanied Perry for an early morning worship service, but I stayed home.

Since we had an overnight guest in the house, we had not let our baby cry for long during the night. It seemed I had been up most of the night with her and she was finally sleeping soundly, so I wearily stayed in bed on a cold rainy morning.

How I wish I would have made the extra effort and awaken Laura for church, because what Perry experienced there was nothing short of a miracle, and I was not there to witness it.

Perry thought it would be interesting to take Rev. Taminga to the new church north of us. The night before we had told him the story of its formation after the measles epidemic. Driving to church, they came to a place where the rain had washed out the primitive road, and they were forced to turn around in search of another place to worship.

As they drove, Perry heard people singing a church song, so they decided to stop and worship there. They found it was an un-organized assembly that was just beginning to meet on the piazza or porch of a larger home.

The group was excited by the unusual presence of two white men and many people recognized Perry as the local teacher. As was the custom, Rev. Taminga was asked to preach, since he was the older of the two. When it became apparent that there was no one in attendance who could understand his American English and interpret his message into Bassa, they turned to Perry and told him to translate.

Perry explained he had not yet mastered enough Bassa, but they were unrelenting. Reluctantly he agreed to attempt the interpretation, thinking they would quickly understand that he was not ready for the task.

God had other plans for this group of new believers. As Rev. Taminga preached, Perry was given the ability to construct complicated sentences beyond his ability, and his vocabulary was unrealistically enhanced as well. He later recalled to me that as he opened his mouth the words would just come out. It was simply amazing and a little frightening.

Rev. Taminga and the people there simply thought Perry had been humble in the assessment of his translation ability. They were therefore not surprised that he could easily and eloquently ramble on.

Upon their return home, Perry was still numb from the experience. He and I wondered excitedly if he would then possess the ability to communicate fluently in Bassa. Unfortunately, this was not to be the case; after the worship service he was simply back to the same point in his language acquisition. While this was a real disappointment, we rejoiced in the apparent outpouring of the Holy Spirit that Sunday morning.

We discussed at length the gift of tongues and what may have happened. Our belief had always sided with the classic Reformed tradition, stating the gift of tongues stopped with the apostolic age. Though not to be restrained, it was given to the early, emerging church in order that they might hear and clearly understand the gospel of salvation in their own tongue.

Apparently in this instance, God again granted speech in a native tongue so the good news of salvation in Jesus could be understood by people beginning to seek the Lord together. What an amazing thing to experience, and it would not be the end of God showing us His miraculous powers.

20
Help Needed

Within a matter of months, I began to physically wear down with day to day care of an infant and upkeep of my jungle home. Without electricity or running water, coupled with becoming a mother and frequent long-term visitors, my time and energy were quickly depleted each day.

For example, when diaper rash became a problem, it was necessary for the diapers to be boiled in a metal bucket on the coal fire. At that time, we couldn't use gas for the generator due to a nationwide gas shortage, so I couldn't use my little washing machine. Hand washing all the clothes and diapers became an additional necessity. My hands became severely chapped and actually dripped blood while writing letters home.

Although I eventually hired some ladies to come to our house and wash the clothes by hand, I despaired of all the work. Coupled with lack of energy, a lengthy recovery from difficult childbirth, and postpartum blues, life had become overwhelming.

After several months Perry set before me an ultimatum. It was time to get help in the home by hiring a Bassa neighbor, or we would consider returning home to the States - and I agreed. It was clear that if we were going to stay in Liberia for an extended time, we should get house help.

For some reason I had not wanted to fit the mold of a pampered missionary and thought I would take care of our home myself. Having hired help not only seemed imperialistic to me, but it would only add to the difference between our lifestyle and that of our neighbors.

Perry's lobby to find house help consisted of the argument that having someone in the home to help would be my replacement for electricity, hot running water, a modern stove with ready and consistent heat, an automatic washing machine, or any other household convenience. His argument made sense, and I did not want my pride to be the reason we would have to resign and go back to the States.

We sought information from others concerning house help. Some advised hiring a woman since they were generally good cooks and companions, but we heard sometimes they tended to compete with the lady of the house. Others thought a man or steward was best to double as a protector when Perry was gone, and it would give someone the opportunity to provide for his family.

In the end, Perry decided we would find a steward. If we could, we wanted to get someone we already knew and could trust. There was a young man named Browne whom we had met the year before while living in the rental house. At that time, he had a job cutting grass at the mission station. Occasionally Rick and Kathy had him do a little housework for them, so they recommended we give Browne a try.

We decided to ask him to work in our home a little at a time, just to see if he might be a good fit. In the end we were quite pleased with his amiable attitude and desire to please. He became a friend and companion of our family working five years in our home. Browne never asked for any of our many possessions and to our knowledge he never stole from us. We explained from the beginning that if something was stolen, he would lose his job and all the income that went with it. If he wanted something, he should ask us about it and not steal.

At the time when Browne started to work in our home, my youngest sister Mary and her friend, Brenda, came for a visit to meet four-month-old baby Laura. They helped train Browne, figuring out ways to explain things to him. He had lived all his life in the village setting, so there were many things for him to learn.

One day stands out in my mind. Since the gas shortage was over for a time, we could run the generator and the electric washing machine. We had Browne watch our demonstration of how to run the washing tub, transfer the clothes to the spinning side to get the water out, then rinse and spin again. Afterwards, we sent him to the clothesline with a bucket of clothespins. He soon returned saying the clothespins were "finished" or all gone.

Curious how so many clothes pins could be used, we looked out the window and burst into laughter. There on the clothesline were numerous bras from three ladies suffering in the hot season. Each bra was spread out down the lines and hung with numerous clothes pins. We quickly displayed how to hang each piece of underwear with only one pin. Browne was a young Bassa man with very dark skin, but we were sure his face turned red that day since our amusement was so obvious.

I'm sure there were times when Browne felt the task I assigned him was completely ridiculous. Yet, he respectfully humored me and completed the job. For instance, at his home there was a dirt floor, but when he came to work at our house, I often gave him the task of washing my beautiful cement floor with soap. Sometimes I even had him use bleach, if a Bassa baby had urinated on the floor. This happened since rubber pants were not readily available.

Browne rose to the challenge of being a steward and became proficient in his duties. He was an expert at stain removal and I often think of him when it comes time to remove a stain. He also mastered using a coal iron, which was no small feat. Seeking the advice of his mother, he eventually developed into a wonderful cook to the point that our Bassa friends and missionary associates requested certain Bassa dishes he made when they came for a visit.

I often gave him the duty of cutting up meat purchased in the market and he would politely ask if he might carry home the parts which I discarded. Of course, I obliged him, knowing it would feed his family for some time.

This put me to shame thinking the food I saw as waste was made into a wonderful meal for my neighbors. They saw it as one of the amenities of Browne's prestigious and enviable job. When Perry or I would prepare the meat, we let our conscience guide us leaving extra meat for our friends in Browne's family. In addition, when we grew tired of our clothes, he was sometimes given the opportunity of first pick.

One of his favorite tasks was to use the mechanical carpet sweeper.

Since we had no electricity, I had brought it out from the States to clean a piece of carpet in the living room. Browne was intrigued with how the brushes rolled the dirt into a receptacle, and he called it "The Machine".

One day when Chief Somah was visiting, Browne enthusiastically asked, "Missy, Missy, I should use the machine just now?" I thought, why not? Browne took it out to the piazza and began rolling the sweeper near the chief. When the chief paid no attention, Browne asked him to raise his feet so he could clean under them. The dignitary raised both feet at the same time, and finally noticed something interesting was going on. Perry and I tried to restrain our laughter.

Finally, Chief asked, "O? Wha' da' thi'?" (What's that thing?) Browne casually replied it was a machine. Then he got excited and ran outside to get a handful of dirt, threw it on the floor, and amazed the chief by picking it up with one swoop of the carpet sweeper. "O! da' thi' fine-o" (O, that thing is fine-o), Chief exclaimed.

He excused himself from the conversation and investigated the rollers on the bottom, with Browne explaining the mechanics. Chief even took the chance to operate the machine and wondered how he could get one. Unfortunately, we had not seen any for sale in Liberia.

It was the perfect time for me to part with the sweeper and offer it as a gift. It certainly would have been a way to honor the local chief, but I was too selfish. I thought I certainly needed it for cleaning the carpet pad where my baby played and would one day learn to crawl and walk.

When Chief left carrying only the chicken we'd given him, I felt a twinge of guilt for not giving him the sweeper. I asked Browne if I should have given him the machine. "Oh, No Missy," he replied. "We use da' thi' too much." (We use that thing too much.)

Browne's family was always a source of learning, as he told us news about different situations they faced. He was married to a woman a little older than himself and had a baby daughter. His wife liked to "make market", selling items on market day to make a little money of her own. Browne's extended family reported she had taken the baby to the market and dangerously let her lay in the hot sun too long.

His family made palaver with her and dismissed her from their

Browne was part of our family as the steward.

village. Browne was then left to raise the baby on his own. When he was at work the baby was tended by Teetee, his mother. It seemed to us he and his wife were separated; but later they got back together, and she was allowed back in their extended family village.

Then a terrible thing happened to Browne's family. His brother's four children died in a house fire. They were not able to escape the blaze, since metal rogue bars were embedded in the windows to keep out thieves. After the tragedy, Browne questioned the safety of our house with rogue bars in every window. We realized we needed to consider what we might do in similar circumstances and we were thankful to have a back door for escape.

Not only was it a necessity to hire Browne, it was also purely luxurious to have a steward help me with household chores. I started out thinking we only needed his help for a couple days a week to wash the clothes, then quickly escalated to having him work all week. On the weekends I missed his presence, having to do basic housework myself.

He washed our clothes and hung them out to dry, then neatly folded them in sorted piles. We could go away and leave the house in his care. When we came home the floors would shine, clean dishes would be neatly stacked in the cupboards, and a pot of Liberian chop would be waiting.

He assisted me in difficult matters when Perry was gone, so it was always good to have him around. He was part of our family and was privy to all that happened in our household, although Perry and I thought we could speak in "high English," assuming it would be over his head.

We told him of the love of Jesus and why we were in his country, but I wondered if the gospel had made a difference in his life.

21

Anomalies

It seemed there were always interesting things happening. Some of them were unusual or exciting, and some were disturbing. Things were often not as they seemed to us, and strange situations felt like the new normal. We were guests in another culture, so we needed to keep an open mind and be accepting

While Mary and Brenda were visiting us, we made a trip to Monrovia. Arrangements were made to meet Dr. Abba Karnga and some other Liberian counter parts at a restaurant. Once we were all seated Perry ordered chicken for each of our guests, since they were unaccustomed to ordering from a vast array of options.

Dr. Karnga sat directly across from my sister. At the end of the meal Mary looked at his plate and then at the plates of the other Liberians. She observed that unlike her own, there were no chicken bones left on theirs. Thinking she needed to find the proper way to dispose of them, she quietly asked Perry what she was supposed to do with the bones. Perry laughed a little and told her he'd tell her later.

What had happened was that the Liberian men had inaudibly chewed all the bones right there in front of us in the restaurant! Many years later in 2004 when Abba was staying with us in our Spokane home, our adult children witnessed this same feat. This time we talked with Abba about the Bassa's habit of eating chicken bones.

He said the practice begins in childhood when milk is no longer available. Bones were part of their diet since they contained the necessary nutrient calcium. I wondered out loud that shards of bone might cut their mouth or possibly puncture intestinal walls. Abba kindly explained that they are trained to carefully chew the bones into the smallest of pieces to avoid problems. And then, he demonstrated the technique as we watched with wide eyes.

We also took my sister and her traveling companion on a cross country trip. We boarded the LAMCO train, which transported raw iron ore from Mt. Nimba on the northern border to the port town of Buchanan. The mining company ran a passenger car, and it was a quick and inexpensive way to travel north.

What a joy to be effortlessly and smoothly whisked on the rail line through the jungle of Liberia, instead of constantly swerving around potholes, bumping over wash board, and sweating in a hot car. On the train ride we observed virgin forests, remote villages, and rushing rivers. While traversing a high bridge over a river, we looked down and were thrilled to see a herd of river hippos.

When we reached the mining area in the north the temperatures were cooler at the higher altitude, and we rented rooms at the company's guest house. There was an Olympic sized swimming pool and nearby restaurants which we enjoyed.

On another occasion with my sister, we were driving to the beach, and came upon the largest python we ever saw. It was stretched out across the road and there was no time to stop. Mary described it as driving over a tree, and that's certainly how it felt from the back seat. We were surprised the snake was able to quickly move into the thick bush, or we would have stopped to look at such a huge one. However, we did get the chance to see it again.

On the return trip home, people from the nearby village waved us down to share some snake meat with us. They had just killed it and were excited, saying there was plenty of "fresh meat". They called it a giant snake and we presumed they had killed the same snake we had undoubtedly injured. We politely refused their generous offer. None of us were in the mood for snake steaks for dinner.

As far as I know that was my only chance to eat snake, and perhaps I should have tried it. My sister and her friend were horrified to think of having snake meat in the car and I didn't like the thought of it either.

I shared with my sister a major tension going on in my mind. My seemingly, lovely, extravagant home situated picturesquely on a hillside among one hundred palm trees was juxtaposed with a cement floored, off grid house, with only screens in the windows, and furnished with a few meager necessities. In our neighbors' eyes we were extremely wealthy. When they came to visit, they felt as though they were visiting some grand estate with a white mansion - and in some respects that was how we lived. Our home was held in great awe and our standard of living was beyond anything they imagined.

The tension was real. My brain had difficulty knowing if I was living the life of a pauper, or if I was living like a queen. As I fussed over saving rainwater from the roof, washed clothes by hand, boiled diapers on my coal fire, and used candlelight at night - it certainly seemed to be more of an underprivileged lifestyle.

We were saddened when our Paramount Chief Somah died of old age. Since the time he had deeded the mission land to us, we had remained on friendly terms. Perry had gotten to know him well because he had resided in a village near our home. Pastor Harry, one of Perry's TEE students, also lived in that village. He kept us well informed of preparations for the dignitary's funeral.

We understood Chief Somah was of the same rank as the chief who had died near our home the first year. It was a relief when Harry told us Somah would not be buried in the same horrific manner.

Extraordinary measures were taken to preserve the chief's body, giving the people time to prepare a suitable funeral for a man of high position. Money and food were gathered in quantities normally not possible for people surviving on subsistence-living. Family, friends, and officials of the area would feast for an extended period until the funeral was over.

It was Pastor Harry who extended us an invitation to pay our respects and visit those grieving. Numerous dignitaries and people paid their respects and so it was only right for us to go to Somah's village as well. My sister and her friend had the opportunity to accompany us and witness this traditional time of mourning. As we approached the town, mourners began to sound off in loud wailings and threw themselves on the ground showing the sincerity of their grief. Venders with their little tables of candies, cigarettes, and personal supplies were lined up to sell their goods at the large gathering.

There were many "quick service" houses in the village to accommodate the influx of mourners. The little structures were quickly assembled by driving bush poles in the ground and building a floor several feet up to avoid nocturnal invasions of reptiles and insects. The upper level was surrounded with palm branches and leaves to make a little room and that is where some guests slept.

Old Man Somah had been dead for more than three weeks before we were summoned. We knew the body had not been buried, and it was expected we would view it lying in state. The heavy odor of formaldehyde was detected as we approached the village. We knew it was from repeated embalmings, which were thought necessary to preserve the body in the tropical climate. A carpet bagger embalmer had been secured, and the family was housing him in the village while his services were periodically needed.

We were taken to a small mud house, which had been newly built to hold the casket. Harry escorted us to a room where a locally made, intricately designed mahogany casket was open. It was lined with a beautiful silk fabric pleated in delicate folds. I was surprised there was a heavy plastic bubble inserted in the casket for viewing - probably to keep flies off.

Somah was dressed in a locally made pin-striped three-piece suit, which we doubted he had ever owned while alive. His skin had a greenish tint to it, and his face was distorted, making me wonder if it was him.

Engulfed by the stench of formaldehyde, we hurried through the viewing area. When we exited the house Pastor Harry rushed over to us and exclaimed, "Doesn't the Old Man look good?" To be polite, we affirmed he did look good. We paid our respects to the family and other people of importance, then headed for home.

To enhance relationships with area officials and local neighbors, we decided to hold a dedication service for the mission station. Missionaries and Liberian co-workers were also invited to attend the event. Of course, a feast would be appropriate for such an occasion, so we kept our eyes open for enough meat to feed a crowd, thinking a goat or sheep on the hoof would do, but none could be found.

Finally, another missionary found a sheep, so he purchased it for us, but the animal got away on our yard. After an hour of running around in the jungle and getting all scratched up from thorns, Perry found it. One might think its wool would become tangled in the foliage, but the sheep in Liberia were of the pure hair breed and did not have wool. Sometimes it was difficult to tell them apart from the larger goats, since they looked so similar, but in Liberia the sheep's ears hung down and the goat's ears stood up.

The day before the dedication, Perry butchered the sheep using the boning skills he had acquired at a meat packing plant for a high school summer job. We hired several local ladies to cook a large meal of traditional sauce to be served with rice.

The dedication service was held under the roof of our car port which was decorated with palm branches and flowers. There was singing in both Bassa and English and appropriate speeches were made. My sister Mary was asked to sing a special number, which everyone enjoyed. It was a truly good time of interaction with our neighbors, and we looked forward to working with them in the future.

For several days after Mary and Brenda returned to the States, I felt the great distance between us. I missed my sister terribly, to the point of suffering several panic attacks - a first for me. With time and the distractions of daily living, I once again became accustomed to life so far from family members. I learned to focus on our lives there and not think so much about family and home, or I became bogged down and homesick.

With baby Laura growing rapidly, it would have been nice to have easier contact with family to share her with them. Short wave radios or ham radios were one option for better communication with back home. Several missionaries from other missions operated ham radios, and we had gone to their homes to try to get in touch with our loved ones.

Perry was intrigued and made getting an operator's license a personal goal. One of the prerequisites was to pass a difficult Morse Code speed test. He got tapes and books and studied the code night after night for several months. Rick from next door also wanted to get a license, so they studied together, although it would be some time until Perry passed the test and purchased radio equipment.

One night as he sat listening to Morse code tapes, he jumped up with a terrible pain in his shoulder. I saw a small hole in his skin and as I was describing it to him, I screamed when a little white worm stuck its head out and quickly went back in. Since it was quite painful, Perry told me to get it out. It was forced out with minimal pressure and immediately his pained subsided.

It looked like a little grub and we decided it must be what people called a "bot-worm" or "mango worm". It was not uncommon for people to get them in Liberia. This could happen when clothes were put outside to dry, and a botfly deposited eggs on the clothing. The larvae would hatch and embed itself under the person's skin. Of course, when it had grown and gotten to the point of wanting to come out, it was quite painful.

The way to avoid bot-worms was to destroy the eggs, by making sure our clothes were sufficiently heated. Hanging them outside in dry season allowed the bright sunshine to destroy the eggs. In rainy season it was a problem since there were times when our clothing hung for days on the clothesline under the eaves, with no hot sunshine, and barely dried. That was the perfect situation for the botfly to leave its eggs. A clothes dryer would have solved the problem nicely, but we did not have electricity.

We had followed the advice of experienced missionaries and shipped out an antique iron. There was a lid on the top, and we placed hot coals in the chamber underneath to heat the iron. In order to be totally sure our clothes were safe in rainy season, I often had Browne iron them. At times a small coal would fall out of a vent and burn a hole in our clothes, so it was a tedious job.

There was a nighttime nuisance going on that we couldn't control, and it drained us of our sleep. Just after the lights went out there would be a commotion in the attic lasting much of the night. We were sure it was rats running back and forth. It sounded as if they were bowling, and all the noise made sleeping difficult.

Thanks to our volunteer builders, all the missionary homes were built to be rodent proof, so we never had a rat in our house. But with so many rats above, it did give us cause to worry they could somehow gnaw through the ceiling boards.

It was thought the rats might reside in the storage shed during the day, so the men cleared it out and many rodents were killed in the process. Still the problem at night persisted. The option of poison seemed to be a disadvantage for several reasons. If the rodents died in our attic, a sickening odor would surely result. In addition, when the storage shed was cleaned the local children had been happy to carry them home for dinner, so they could unknowingly take a contaminated rat home and become sick themselves from the poison.

Our Bassa friends nodded their heads in sympathy over our nocturnal invasions. They suggested we get a cat, but they cautioned us that good cats were hard to find. Perry saw a nice, big cat in Pastor Alexander's town and inquired about it, but it was someone's cat and they were not willing to give it up. Alexander put out the word that the white people needed a cat, and we waited.

Our Bassa neighbors said, "Remember 'chicken calls cat'". We didn't quite understand what that meant, so they simply explained the Bassa word for cat "Soo-da", means "chicken calls". More investigation uncovered their local custom. It was quite simple, when someone got a cat, they must trade it for a chicken - otherwise, the cat would not be good at catching rodents. That made perfect sense to everyone, except us.

Eventually, we received news that someone had a kitten for us in a neighboring village, so Perry got his motorcycle and rode off the yard carrying a chicken under his arm. He returned home, pulled a bundle of fur out of the hiding place in his shirt, and asked, "Laura, what's this?" Laura wasn't even two years old, but she said "Kitty." Our little daughter loved the kitten immediately and "Kitty" became the official name.

Kitty lived with us for nearly eight years and she was an excellent cat in every way. Upon her arrival the problem of rats bowling in the attic stopped.

Much to Laura's delight, Kitty enjoyed being part of our daughter's play, and was content to be carried around in a basket. Kitty produced litter after litter of beautiful kittens, and Laura had the official job of taming the new kittens by playing with them most of the day. Everyone was pleased with the kittens they received at the mission, and we of course ended up with extra chickens to pass on to our guests.

Kitty added to her uniqueness by accompanying Perry when he would leave the house with the pellet gun. She had learned he liked to do a little target shooting by practicing on the many lizards in our yard. Perry called her his retriever, since she would wait by his side until the lizard fell, then off she'd go to claim her prize.

I too used the pellet gun, shooting at snakes in the nearby palm trees. The ground keepers thought it was great sport. They would rush to the house saying there was a snake hanging from a tree and wondered if I would like to shoot it? We once arrived in an interior village and the people remarked, "O are you the white woman who shoots snakes in the trees?"

I awoke one night to a deafening noise. I lay paralyzed in fear, wondering how Perry could sleep. I could not identify what it might be or where it was coming from, but it had a definite rhythm and cadence. Then it occurred to me that someone was using a hacksaw on a metal rogue bar in our window! The rhythmic noise was the saw blade being pulled back and forth. I could not identify which window was being sawed, but it was so loud it must be nearby.

I quietly woke Perry and he too was startled by the loud noise. We

Laura and her Kitty

had to chase the thief away and protect ourselves. By the light of the moon we could see no one was sawing the window bars in our bedroom, so we crept around the dark house trying to discover which room the thief was breaking into. This rogue certainly was not a quiet one, and I could not imagine one being so stupidly noisy. Was someone trying to frighten us?

We could find no evidence of someone trying to break in throughout our house, and still the rhythmic noise continued on and on. We bravely turned on a flashlight and called out to leave us alone. Still the sawing noise continued its cadence without interruption, and I put my hands over my ears.

We called out to the night watchman, but he did not answer. We wondered what had happened to him, had "they" gotten to him first? How creepy! Was someone playing a trick on us at 2:30AM? What was going on? After a second search in the house, we then turned on our battery-operated lights and checked each room again. We looked outside shining flashlights, still the eerie sawing noise continued. We almost felt trapped in our house while someone was playing a cruel joke on us.

Perry bravely went outside to look around. Being frightened, I locked the door behind him so no one could force their way into the house, and to this day he teases me that I locked him out. I stood by the door the whole time waiting for him to come back and was ready to unlock it only when he returned. After looking around the exterior of the house, he came back without a clue as to what might be going on, other than the noise was coming from our house.

It was impossible to distinguish the direction of the source. We yelled out, "Bā moo!" (Go away!) and other Bassa phrases. Still the undisturbed noise sawed and gnawed on and on into the night. Would the deafeningly racket never cease? It was amazing our baby remained asleep through the commotion, since she was normally such a light sleeper. The night seemed full of mystery: What was the source of the noise, how could the baby still sleep, and where was the night watchman?

We began another systematic search of every area of our house. Perry even opened the attic access in the ceiling and that's when the noise suddenly grew louder. Finally, we had something to go on and were confident we had at least found the area where the noise was coming from. We listened closely, what could it be?

The attic was secure, and it appeared no one could break into it, so how could this be? Was someone trying to saw through our valuable aluminum roof and steal sheets of roofing in the middle of the night? No, Perry had checked the roof with a flashlight when he was outside. Now with the attic access open from above, were we vulnerable to someone attacking us from the attic?

Standing on a chair and shining our strongest flashlight around, Perry finally saw the reason for our disrupted sleep. It was a fat rat, lying on his back on a rafter pole. Its back legs were positioned up to balance itself on the roofing, while it used the front claws to scratch open numerous mud-wasps' nests stuck to the roof. With a rhythmic motion it would drop the larvae in its mouth, go back to scratch the next one out, and eat it as well. The scratching on the metal was evidently reverberated across the whole roof and it was surprisingly loud. All that noise from one rat!

The beam from the flashlight did not intimidate the rat in the least. Unafraid, it did not hesitate, but continued its meal of grubs, apparently now using our light for its own advantage. We yelled at it, and it turned and looked at us with a curled-up lip, almost appearing to smile. That raised our tempers some and we attempted to hit the nasty rodent with a broom but couldn't quite reach it. Still, it completely ignored us, all the while maintaining its rhythmic scratching and eating.

Perry finally got a great idea and put Kitty in the attic. She was still quite small, and I seriously feared for her safety next to the huge rat, but apparently as soon as it smelled Kitty, the nocturnal intruder instantly fled, and the deafening noise stopped, never to return. What a relief!

While Kitty was still small, our neighbors Rick and Kathy came home with a German Shepherd puppy and they named her Schatzi. She was a wonderful dog and got along with Kitty amazingly well. They would curl up together and take naps, and romp around the mission station playing. One day I looked out the kitchen window and saw Schatzi pick up Kitty's head in her mouth and gently swing her limp body from side to side. I was afraid something dreadful had happened to Kitty, but when Schatzi released the cat, it walked over and affectionately rubbed against the dog's leg with a purr.

Suddenly the dog-cat romance ended when they both came of age and had their first litters. Then they would scrap and warn each other of their prospective territories. In later years we inherited Schatzi and she stayed with us as a member of the family defending us many times from intruders to our home. Kitty was also with us for many years, and everyone was saddened when she disappeared.

We also raised rabbits and chickens in pens by the storage shed. The chickens were beautiful, robust Rhode Island Reds which became so large we called them turkeys, and they were excellent to eat. Some of our female rabbits had been purchased from Larry before they left the country. They were our breeding stock and Perry had bought a buck in Monrovia from a Dutch businessman leaving the country. We named the father of our future rabbit litters "Woody" after the Bassa word for rabbit. True to the commonly held assumption, we soon had many baby rabbits.

Perry built rabbit cages and bought some from other missionaries. The cages lined our carport where the rabbits would be safe from the rain. We knew that we could tolerate eating rabbit and hoped that the Bassa people would try to raise them too as a protein supplement in their diets. We attempted to expand their palettes with samples of free meat. They did like the meat, but raising them was a little more in animal husbandry than they were used to. Perry thought a bamboo rabbit cage hanging from the support beams in their outdoor kitchens might work, but the idea never took off as we hoped it would.

Part of living in a third world country was dealing with fuel shortages. At the beginning of our first year back, there were serious lack of imported gasoline, kerosene, and cooking gas. We had to always be thinking of ways to conserve, and it was nerve-racking to think of running out.

We came to the point of sharing a refrigerator with the other family on our mission station, since kerosene for the refrigerators was impossible to find. One week we would use the frig together at their house, and the next week we would all share our frig. Kerosene usually cost $3.25 a gallon, however during shortage times the price could jump to $5.00 a gallon, if it could be found.

Gasoline was also lacking in the country, so we tried to save by traveling together for supplies, however most of the gas was reserved for the mission work to go on. We were even concerned that thieves would come and try to break into our mission warehouse. There was no hint as to when the commodities would be available again.

With bottle gas for my kitchen stove also a shortage, I did not use it except rarely to make popcorn for a snack at night. All meals were prepared on the coal pot in my outside kitchen. Using the coal pot was a painstaking task, which I certainly disliked. First the locally made coal had to be lit, and then I had to wait for the coals to get hot enough to cook. If I got busy with the baby, guests came to the door, or I just waited too long, the coals would cool down too much. Cooking on coals was a time consuming, dirty and frustrating job when there were so many other things to do. My steward, Browne was given the job each day of lighting the coal pot, cooking on it, and heating water.

While in the States for Perry's final year of seminary, we had done a little research on cooking alternatives and were impressed with the idea of a mud stove. Perry took off with the idea and created a wonderful three burner mud stove out of termite mud. Simply, it was a life saver.

A counter high base was first constructed with termite dirt and given time to harden. On top of that he formed a heat tunnel with more termite mud, which made for easy modifications through trial and error. The tunnel connected the stove's largest burner to the smaller ones. Hot coals were put under the largest burner and the heat traveled down the tunnel past the smaller burners and out the chimney. But there was a problem, since the little burners didn't get hot enough to cook.

We fortunately discovered a Peace Corps model which used a high ridge under each burner to pull the heat up to the cooking pot, otherwise the heat wave bypassed the pan on its way to the chimney and the pan would not get hot enough for cooking.

Making dinner on the coal pot in my outside kitchen. Back door led to the inside kitchen.

We also discovered a lid had to be placed over an empty burner, so the heat wouldn't pass up through the burner's hole. Eventually we got the stove to work remarkably well, and Browne was always proud to take our guests around to the side of the house and show them "his" cooking stove.

To the right of the stove's base, we created a coal bin with termite mud. Moving the coals and placing them under the burner was a very dirty job, and it seemed my fingernails were always black. I tried using some big tongs to grab the coal, but it was quite time consuming, and not nearly as efficient as the fireplace shovel my father-in-law sent us. What a wonderful tool it was - nearly life changing! Browne saw the little shovel as so valuable that he thought we should store it in the house so thieves wouldn't take it.

Perry also designed a mud oven, which worked equally well. He found a sheet of heavy steel in the LAMCO scrap yard and commissioned a welder in town to make an iron rectangular box with a hinged door on one of the smaller ends. The metal box went on the mud slab next to the coal burners and we encapsulated it with termite mud, leaving an air space on all sides.

Coal was burnt under the oven, but it was necessary to have a thick mud layer between the coals and the bottom of the oven, otherwise the floor of it became a frying pan. Hot air from the coal fire was forced up and around the sides of the metal oven exiting through a chimney in the back center. It had been tricky to get the chimney placement correct and we moved it several times. The chimney was shared by the stove creating an air channel for the heat. We even put a thermometer in a hole in the oven door which came from a rusted-out camping oven.

It was remarkable how well the oven worked, and it was a great joy for me. I learned how to keep the temperature consistent and baked all kinds of things including pies and bread, and on the floor of the oven I could even bake flat bread and pizza dough.

When plotting the placement of the houses, Perry had noted a well-used African foot path close to our house site. He was told it was used by farmers going to their nearby fields over the hill. We later realized it was also a well-used road to villages beyond. That fact should have been enough to move the foundation of the home even 10 feet, but we were culturally inexperienced and wanted the big tree by our front door.

We thought we would move the path by simply re-routing it. We were told during the construction phase the builder attempted to move it a short distance away for safety purposes, but the people continued to take the original trail.

People traveled the path throughout the day passing within feet of the corner of my kitchen and piazza. Sometimes we would look out and see huge loads being toted on someone's head within feet of our house. The bundles would bob up and down as the person walked along. They came so close I could have reached out and touched them from my kitchen window.

Most called out a greeting echoing through the home, or would often stop and look in the windows asking, "What are you doing?" Of course, we felt as though this infringed on our privacy. We put the customary sticks on the trail and cut a nice path down to the dirt indicating the route was being changed to circumvent the house. After all, we needed our personal space! However, our desire for the new path was not the shortest route, and people simply refused to take it.

I fretted about the African path wondering if the local chief was needed to make the desired change. But as time went on, the travelers became my link to news of the day. They would report how their rice farms were growing and ask what I was doing in my house. This was the friendly, neighborly thing to do and a friendly neighborly response was certainly due. Occasionally people would stop and ask if so-and-so had passed by, as they were looking for them. At times they reported local happenings, like who was sick, and friends would even stop to play with our children.

I would ask if anyone had bananas or something else for sale, and the word would get passed. After a while someone would arrive selling bananas. When I was cooking the smells would waft up the path and people would tell me I was embarrassing them, since it made them hungry. It was not uncommon for people passing by to speak of their hunger and need for food. There would also be several times when a passerby would intervene for me in dangerous situations with snakes.

At times people caught in a down pour would hold up under the eaves or take refuge in my piazza sipping a cup of hot tea until deciding to head for home. Children often arrived under huge leaves used as natural umbrellas, and the leaf would be seen bouncing past my window when they ran home.

In America we live shut up in our houses and sometimes don't even know our neighbors. It was difficult to transition back to our individualistic society. We had learned from the Bassa people how valuable a close-knit community can be.

22

Dangers

The jungle was all around us. With it came dangerous wildlife, and we were intruders in their habitat. To make matters worse, we were inexperienced and unaware. Most people carried a cutlass when they walked the jungle paths, and there were often reasons to use it. Praise God! He always provided protection when our family needed it.

One night as I sat at the kitchen table writing letters, Schatzi started to angrily bark just outside the window. Then came the blood curdling scream of a large jungle cat near my house. In fright my hair seemed to stand up straight. Suddenly, I saw the silhouette of a large leopard leaping across my front yard with the dog chasing closely behind. The scene was illuminated by car lights as Perry happened to drive up the hill at just the right moment.

He proceeded up the driveway, parked the car in the carport, shut off the engine, and opened the door. I called to him that I had just seen a leopard in the yard, and he should be extra careful walking to the house. (He was roughly 30 yards away.)

He responded he had seen it too, but he thought it had run into the jungle. There was silence for a few seconds as we peered through the darkness listening for any movement, then I heard him slam the door and quickly come to the house.

I unlocked the door as he came running up, and his eyes were wide in amazement. "That was a little frightening after seeing a leopard in our yard," he exclaimed.

"Oh yes it was!" I told him. "And, I even 'got' to hear it scream close to the house!" We called for Schatzi, but she didn't respond. The night was eerily quiet. She appeared the next morning, presumably our defender with a few deep scratches on her head from a battle with the leopard. Perhaps it was seeking an easy meal with one of our chickens and rabbits, but it never returned – as far as we know. The night watchman believed he saw one several times as well.

One day while cooking dinner, I found myself in a dangerous situation. Perry was gone to Buchanan and I was home alone with Laura. It was that busy time of day around 5:00 PM with ongoing meal preparation, and a sauce was bubbling outside on the mud stove. My daughter was unsettled with hunger, so I put her in the highchair and offered her some rare Cheerios.

While she was entertaining herself, I continued with food preparation on the coal pot going in and out of the kitchen's back door. Being consumed with my daily routine of maintaining the coal fire, I was unaware of the dangerous situation going on very near me. Normally while I cooked Laura would have been at my side, playing on the outside kitchen cement slab. Praise God she wasn't that day!

My attention was finally diverted from cooking when I noticed a rat dying on the cement about three feet away. It was convulsing and gasping for air. I wondered if it had rabies but was unafraid since it apparently could no longer get up and chase me. I thought when Perry got home I would have him dispose of it.

The next time I pushed the screen door open and took a step out the back door, I heard a hissing sound. I thought it was only the rat defending itself or drawing its last breaths.

To my horror - I was instead face to face with a green snake hanging from the palm tree next to the outside kitchen. I had not personally seen a green mamba before, but I recognized it immediately from our much-used snake book and from Perry's description of the one he saw while cutting the survey line.

It was a slender, bright green snake with its head held high, big round eyes, and dorsal scales a little darker than those on the belly. I also knew the green mambas were aggressive and deadly with highly neuro-toxic venom. Our Bassa neighbors called them the "seven step snakes" – When the snake bites, you only get seven steps before you die. The thought occurred to me that I could be dead before Perry got home. Also, should I get Laura out of high-chair or leave her there?

I felt quite fortunate the screen door was still between me and the snake, but I had opened it and had taken one step down leaving my foot and ankle exposed. I froze for a second, then quickly withdrew my foot, while the snake hissed and lunged towards me with lightning speed. The screen door was pulled shut quickly and locked.

I frantically grabbed the cutlass from behind the refrigerator and stood behind the screened doorway waiting for a chance to go out and chop the dangerous snake's head off. It was a brave thought, but not too rational, and downright dangerous to think I could kill such a quick moving snake. Then reason set in and I instead went for the camera. The snake hung there for some time moving its head from side to side as if to focus through the screen better.

All the while I was so thankful Laura was locked in her highchair. She contentedly savored one Cheerio at a time, and I was giving her more and more to distract her. No problem if the extra Cheerios spoiled her appetite and she didn't eat a lot of supper. I needed to attend to a more serious matter and never mind if the sauce burned outside.

The situation I found myself in was exactly why we had decided to hire a steward for protection, but he had already gone home for the day. After some time, I began to figure out what was happening. It appeared the snake had poisoned the rat up in the palm tree. The rat became paralyzed with the venom and fell out of the tree, so the snake was simply going to claim its prey.

After taking pictures so people would believe this was really happening to me, I watched and waited. Then, suddenly, the snake was gone and so was the rat. I never saw exactly what happened, but I was now hesitant to go outside and resume my cooking. Making sure the outside kitchen was safe, I ran outside, grabbed the pan of spaghetti sauce and ducked back safely inside. That afternoon became a good time to use the hoarded cooking gas I was saving for an emergency, because an emergency was exactly what I had on my hands.

Soon people began to pass by my kitchen window on the African path after working all day on their rice farm. I told them what had happened, and some brave men took their cutlasses up on the roof and looked around, but they saw nothing. They also scolded me, saying hadn't they told us it wasn't a good idea to have a tree growing so close to our house? I replied that this type of tree doesn't have the roots that destroy building foundations.

"That's not the thing we're talking about," they said. "We were talking about snake business. Snakes live in the trees and it's too dangerous to have them so near your house. Tomorrow we will come and cut it down and then you can eat palm cabbage."

The next day a group of men went to work cutting down the stringy, fibrous wood of the tree, even digging out the root which did not have a tap root but many tubal fingers. Browne made a delicious palm cabbage soup from the "heart" of the tree where the branches are formed. We shared the rest of the cabbage with the laborers and their families.

They taught us a new **Bassa proverb that day. "If we had money like a palm tree has roots, we'd be rich." Indeed, we were already rich – we had our lives. It wasn't the first or last time God protected us from a snake.

When Laura was still developing into a steady walker, she wanted to play outside. I sat on the front step while she roamed around the yard not far from me. Suddenly our steward came storming out of the house with the cutlass and yelling at me. He told me I wasn't taking good care of Jonja. I knew I was a good mother, so those were fighting words, but he picked

---

**For the Bassa it is a natural thing to "throw" or use proverbs in everyday life experiences. Rev. Dr. Karnga has recorded[22] many traditional Bassa proverbs complete with explanations. In the same spirit, I will occasionally site or throw a proverb, with the hope that I am applying it properly.

her up and took a few steps around the side of the house to point the cutlass at a night adder just a few yards from me - lesson learned. God had blessed us by protecting her and giving us Browne to guard us from unknown danger.

Snakes blended into their environment so well and could not be seen from even a short distance away. I had to stay close to Laura and constantly look for danger, not only from snakes but also from scorpions, ants, and any number of other things from the nearby jungle.

Only a few days later, Browne again found a night adder in the coal bin. Several times that day both he and I had shoved our hands into the coals and threw them on the fire. We shuttered to think how close we had come to unknowingly antagonizing a hidden snake.

Night adders were not long snakes, but short and thick possessing scales with a velvety brown texture and a series of black patches down the back. They were not seriously dangerous like the green mamba, but a bite could cause painful swelling, and for a young child it was considered deadly.

I had always wondered about the verse in Luke 10:19, *I have given you authority to trample on snakes and scorpions.* Perry came home one day and said the people following him on a jungle trail had admonished him to watch where he was going, since he had unknowingly stepped on a snake.

I was quite surprised this happened since he was always observant of his surroundings, especially in the wild. I asked him if it was a dangerous snake. He said he was told it was black and if it had bitten him, he would have died, so it was probably a black cobra. Frightened, I scolded him and said he'd better be more careful.

Sometime later, we were out on the jungle paths and the Bassa person behind me started yelling. "You stupid white woman, you stepped on a black snake and you didn't even see it. You were looking at trees and flowers, you better start looking on the ground for snakes." I was shocked. I had stepped on a snake and not realized it at all.

If you make the most High your dwelling... then no harm will befall you...He will command his angels concerning you, to guard you in all your ways; they will lift you up in their hands, so that you will not strike your foot against a stone. You will tread upon the lion and cobra...I will protect him, for he acknowledges my name. Psalm 91:9ff

An encounter with a gaboon viper occurred when I had an eerie feeling there might be a snake seeking the shelter of our home after a sudden rainstorm. Before running briefly to the clothesline, I told Laura to stay inside. She was generally obedient, but then I saw her toddling towards me and ran to scoop her up.

After chastising myself for being so jumpy, I noticed something dark behind the broom leaning against the house. A large viper was coiled there. I had earlier used the broom to sweep my outside kitchen, and both Laura and I had just walked past it. Once again, the Lord had been protecting us, and we knew it because we saw the dangers He kept us from.

I was home alone and hesitant to go back inside with the snake nearby. God promptly provided a man on the path who was carrying a cutlass. He killed the snake and said it had probably come for the nearby baby kittens, which Laura had left in a basket near the door

We had yet another experience with a snake one evening. Perry and I were trying to make popcorn on the coal stove in the outside kitchen, a rather tricky task. There was a down pour of rain at the time and our cat kept looking at something just off the edge of the kitchen's cement floor. Perry got the flashlight and we were surprised to see a large night adder lying along the cement. Perhaps it too was seeking shelter from the rain, but it was a false sense of shelter, because Perry went after it with the cutlass.

While giving a ten-week exam in one of Perry's TEE classes, an unwelcome guest appeared. Perry came home and told me the students got so upset with the guest that they killed him, and they were rather nonchalant about the killing! He was of course teasing me. What happened was that during the exam one of the pastors looked up and said, "Look at that snake."

Looking over his shoulder, Perry was shocked to see a green snake looped around a rafter pole above him. Its head hung down looking over his shoulder, as if to get a better look at the exam on the podium. I immediately asked if it was a green mamba, but no - it was a longer, skinnier snake, and a different shade of green.

One of the students stepped outside, came back with a stick and said, "Excuse me," before climbing on a chair and hitting the snake. It fell to the floor and was quickly killed from whacks with the stick. Then the student calmly took his seat, and everyone resumed their test. Perry had to ask him to please remove the carcass from the classroom.

Our first year in Liberia we had purchased a paperback book in Monrovia entitled "West African Snakes" complete with pictures and descriptions. Beside each picture we briefly noted an encounter and the date. The spaces began to fill up and we eventually lost track of all the dangerous reptiles we saw. Yes, God and his angels were on guard watching over us. His necessary vigil would need to continue, as there would be other incidences with snakes to come.

One evening as Perry sat in our living room chair, he felt a strange stinging on his arm. In a short amount of time it began to go numb. Examining the area, he found a tiny gray caterpillar, the size of a grain of rice. We scooped it up with a piece of paper and saved it in a bottle in case the situation called for medical intervention.

Quickly his whole arm became numb and he was unable to move it. He commented that he could have surgery on it and he wouldn't feel a thing. Naturally this was quite alarming, and we went to bed worried. Who knew how this would turn out.

The next morning, we were greatly relieved. The numbness had disappeared, and he could freely move his arm again. We thought about the potential this little caterpillar held for the medical world. Perhaps people who needed surgery could have this form of anesthesia, instead of going fully under.

We heard of many unusual remedies from the jungle flora that went undiscovered by the modern world. Sadly, much of the virgin jungle is being destroyed and some of God's treasures for His world will go with it. I would even submit myself to an herbal treatment from the jungle in the near future.

We had another nocturnal invasion of driver ants at Number 1. We noticed they were trying to get into our house in the early evening. We wanted to sleep instead of vacating the place, so we spread kerosene around the exterior to steer them away. That seemed to work, but I worried the kerosene would evaporate during the night allowing the pests to enter our home.

Since they were swarming just outside Laura's bedroom, it seemed to me the ants could get into her bed and bite her. At that point in time she was waking a lot in the night, and we were attempting to let her learn to put herself back to sleep. If she cried, how were we to know if she was crying from ants in her bed, or if she was trying to wake us for no reason?

Her father thought she would be fine, while I was quite worried over the potential situation. We compromised in a most unusual way. We put the legs of her crib in large cans of used car oil, just as we did the rabbit pens! With our baby reasonably safe from an invasion of ants, we went to bed - but not for long.

By detouring the aggressive ants from our house, they were sent in the direction of the chicken and rabbit pens. Our night guard awoke us at 2:30 AM saying the ants were in the baby chick's pen. We went out and picked ants one by one out of 53 chicks' fluffy feathers. Perry drove the car around so we could work with the light from the headlights, and all the while baby Laura slept safe in her crib.

While we were pulling the ants out, others swarmed around our feet biting us in defense of their newly claimed territory. We poured kerosene on our legs and feet to keep them off. Some of the ants' pinchers were buried in the flesh of the little baby chicks and it quickly became a bloody mess. In the end, we were pleased that only five chicks were lost.

Making matters worse, the chicks weren't ours. They belonged to our watchman, since we had convinced him to raise chickens for a cash profit. This whole episode discouraged him, and he felt his earnings were killed by the ant invasion. It was a real blow as we struggled to help people get ahead, but he repeatedly commented on how impressed he was that we would get out of our bed to help him save his baby chickens.

Driver ants were a true fascination - when they weren't aggravating us or destroying property. It was easy to imagine their colonies contained millions of ants, which God made in many sizes with separate duties. They traveled great distances in long columns protected by larger sized warriors on either side of their path.

The ants could join their bodies to make a chain or bridge, while fellow ants crossed over. They could dig tunnels below foot paths, and they could build shaded canopies from minute pieces of mud to protect themselves from direct sunlight. We observed a moving black ball in the driveway during a heavy rain and ran out to see what it was. To our surprise, it was a ball of driver ants in standing water, rolling around to protect themselves from drowning.

When the driver ants received communication of an area worthy of food, they would swarm searching every square inch. Due to the sheer advantage of millions of ants invading an area, they could even subdue small rodents finally wearing them down with hundreds of ant bites. In the end only bones would be left, in fact any carnage in the jungle could be consumed by them. We were told driver ants could debone a human in four hours, a gruesome detail when a quadriplegic was tragically attacked by driver ants one night and did not survive.

Another danger we faced was in human form. In third world countries there is often little treatment for those who suffered from mental illness. We sometimes saw these unfortunate individuals in the markets or villages and knew it was best to leave them alone. These people were often drawn to us seeking help, perhaps since we looked different with our white skin and straight hair.

In later years, a man was a threat to our children and me in the Buchanan market. The market ladies urged us to quickly leave, and I felt compelled to do so. I witnessed the man receiving corporal punishment as I drove away.

A troubled man often came to our mission compound. People called him the "Circle Man", so named due to his habit of incessantly walking in little circles. He would mumble threats with bizarre warnings of coming doom. We were not too sure about him, so Perry told the ground workers to keep an eye on him when he was there.

I was resting one day when he came close to the bedroom window. He was talking out loud and seemed to be in conversation. I thought I heard him say, "Ok, I'll kill them all today." I jumped out of bed, could my ears have heard correctly? Perry was gone, so I had the mission ground keepers kindly escort him away. It took some time for him to leave the property, since he could not refrain from walking in circles and in a sense spiraled down the driveway.

We were not too alarmed by him, since he wasn't aggressive, and it was apparent he was deeply obsessed with walking in circles. It did give me cause to wonder if he could suddenly break away from his trance and do us harm. He would come and go from our area, and from time to time we would see him along the roadside relentlessly walking in circles.

Unbeknown to us, Circle Man regained his sanity and came to our door one day. I didn't recognize him in his healthy state. He was clean shaven, had gained weight, was well spoken, and polite. He said he was hungry and asked for food. I looked into his eyes and saw the deep-set hunger I had learned to identify. Unaware, I invited him to take a seat on our porch and went in the house to ask Browne to bring the man something to eat.

When my steward saw who it was, he hurried back inside the house and locked the wooden door behind him. He advised me to not return to the piazza saying, "Missy, that's Circle Man. Stay away from him. He's dangerous!"

Our guest must have heard us, since he called to us saying he wasn't crazy anymore and was now healthy. Browne and I went together to talk to him, keeping our distance in the doorway. Browne said, "Aren't you Circle Man". He affirmed he was, adding his name was Sam.

He went on to explain he suffered with mental illness and some of the difficulties he endured. Due to constantly walking in circles, his feet had become so damaged that he could barely walk at times, still he had a strong inner drive to continue pacing in circles and could not stop himself. He had dealt with severe malnourishment and dehydration, and suffered from a variety of other problems, including unkind people and dizziness.

He added that when he was crazy, he liked to "visit" our mission, since he knew people would not harass him there. He told us that the devil started to torment him, and he added, "You know this is Devil Country. Well, the devil had me sit on his council. They ordered me to kill your whole family! I could never do it because there were so many angels with swords surrounding your house!" The explanation certainly surprised me, but doesn't Psalm 91:11 say, *For he will command his angels concerning you to guard you in all your ways*?

Sam went on to explain he met a kind nurse, who invited him to go to a Christian clinic, and there he received medication which made him sane. But most important, it was there he gave his life to Christ. He explained he was two new men both physically and spiritually.

What a wonderful story Sam told, and we rejoiced with him! He could continue to receive medication from the same clinic, but at that time was out of money to make the next purchase. He asked if I would please help him. Of course, it was an easy decision to make, but Browne admonished him to use the money on medication only, since he had heard Circle Man sometimes used alcohol to reduce his suffering.

Sam thanked me profusely for the money and food and apologized for the nuisance he had made of himself in the past. He left without incidence and I never saw him again.

Sometime later, Browne came to work saying he had sad news. Sam must have run out of medicine, so Circle Man was out walking his circles on the tar road, when he was tragically hit by a truck and suffered fatal injuries.

23

Joy in the Morning

Laura with bush-school girl

Although I knew God had called us to Liberia and I found great happiness in being a new mother, I had to admit I was in a dark place. Having a baby was a wonderful answer to prayer for me, and I knew I was doing a good job caring for her. The saying that "pride swelled up in her chest" was a mystery to me, until I held my baby in my arms. Why was it then that I felt so incredibly sad?

Worst of all, it seemed my prayers weren't being heard, and when I read the Bible, I felt empty. My husband tried to encourage me, but even that made no difference. How could I stop the emptiness - did I even want to?

One thing I realized was that the absence of our family contributed to my mounting depression. They were not part of our intimate lives and could not offer the unconditional love and guidance a new mother needs.

We lived a secluded life in the jungle with another missionary couple, who did not yet have a child, and while they were thoughtful and kind - I somehow felt very alone. Other missionaries with children were not around to give encouragement and seemed to pay little attention to my baby. It seemed like there was no one to support me.

Several other personal difficulties added to my situation. There was the problem that our Bassa neighbors were not impressed with my mothering skills, my physical recovery from childbirth was lengthy, I missed the excitement of going with Perry to the villages, and I lamented the loss of my occupation as a dental hygienist. In addition, it was during this time that I also suffered with reoccurring boils, which were overwhelmingly painful and physically draining.

Usually home without a vehicle, gave me a trapped feeling, but I reasoned, "Where would I go, if I did have a car." I also worried about what I would do if an emergency occurred with Laura. This was not a manufactured concern since she often spiked a high fever with ear infections or malaria.

I lost track of how many times her temperature quickly rose to an alarming 106° with ear infections, malaria, or after immunizations We gave her weekly medication to prevent malaria, still she suffered with it several times as a baby.. I would anxiously bathe her to bring the fever down. These factors coupled with the lack of sleep most mothers of infants experience, left me unable to shake deep discouragement and futile feelings.

I began to despair of life itself and lost an alarming amount of weight. Although Perry knew I was having a rough time, I couldn't share with my husband the depths to which my depression had reached until years later. My mind began to linger with fantasies of how I might escape life, not to leave my husband or child, but to get away from a trapped feeling.

When others were around, I groomed a pleasant façade and made sure I had a smile to hide behind. At Laura's well baby checkups, it did not occur to me to ask the doctor for help or tell him of my desperation. As the months slipped by, my depression lingered and festered. It seemed my state of mind was beyond my control, but thankfully I did not consider harming my child.

At that time postpartum depression was not broadly known, in fact I had never heard of it. The term "baby blues" was common, but it seemed to be short lived. It wasn't until years later that I heard about postpartum depression on TV and realized that was most likely what my problem had been for twelve long months.

In fact, one in seven women will experience something more extreme than the typical baby blues. Women who give birth and struggle with sadness, anxiety, or worry for several weeks or more may have postpartum depression (PPD). While the baby blues tend to pass quickly, PPD can be long-lasting and severely affect a woman's ability to get through her daily routine. Treatment with medication is often successful[23] and perhaps would have relieved me of much turmoil.

Considering my emotional condition, Perry and I decided we needed to go back to the States for a visit. We hoped that going home for Laura's first birthday might be a good break for us all, but especially for me. We also wanted our families to meet Laura before she got any older. We didn't tell our missionary team, but Perry and I realized there was a real possibility we wouldn't be able to return to the mission field.

Literally, I needed to snap out of it, and God knew I had sincerely made every effort to the best of my ability. With His help, all things are possible, and He did come to my aid.

Our trip home was exactly what I needed. My symptoms simply vanished from the time we met our parents at the airport. It seemed to me that having the support of our family and especially that of our mothers was all I needed. Their felt love and excitement to meet Laura and their encouragement to me as a mother were powerful healing factors. I still remember them telling me, "She looks so healthy and happy," and that was what I needed to hear. While in the States, I gained an attitude of peace and joy, and we were able to confidently return to Liberia.

It is a common fallacy that missionaries are super Christians. They are only ordinary people who have received God's unique call on their lives. They respond positively to the call to go and spread the good news of His salvation, but it is God who gives them the desire to go and equips them for the call.

The calling, preparation, and arrival are often spiritual high points in their lives. Once they finally got on the mission field the testing and difficult times often began. We saw this happen with every missionary who arrived in Liberia, and I suspect it is true in other areas of the world as well.

Most missionaries would start out on a high when they arrived in country and everything was exciting and new. Then somewhere along the line, they would experience a plummeting low, leaving them feeling defeated and devastated. This often happened around the time of a first illness or when cultural and spiritual props were missed. For some they missed the sound of the organ playing in church and the singing of the congregation. Others missed the fellowship or a family dinner after church, but for me it was group inductive Bible study.

After taking Laura to the States, I decided to be proactive and find what I needed to be healthy. I mentioned my desire for Bible study to other missionary wives on our team and was pleasantly surprised they too had been thinking of starting a Bible study. Like me, most of the wives lived some distance from other missionaries, so we set a plan in motion. Marty offered to lead a study on Romans 8. It sounded like a deep place to jump in, but that's exactly what we did, and we loved being in God's Word together.

Once a month before our scheduled meeting, the wives expected to find their Peugeots ready and waiting in the car port, with the husbands' schedules cleared and available for babysitting. It was interesting to hear the fathers recount their experiences of being home all day with their children and without a vehicle.

One time the men thought they would get together for a meeting on our Bible study day. They figured they would multitask by holding the meeting and watching the children at the same time. The mothers were not surprised to hear the meeting was a disaster with babies crying and needing constant care, giving little time for the fathers' meeting.

The ladies took turns hosting the Bible studies at their homes, and sometimes I would have to drive three hours one way over terrible roads to get there, but God always kept me safe. Carpooling with other wives

Ladies Bible study group, notice the lappa suits

was sometimes an option, and other times I would bring along a local friend as a companion for the trip. The monthly meetings continued throughout our time in Liberia using several different types of Bible study and rotating the discussion facilitators.

Toward the end of our years in Liberia, we encouraged the Bassa wives of mission workers to attend the ladies' Bible studies with us. We not only enjoyed their fellowship and insights into God's Word, but we hoped it would encourage our Bassa sisters in Christ to provide Bible studies for their friends.

Not only did the Bible studies maintain my spiritual state, but my Bassa neighbors began to accept my mothering skills. With my baby's rapid growth and development, mothers asked for advice on nurturing their babies. I was sickened to learn that when busy mothers needed to regain their own strength, they would sometimes switch from nursing to feeding their babies water rinsed through boiled rice. It was not surprising that the children became malnourished. I found it a privilege to give them advice and help them with their babies.

Fathers in Perry's TEE classes even approached him for advice on how to keep their children healthy. He told them to care for their pregnant and nursing wives by providing more meat for them to eat. They should also allow mothers to stay behind in the village to nurse the babies. With better nourishment they would grow faster and stronger.

Perry helped men re-evaluate the care of their families. He explained that meat not only quenched the father's appetite, but protein provided necessary nourishment for children to grow and develop. As a result, we had the joy of seeing the welfare of children improve. They were strengthened not only in our immediate village, but also in a wide range beyond our mission home through Perry's TEE students.

Typically, missionaries spent a certain amount of time on the mission field and then traveled back to their home country in order to raise support. Several options were made available by CRWM, beginning with two years of work abroad followed by three months of "home service", two and a half years of mission service with six months back in the States, or up to three years overseas coupled with nine months in the States. Our family took several two-year terms with three months in the States.

Practically speaking, many plans are set in place to make home service as productive as possible. After experiencing a year long bout of post-partum blues, we began to pray that God would bless us with a second child, who would be born during home service.

Our prayers were answered! Not only with a new family member, but the due date for our second baby landed right in the middle of our time in the States. The baby would be born in the security of our families with medical care in a stateside hospital.

I saw God's timing as perfect. This baby was nothing less than a personal blessing straight from heaven. After feeling spiritual distance and struggle with postpartum depression, I was humbled by God's blessing for us. It seemed my Heavenly Father was proving His love for me and caring for my family in a special way.

If I again struggled with lingering difficulties, we would be in the States close to family and friends. I realized God had not abandoned me and rejoiced under the shelter of His wings.

That shelter would soon drop, and life would feel much different to me. Unbeknown to us at the time, a difficult season was ahead before we even left the field for home service. Would the experience be used to glorify His holy name, or would it tear me away?

We are not privileged to know how or why the Lord chooses His plans for us, but His will is *good and perfect*, Romans 12:2b. God is never finished with His refining work in our lives, and we should never choose to be left to our own ways and desires. We can only make ourselves available to Him, trusting He will always lovingly care for us and *work all things for good to those who love Him and are called according to His will*, Romans 8:28. We must know and rest assured that whatever comes, the divine intruder only seeks to draw us ever closer to Himself and bring our Savior and Creator the honor and glory.

While I was pregnant, Perry and I undertook an important project. It was a known fact that slash and burn farming used throughout the country was destroying virgin forests and the earth's ecosystem. Rick encouraged his agriculture students from the churches to plant upland demonstration plots with a better farming technique. If the Bassa farmers could be convinced to use fertilizer, it would mean better producing crops grown on the same plots of land year after year, which would save our God-given environment.

Under the guidance of Rick and only slightly aware of the labor required, Perry and I asked our Bassa neighbors if we could grow a small rice farm next to theirs. They agreed and we choose a demonstration plot a short distance from our home.

The first step was for Perry to work alongside the men clearing the jungle of trees and brush with only a local cutlass and small axe. It was a long and difficult task. After the fallen trees and underbrush had dried for a lengthy period in the hot sun, the men burned it all in a raging fire. Tall flames from our field seemed to come dangerously close to the house as it lapped up the dry timber, but a band of thick green jungle was enough to stop its progression.

It was the ashes from the fire that were traditionally used to fertilize the Bassa fields. We knew from experience it would be inadequate to produce deep green, healthy rice stalks laden with rice kernels. Our small plot enriched with fertilizer was to be an example of better farming.

When the planting season started and the women went to the field, I grabbed my locally made hoe and tagged behind. It was their task to "scratch" rice seeds into the earth with the ashes. The work was long and hard in the tropical sun.

My neighbor lady tied her young baby on her back, then hand scattered rice seeds on the ground. With her legs held straight, she bent from the waist at such an angle that the baby was nearly upside down. Working with quick strong strokes, she used a short-handled hoe to cut deep ruts in the orange soil between her bare feet and cover the scattered seeds.

I took my place beside her and did my best to keep up while adding little white balls of fertilizer. It seemed to be a competition, and she put me to shame quickly outpacing me. The task proved too much, and Perry had to complete our area.

When our rice sprouted and began to grow, immediately a difference was evident. It grew tall and strong with a beautiful dark green color, while the field next to ours had an unhealthy yellow hue and shorter, flimsy stalks. With our beautiful rice, grew equally healthy weeds. Like little sins in our lives, they grew unnoticed and then attempted to take over and drown out our anticipated harvest. Weeding was our next step as upland rice farmers and that too was the woman's job.

One morning, while Perry did his office work at home and Laura hopefully napped, I took the opportunity for a much desired and rare break from the duties of a full-time housewife and mother. Nearing the end of my third month of pregnancy, I set out to our rice plot to hoe the weeds.

After a long, physically exhausting morning, I was glad to begin my short trek on the shaded trail back to our house. As I walked, I felt severe cramping in my womb and began to worry all was not well with my cherished baby. I anxiously wondered if I had worked too diligently in the hot sun. Maybe I was dehydrated. I stopped in the shade, took a long drink and breathed deeply trying to relax the angry muscle. By the time I reached the house, I knew I must go to bed immediately in an attempt to

Rice harvest from our test plot

save our future baby.

Seeking medical advice, Perry made a quick trip to the ELWA hospital over an hour away. Dr. Befus said there was nothing that could be done, but I was right to go to bed, and should stay there to ease any future guilt. He said I shouldn't feel bad about working hard in the hot sun. Hard work can not destroy a healthy fetus, and he concluded by telling Perry he may need to take me back to the hospital.

The next day our worst fears were realized. We wept as we buried our little baby in a match box near a large flat rock in the back yard. Perry said, "No matter how small this baby is, it is still our child."

I was devastated. Not only had I lost our baby, but how could God withdraw His special blessing so perfectly timed? The blessing had indicated He heard my pleas for help when I couldn't pray anymore, and it had demonstrated His attentive and constant love for me as I battled life in a place far from home. This child would have been delivered during home service surrounded by a loving extended family, which I believed God intends everyone to have. Now that there was not a baby to be born, what did that say about God's love and care for me?

My grief grew much deeper than I had imagined it would. I knew people who had a miscarriage experienced sorrow, but I thought their mourning was tempered as they realized it was a deformed baby or that something else went wrong. I thought they would reason through their loss and that it would not be that hard to accept.

That was not how I felt. Though I searched God's word, I could find no solace in the scriptures. It seemed the pain would never leave, and I could never be happy again. I felt I would always have our loss constantly on my mind. Even if I could be happy again, I didn't really want to be, because I wanted the baby so much. In addition, I was frightened by the possibility of plunging into another prolonged season of depression.

A couple of days after the miscarriage, I awoke very early one morning weeping with a heavy heart. My crying grew stronger as daylight began to show on the horizon. Sensing the need to cry my heart out without awaking my family, I stepped outside as a cool mist from the evening dew was still rising in the morning light. The hem of my long white nightgown gathered the dew as I strolled the pineapple patch allowing the tears and sobs to flow.

A new day was beginning, another day to live without my precious baby growing inside. As much as I felt like life should come to a standstill or - even more - go backwards, it certainly would not. Life would go on - a new day was dawning, and it would be without my little baby. I cried for the baby we had lost, for the years of love it would have received and given.

Hidden deeply within, I wept for fear that my God had somehow abandoned me. Could this be a punishment for something I was unaware of? Perhaps that too was a possibility I needed to contemplate.

Consumed with pouring out my emotions, I was shocked to see Dabo coming toward me. She was the elderly local midwife. She asked me what I was crying about, and I told her in Bassa my little baby had died. She thought I meant Laura had died and started to cry with me.

After I cleared up the misunderstanding, she admonished me yelling, "You should be happy you didn't bleed to death as many Bassa women do when they miscarry. There will be other children born to you – Stop crying!" Instead of giving me sympathy, she was disgusted and stomped away. I felt stunned, realizing the aversion some might have for my sheltered life with readily available modern medicine.

With my tears quieted and my heart numbed, I returned to the house to resume my search of the scriptures. I needed an answer for "Why?" Why would God permit this miscarriage to occur? There had to be some explanation and I knew God's Word would hold the answer.

That morning the words of 2 Corinthians 1:4-5 leapt off the page and profoundly spoke to my soul: *Praise God, the God of all comfort, who comforts us in all our troubles, so that we can comfort those in any trouble with the comfort we ourselves have received from God.*

These verses allowed me to open my heart to God's healing. How wonderful that He is the God of all comfort, who comforts us in all our troubles. Comfort is a given, I didn't need to doubt it or look for it. It is just there, available for all situations, for all troubles.

My question of "Why?" was clearly explained: "So that" I could comfort those in trouble, because I had been comforted. I gained the hope of being a vessel of understanding and healing for others because God willed that for my life. At the time, I thought it was a little strange that this "clicked" for me and brought me out of deep grief, but I was so relieved to think I had found what God was doing in my life that I didn't question it.

Perhaps there was relief in simply understanding that God had not abandoned me. I still mourned deeply within from the miscarriage, but I knew God was working and had a plan. I didn't want to be outside His will, even though at the time it didn't seem like He had such a good plan. The seeds of joy and contentment that I felt that morning were tangible, being lifted from despair by God's Word.

As time went on, my physical health became a cause of concern for us. The doctor had told Perry to take me to the hospital if I didn't recover from the miscarriage within a couple of weeks. Six weeks had passed, and I had not fully regained my health. I resisted returning to the same hospital for a surgical procedure where I had been left unattended, my roommate had died, and another missionary wife had received questionable care. I felt with a little more time and rest, I would surely recover. Perry threatened to force me in the car and take me to the doctor.

Dabo again visited us in a timely and providential manner. I thought perhaps she might be able to help in this matter. There is an old Bassa proverb which says, " Nyonnon-soa se-deh kon ni, okonnon dio-dyoa - The old lady might seem to have nothing, yet she has her Dio-dyoa." The dio-dyoa is the seed of a certain tree, used to cure skin diseases. It is precious since it can only be found with a few aged women.[24] In this case, our aged resident midwife held the key to a natural remedy for my problem.

I asked what she did for women with prolonged bleeding after a miscarriage, and she replied "I told you women die from bleeding business. White lady, you could die! You better take fever leaf." It so happened that God had allowed a fever leaf bush to grow in our yard. While working on the mission grounds, Taa had carefully groomed the bush and sometimes people came from the villages to pick its leaves.

I knew I was not allergic to it since I had used it to flavor Bassa dishes, still we wondered if I dared to try it. I had failed to ask Dabo the all-important question of how much to take, so we decided to try just a little. Perry brewed me some tea from the leaves and I drank it.

There must be something powerful in fever leaf because an hour after drinking it, my condition had improved and in fact that was the end of it. Perhaps the plant was high in vitamin K, which promotes blood clotting. We were thankful for such an amazing, easy result, but wondered too if everything was actually alright. Could the fever leaf be masking an underlying problem? Evidently everything was as it should be, since another child was soon conceived!

We found ourselves approaching the end of our first two-year term and looking ahead to "home service". After being apart from our families and home church for a couple years, we were eager to have some down time and enjoy a complete break from the mission field and our remote lifestyle. To help schedule our home service, the CRWM home mission office made contacts for us and set up speaking engagements at supporting churches, which they did for all missionaries.

When we left for home service, I was beginning the second trimester and Laura was one and a half years old. Perry's mother made arrangements for us to house-sit their neighbor's home. It was the perfect situation giving our little daughter the opportunity to live across the street from Grandpa and Grandma Tink', and my parents lived only 25 miles away.

Home service was nothing less than grueling with travel, meetings, and speaking engagements in different churches each week, not to mention sleeping in strangers' homes with the hope that our young daughter would be on her best behavior. This left little time to resolidify family ties. It was especially difficult to keep such a schedule with a child, but we did our best and it was truly a joy to meet the people in the churches who supported us.

Occasionally, Laura enjoyed a new opportunity of staying with grandparents while we were gone. We spoke at a cluster of supporting CRC churches in the Ripon, California area and flew to another church in Grangeville, Idaho, meeting up with former seminary classmates and dear friends along the way.

After spending time with supporting churches and squeezing in time with family, we were eager to return to our lives overseas. There was a running joke among missionaries – The mission board makes home service so busy and difficult, that the missionaries beg to go back to the mission field.

At the end of home service, I was again seven months pregnant when we readied ourselves to return for our third term. The natural desire to be surrounded by family and have the best of medical care available had a strong pull. I was emotional as our parents helped us pack, and I shared with my mother that I would have preferred to give birth in the States.

Later at the airport, Perry's mother was overcome with emotion facing the fact that we would soon take her only grandchild away. She said it was even more difficult to say goodbye with another baby on the way, and her grief was shared by us all as we tried to console her. These conversations with our mothers only proved the deep love we had for each other and how difficult the separation was.

With God's call upon our hearts, nothing could change our minds from the commitment and privilege of training the Bassa pastors. Though it was difficult to be apart from our extended family, we knew we were doing the right thing. I was reminded of the man in Luke 9:61-62 who told Jesus he wanted to go back and say goodbye to his family before he followed the Lord. Jesus told the man he must not look back in order to follow Him.

Even while traveling back to Africa we faced temptation to turn around and go back. The day we flew out of Sioux Falls, a fierce blizzard raged across the vast Midwest prairie delaying our arrival in Chicago. We had to rush through the airport, since there was a chance we could still make our connecting flight to Amsterdam.

Pushing Laura in a little umbrella stroller, I ran behind Perry with my big belly bouncing from side to side. It was a long run and we just barely made it. Crossing the Atlantic, I began to suffer the familiar pains of labor, probably as a repercussion of our long run. I pressed my face to the window and cried, wishing I was flying home in the opposite direction.

Frightened our baby would be born too soon, we did everything we could to ease the contractions. Perry completely took over the care of Laura, and I kept myself well hydrated and relaxed on the plane. Arriving in Amsterdam, we providentially had reservations to stay in a hotel until the next morning, when our flight south to Liberia would leave.

The strong contractions were unrelenting in the hotel and we were frightened. We decided that if they continued into the morning, we would make alternative plans. I spent much of the night in the bathtub, praying and using hot water to relax the powerful muscles surrounding my unborn child. By the morning the danger seemed to have passed, and we prayerfully flew down to Africa believing God would protect our unborn child.

24

Baby Michael's Arrival

Back in Liberia, the official at Roberts International Airport stamped our passport and said, "Welcome home!" Indeed, it felt like we were home. The high heat and humidity, the hustle of the luggage porters, and the sounds of Liberian English were all familiar and welcomed.

The missionary who picked us up at the airport casually reported a small animal had apparently died in our well and contaminated the water supply – I thought, "Here we go – back to missionary life." He added the carcass had been removed and the water was treated by adding a bottle of bleach to the well. Afterwards, the well was flushed, so the water was once again safe. This seemed logical to me, since I remembered my father doing the same thing when I was growing up on the farm.

It was peculiar though, we noticed the water coming from the kitchen and bathroom faucets smelled clean, except for the shower water. In fact, it smelled so strong that I gagged while taking a shower. To cover the stench Perry splashed on aftershave, and I used my precious Avon scented bath powder, however the odor in our hair couldn't be masked. We again flushed the entire system, but still the shower water was simply nasty.

Since we had been on home service for an extended period, it was a lot of work to restore and clean our home. Browne came by the house hoping to be our steward again, and I put him to work. Without glass in the windows, the house had been open to the elements the whole time we were gone. There was heavy dust everywhere and a little mold growing in some corners, so I had him clean from ceiling to floor with soapy bleach water.

Meanwhile, I opened the 55-gallon steel drums, which contained our belongings and were sealed before we left for the States. All the missionaries did this when leaving for home service to keep possessions safe and dry. I carefully unpacked items and put them in their place, trying to take it easy and not stimulate labor contractions, which seemed eager to flare up.

When Browne was cleaning cobwebs in the shower stall, he began to gag and jumped off the chair, exclaiming in Bassa that something was rotten. He had happened upon the source of our stinky shower water.

In our shower bucket was a dead, decaying lizard! Just imagine, each night before we showered, I stood on tiptoe to pour boiling hot water into the bucket hanging from the ceiling. Cold water was added and the two were stirred together. Then, standing beneath the shower head attached to the bottom of the bucket, the valve was turned open, and without knowing it we bathed in decayed lizard water! No wonder it was so foul. I was fortunately bathing Laura in a plastic tub, so she wasn't exposed to the filth.

Through the years there were many gross stories that missionaries liked to tell. We all prided ourselves on being a tough crowd, but that particular story normally grossed out even the most seasoned missionaries. A familiar saying goes something like this:

When a first term missionary finds a bug in his soup,
he throws the soup away.
A second term missionary spoons out the bug
and eats the rest of the soup.
Thereafter, the missionary eats the soup,
bug and all, considering it extra protein.

Soon after our return a dangerous, life-threatening illness began in our precious daughter, although we didn't realize it for some time.

Having just turned two, Laura was ready to be a "big girl" and be potty trained. She wanted to wear the pretty underwear she had helped pick out in the States. Laura was known for her mild manner, but one day a temper reared its head as she sat on her little potty chair, and she slammed her left heel against the cement floor. I saw her do it and knew it had to hurt. But it took some time to discover the magnitude of her actions.

Shortly after this she began to get sick and run a fever. We knew something was wrong with her and took her to the doctor at ELWA. Laura was no stranger to ear infections, but it was not the problem that time. We returned to the doctor a second time sure our unhappy little girl was not well, but again nothing was discovered. Her malaria smear was negative, so it was probably a virus. However, a new symptom had developed - she was walking with a little limp. It could have been a huge key, but we didn't realize it at the time.

In a couple days, she became seriously ill and even lethargic, so we rushed her back to the capital city. On the third trip, we searched out Dr. David for a second opinion. He was a CR missionary doctor who had worked at ELWA and was at that time an instructor and pediatrician at JFK hospital. It was difficult to get in to see him, but we were persistent and tracked him down. He closely examined Laura, who was 26 months old, but couldn't find a reason for our concerns.

Just as it seemed the examination was over, the doctor began to systematically feel all over her body from head to toe. He suddenly became alarmed when he felt her left heel. It was hot with no apparent sore in the area. The doctor took a needle biopsy of the soft tissue and told us he feared she had osteomyelitis, a bone infection which can be very serious.

He told us to get Laura on cloxicillan, a powerful antibiotic. Perry went to eight pharmacies in downtown Monrovia in order to accumulate enough medicine for her. It was quite expensive, but that was not of any concern to us.

A few days later we returned for the doctor's re-examination, and he was not assured the infection was responding to the medication. Laura's heel was still quite warm, she could not walk on her left leg, and our little girl was not feeling any better.

The doctor informed us the biopsy had returned positive for infection, and again warned that we had a very serious condition on our hands. He felt sure osteomyelitis had set into Laura's heel bone, which could result in a crippling condition. We were told to not allow her to walk, which could possibly further damage the bone. Then quite seriously and tenderly, he told us she might not survive. I felt a surge of panic rush through me, but I knew she was that sick.

He added we needed to take her to the States for intravenous treatments. In addition, he could not allow me to travel on a plane, since I was seven and a half months pregnant and still experiencing intermittent premature labor. There was no question that Perry should get treatment for Laura in the States or possibly in Europe. I would therefore stay behind and have the baby alone in Africa.

In the end Dr. Van Reken changed his mind. He said Laura could stay in Liberia, if we could find enough of another rare antibiotic, Dalacin C (Palmitabe) or Clindamycin by the UpJohn company. We would have to give Laura an oral dosage exactly every four hours and that meant even waking her up in the night. The doctor prayed with us that we would be able to fill the prescription in the pharmacies downtown and that God would grant her healing. If we couldn't find the correct medicine, Perry and Laura would leave on the next flight out.

While I held Laura in the hot car, Perry again scrambled from one pharmacy to another sometimes buying one pill at a time. We needed enough medication for a few days when our next doctor's appointment was. The pills were very costly, but we would have paid any amount to save our beloved daughter. The pharmacy owners promised Perry they would restock their supply for him.

In a third world country it was impossible to tell if the pills had passed their expiration date. We could only earnestly pray and trust God had provided a diagnosis and medication potent enough to be effective against her particular infection.

A few days later, we thought it appeared she was responding to the treatment as the fever dropped slightly and she felt some better. The doctor confirmed our hopes, he too felt the antibiotics were working. Perry returned to the pharmacies to purchase additional medication and took it upon himself to faithfully administer the treatment giving her each dosage exactly four hours apart.

Laura limped for nearly six months, and it grieved our hearts to watch her. The doctor told us she would probably be crippled her whole life, but at least the infection had not spread, and we should be thankful she had survived the ordeal.

Time passed and God saw fit to answer our prayers by graciously renewing the site of her infected bone. She eventually walked without a limp and has been able to lead a full life, including playing basketball in high school and running cross country and track in college.

The question of where to give birth to our second child was a bit of a mystery. We could always return to the missionary hospital where Laura was born, but we wanted to see what other options were available. Within a half hour's drive from our home was a hospital at Firestone rubber plantation, so we asked for a tour. The buildings seemed run down and old. The delivery room had little equipment with a cement floor and an old-style table in the middle of the room. I asked if expatriates gave birth there and was told a white baby had not been born at Firestone for many years.

We knew we could go to LAC plantation where Perry had been hospitalized, but once labor began it would be too far to travel and road conditions were poor. One missionary was planning to give birth at home and our missionary midwife would attend her, but remembering the birth of my first baby, I was not interested in a home birth.

On the outskirts of Buchanan was LAMCO mining company's seaport including their hospital. We interviewed the Scottish midwife, Elizabeth Aghion. She had many years of experience and I liked her, so we decided on LAMCO hospital.

Two weeks before my due date, Perry expected Laura and me to travel with him to Buchanan for his BMA (Bassa Ministerial Association) meeting. I demurred, saying I was in no condition to travel one hour over bumpy, pot filled roads. "You won't have a car, what will you do if you go into labor?" he questioned me.

I reluctantly packed an overnight bag for the family and, just in case, included the birthing essentials. We planned to stay the night at our mission's guest house. Buckling a pillow over my pregnant belly to protect it from the jolting ride, Perry drove with extra care, but I still felt each pothole with painful clarity.

After we arrived at the guest house, I experienced a burst of energy and completely cleaned and rearranged the guest house kitchen cupboards. I also quickly decided to make a minor trim to Laura's hair. This seemed strange to me, but I reasoned certainly it was too early for the nesting instinct's adrenaline rush.

Mark and Pat invited us over for dinner at their nearby mission house. Afterwards the men went to their meeting, and Pat's eyes sparkled with an idea. She joked, "Since it's April Fool's Day, we should go to the guy's meeting and tell Perry it's time to take you to the hospital." She thought it would be humorous, but I knew the joke would be on her.

I was going to tell her, "The joke's on you! We need to go to the meeting and get Perry, because I really am in labor," but then our husbands came back. Elated Perry was there, I jumped up saying, "Come on, Perry. Let's go to the guest house."

They questioned, "Why are you in a hurry. It's such a warm evening. Don't you want to stay and have some cold lemonade?" Perry agreed, after all they had an electric refrigerator which made the extra hard ice, much colder than our kerosene refrigerator could produce. He thought it would be a treat to cool off, while enjoying conversation with our friends.

Normally I would have felt the same way, but I was anxious and could not catch his attention. No one seemed to notice how uncomfortable I was. I couldn't sit down, was constantly pacing, and my repeated trips to the bathroom were ignored. At times I leaned on the back of a living room chair panting out contractions, while the others visited nearby. It seemed they had grown accustomed to my problems with premature labor pains and the misery of late term pregnancy.

Perry finally took his last sip of lemonade and I immediately insisted we get Laura and leave. With a questioning look in his eyes, we made our way to the door. Mark and Pat stopped us and said, "Well it won't be long now. Are you two up on the Lamaze method?"

I said, "Well we'd better be!" then grabbed Perry's hand and led him down the steps.

As we crossed the lawn to the guest house, I told him, "This is it, the baby is coming. I'm in labor!" He asked if I was sure, and I assured him I was serious, adding I was glad he had urged me to go to Buchanan with him or I would have been home alone.

At the guest house I paced around the kitchen table with each contraction. We were waiting to leave for the hospital until the final dose of Laura's important antibiotic was given. Perry said God timed it that way because He knew we would be busy in the delivery room that night and wouldn't be around to give Laura her medicine every four hours.

We notified our Mark and Pat that I was in labor, asking if Laura could spend the night. They said they suspected labor had started, since they watched me circling the guest house table. After taking a picture of our little family just before leaving, we put Laura to bed, and one of them came to stay with Laura.

On the way out to the car I leaned on the hood to breathe through another contraction. Suddenly, I realized red fire ants were crawling up my legs and biting me. I stomped my feet to get them off and removed my sandals since they were full of the nasty ants. We bounced across town over the pot-filled roads, stopping occasionally during contractions, and finally arrived at the LAMCO mining company hospital, which we were glad was nearby.

Perry dropped me close to the hospital door, but the night guards refused me entry, since I wasn't wearing shoes. It didn't help to explain that they were full of red ants. When the next contraction came upon me, they hurriedly unlocked the doors and rushed us inside.

Through the night of labor, I used headphones and sometimes sang along to the calming praises of Maranatha! Music. The nurses laughed to see a lady in the delivery room singing, but it was wonderfully relaxing. For our second baby, we were surrounded by staff and the midwife

Kathy, Laura -2, and Scottish Midwife who delivered Michael

checked us frequently with helpful advice, saying the baby would be born before midnight.

Although I wanted a quick delivery, I did not want my baby to be born on April Fool's Day. However, it was not my decision to make. I ended up laboring through the night. At 4:28 AM Perry announced, "It's a boy!" The baby weighed in at 9 pounds 6 ounces.

On that eventful night as we drove to LAMCO hospital, I reminded Perry that if we had a boy we had not decided on a name. This was not to be a problem, however, because right after he was born, Perry looked at me with tears in his eyes and said, "His name is Michael". He somehow knew "Michael" was to be his name, although it had not been on our top three list.

Since we were Americans, the staff opened the expatriate wing of the hospital. Otherwise, I would have been in a large crowded ward. When we realized my baby and I would be the only patients in the wing, Pat offered to spend the night with us. How wonderful to have her assistance. She had to go and bang on the locked door of the wing several times in the night when I needed a nurse for medication.

Michael was ravenous and unhappy even though I had fed him, so the nurse brought an IV bag and a little medicine dose cup. She showed us how to get him to drink from the little cup. He carefully sipped the water and was more content afterwards. I had never seen a newborn baby drink like that before. The African nurse explained that if a mother dies, babies can be fed that way and survive. When they start nursing, they lose the ability to sip from a cup.

The day after Michael was born, Perry paid the bill of $115 ($15 for delivery, $100 for one night in the expatriate ward) and we traveled home to Number 1. Our newborn held his head up the entire way home over the bumpy roads. Afraid he would get whiplash, I kept pushing his head down, but he would pop it up again as if to look around.

When our Bassa friends came to see Michael, again they remarked, "I praise God you didn't die with your baby!" How sad to think women entered such a treasured time in life with the fear of death, but it was certainly their reality.

We realized his name was as difficult for the Bassa to say as Laura's name had been. Our local neighbors gave him the Bassa name "Ga-ma-sau", meaning "man is a rock". That name was chosen since he rapidly grew into a big, strong baby. His well-baby checkups at the ELWA clinic showed his growth rate off the charts. The doctor even suggested I was feeding him too much, but I ignored his comment. I knew that was not the case. Also, Michael was a strong baby and achieved his motor skills much earlier than normal.

Shortly after we got home from the hospital, I began to feel ill, got a mild fever, and had to go to bed with nausea and general weakness. After a while, the whites of my eyes and skin took on a light-yellow shade, so I wondered if I had gotten hepatitis. I changed my diet to bland food, no fat, and ate primarily oatmeal. Many years later when we were living in the States, blood work revealed I had indeed had hepatitis A. Possibly it was something I contracted in the hospital from contaminated food.

There was the concern that having another baby in Liberia would throw me into postpartum depression again. The second time around, however, I experienced the opposite reaction. I found myself being joyful and thankful for two healthy children. No doubt – It was my positive response was an answer to prayer.

There were several other factors that also contributed to my emotional wellbeing. It helped that by the time of Michael's birth, the Bassa mothers in our community were seeking my advice for feeding their babies and children, rather than criticizing and laughing at me. In contrast, before Laura was even born, they were doubtful of my ability to nurture my baby and told me so.

Another difference between our two babies was that Laura was a light sleeper and often cried in the night. When the rainy season came, it was nearly impossible to hear if she was crying with heavy rains on our aluminum roof. It seemed I would lie awake much of the night straining to hear if she was crying and became sleep deprived myself.

Desiring a different nighttime routine for our home, I prayed before Michael was born that God would be pleased to bless our new baby with good sleeping habits. I prayed that by the time the heavy rains started in June, baby would be sleeping through the night.

God's answer to my prayers was that Michael enjoyed sleeping. At first, he was barely awake long enough to be bathed and fed, and we had to keep him awake to play with him. This allowed not only for an easy transition for Laura, but by the time the monsoon rains came, we were used to Michael sleeping through the night.

Baby Michael Six weeks old

When Michael was six weeks old, I pulled out the Baptismal clothes Perry's mother had sent and panicked thinking it was too small. We quickly called everyone on the mission radio and asked them to please come for his baptism on Sunday. I literally had to shove him into his clothes, and he growled in disapproval and discomfort through much of the worship service, but he looked so cute in his little outfit.

The baptism was held on our lawn with some missionaries and Bassa colleagues present. The missionaries sang "Welcome to the Family" accompanied by guitar. Perry baptized him and shared a message from Acts 2:14ff. (See the liturgy and sermon notes in Appendix F)

Laura was also baptized as an infant. For both services, we had the mission workers build a circle with palm branches on our lawn where we sat with our guests. Holding the baptisms in one of his student's churches was not an option. There was the danger we would show favoritism towards one of his students, so our babies' baptisms by sprinkling were held on the mission grounds.

Our Bassa village neighbors and the students in Perry's TEE classes were accustomed to holding and playing with Laura. Now they eagerly grabbed Michael out of our arms. Michael soon became known for being a cuddly baby, whom people loved to hold.

This was a wonderful time in our lives. We were blessed with two healthy children and a privileged call from God to teach pastors everything from the gospel of Christ down to healthy family living. We will always look back fondly on those days, missing the blessing of friends and neighbors calling at our home uninvited, the opportunity to teach those who were eager and innocent, the pastors sitting on the edge of their seats passionately waiting to hear the gospel of Christ, and the enthusiastic worship of the Bassa believers.

Comment on Infant Baptism:

Infant baptism is a strong part of our Reformed faith stemming from the promises of a covenantal God, who promised to be a God to us and to thousands of generations after us. *Know therefore that the Lord our God is God, the faithful God who keeps covenant and steadfast love with those who love him and keep his commandments to a thousand generations…*(Deuteronomy 7:9).

Throughout the Bible, starting in the Old Testament, God always worked through families placing a sign upon the children that they were His (Genesis 17:9-14, Colossians 2:11-13).

In the New Testament, Jesus called the children to Himself and in Greek it reads, *He thoroughly blessed them*, Mark 10:16, meaning He called them to himself. In many Bible passages the children of believing adults were baptized as part of the household of believing parents. (Acts 2:39, 11:14, 16:15, 33, 18:8, I Cor. 1:16, 7:14)

Bassa neighbor ladies take turns holding Michael

Historically the Church of Christ baptized the children of believers. It wasn't until recent history in the timeline of the church that the ana-baptists protested the baptism of children, calling for baptism at the time of personal confession. Ironically this theological persuasion is now called Baptist.

Reformed Christians also hold to believer's baptism, but they understand from the Bible that after God works in a believer's heart, He also works through the believer's family by calling their children to Himself. When they reach the age of discernment a personal response of accepting Jesus as their Lord and Savior must be made, but before that God had His sign and seal upon them.

As the recipient of infant baptism, I have always known that God loves me and called me to Himself. My faith was nurtured in the church, by loving parents, and extended family. There came a time in my life when I felt the desire to make a personal confession of my faith recognizing that my family's faith could not save me. I needed to acknowledge that Jesus was my personal Lord and Savior, and this I did in the 8th grade at a Bible camp. The following year I made public profession of my faith before my church congregation.

25

Ministry & Travel

"The Call is Our Strength" became a rallying point for us when homesick, overcome by heat and humidity, or unable to endure yet another road pothole. Above all the personal triumphs and challenges, the call we felt from God was our incentive to continue living in Liberia to train Bassa church leaders for their ministries. After five years, our missionary team had trained 444 officers in the Church of Jesus, and we were committed to opening new teaching centers for many more who had requested classes.

Perry was unanimously elected to be the first director of Christian Extension Ministries. CEM was an organization of CR missionaries and Liberian staff, who worked together to develop and teach classes equipping the Liberian church not only with theological courses, but with training in agriculture, health, and literacy. Bible translation and a scholarship program also took place under the umbrella of CEM.

Being the director meant Perry's responsibilities included overseeing all CEM ministry programs, personnel, and finances. He also interviewed people to fill CEM positions and make sure they received training as needed. It seems that wise appointments were made since most of them are still serving in their original ministry positions.

CR missionaries also had a field council with a leader to oversee missionaries and report back to the mission headquarters in Grand Rapids. The position of field leader was rotated among the missionaries.

As the CEM Director, Perry had to drive one hour to Buchanan a couple times a week to oversee the CEM programs. He also was given the task of general contractor to build a CEM office complex in Buchanan, which was located down the road from Mark and Pat's mission home. The office building was designed in the shape of an "L" with an interior courtyard. There were several offices, a large conference room in the corner and a soundproof recording booth for TEE classes. Additional offices were added a few years later.

In addition to being the CEM director, Perry continued his first love of teaching three TEE classes in our home area on Mondays, Thursdays, and Saturdays at 10:00 AM. He had roughly 20 students in each class. In one of their courses they studied the first four books of the Bible. At the beginning of our 3rd term, Perry led his TEE students through a study of the Old Testament Prophets.

He loved teaching and reported in a letter home that the students were doing well and had mastered reading the Bible in Bassa. They were able to use written study notes, and no longer used cassette tapes to prepare for class. As always, the final goal was for the pastors to learn to prepare good sermons using only God's Word and highlighting Jesus saving activity on the cross. They had no other resources than the Bible available to them.

Perry taught his students that the Bible is the inspired Word of God as a revelation of Himself. Because it is God's Word, it exposes our rightful relationship to Him. Basic sermon preparation must begin with reading the whole story or message in a Biblical text in order to discover how it reveals God or points to Christ.

He emphasized it is not correct to read the Bible as though it is written to oneself personally, since we are not the original recipients. The pastors were trained to first consider the original intent of the letter, who the recipient was, and what it meant to that person. In that light, they (and we) could consider what the passage was saying to the original church, and finally what it means to people of their churches.

Above all Perry stressed the pastors should faithfully preach the Word, as if God himself is addressing the congregation. Another important aspect of the TEE classes was to train the pastors to work together and critique each other as brothers in Christ. *As iron sharpens iron, so one person sharpens another,* Proverbs 27:17. They learned to enjoy this fellowship of pastors and many groups are still meeting now, years later.

Periodically, translation of portions of the Bible were completed and put to print. Perry and I felt it was important for the pastors to receive copies. We stockpiled books as they came out and made them available to his students. We also had them for sale in our house, and they made a fine gift for visiting dignitaries.

Each Sunday we continued to visit Perry's students' churches. At the worship services, Laura and I wore scarves appropriately tied and would sit on the left-hand side of the church with the ladies and girls. It was not unusual to sit shoulder to shoulder with sisters in Christ and when the drums started to play the rows would sway together to the music clapping loudly with the rhythm.

The tight seating was uncomfortable for me, but again I had different personal space expectations, so it was to be ignored. There were several times a lady fell asleep with her head on my shoulder and often there was a request for Laura to sit by others. She would sometimes oblige them, but other times we would smile and say she was going to sit by her 'ma'.

When Michael got older, he joined his daddy on the right-hand side with the men and boys. Typically, Perry's student would invite him to sit on the stage behind the pulpit. They would insist Michael go with his 'Pa' and

Michael sitting alone behind the pulpit

provide a chair for him as well. There he sat in front of everyone from the time he was two years old. His blonde hair was a local curiosity and people were undoubtedly distracted. Occasionally he would start swinging his legs or even fall asleep, and it was very cute. What made me nervous was when it was Perry's turn to preach, Michael was essentially unsupervised. I worried if he would cause a disruption, but it never happened.

I enjoyed using my training in the medical field to help neighbors with various ailments. Occasionally, our porch would become a type of treatment area to soak and bandage infections, encourage mothers with babies failing to thrive, or treat children with a deep thorn. I somehow became known for digging out splinters and removing dead skin, so some of the children feared coming to see me. Using numbing jell for teething babies helped to anesthetize the area, making the ordeal more tolerable.

Margaret invited me to teach a class on oral care to the Village Health Care Workers. I enjoyed getting back to my dental hygiene profession and demonstrated how to brush and floss. People did not always have those items, although toothbrushes were available in the markets. I would often see people cleaning their teeth with a stick frayed on one end, so I concentrated on daily cleaning teeth, no matter what type of instrument was used. When a part-time job at the LAMCO dental office was offered, I considered applying for it. It would have meant a long drive and no childcare was available, so in the end, I was content to be a stay-at-home mom, which is an important calling.

The mission handbook called for missionaries to take a yearly vacation, but there was little to do and few places to go. Sometimes we stayed in other missionaries' homes for a change of pace, but when Michael was a baby we decided to get out of the country and flew down the coast to Abidjan, Ivory Coast for vacation.

We treated ourselves to a cold Coke with ice at the airport restaurant and even gave our children a sip. Soon after, our family developed terrible sores in our mouths. While on vacation we were miserable and could hardly eat or talk. We called it "Mung Mouth" and assumed the ice in the coke was contaminated. It took much of the vacation to get over it.

It was interesting to see a country in Francophone Africa. We were surprised by the modern tall buildings, loved the smooth wide roads, and felt the language barrier, not being able to speak French. We stayed in an air-conditioned mission guest house, but it was hot and uncomfortable most of the time. Dogs barked nearby throughout the night, and there were no mosquito nets on the beds, so mosquitoes swarmed us all night.

The kids were sick most of the trip and Laura spiked her infamous 106°F fever. Perry fearfully rushed her by taxi to the hospital, where she was diagnosed with malaria and given an injection of chloroquine and aspirin. She suffered through the night, presumably with some reaction to the medication. When the vacation was over, we were thankful to return home to our humble dwelling in the Bassa jungle.

When it was time for us to purchase a new mission vehicle, Perry and another missionary went to Monrovia only to find our mission's standard white Peugeot station wagon was not available. Due to the Liberian dollar being devalued, the Peugeot dealer had postponed importing vehicles. There was the option to get a Peugeot sedan, but we hauled a considerable amount of fuel and the sedans didn't have the space for tanks.

After shopping around, they found an air-conditioned 4x4 Nissan Patrol and the dealership was offering a discount for the US dollar. This vehicle was certainly a step up from what the other missionaries were driving, although not the first car with AC and the 4x4 option.

Missionaries are a strange breed, and some stated they were not pleased with our new vehicle. It was suggested we should refrain from using the AC, since others did not have it in their vehicles. It seemed there was a mentality that missionaries needed to suffer and suffer alike to be good missionaries. Being thin skinned, I wasted emotional energy considering these comments.

It was a true luxury to have AC in the vehicle. When we arrived some place, we weren't all wet from perspiration, and without the windows rolled down for ventilation, we could enjoy pleasant conversation while driving. In the future, this vehicle would play a role in several potentially serious encounters with officials for both Perry and myself.

Our team of missionaries frequently experienced undue harassment from police and military, including anything from arrests to soliciting bribes. We used to joke that we expected to be pulled over and harassed by police every time we went into Buchanan or Monrovia. Payroll was often not met for men in uniform, so we could hardly blame the officers for seeking money for their families. It was extremely nerve-racking to have someone in uniform pull us over. We never really knew how serious the situation would be, or practically speaking how long it would take.

Checkpoints were set at regular intervals along the paved roads to monitor traffic and all vehicles were required to stop at them. It was a nuisance for those of us accustomed to traveling freely whenever and wherever we so desired. But being guests and temporary residents in Liberia, we had to politely stop and respectfully respond to the officials who were supposedly only doing their jobs.

They normally asked us where we were going and where we were coming from. They had the authority to ask us to get out of the vehicle and search through our belongings. Once I was perturbed when they went rifling through my baby's diaper bag, which really seemed unnecessary. But it was important to hold our tongues and comply. Resisting their authority would only delay our trip.

We understood the businessmen freely offered bribes to hurry the process along, but missionaries throughout the country held together and were in good standing with officials without paying bribes. It seemed we only had to slip in the fact of our missionary status, and we were sent on our way.

There were also times when the officers had reached the end of their shift and needed a ride home. Of course, our half full mission vehicles were more comfortable than a crowded taxi, so in a sense our vehicles would be commandeered.

One day an overwhelmed missionary unfortunately responded in anger to those on duty at a check point in Grand Bassa County. There was no excuse to yell at officials and defiantly drive away knowing the officers were not issued a vehicle to pursue them. From that time on, missionaries endured lengthy interrogations at that gate. We were often delayed for long periods of time, being ignored while cars behind us were waved past to resume their journey.

Perry traveled the main road a lot and caught the brunt of the officials' collective disgust over the incident. They knew he was a "big man" in the mission, so he was taken into headquarters and questioned as to why he was allowing such a volatile person to be part of our mission. His years of travel and genuine good relations with many individuals stationed at the checkpoints was "spoiled", as they say in Liberia, by just one incident when a person lost control and let anger rear its ugly head.

They even suggested Perry beat the person to teach missionaries to show respect. Perry could fortunately tell them the missionary was not technically with our mission, but it mattered not to them. They required his repeated apologies whenever he passed through the area. Their response was that words weren't enough, meaning you pay us a bribe and we'll quit hassling you. After a year passed, mutual respect was renewed, and Perry was again waved through the gates without undue bother. It was a good lesson for us all to learn.

In another road incident, a chance encounter with a drunken soldier brought danger, but also amusement to our lives. We needed to get Michael's US passport finalized, so we took the kids to the embassy in the capital city. Afterwards we met up with Mark and Pat and went in one car to a restaurant. Along the road a soldier with a gun waved us down, and we were obligated to stop.

In the pouring rain he requested a ride but was shocked to see our seemingly empty car was packed with children in car seats. There was no choice but to squeeze into the front seat and I do mean squeeze, since he made the fourth adult on the front bench seat. In the process of getting settled, he handed Perry his M16 rifle and was just able to latch the door, but still some rain came in.

We proceeded on with babies crying in the back, rain pouring down, windows blocked with condensation, and the wipers on extra high. We had only traveled several blocks when the soldier yelled out, "Silence!" However, the babies only cried all the harder. The man held his head and said he had a terrible headache, so he demanded, "Stop!"

He jumped out, slammed the door shut, and started running down the road. We quickly caught up to him with Perry holding his rifle out the door saying, "You forgot something!" The shocked man's face turned several colors as he grabbed his weapon. We continued on our way, but once we were a little way off and felt safe, we exploded with laughter.

The following year we decided to drive to Sierra Leone for our vacation and visit some CR missionary friends across the border. During the trip we found ourselves in a serious situation with Perry almost being thrown in jail.

After spending five hours at the Liberia/Sierra Leone border, the road turned into a little dirt path through the jungle. There was a fear that we had gotten off the main road, except there had been no alternative turnoffs. We then came upon a long, thin stick mounted several feet high across the road with a makeshift hut nearby.

Accustomed to West African road signs, we stopped at the official check point gate. It was manned by stern Sierra Leonean soldiers with guns. They detained us, thoroughly searching our belongings, making us stand at attention, and harassing us. All the while I was aware there was no restroom, and I needed one desperately.

The situation became serious when they threatened to confiscate our vehicle and arrest Perry. Several hours of interrogation passed, while they tried to intimidate us into giving them the vehicle. Although all our vehicle paperwork showed our mission and we were the rightful owners, they accused us of stealing it. They also said the title listed it was a white vehicle, but they maintained it was the wrong documentation since there were red and orange decals across the doors.

Perry held his typical controlled demeanor, politely and respectfully responding to their query. Occasionally our young children would cry or fuss as we stood at attention in the heat and bugs, and the agitated officials would yell "Silence!"

I was fearful and prayerful, and tried not to cry. They threatened to haul Perry off to jail and they tossed out nasty comments about how I'd

then be alone without my husband to defend me. Their intimidation was some of the best we had experienced, but we too were experienced and held our cool, although I had to blink back tears at times. They put up a good front, apparently wanting a new vehicle for their squadron.

Perry finally turned to them. "Gentlemen," he said while taking his pocketknife out of his pocket and twisting the blade up. For a split second I wanted to intervene and tell Perry he couldn't fight the group of soldiers with a short jack-knife. But he continued, "Let's go over to the truck and scrape the sticker off the door. You will see what it looks like then." The soldiers said, "O! No-No don't do that!" and they refused to let Perry remove the decal. Apparently, they didn't want their potential vehicle damaged.

Perry said, "Look at me, do you say I'm a white man?" They agreed he was a white man. "And look, you see I have on a blue shirt, but still you call me a white man. You all have green army clothes, and yet you tell me you're black men. You see, the truck is white, and it has orange clothes."

The fierce soldiers slowly cracked a grin, then broke out in laughter and gave Perry a high five. It was an admirable palaver - won by a clever refute. The white man had made a valid point and come to the point of nearly disfiguring his vehicle.

We were sent on our way, but we were thoroughly shaken by the experience. I said I wanted to turn around and go home, but that meant we would have to travel back past the same check point and soldiers. We decided to continue our journey. All together the 250-mile trip took us twelve hours, including five hours at the border crossing, numerous checkpoints along the way, and terrible road conditions.

The next morning, we finally met our friend, Stan waiting by a dock in a speed boat. Our flashy vehicle was parked in a secure lot with other mission vehicles, and we took off down river in the speed boat. He drove at top speeds for 45 minutes, finally reaching his family's home and place of CR ministry.

They were part of a church planting team among a Muslim tribe on the Atlantic coast. It was a thrill to visit the work there and meet the other missionaries, but again it was even more thrilling to arrive safely home at the end of our vacation.

I planted beautiful hibiscus around our house just by shoving sticks in the ground. In the moist tropical climate, they quickly took root and grew into bushes supplying us with many flowers. The hummingbirds gathered nectar from the blossoms and I often swung my children in the hammock, while we watched the fascinating birds and waited for Daddy to come home.

There was another improvement we decided to make to our mission station and that was to plant an orchard. Looking to the future, it seemed it would be wise to provide a cash crop to help sustain national staff and revenue for the CEFL. We first got the idea when visiting an orchard in our region when my parents were visiting. The expatriate owner had a wide variety of trees, and said he was selling produce for a profit, although getting the fruit to outside markets was often difficult.

It was not easy to find trees for our orchard, but we put the word out. Peter, a CEFL worker, said he had heard the Central Agricultural Experimental Station in Suakoko had fruit trees available. Perry left the next day with the vehicle full of Bassa men interested in agriculture. They were able to purchase 100 trees of orange, cocoa and coffee, but could only get 50 German plum (mango) trees.

The drive north to Suakoko went well, traveling on the main tar roads. For the return trip the men decided to take the straight route home traveling on interior dirt roads with questionable road conditions, and they would get to see some new territory. Their map was not detailed enough, and it was the days before having GPS to guide them, so at every crossroad someone would jump out and ask for directions. They traveled past typical villages and farms, but mostly the orange dirt roadway was disappointedly hemmed in with thick growth of jungle.

When they came to a wide river with an un-improved log bridge, they stopped to take a better look. The bridge inclined to the opposite bank and was supported with huge long round logs on the bottom resting in the dirt. The vehicles drove over planks nailed perpendicular to the logs. As Perry proceeded across the bridge, one of the logs behind them started to slide down the bank, tilting the bridge to one side. It was certainly frightening. It seemed unwise to stop, so he coaxed the vehicle to steadily climb the logs sloped across the river.

Suddenly something flashed across the rear-view mirror. Perry's eyes widened as he watched the top planks fly off the bridge behind them. Evidently when the angle of the bottom logs shifted under the weight of his vehicle, the top slats were sent flying. He increased his speed fearing the bridge would totally collapse.

When they got to the other side he was shaken, so he stopped the truck and got out. His passengers wondered why he had stopped and were astonished to see the entire bridge had collapsed behind them! The bridge was simply gone. "God blessed us-o," was the commonly repeated phrase by the passengers in the truck.

Treacherous bridge crossings weren't uncommon as we traveled through the bush. Several times we came upon questionable bridges where the large support logs had slid down one side of the riverbank. The bridges were rectified by placing another set of logs diagonally from the weak bank to the bridge. It was a challenge to drive across the log bridge and maneuver unto a second set of logs to reach the other side.

Even though taxies and buses used bridges in that condition, it seemed a bit of a risk for us to cross, but a few times there was no choice. The trick was to turn the wheels just at the right time from one set of logs to the next. It was helpful for someone to direct the driver, but we triumphed and made it safely across every time.

My parents' first visit to Liberia was for Christmas when Michael was a baby. The day my parents arrived, I insisted we leave an hour earlier than normal to meet them. I wanted to have the thrill of seeing them step off the plane and didn't want anything to go wrong to cause anxiety on their part. Leaving on time, we were only a short distance down the road when a flat tire developed. There was no spare, so it was necessary to hail a taxi and go back to the mission to get another vehicle.

In the end we arrived at the airport half an hour late. As Perry swung the car around, there were my parents standing outside with a swarm of people around them. My mother had a huge smile on her face and waved to us.

While going through customs, they had met a man whom they called "Chiefy". He was a Liberian man who had clearly been a huge help to them making their way through the airport and was even waiting with them outside. There was none of the usual hassle from baggage carriers, and that was a big clue to us that this man was of some distinction. He had endeared himself to my parents, so we thanked him kindly before beginning our drive home.

My parent's acquaintance turned out to be a man of true integrity, who would later re-enter Perry's life when he was at the port to get mission items cleared through customs. This man kindly recognized Perry and was indeed a type of "chief" at the airport. He opened many doors to quickly process port customs without the usual expectations of under the table bribes. My parents' chance encounter with him and their genuine friendliness to stranger was God's plan to an open door of blessings.

When they arrived, it was a comfortable time of the year for us, yet for them the heat and humidity felt overly oppressive, since their blood was still thick from the winter months. They had left below zero temperatures in South Dakota and arrived to 90° F with equally high humidity. That was nearly a 100-degree shock to their bodies, and the night temperatures falling to 73° F were of little comfort to them.

We had some vacation time to spend, so we took my parents to Nimba County in Northern Liberia. The temperatures were cooler at the higher elevation and we had the fun of watching a Liberian rodeo rounding up cattle. We also visited a leprosarium run by a long-standing mission in the north. How incredibly sad to see the effects of the disease. Some with fingerless hands made beautiful carvings from the native red mahogany and sold them to earn a living.

My mother loved my beautiful "Butterfly" treadle sewing machine which was manufactured in China. It was foot powered and therefore easier to operate than those with a hand crank. The machine was a source of contentment for me until we departed Liberia. Mom and I completed several sewing projects together using foot power.

One day we walked past a store displaying a treadle machine. Before we left town, my parents purchased one still dismantled in a box. They transported it home with them as luggage on the airplane.

The missionaries from several ministries gathered another time at our hut on Silver Beach for the baptism of a missionary child. If we had been on a beach in the States that day, a red flag would have been waving, meaning no swimming allowed due to an unusually strong undercurrent. No such warning system was in place on our African beach, so the situation had to be assessed on our own. Our carload arrived early, and we found the undercurrent was exceptionally strong. In fact, even the men could not stand in water over their waists without being pulled over.

A carload of missionaries drove up, and a couple of older boys jumped out of the car running straight for the irresistible waves. As they ran past, I yelled above the ocean surge, "Don't go out - the undercurrent is very strong and dangerous today!" But, they ran into the deeper water.

Realizing they were headed toward danger, I immediately turned and ran up the beach, yelling to Perry some distance away that the boys were heading out too deep. He took off running for the water and as he dove in, I turned to see the boys already struggling and trying to swim back.

One boy yelled to Perry, "I'm OK, but help him." Indeed, I could see the second boy was already panicking and yelling for help. I gasped as I watched him go down for the first time. Perry saw it too and keeping track of the boy as he swam, counted each of the three times the boy surfaced and went down. Finally reaching the spot where he last saw him, Perry took a deep breath and dove to the ocean bed.

Searching frantically underwater he noticed little puffs of sand on the ocean floor. He followed one after the other and finally came upon the boy's body. He appeared lifeless, not moving at all, but laying on his back, bouncing along the sand floor, and being pulled swiftly feet first by the current.

Perry knew it was his only chance to catch him and swam as hard as possible to get close. He was able to reach out and grab the boy's golden hair in his fist. Pulling the lifeless body towards himself, he gripped the boy under his left arm. Sensing they were now being caught together in the under tow, Perry crouched down and blasted them off the seabed, out of the undertow, and to the surface.

Once above water Perry gasped for air while positioning the limp boy in the towing hold - as he had been repeatedly taught by his instructor, a former member of the Marine Corps. Towing the boy, Perry headed for shore swimming against the strong riptide. As Perry pulled him along, the boy seemed to revive and moved a little, but then became motionless again.

The boy's father met them part way and tried to take his son from Perry, but Perry was trained and confident and had to push the father away. He told him, "No I've got the rescue hold on him and I know what I'm doing." They swam to shore and dragged the boy out of the water.

Once the boy was on the beach, there were differences of opinion on how to proceed. Perry knew exactly what to do. Not only had he been taught well, but he had in fact saved two other people earlier in his life. He lost no time and rolled the boy onto his stomach, pushed on his back, and rolled him back over. Soon the beloved son vomited up sea water from deep within, followed by a gasping for breath. Perry was pleased and said, "He'll be OK now."

Later on the beach, we crowded around to witness the baptism, and thought of the dramatic rescue we had just experienced. It was a picture of Christ rescuing us when we were dead in our sin and separated from God. We rejoiced in His claim on our lives, thankful for Christ dramatically delivering us from the depths of sin.

26

Godly Interventions

Perry's parents made a second trip to visit us. His father, Virgil spent much of his time auditing the ministry's books, and he held enrichment seminars for the CR missionaries. Just before they were to return home, there was an attempted coup d'état in Monrovia to overthrow the president. It was a frightful time and we kept our white faces off the roads and safe at the secluded mission grounds.

Commissioner J. Tah Wah Freeman came to the mission to check on us and said, "This is why I granted you this land and wanted you living a distance off the tar road, you are safe here. It will be best for you to stay here and not go to the car road."

We knew from the radio that the coup was unsuccessful. President Doe was not run out by the rebel army under General Quiwonkpa, who was in fact captured and killed.[26] There were curfews at 6:00 PM each night and the soldiers were restless maintaining order.

At one point we felt fear when semi-automatic rifles were fired in our nearby village. Old Man Pau told us the women and children ran and hid in the bush when the soldiers entered their town. They made a nuisance of themselves ordering people around, but in the end merely confiscated chickens for their dinner.

On the day Perry's parents were scheduled to depart, the radio announced the airport was still closed, but we could not persuade them that their airplane would not be flying - It was simply unthinkable. Local political tensions had lessened, so their son reluctantly indulged them and dared to drive to the airport allowing them to see for themselves. They endured many extra checkpoints manned by stern soldiers. At one point they were required to leave the vehicle and walk in front of the soldiers for inspection.

They all returned shortly thereafter saying the airport was indeed closed, in fact deserted, and guarded by army tanks. Perry's mother was pale and quite disturbed, since she'd seen an army truck near the airport full of dead bodies with arms and legs hanging out. The situation was real, worse than we had thought, therefore we resumed our seclusion at the mission station.

His parents ended up staying nearly two weeks longer than intended, solely due to the airport being closed. We sent messages through amateur radio contacts informing relatives in the States we were alright, and to let Mom and Dad's employers know they were stranded in Africa!

It was during our seclusion that we witnessed a miracle from God. Our neighbor Zah-kpá was an older man, who had spent his life as the village basket weaver and blacksmith. The talent of finding iron ore in the hills had been passed down to him, and he had made a little smelter to refine it.

I had placed several custom orders for baskets with him, and I still use the iron hoe he made for gardening. Another order for bamboo sleeping mats took two attempts, but he finally gave in to my peculiar measurements and made some unusually long ones according to my specifications. They were hung in our piazza for shade from the blazing sun. The mats were quite the conversational piece when village people visited and watched us roll them to the ceiling by simply pulling a cord.

Perry's mother worked in a doctor's office and watched me treat Zahkpa for an arm infection. He had also sought healing from the local witch doctor, who packed it with mud mixed with dung. When the infection became severe, he returned to our house for help. Perry told him to step outside and remove the country medicine. I then washed and soaked the wound, treated it with antibiotic ointment, bandaged it, and sent him to the doctor in Buchanan. The arm began to heal, but shortly thereafter we received word that he was once again quite ill, and we were asked to visit him at his house.

Zahkpa demonstrating basket weaving

Assuming his arm was again infected, Perry and I went to check on Zahkpa while Grandpa and Grandma stayed home with the kids. Since we were sequestered on the mission, we made our way down the back path past the mission well. From there we could ascertain if the village was safe to enter.

There seemed to be no soldiers, so we visited Zahkpa laid up in his sparsely furnished house. As we stepped in his room there was a heavy stench in the air. He told us he couldn't walk due to sores on the soles of his feet. Using a flashlight in the dimly lit mud home, we could see two holes so deep his bones were visible. The skin around the area was awful looking, and explained the source of the rotten smell.

Zahkpa's family wanted us to take him to the hospital, but Perry explained we couldn't go out on the road, since soldiers were edgy and had recently shot up cars at the nearby police gate. We prayed with him for God's healing and told him he should not put country medicine on it. Later, I had Browne take some clean bandages and Epsom salt to him, giving him instructions for how to soak his feet.

Early the next morning, we were shocked to hear Zahkpa yelling as he walked up the gravel driveway with bare feet. He rushed up the steps to our piazza, threw himself onto a chair, and held his feet up in the air. It was amazing - the holes in his feet were gone, his soles looked as if nothing had happened! We were unnecessarily shocked - hadn't we prayed for

God to heal his feet?

"I bless you, I bless you - you healed me!" he exclaimed.

We emphatically told him, "No! We didn't heal you. We can't heal people. We prayed to God, and He healed you. Only God can heal like that!" Acts 3:16 describes a similar situation: *And his name [Jesus] – by faith in his name – has made this man strong whom you see and know, and the faith that is through Jesus has given the man this perfect health in the presence of you all.*

Zahkpa had not been a man to go to church, but after experiencing this healing, praise God, he started attending the local church.

Perry witnessed another answer to prayer when he and Joe, a fellow missionary, made a short walk to a church conference. As they passed through the village, they noticed a large group of people gathered in a kitchen looking at a man's hand. Joe was immediately drawn to the situation and went to see what was going on.

The man's hand was grossly swollen, looking like a catcher's mitt with no fingers. Joe told Perry, "We have to pray for this man," and he intensely prayed out loud for God's healing. Perry and Joe then left and attended a session at the conference just up the path.

When they returned about two hours later, the man was still the center of attention. But this time the people were marveling at the change that had taken place. As Joe and Perry broke through the crowd, they too were amazed to see the man's hand had greatly deflated to nearly normal size. It was truly amazing!

Joe noticed part of a thorn imbedded at the base of the thumb. He pulled it out with his fingernail, and pus gushed out. Undoubtedly this was the reason for the hand swelling, but the rate at which the swelling decreased was truly an act of God in answer to Joe's prayer.

God's miraculous protection was certainly extended to our children. It was pointed out to us again when Perry and I were working with the mission ground keepers. The jungle had a way of slowly creeping into our yard, and we were attempting to push the borders back again with sharp cutlasses in hand.

It was one of those very hot days, so Laura and Michael were stripped down to underwear and diaper. They were playing with their little wicker chairs in the shade of a palm tree, but suddenly picked them up and moved some distance away. The chairs were a struggle for them to carry, so I wondered what made my babies decide to move out of the shade and into the hot sun.

Suddenly my question was answered when a large black hooded cobra dropped from the tree branches to the very spot where our children had been playing! The Bassa workers sprang upon the long cobra and chopped it into pieces, saying "That snake is bad-o, we can't even eat it."

I thought of the verse from Isaiah 11:8, *The nursing child shall play over the hole of the cobra, and the weaned child shall put his hand into the adder's den.* Clearly God, who was our shield and protector, had sent His angels to usher our children to safety.

Letters home show that both our children endured prolonged illnesses with many things from ear infections to malaria, and Laura continued spiking 106° temperatures with a multitude of ailments.

Taa & Browne with Michael at rice harvest

Michael too entered a dangerous stretch of un-known illnesses and endured a spinal tap to check for meningitis. Normally this procedure is done under sterile conditions, however Perry was asked to assist by holding his son down on a dirty, bloody ER bed. I quickly grabbed a lappa from my bag and inserted it under my child. Then, I was discharged from the curtained off area to maintain a sterile environment. In the end, one-year old Michael was diagnosed with a simple case of malaria. Here again we know for certain that our Heavenly Father was protecting our family from further harm.

While our children were young and Perry was gone for several days, I found myself quite ill with severe pain in my lower right abdomen. I used our excellent resource book "Where There is No Doctor" to assess my symptoms and was alarmed to learn I was most likely having an appendicitis attack. The book said to seek medical attention immediately. I found it hard to believe at first, but the pain grew steadily worse. Apparently, I needed to face the facts and make a plan.

This happened on a Saturday, so Browne and the mission yard workers were not around to assist me. My young children and I were home alone without a car. I contemplated walking down the driveway to the tar road and hailing a taxi to go to ELWA hospital, but I honestly couldn't walk that far in such pain. I was finding it difficult to walk down the hall to the bedroom to check on the children.

I reasoned someone would eventually pass on the path. I would ask them to charter a taxi for me from the road and have it come up the driveway to get me and the kids. Most taxis passing by on the road were already full, so God would have to provide three seats for us.

Strangely, not a soul passed on the highly used African path near my kitchen window. The mission was eerily quiet, not even a breeze moved the leaves, and my children were uncommonly quiet enjoying each other's company for a prolonged time. I felt as though time was standing still while the pain increased.

In the quiet I prayed fervently that someone would come and help me - suddenly a car appeared at the bottom of the driveway. As it approached the house, I could see it was a carload of missionaries I knew. But, the car stopped in the middle of the mission and stayed there a distance from the house. It seemed they would drive away without greeting us, so I limped outside and waved them over to me unable to go any further.

I told them I was home alone for a couple of days with my children and in extreme pain. I was quite sure I was having an appendicitis attack and needed help to get to the hospital. Incredibly, they told me they couldn't take us, since they had no room in their car. They had just stopped to show their guests the beautiful mission station. They stated they were on vacation and hadn't intended to "bother" us, adding they were not heading towards the hospital.

I was shocked but did not panic – I said nothing more, I did not plead. I should have insisted they help me and make them realize I was in a serious situation. Perhaps I was too astonished by their selfish response. They suggested I get a taxi and said good-bye. I said nothing, but simply let them drive away, taking my hopes of rescue with them. Perhaps God had someone else in mind to help me - how could I have dared to take that chance?

Tears of panic flooded out as I limped back in the house and knelt on the living room floor with my hands stretched to heaven. I cried and pleaded with God in loud whispers, so I wouldn't frighten the children. "Please have mercy on me and my children. You know what is wrong with me, is it not your desire for me to go to the hospital? If I pass out the children are too young to be alone! Perry will not be home for days, and I can't reach anyone on the mission radio. You know all this, You know what is wrong, You know what I need! Heavenly Father, what is your plan? May it be your will to please heal me now! Now Lord!"

"Mommy?" Laura came to see what the commotion was about. I reassured her I was praying, and incredibly she accepted that. I asked her to go back to her room, lie down with her brother, and take a nap. Much to my surprise they obeyed without hesitation. I prayed until I was exhausted, then laid on the couch for some time praying and weeping, then I must have fallen asleep.

I awoke suddenly and noticed the pain had greatly subsided and later it finally disappeared altogether, except for a sore spot remaining for some days. I thanked God for answering my prayers but was never certain of what was wrong. I thought I must have misdiagnosed myself and I wondered - had it really been that bad?

Roughly ten years later, a surgeon marched into my hospital room after surgery pushing the door shut behind him. He seemed angry at me. "So! You think you're a pretty tough cookie and can tolerate pain!"

I fearfully nodded, "Yes". Silently I searched my memory and it was true, I was tough and had endured several different types of overwhelming pain in my life.

The doctor continued, "Your appendix ruptured in the past and obviously you didn't seek medical help. It was a mess for me to clean up. You're lucky you didn't die from it! When you have pain like that go to the doctor."

Shocked, I recalled my pain in Liberia and quickly told him the story from my past. In the end the doctor told me he was sorry for what had happened. He was a Christian man and thanked God with me for saving my life when I was home alone with young children.

I asked the doctor if the long-term penicillin injections I was receiving at the time (as a repercussion of rheumatic fever leaving scar tissue on my heart valve) would have warded off such an infection, and he thought it could have. Perry had providentially given me that monthly injection just before he left. Unfortunately, the scar tissue the appendicitis left behind causes difficulty in my life. As my mother has taught me, it is a thorn in the flesh reminding me of God's faithfulness and His personal answer to my prayers.

Often People don't believe us when we say Perry was struck by lightning twice and lived to tell about it, but I must add it to the account of God's miracles. Although the hits were indirect strikes, still they were quite dangerous and had enough power to kill.[27] The first incident occurred one day during a torrential downpour. Perry ran about 100 yards home from his office for lunch. He safely reached the house, but was drenched, so he went to the bedroom to get dry clothes. I was folding laundry by the bed and he came in the bedroom dripping water on the floor. He stood next to the light switch, which didn't have a face plate.

Suddenly there was a bright flash of nearby lightning followed by a very loud crack. Simultaneously, I saw bizarre blue "fingers" burst out of the light switch and strike him. Perry yelled and leaped backwards landing against the wall. There was a red mark on his back where I'd seen the fingers zap him, and the light switch was blackened with an electrical stench in the air. It was remarkable that Perry was OK, other than being shook up.

The second encounter with lightning involved our children when they were older. Perry and the kids were caught in a downpour while walking home. He picked up Michael, being the younger of the two, and they ran for home. There were lightning strikes all around and they were thankful to reach the house safely.

I had unplugged the mission radio, a common precaution, and laid the coax across the kitchen counter. Perry was still holding Michael and standing in a puddle of dripping water when the radio antenna received a jolt of lightning. The electricity traveled down the coax, and again leapt with a flash of blue fingers zapping Perry's arm and Michael.

Laura also felt a shock since she was standing nearby in the same puddle of water. They all screamed and yelled yet escaped basically unscathed. The bottoms of Perry's feet were burned, and again a red mark appeared on his arm where the flash had been discharged. Certainly, our radio for communicating with the other missionaries would have been damaged if it had still been attached.

Some Godly interventions we recognize right away, while others may happen unaware. It is our Heavenly Father who watches over us, and it was God who protected us many times from unknown sources with possible tragic outcomes. Matthew 10:29-31, *Are not two sparrows sold for a penny? And not one of them will fall to the ground apart from your Father. But even the hairs of your head are all numbered. Fear not, therefore; you are of more value than many sparrows.*

27

Missionary Life

Several new and important responsibilities were added to our already overwhelming schedule. Perry was honored to be unanimously voted as chaplain for the CEFL. In this capacity he became privy to the interpersonal relationships within the Bassa churches, settling disputes, giving advice, and visiting pastors when they were ill.

I remember several times when a precious day off with family was interrupted by a carload of church leaders driving out from Buchanan to have Perry mediate their differences of opinion. The leader of the Bassa pastors remarked to me that Perry's role as a chaplain was exceptional because he could see through cultural differences and offer sound advice.

The distance we felt from our families didn't diminish as time went on. In fact, we felt it more acutely. Three of my siblings married without me being able to travel home for their weddings, a fact which even now brings tears to my eyes. Two of our grandfathers died and were buried in our absence, and our children were growing from babies to young children without really knowing their grandparents or other family members.

To partially remedy the separation, Perry renewed his study to become proficient with Morse code, and finally received a short-wave ham radio license becoming an amateur radio operator. To achieve this, he took a test on radio theory and a second proficiency test on Morse code, which was deemed more difficult. He successfully deciphered 13 words or 65 characters of Morse code in one minute to pass the test and was awarded the call sign EL1AG. He purchased a ham radio in Monrovia, but then the tricky and difficult task of constructing an antenna began.

His short-wave antenna consisted of three parts. Each part was made from thin bamboo poles in the shape of an "X". They supported three graduated squares of strung wire. The middle square was the actual antenna with each side ten feet long. The largest back square was called the reflector antenna, and the front was the director. It focused the signal to obtain a stronger signal.

It was quite a feat to erect the large, ungainly antenna on a pole in our back yard. Browne always laughed so hard recalling how he and I were to hold ropes while the antenna was rotated into the air. We were instructed to not let go, no matter what.

On the first attempt to rotate the contraption up, the pipe suddenly bent at the pivot point. When the tension unexpectedly released, Browne and I were sent skiing on our back sides across the muddy yard. The Bassa neighbors standing around watching said it was the funniest thing they had ever seen as we went sliding past them. It was not that funny to me because it was a huge disappointment and my legs were filled with cuts and coated with thick mud from sliding across the ground in a skirt.

Eventually the pivot was reinforced, and the antenna was installed successfully. Then, Perry began the painstaking job of tuning it by lengthening and shortening the wires. Finally, everything was just right, and he became an actual ham operator sending his messages across the air!

What a joy it was for him to use the short-wave radio from our living room in the jungle. He would send out a request across the waves searching for a ham operator in the States who could make a phone patch.

Technology was somewhat archaic in the 1980's, so we had to get our ham call attached to a telephone. A helpful ham operator in the States would dial our parent's number, but it was necessary for a telephone operator to intervene, so we could request a collect call. (We had to pay for long distance calls in those days.) If someone was home, they would then accept the charges, and finally we would be able to talk. It was necessary to say "over" each time we completed our part of the conversation and sometimes the quality was quite distorted, but it was a true wonder and blessing to talk with family back home.

Unfortunately, it was quite rare to have this opportunity. Atmospheric conditions had to be just right, the signal had to be strong enough with an operator in the States, and lastly family had to be home to answer their phone.

Early on we had a good laugh when a ham operator in the States found a catchy name to go with Perry's call sign letters, EL1AG. "EL" is Liberia's call prefix, so the operator named him "Liberia's One African Gorilla". Ham operators usually had a catchy name to go with their call signs, so we had been trying to come up with something unique. The African Gorilla name stuck, being recognized by other operators in the States.

We also became involved with opening a clinic in our immediate area. Since there was no local medical care, Commissioner Freeman asked our mission to establish a clinic at the Number 1 Government Compound. CEM responded that they didn't set up clinics. A trained physician's assistant then moved into the area and began a "black bagging" business, going from village to village treating people.

Still there was a heartfelt need for a clinic, so under the guidance of Kathy, who lived with us at #1 and was our mission's community developer, a committee of church representatives was formed in our area. The purpose of the committee was to start a Christian clinic. CEM then approved one since a local committee would be in place to manage it. They hired the local black bagger as the acting PA after he gave an impressive interview.

The clinic not only functioned as a place for sick people in the area. It also assisted the locally trained Village Health Workers and Traditional Birth Attendants in several ways. They could refer patients to the clinic for further care, and they were also able to purchase and replenish their medications at the clinic's pharmacy. Since it was no longer necessary for me to provide medications from our home, I missed my contacts with them.

Clinic staff included the PA, a person trained to fill prescriptions, and another person who handled the money. At first the clinic was only open one day a week. It was around this time that Rick and Kathy and their little boy Nathan left Liberia for a new opportunity and a teaching fellowship in the States. Our mission compound seemed quite lonely with their empty house sitting on the hill, and the Bassa people were also sad to have them leave.

Handling the money at the clinic and making the books balance was an overwhelming job for the clinic's clerk. He was the only suitable applicant for the job but lacked experience and training. Since Kathy had moved away and was no longer available to assist him, the clerk asked if I would help him sort out the financial records.

He arrived one hot afternoon and we sat on the piazza going through the books while sipping cold lemonade. As we concentrated pouring over the accounts, it seemed to be getting dark in the middle of the day, making it more and more difficult to see the numbers on the page. We leaned forward trying to see the figures written down. That's strange I thought, the sun shouldn't be going down yet and there wasn't a cloud in the sky.

I looked up and startled to see the light of the sun was blocked by swarming driver ants covering the screened walls. It was obvious our home was being silently invaded. The ants were even crawling on the ceiling. It would be impossible for us to continue our session. The clerk taking it all in stride gathered his papers, excused himself, and said he would be back another time. I noticed as he walked through the screen door many ants fell on him, and he was occupied with picking them off as he walked down the driveway.

Our attempts to rectify the clinic books had come to an end. It reminded me of a Bassa proverb our Bassa father had told us: "Pee-nyuehn ni se hwio xwadaum - Night must come to end the pleasures of the day." To the Bassa this meant that just as everybody must go home when the night comes, so also something that is useful to the community can be brought to an end by something or someone not so worthy.[28] In this case, the massive ant invasion was the something not so worthy, and it had brought to an end something useful for the community clinic.

The ant invasion was full blown. The front half of the house was black with a wave of driver ants, so it would be futile to spread a kerosene border around it. That would only lock them in the house, a lesson I had learned from the past. I quickly grabbed a few overnight essentials, dismissed Browne with a paid day off, and got the children out the back door just ahead of the swarming ants.

We drove to the end of the driveway where Perry was working in his office and informed him, "Drivers are invading the house, let's go to Buchanan." He finished up a little office work while the children played in the nearby palaver hut, and we took an impromptu trip to Buchanan spending the night in our mission guest house. Returning home the next day, there was no evidence of the ants' invasion, and as anticipated we found they had purged the entire house of any bugs and cockroaches - that was the advantage of a driver ant invasion.

Since we lived near the clinic, it was a chance for me to get involved and use my training and experience in dental offices to help the new clinic run smoothly. One day the staff was complained there was no clean water, no good water source in the immediate area, and no money to dig a well.

Telling them I had a solution, I went home and brought back a big plastic barrel and a small plastic pail, which fit perfectly in the barrel's top opening and could hand in the inside on the top rim. I told the staff we were going to make a water filter, and it would clean the water from a nearby slough.

They had no experience with a filter, so it was a totally new concept for them. Using a jack knife, I proceeded to make a small hole in the bottom of the bucket. Then I cut a round circle from an old rubber inner tube and made a small opening in the middle to form a washer.

They all watched carefully when I pulled a "candle' filter out of the box. It was a manufactured semi-porous stone about two and a half inches thick and six inches long used to filter water. I inserted the threaded end of the candle into the rubber washer and through the hole in the bucket. A nut fastened below the pail held the candle in the middle of the plastic bucket and secured a waterproof union.

Using the same method, we also installed a valve in the lower side of the plastic barrel. I carefully washed the barrel and bucket with bleach water. Then I hung the bucket inside the barrel, with the top of the bucket hanging on the top lip of the barrel and put the lid on it.

The staff laughed when I told them we'd put muddy water from the marsh in the bucket, and the result would be filtered water clean enough to drink. In fact, they were half mad and rebuffed my idea of having them use dirty water.

The fact that our family was using the same method in our house and drank the water seemed to soften them some. I filled the bucket with slough water and waited. There was a slow dripping sound on the inside, but the staff said it would never work and simply walked away to resume their duties. I had other responsibilities too, so I took my children home.

The next day I ventured back to the clinic and the PA came bounding out the door. "Missy", he said "We have clean water, let me show you." He proceeded to carefully explain step by step how to assemble a water filter, and yes, he had learned the lesson well. He had even discovered how to brush sediment off the candle so it would work more efficiently.

God's grace, we met this PA again twenty-five years later. He was still faithfully ministering to his people as director of Bassaland CEM clinics.

CEM opened another clinic in a remote area north of us. Perry and other CEM staff filled our truck and drove the distance for the opening ceremony. Shortly thereafter everyone from our vehicle, including even the Liberians, came down with similar symptoms of low fever, reduced appetite, nausea, and vomiting. One of the missionaries went to the LAMCO clinic and it was confirmed he was suffering from hepatitis, so we figured everyone had the same thing. Later, their eyes and skin turned yellow, and stools were pale.

Upon the diagnosis, I immediately changed Perry's diet to no fat and had him eat mostly boiled oatmeal. He was sick, but it wasn't the worst case among those who had traveled together. We always supposed Perry had contracted hepatitis and expected it was type "A", which is food borne, but we were wrong. Twenty-five years later it nearly cost him his life, which happens in the last chapter.

Our day to day existence at the mission included visits from the Bassa children in the nearby town. They were in the habit of coming Sunday afternoons when I taught Sunday School for my children. I provided a snack and used flannel graph figures, which the missionary wives shared.

When village children came to play, they showed Laura and Michael how to tie baby dolls on their backs, eat raw palm nuts, and sleep on the floor, only to be awakened when someone crowed like a rooster. Laura treated them to tea parties with her toy dishes and had them play church, encouraging everyone to sing as loud as possible. Michael shared his Tonka truck and the boys moved dirt in the yard while Browne surveyed the area for snakes.

It was through these daily encounters that our children learned Bassa, and sometimes understood Bassa better than Perry and I did. They even developed their own little language between the two of them using a mixture of Bassa and Liberian English. Unfortunately, after our relocation to the States, they teamed up and decided to quit talking Bassa, and we could not persuade them otherwise.

We were always surprised when Bassa people would ask us if Laura was a "ma" or "ga", boy or girl. This would often happen when we visited Perry's students' churches and Laura would be dressed in a pretty dress and have pig-tails in her hair. I asked the ladies in my town why people didn't know she was a girl. They responded, "Well, of course it's because you didn't bore her ear." From then on Laura wanted earrings, and the next

Laura with her pet goat

time we went to the States she got her ears pierced at the age of five.

While Michael was still young, our family somehow became the dreaded hosts to some nasty pests – scabies. This is a highly contagious skin parasite that is incredibly itchy. The little female mites burrow into the skin and deposit eggs and excrement. After a couple weeks red itchy, pencil-thin trails can sometimes be seen due to a person's allergic reaction. The itchy rashes usually appear between fingers, around the wrists, elbows and abdomen and the irritation seemed to intensify during the night. To get rid of them everyone in the family must be treated at the same time and everything laundered at high temperatures.[27]

Our scabies episode began at the onset of rainy season. This was significant because putting sheets, towels, clothing and everything else in the hot African sun was not possible, nor was a clothes dryer available. With the torrential rains coming, there was little sunshine and eventually it seemed every bed and all our clothes became infested with scabies and an opportunity for re-infestation. The mites can live for a couple days on surfaces, so we placed as many items as possible in plastic bags for a week to exterminate the scabies.

Whenever anyone entered our home, I had to humbly announce that we had scabies. To the Bassa guests, we simply said we were embarrassed. That was the only explanation needed. People startled at the revelation, and few desired to stay for a lengthy visit. Guests were directed to sit on particular wicker chairs, which I promised were uninfected having been reserved solely for guests.

During rainy season, we took the treatment for scabies and I devised a plan to rid my house of this "embarrassment". I carefully bagged certain items in our house and boiled our sheets and clothes. Even finding garbage bags was difficult. It was an unnecessary luxury, but we finally found some in the capital city.

Unfortunately, it was impossible to stop the chain of infestation and we did not completely rid ourselves of them until dry season returned - enduring several months of sleeplessness due to the intense nocturnal itching. I was concerned that our steward would contract scabies, but that problem was satisfactorily avoided.

One day we sensed the "mid-dry" in the rainy season was upon us, and the sun promised to shine for a length of time. This would create enough heat to eradicate the critters. My steward quickly got all the chairs, cushions, mattress pads and towels out to the bright sun for the day. Our infested clothes and bedding were boiled and hung in the sun to dry, and each person in our family was treated with benzyl benzoate. All the work and organization were rewarded with success, and from then on we were scabies free. Hallelujah!

Folding clothes one day in my bedroom, I distinctly heard a smacking and chewing sound. I looked at the window thinking someone was watching me while eating something chewy like sugar cane. It would have been unusual for someone to be bold enough to gawk in the bedroom window. People did look in kitchen windows, but not in bedrooms. However, no one was there. I listened again. Yes, there was a definite munching noise. I found the kids playing nicely in the next room and they were not eating anything.

Back in the bedroom I followed the chewing noise to the shelf where my folded clothes were placed. The sound seemed to expose a hidden world of people chewing juicy bubble gum, how strange! But then - how maddening! Moving my clothes aside, I discovered termites! They had cleverly hidden tunnels up the board shelving and were feasting on my cotton underwear. Though exposed they fearlessly continued their destruction and smacking their juicy jaws.

A careful search of adjoining rooms uncovered termites in the children's books, and even their clothes. They had no doubt entered through a crack in the floor. What a terrible mess it was to clean up after termites. They had manufactured mud to make tunneled trails everywhere leaving deep grooves in some of the moldings and wooden furniture.

Following the termite trails outside, we found their cone shaped mound in the jungle nearby. Driver ants often took up residence in abandoned termite hills, which were built above ground up to six feet tall with extensive tunnels for ventilation. There was a dangerous element to them since snakes like the green mamba often made their homes in them. The best way to destroy their colony was by tearing down the mound and removing the queen. The termite queen typically lived below ground level in a secure, mud-layered, football shaped cocoon.

Considering both driver ants and termites had made recent invasions of our home, we decided to slow their progress. While I was preparing dinner that day, Perry came to the house for matches explaining he was going to burn the termite mound and destroy their colony. This sounded reasonable to me.

Shortly thereafter I was alarmed by a series of loud explosions coming from different areas around the mission and even from the nearby jungle. I went running outside and found Perry with a happy, yet shocked, grin on his face. He explained he had poured a good amount of gasoline on the offending termite hill and letting it soak had gone to the house for matches.

He lit one, threw it on the mound and KABOOM! The termite hill exploded with fire. Several seconds later there were other deep explosions around our yard where termite hills had formerly stood. It was fascinating to think the mounds were connected with underground tunnels and the gas fumes had traveled through them creating the chain response! After the bombing incident Perry no longer used gasoline, considering tunnels could have been under our house and caused an explosion too close to home.

Another pest more dangerous than termites or ants tried to invade our home as well and we unknowingly carried it in the house. It wasn't unusual to purchase a large stalk or bunch of bananas along the roadside, in the market, or from a salesman at my door. The many "hands" or groups of bananas would ripen at a nice pace for our family and guests to consume.

Picture a long stalk of bananas hanging from a hook in the ceiling with yellow bananas on the top and greener ones at the bottom. My steward warned me against hanging the bananas in the house saying simply it wasn't a good idea.

It took a while for anything to happen, but eventually the danger of hanging bananas caught up with me. One rainy morning I sleepily flipped pancakes, luxuriously using my inside stove and cooking gas. Suddenly and without knowing why - I began to scream. Almost as an afterthought, I noticed a huge hairy spider on my kitchen wall. It was the size of my hand with the fingers spread out, and Perry immediately went after it with a flyswatter, which seemed flimsy compared to the spider. The thing began to take enormous jumps on its spring-loaded legs, and we bounded around the room after it, while the kids laughed at the fun.

Perry was disposing of it when Browne walked up to the house. And then the scolding began, "I told you to not have bananas in the house. Any kind of thing can live in the big bunch of bananas." With that he grabbed the stalk of bananas and hung them in my outside kitchen.

From then on, that's where stalks of bananas were hung. Travelers on the African path were not the only ones who would notice them and request a handout. One night we heard something slobbering over the ripe bananas. Half afraid it was a dangerous wild bush cow, Perry shown the flashlight through the window, and we saw beautifully colored fruit bats helping themselves and slobbering over the readily available fruit. After that, it was always a quandary where to store the bananas. In the end, I harvested each "hand" as they began to ripen, washed them, and took them in the house to avoid attracting bats.

A discovery decades later would reveal fruit bats were the natural hosts of the Ebola virus, although the disease first appeared in 1976. The virus for hemorrhagic fever is transmitted through body fluids of bats or primates to humans resulting in high casualty rates.[29] Praise God, He undoubtedly protected us from such a disease.

There were times when we craved food from the States. In particular, I loved Grape Nuts cereal. I loved the crunchy nuggets for breakfast and often missed it in the morning. Once Perry came home from the capital city with a wonderful find – a box of Grape Nuts!

Laura and Michael with local girls
Notice bananas hanging outside

I disciplined myself to wait until the morning to eat them and made a fresh batch of powdered milk to sit in the frig overnight, since it was much better that way. In the morning I sat down to breakfast with the bowl of cereal, not minding a little musty smell coming from the box, we were used to that in humid Liberia.

I took my first bite trying to ward off the musty flavor but looking into the bowl noticed the carcasses of bugs and worms beginning to float to the top of the milk. Disgusted and sorely disappointed I had to spit everything out. Funny how I never craved Grape Nuts again. I also loved Butterfinger candy bars, which ended in disaster upon the discovery of worms tunneling through it.

One day I decided to use the electric hand mixer and hooked up an inverter to change battery power to AC so it would work. With the kids standing on chairs to see the mixer work, I turn it on only to have cockroaches hiding in the interior splattered everywhere. How repulsive, of course that kitchen appliance was never used again.

Growing up in South Dakota had not afforded me much, if any, contact with African Americans. When we went to live in Africa suddenly the tables were turned. I was then seen as a rarity, since other white people were not common. One advantage was that it was always easy to find Perry's white face in a crowd. He also stood above a crowd, since Bassa people were not overly tall.

It was a surprise then for me to look out my kitchen window one day and think, "Wow, that's a very tall person walking up the driveway. I haven't seen such a tall person in a long time." When the man came to the door, I startled realizing he was Caucasian. Apparently, I had come a long way from my sheltered childhood, to then becoming so accustomed to seeing African people that the skin color was completely escaping me, and I was glad for it.

The white man at the door introduced himself as a Peace Corps volunteer from our home state of South Dakota. He had somehow heard that we were from the same state and wanted to meet us. He spent the weekend at our home, playing with our children, and enjoying western food. But when we prayed before meals, he did not pray with us, only looked straight ahead. He told us he didn't believe as Christians do, but of course we enjoyed his company anyway.

It was impressive to hear of the many community projects under his care. He had taught children in the public schools, had classes for adults to learn to read, dug wells, put in latrines, and encouraged people to use them. It was fun to compare notes with him and learn how he was accomplishing everything, but it seemed there was something empty about it. He was giving humanitarian aid, whereas our team of missionaries were supplying those things coupled with the gospel of Christ, spiritual training, and fellowship.

One day a TEE student of Perry's invited us to a baptism, which ended in an alarming manner. After first worshiping at his church, we slowly walked a path to the river singing church songs to the beat of the drums. At the riverbed the new believers lined up in proximity, customarily almost touching chest to back. They ceremoniously wore white clothing for such a holy day and maintained a prayerful attitude as they waited.

The pastor went first into the river wading up stream where he planted a tall wooden cross. He said a short prayer there, then waded downstream planting a similar cross, and prayed there as well. Perry explained later that the crosses and prayers were to keep out any river spirits.

As each new believer entered the water, they were baptized in the customary manner. With the help of their pastor, they leaned backwards while plugging their nose, and the pastor dipped them completely in the water before helping them get upright. But what happened to many of them when they reached the shore scared me and was most unexpected.

Some of the people threw themselves on the ground where they screamed, yelled, convulsed, and seemed almost incoherent. One young man even foamed at the mouth. People didn't seem to take much notice of this, and in fact kept their distance except to push the wet believers with a long pole to keep them from hurting themselves or rolling back into the river. My children became frightened and began to cry, so I carried them away from the strange responses and we waited in the car.

The pastor later clarified that the people were experiencing demons leaving their physical body. When they were baptized into Christ, His Holy Spirit filled them, and the demons had to leave, sometimes unwillingly.

Spectators didn't want to be close to the newly baptized for fear the spirits would jump into them. He further explained as Christians we don't have to worry about that happening, since we are filled with the Holy Spirit which is stronger than any other thing in the spiritual world.

He commented that people were always anxious about what would happen after they were baptized, and whether a demon would make a scene while exiting. On the other hand, witnessing an exorcism often encouraged people to become Christians and be baptized. After all, who would want to have such a horrible thing dwelling inside?

Each Christmas we anticipated a special time with our neighbors in the village. No, we didn't bake them cookies, although they would have enjoyed a special sweet treat. Each year on Christmas Day we went to the village with an overloaded wheelbarrow of rice, cans of oil, and bags of smoked fish to distribute to our neighbors.

We explained to them that we gave them gifts, since Jesus came to Earth to reclaim His Kingdom which opposes hunger, sickness and sin. On Christ's birthday we didn't want anyone in our village to be physically hungry or needy because that is what He would want. Perry also carried money in his pocket and those without meat at their house got enough change to buy some fresh fish. I saved large powdered milk tins or cans throughout the year and gave each household one full of rice. Some years we also gave out clothes and flip flops.

Perry and I hosted a CEM Christmas party one year for all missionaries and Liberian staff and their spouses. We decorated our back patio with a palm branch wall and Christmas lights. Everyone came dressed in their finest and it was a wonderful time of great memories with our brothers and sisters in Christ.

We were thrilled when Gil and Jan, from Perry's home church came to Liberia. They were a connection with home, even though they would live three hours away in the Vai area on the other side of Monrovia. CR missionaries were evangelizing the area and had requested a teacher for their children. Jan had volunteered for the position and took a year off from teaching elementary school.

Gil was a professor of ornithology (the study of birds) at Sioux Falls University and planned a sabbatical project while they lived in Liberia. He did a significant study of the pesky rice birds, which would fly in and destroy a rice field in no time.

Liberian family members had to spend incredible amounts of time from sunup until sundown in their rice fields shooting the little rice birds with slingshots. After studying the situation, Gil designed a bird cage easily woven by the local people. The trick was to catch a rice bird, keep it

Delivering rice and Christmas gifts to our village.

alive, and put it in the cage. The little yellow birds were so gregarious they would attract others to enter the cage with them, and thus be caught. It was a simple, good solution, unfortunately I am not aware if it was adopted by the people.

Gil and Jan came to visit us just before an annual TEE conference, so we invited them to attend the opening worship service. Perry was the chair of the conference planning committee, so it was exciting for them to see a small part of his work.

When we arrived at the conference, excitement was very high among the students as they anticipated the fellowship and teaching ahead of them. We all packed in the hot humid church with no room to spare. Somehow Jan and I got separated on the women's side of the church. When the music started, people jumped to their feet to worship God. Everyone sang and clapped enthusiastically, and each row swayed together.

I was not sure how Gil and Jan might react to African worship. What would they think of sending missionaries who were swaying and clapping to the music of drums in church?

I looked back at Jan and saw the biggest grin on her face. Tears came to my eyes as I watched her standing side by side with exuberant African sisters. There was no choice for her but to sway with her row to the tempo of the African drums. Those next to her were singing and clapping, and none of them minded her clapping was a little off beat. The head tie we had struggled to get properly on her head was already hanging at an angle, but she was worshipping God like she had never done before.

Gil and Perry sat on the front platform and had cooler seats since they weren't sandwiched shoulder to shoulder with their neighbors. Gil too had the happiest look on his face, clapping to the rhythm and absorbing all that he could.

How wonderful it is to worship in another culture and experience their unique forms of praising God. What a wonderful God we have! He created so many different people and cultures, He sent us the Bible which is applicable to every people group, and He is pleased to accept the wide variety of worship they offer Him.

28

Devil Country

★*Discretion is needed - This chapter may not suitable for children.*

Browne came to the house one morning stating that everyone in the village was greatly alarmed and seriously afraid of the "Heart People". They were reportedly running a campaign at night to harvest beating hearts for their society business. Everyone was told to be certain their doors and shutters were locked, and not go outside after dark.

There was even the fear that the heart people would break down the mud walls of houses to get to their victims. Browne said, "You know, our houses are not so strong like your house with cement walls. This is Devil Country and the heart people will be out tonight. I am not sleeping all night in order to watch over my house and keep my family safe." Browne was quite scared and jumpy all day. He asked to go home early to make sure his family was safe. I sent him on his way, and he literally ran down the driveway to his home.

We had heard several reports of the heart people, also called the Leopard Society, capturing people just north of our mission, but now it was apparently going to happen close to our town as well. We were told of dismembered bodies left hanging in the jungle.

Abba Karnga providentially stopped for a visit that day, so I asked him about the heart people and the leopard society. His demeanor and reply were quite serious but calming. He said, "You are a believer, so you have the Holy Spirit in you, *Greater is He who is in you, than he who is in the world,* (1 John 4:4). *Be continually filled with the Holy Spirit* (Ephesians 5:18). With the Holy Spirit dwelling in us, we were protected and there was no room for evil spirits to enter uninvited. Still you should be careful, but not afraid." His explanation gave a sense of relief.

That night, certainly by oversight, we went to bed with our backdoor unlocked. How it happened we don't know. It was a little disconcerting in the morning to discover the possible danger we had placed ourselves in, but it was also a testimony of God's constant protection over us.

That same morning, the town chief and a group of men showed up at Perry's office door. A family had reported a man was missing from a neighboring town. The men formed a search party, since they had been informed of the general area to which the man would be taken. They were visibly shaken and asked if Perry would join them, meaning would he drive them in the car. He agreed, so they told him to get his cutlass, and drive them to the evil area just south of us. It was rumored the heart people were prowling there.

Perry joined the posse, which spread out to look for any clues of the missing man. They walked in a line through thick jungle, each man swinging a cutlass to make his own way and calling out to each other to keep track of their positions. They had searched through the morning, when Perry unfortunately and suddenly came to a small clearing.

Just ahead he saw a horrible and unforgettable sight. A man's body was hanging from a tree. His hands were tied to a branch, and the body hung just above the ground. There was blood everywhere.

Perry advanced no further but called to the other men. They came running and pushed past him to examine the scene. There was an incision on the left side of the body, and it was explained that the heart could be retrieved from that angle while it was still beating.

A beating heart was a requirement of the leopard men to make powerful medicine, most likely used against another person. Physically sickened by the incident, Perry drove the search party to the commissioner's office to report the horrific crime.

What evilness there is in the world. Satan sorely tempts the person not filled by the Holy Spirit. Romans 6:11-14 explains: *You must consider yourselves dead to sin and alive to God in Christ Jesus. Let not sin therefore reign in your mortal body, to make you obey its passions. Do not present your members to sin as instruments for unrighteousness, but present yourselves to God as those who have been brought from death to life, and your members to God as instruments for righteousness. For sin will have no dominion over you, since you are not under law but under grace.*

Our experience with the work of the evil one was not over. Browne did not come to work the next morning, but his brother Uriah arrived to inform us the family was desperately searching for Browne's three-year-old daughter. He asked if we would meet him at his town, and we hurried there to learn more.

Browne was certain his little girl had vanished into thin air, since he had securely locked the doors and windows before darkness fell. The family wondered if the heart people had "strong medicine" enabling them to pull her through a wall or door. Would they find their little girl, or would they find a dead body?

The scene at the village was chaotic. Everyone was scared, searching the village and surrounding bush for her, but afraid to go too deeply into the jungle alone for fear the heart people would grab them as well. It seemed we were helpless and up against an evil force we could not control.

We had Browne gather the people together and sit in the kitchen to pray for God's protection and her release, which they gladly did. We returned home with a heavy heart. That night it rained and stormed with a forceful wind. It was a long and pitiful night as I lay awake praying for the child's safety.

Uriah returned in the morning with an update. Browne's daughter suddenly showed up in the early morning crying on the side of their house under the eve. She was completely dry, indicating she had not been exposed to the rainstorm.

When asked where she had been, she didn't know. Apparently, she had been given the "forget medicine" made from a plant in the jungle, which left people incapable of remembering recent happenings. (Perhaps this plant variety is like our modern medicine Versed, used for conscious sedation during medical procedures and surgery.)

Our God-fearing neighbors claimed the prayers offered to God the day before were responsible for her safe return. They reasoned some of the prayers were prayed by the woman (myself) whose name meant "God is all powerful". This proved to them that God is stronger than the evil heart people. Indeed, He is the all Powerful One!

Browne's family pressured him to seek out the advice of a Christian fortuneteller or soothsayer. Our steward came to work the next day asking me for a large advance to cover this service. I refused to forward him the money, saying I didn't want to be part of the superstitious dealings. I felt bad to not help him, since he had been a loyal employee, but he seemed to take it in stride in the end.

Browne found the money elsewhere and the fortuneteller determined Browne's step-grandfather, Old Man Charlie, had an evil spirit in him. He said the evil spirit in Charlie took Browne's daughter and fed her to the society's dragon. In addition, they were told this same spirit was responsible for the fact that Charlie's adult son had epileptic seizers. Using that "evidence" alone, Charlie was arrested by the local police and thrown in jail, where he was repeatedly beaten for his alleged crimes.

I had seen this elderly man and his wife nearly every day as they walked the African foot path leading to their rice farm behind our home. They would often stop to talk and play with Laura and Michael. Had our children been in danger when Charlie passed the house?

I told Browne it was hard for me to believe Charlie would do something like that. He replied that he was surprised as well. But he reminded me, it was done by the evil spirit Charlie allowed to be in him. He added information from the Christian fortune teller was certainly true. I was surprised the man was considered a Christian, but Browne assured me he went to church and everything.

It was interesting to learn, the testimony of these soothsayers held up in the courts of law. We had to wonder, did they genuinely have powers, and did they call on the name of our Lord Jesus to receive their visions? On the other hand, perhaps the devil worked through African fortune tellers, where people confidently believed in that type of thing.

Another shock came weeks later when Charlie confessed to the crime of kidnapping Browne's daughter. He said he had taken the little girl for his society's devil business, but they discovered she was not his blood relative. In fact, she was his step-grandchild, and so she was rejected and thankfully returned safely to her village.

Moreover, Charlie also confessed to committing some other murders. We wondered if his confession was forced due to torture at the jail. But Browne had learned that Charlie was given a truth medicine harvested from the jungle, and as a result he admitted he had killed people in the past for society business.

Old Man Charlie was released after some time and rented a sleeping room in the town not far from our house. One day I startled to see him only feet from me as he passed on the nearby foot path going to his rice farm. He greeted me politely and went on his way.

For me, it was certainly unsettling to have a potentially violent serial murderer and kidnapper walking within feet of our house on a regular basis.

I told Browne to tell him to use another route to go to his field. But Browne told me not to worry, and others from the village assured us as well. Apparently, the authorities had made Charlie eat some country medicine, which would cause him great harm if he were to ever get involved in bad behavior again. We were assured we would certainly be safe from the evil possessed man passing our house twice a day. Still, we sent word to him that he should find another path to take to his farm.

The situation was almost more than I could handle.

29

West Africa

We had the privilege to travel to several other African countries starting when Laura was three and Michael was just over a year old. In fact, we traveled so much that each page in Laura's passport was eventually full of custom stamps. We had to take her to the US embassy where accordion pages were pasted into her book allowing for more travel. Perry and I had been issued thick passports, but it seemed children were given thin ones.

At the beginning of rainy season three families from our team went to Nigeria for a missionary conference and a grand tour of Christian Reformed mission sites, which had been active for over 50 years. We arrived in Lagos late at night, where a missionary from another mission picked us up and was to take us to a mission guest house for the night. Since there were too many people for the mission van, three adults had to go by taxi. Perry and I were randomly assigned to go in the taxi with our children and another lady from our group.

When one of the wives showed apprehension about being separated from her husband, Perry persuaded me to switch places with her. Perry and Michael went by taxi to the mission guest house arriving within 20 minutes. Laura and I set out with our luggage and another couple in the mission van. This was thought to be the safest transportation to the guest house, in reality we were setting out on a troubling three-hour journey.

As we left the airport, it was readily apparent the van was in poor shape. It kept overheating, and we would sit along the side of the road waiting for the engine to cool. There were many people walking, and they would stop to see what we were doing.

In the African culture, it was not rude to hang around and stare in car windows, even if someone was in the car. Thus, a group of people gathered each time we stopped. Although our children were somewhat used to this, they were tired and began to cry from the piercing stares and unrelenting requests for money. The gawkers assumed we had a lot of money since we were white, traveling in a private vehicle, and the driver had placed a tall stack of money on the console in the front seat.

When the engine would overheat, the missionary driver would jump out of the van and open the hood, leaving the stack of money vulnerable for anyone to simply reach in and grab it - Of course it was a very warm evening and necessary to have the windows rolled down.

My fellow missionaries in the back seat were alarmed and asked me to put the money in the cubby hole, which I did. When the engine cooled and the driver got in the van he requested the money be put back. This happened several times, and we couldn't figure out why he wanted the money be taken out and replaced on the console where it was vulnerable. It seemed he was upset with us for safeguarding it.

The van's engine was between the front seats, so it was very hot in the vehicle when it overheated. We joked that it was so hot perhaps the money would burst into flames sitting on the engine hump. Putting it in the cubby hole would not only be safer, but also cooler.

It took a long time for the engine to cool down each time, and my leg next to it got a sun burn. We were carrying several water jugs and offered some for the engine once the steam was gone, but strangely the driver didn't take us up on our offer. The driver then admitted he was lost on Lagos' complex road system. He asked directions of random people, but they didn't know.

The van finally died, so he waved down a taxi for us, and paid our fare to the mission guest house. This felt like a great relief - however it was the beginning of phase two of our troubles. We were happy to be on our way in a nice taxi, and as it sped away we wondered how long the stack of money would last without our protection.

It was difficult to converse with the driver, since he was French speaking, but we soon had the impression he too didn't know where to go, since he was asking for directions. He brought us to a mission house, but the Nigerian family living there had no idea where we were supposed to go. They did however point down the road saying there was another mission in that direction.

We began to panic realizing we didn't even know the name of our destination. I said a quick, anxious prayer, and suddenly recalled the name of it. By this time the taxi driver had taken the opportunity to hurriedly dump our luggage on the curb, tell us to get out of his car, and then drive away.

What a predicament we were in. The other missionary's husband took his young son on his shoulder, left the rest of us on the side of the road, and walked away to see if the nearby mission could help us find our way. We didn't know where to go, luggage was piled up by the street, and we women and children were left alone and in tears. We were concerned for our safety as well since there were many people walking by even though it was after 1:00AM.

This was a fearful time for me, being left behind. The other wife and I decided to sit on our suitcases so they wouldn't be stolen. We knew the crime rate in Lagos was very high and there we were sitting defenseless. Laura and I didn't even have identification since Perry was carrying our family's documents. I shed a few tears realizing we were lost in a large city, and of course created the scenario where I might never see Perry again.

After some time, the man came back and told us he had talked to someone, who told him of a place where white people stay. He turned around and walked rapidly away to keep up with a person leading him, but quickly returned when his wife yelled at him to help with the luggage.

I had all our family's luggage and those were the days before there were nice wheels on the suitcases. I tied my three-year-old on my back in African style, and found it was quite a struggle to manage two big suitcases, too heavy for me to lift. We had several blocks to go, so I pushed one suitcase ahead, and then went back to get the other one. Sometimes the man would come back and help me catch up with them.

Finally, I saw the silhouette of Perry running across a lawn behind a high metal fence. He seemed to be running in the wrong direction, so I yelled "Perry I'm over here", but he was running on a sidewalk to the gate down the street. How thrilling to find my husband back and be told my baby was safe and sleeping. What a wonderful man Perry was, taking all the luggage for me - But how quickly my mind-set changed!

While we were walking the short distance to the guest house, he told me one of Michael's shoes had evidently come off in the taxi, so he was left without one shoe. It had been a long night and I suddenly became angry Perry had not noticed the missing shoe. After all we had went through to find shoes for his very wide foot, that should have been a top priority. I further reasoned he didn't even have to worry about carrying our family's luggage as I had to. Thankfully, I softened realizing I was overreacting about an accident.

It was a problem though, what would our active baby boy do without shoes? In Africa you can't walk around without shoes for fear of catching parasites and germs on the ground.

Perry said the missionaries at the Lagos guest house had been quite worried about us when we didn't show up in the van. The road we took was known for having one of the highest crime rates in the world. They had sent out two cars in search of us, knowing the van's engine was not good, but they couldn't find us since we were lost.

Finally going to bed about 2:00 AM we found out we were not alone in our room. Not only were our restless children sleeping with us, but due to holes in the screens, mosquitoes plagued us throughout the night. They buzzed in our ears and bit us wherever the osculating fan didn't blow them off. How I wished I had packed a mosquito net. Meanwhile, a couple of dogs barked continuously in the yard below.

After laying down for three hours we headed to the airport and flew to the conference site high on the Jos Plateau. As we exited the plane, we were surprised to find great relief from the tropical heat and humidity. The higher altitude felt so good that some commented they could kiss the ground.

We attended a couple of conferences and met Nigerian missionaries.

They spread the word that Michael needed shoes. A Nigerian missionary graciously searched through the market and found exactly what we needed. We also went to a zoo, got to ride in mission airplanes, and visited Nigerian mission sites. Most sobering of all, we went to the graveyard where many missionaries and their children were buried. What a sad memorial to the cost some have paid for the gospel of Christ. *

Nearly a month later we set off for Abidjan, Ivory Coast to attend a Mennonite conference for missions to African Independent Churches (AICs) hosted by Dr. David Shanks. This continuing education conference was attended by missionaries from 20 other African countries all doing the same type of work.

Other missionaries confessed envy when they heard of the cooperation and eagerness of the church leaders we were training. They were not finding the same response from churches in their areas. The

---

*When Laura was three years old and we went to a mission conference in Nigeria, we heard of a new CRWM endeavor among the Avadi people, an unchurched people group in the northwest area of the country. Missionaries later moved there and did evangelism, but there the people showed little interest in the good news of Jesus.

Twenty years later after most CR missionaries were gone and were replaced by Nigerian evangelists, the Avadi people responded to Jesus' irresistible love. Churches were established, and there was a need to train the emerging believers and church leaders. Our daughter Laura had the privilege to go to that area of Nigeria as a missionary some 23 years later.

She and her husband Matthew and their two young sons ministered at the CRWM Warari Bible School for nearly four years, teaching new and illiterate Christians more about God's Word. They lived a solitary life in a remote area about 300 miles off the Sahara Desert and endured temperatures reaching 115° F at the peak of hot season, with a low of 95° F at night. Perry and I had the wonderful privilege to visit their remote home and witness their genuine love and care for our brothers and sisters in Christ.

Case, another missionary who lived in the same area several months each year teaching evangelists, told us of a miracle God was working on the campus. The students planted their crop of sorghum (Guinea corn) on the grounds of the Bible school and God blessed their yield, sometimes as much as 10-fold! God was showing his power and mercy to the new body of believers. The neighbors next to the campus noted the bumper crops and planted close to the border of the school grounds. Their crops were blessed as well, but the blessing diminished as the distance from the school property increased.

conference attendees presented papers describing their ministries to AICs, followed by discussion. Perry presented his paper summarizing the Bassa independent churches and our work among them. (See Appendix G) It was a valuable conference and we learned a lot. Several at the conference had written books on the subject, yet they were humble and eager to learn from missionaries like us, who were learning as we went along.

There were other opportunities to share on the African continent what God was doing in Bassaland. A few years later, Perry was invited to train Mennonite missionaries in Ivory Coast. He also had the opportunity to travel with Rev. John Innis to Ghana, where they spoke at a mission conference held in a colonial built university. Mark, Abba, and Perry later represented our ministry to the Bassa at a large conference in the Congo, formerly Zaire.

Our mission team invited the Professor of Missiology from Calvin Seminary to go to Liberia as a consultant to analyze the Bassa churches and the work we were doing amongst them. He was to be a fresh set of eyes having spent many years working in Nigeria to establish churches.

He observed several TEE classes which Perry taught and later told him he was a gifted teacher. The professor advised him to get out of administration, saying his gift of teaching was being wasted. A couple weeks later, a trusted colleague informed me that Perry was an exceptional administrator, sensitive, tactful, and respected by Bassa church leaders in the CEFL.

At the time we were searching for direction on whether we should move from the jungle setting to the city of Buchanan, where the hub of our mission work was. The comments from these respected missionaries only increased the pulls we felt to both stay to teach local pastors and to move to town allowing Perry to be the full-time director.

In the end, it was the CEFL who made the final decision. They asked us to relocate to the city of Buchanan for day to day oversight of CEMs programs and fulfill obligations as the CEFL chaplain, and we made plans to comply.

30

Redeemed

★Discretion is needed - This chapter may not be suitable for children.

One typical trip to Monrovia became a desperate situation for our family – one that I shudder to write about even now. It all began with an earlier episode when Perry was driving our unmistakable vehicle in Monrovia. He and Ron, the CRWM West Africa Director, were making their way across town and needed to cross the busy double lanes of Tubman Street in the Sinkor area. At that point there was a wide sweeping curve in the road, and oncoming traffic was not easily visible.

When it seemed all was clear to proceed, Perry cautiously pulled out to cross the lanes. Suddenly Ron shouted "Stop!" and Perry slammed on the brakes. The front of the truck had only entered the first lane, but hearing sirens blazing he quickly backed up to clear the road.

Simultaneously, President Doe's motorcade whizzed around the corner and passed by going about 80 mph. "Whew, that was a close one," was the feeling. Knowing how things can go, the incident worried Perry for some time and sure enough it came back to haunt him.

Sometime later, months down the road, our family made a trip to the capital city. We finished our business early and were headed out of town, when a passenger in a taxi next to my side of the vehicle began waving his arms and yelling at us. I did not recognize the person, so I averted my attention. Things like that happened frequently.

The taxi switched lanes and came to Perry's side of the road motioning him to pull over, which he did. Although troublesome, again this was not overly uncommon. I wondered what they wanted; perhaps a ride since it seemed to me we had done nothing wrong.

Perry was harshly ordered out of the vehicle. The man said he was the government official who drove the lead vehicle in the presidential motorcade. He claimed to have witnessed Perry attempting to interfere with the president's entourage. Perry was placed under arrest, ordered to drive his vehicle to the Monrovia police station where he would be questioned.

Trying to speak in code to me with Laura and Michael curiously listening, Perry assured us he would politely explain what had happened that day and then we would be on our way home. At the police parking lot, he parked the SUV in the middle of an empty area under a light pole, even though it was mid-afternoon. There was no chance for a parting kiss since the security officer stood waiting at Perry's door. My heart sank as I fearfully watched him walk away with the stern officer.

Time dragged on and on. The children asked why their father was taking so long. I assured them everything was OK. Laura watched me carefully. I could not restrain my desperate, silent prayers. I rested my head on the dashboard to control my body from shaking in deep anxiety. I knew without a doubt Perry was in serious danger.

Hours passed and more activity began to happen around us in the parking lot. Many cars came and parked, then others left. I surmised a change in shift had occurred, I prayed this would be to Perry's advantage as new people might view his situation differently.

Several times I grew apprehensive as squad cars circled the vehicle. I nodded to them, as if everything was alright and prayed they would not bother us or ask me to leave. What would I do then? I couldn't let myself think of leaving without Perry.

Our children began to cry in fear. I climbed in the back seat and held them close, rocking them, and singing songs to calm them trying to assure them and myself that he would soon be coming back to the car. I'm sure Laura felt my body quivering and kept asking what was wrong.

Darkness came, and we felt hunger. Since I had purchased some crackers and cheese, I opened the tailgate to get them out, but quickly pulled a folded lappa to my face, silently sobbing in prayer for my husband.

In such frantic situations there are few words to pray. That night my silent, desperate, repeated words were, "O Lord, my God, Help Perry!" Even when I was calmly dealing with my children, my brain was repeating that phrase. I knew I must control myself, the children needed me, and I needed to keep a level head. Still the seriousness of the situation was a drowning weight upon my heart.

While we waited in the vehicle, Perry was first ushered into a large room with rows of desks and a podium in the front. He thought it might have been used for training or for squad briefings. He was questioned there by a group of men led by the arresting officer.

He felt reasonably safe there since others in the police force were constantly coming and going. When he asked what the charges were against him, they were explained and written in a binder of records. Perry then countered with his explanation of the incident - however that appeared to only increase their agitation and anger.

He was then pushed out of the public room, down a hallway, and into a large holding cell with no windows. The arresting officer came to the forefront yelling at him and saying he was a Krahn man from the same tribe as President Doe. It was his job to protect the President of Liberia, but Perry had almost caused him to have an accident while driving in the motorcade at 80 mph.

He yelled at Perry to confess to this crime. Perry explained he had only begun to enter the street when he heard the sirens and had quickly backed out of their way as they came around the corner. He said he had a witness and offered to take him to the place where the incident occurred. He would show him exactly what had happened, but this only further enraged the officer.

Others crammed into the holding cell, yelling for his admission of guilt, threatening to beat him if he didn't sign a confession. Perry tried to calmly tell them that Liberia and the United States had a treaty, which gave Americans the right to have a US Marine escort when being questioned. The officer suddenly gut punched Perry saying, "Here's your Marine escort. You missionaries come here to live in our land, and laugh at the people, and take advantage of them - look who's laughing now."

Perry bravely responded, "You have no idea what we left behind to come here. We have come to serve you and your people, and to explain the way to God and salvation through Jesus Christ." The officer responded he was Muslim, and others around him added they were as well. He said he didn't want to hear any more about God from a Christian missionary. Perry repeated his request for a Marine to be present.

The accuser had obviously orchestrated certain people to remain in the holding cell with him, and they jeered at Perry for being a Christian. There were four of them and they pulled off Perry's shirt, while threatening a beating if he didn't sign a confession.

He repeated, "I want a United States Marine escort." Their response was to punch him in the stomach again. Crumbled over, they began to remove his pants, but Perry resisted and offered to remove them himself, thinking he might retain his dignity and avoid being stripped to nothing.

One of them began to slap his night stick on his hand before he delivered a swift blow to Perry's upper thigh. Then another man applied his stick to the other thigh. After that a barrage of attacks followed to the chest, back, buttocks, and stomach. Suddenly a new officer came to the cell and yelled, "Hey, what's going on? Get him out of there."

They dragged him back to the classroom without his clothes, while snarling in his ear that if he told anyone about the beating, they would someday find him and kill him – a threat meant for Perry to believe.

Finally, another man passed through the room asking questions, and wondered if Perry was alright. Because of the pain, all Perry could respond was, "I am an American citizen, I request a United States Marine escort. I request to go to court."

The man left and three minutes later a new commander from the change of shift entered the room. He simply took the book of charges, emphatically crossed out the accusations against Perry, and said, "There will be none of this!" He told Perry to put on his clothes and get out of the police station. As Perry hurriedly dressed, he witnessed his accusers being reprimanded and belittled.

I first thought I saw Perry leave the building in the dark, but it was some distance away and I lost sight of him behind some cars. After some time, he slowly walked up behind the truck and I unlocked the door. He would say nothing, so I slid across to the driver's seat and drove us home through the night.

I noted he would grimace when we hit bumps, so I took my time driving to avoid the potholes. As we approached the police gates, we were especially worried about any additional trouble, but no one bothered us. Little could be said on the way home with Perry hunched over in the seat, and the children listening carefully, sensing their daddy was in pain.

For some time after that Perry did everything he could to hide his bruised body, even from me, and I never witnessed the full repercussions of his beating. When he entered the bathroom to shower, I heard the unfamiliar click of the lock, and he only undressed in the dark. He wore long shorts covering his thighs and t-shirts covering his arms even in bed.

When friends came a week later encouraging us to go to the Number 1 beach with them to buy fish and do a little swimming, Perry emphatically refused to go along. "Is something wrong with Perry?" they questioned me.

Respecting my husband, I did not press him for details. It was apparent he needed time to recover from whatever had happened. He did tell me bits and pieces, but I knew one day he would reveal what really happened.

Two weeks later, our family attended a long-anticipated reunion with other missionaries at the beach, but Perry decided we should leave early. Our excuse for leaving was that he was not feeling well. In reality, too many people were pressing him to go swimming and he was not ready to take his shirt off.

Sometime later I saw faint bruising throughout much of his back and commented on it, but he quickly turned away. He responded that he thought it was gone and he didn't want to worry me.

Why the secrecy after such a horrible ordeal? Perhaps some might be prone to expose what happened. Of course, there are several ways to handle the situation, and the police officers had entered a serious threat on his life.

In addition, if our colleagues found out or if I had been given evidence to substantiate what I knew, we would have faced the one thing we all dreaded – the fear of brutality. Perry thought it best to avoid the collective anxiety that could have resulted. Perhaps if I or others had known the full details, we might have gotten to the point of abandoning the work of the mission and gone home.

It was Perry's decision to make, and at the time he did not entirely disclose what happened to him. He did tell us he had been arrested and detained for some time, but there are some things that are too shocking for the brain to believe. The missionaries were all smart enough to know what may have happened - if we dared to face it. Once the bruising was over, the evidence was gone. Given the fact that this was an isolated incident and not a trend to threaten missionaries in general, the vital work of the mission would continue without hindrance.

After the beating Perry avoided every occasion to return to Monrovia, sensing retaliation, until several months later when a car came screaming up the driveway. Our co-workers jumped out saying they needed Perry to go to Monrovia with them. Abba, Mark, and several others were in a Buchanan jail over some minor dispute with a local Buchanan government official, and they were threatened with a beating.

The idea was to take Perry as the CEM Director to the Executive Mansion in Monrovia and request the men be released. Perry privately voiced his apprehension to me as he changed shirt, then rushed off with the others. I rushed to the bedroom to pray for God's protection and the release of our friends.

In Monrovia they were ushered into Vice President Harry F. Moniba's suite. As introductions were made, the VP commented, "So which one is Tinklenberg? We've been hearing of you and CEM, and the good work you're doing for our people." He had a steward bring his guests hot tea and Cokes, while they stated their case and asked for their colleagues' release.

The VP stood up and went to a bank of radios behind him. Using one of them he gave the order to release the men from the Buchanan jail. He chatted with them for 5-10 minutes more, and the encounter was simply over.

As Vice President Moniba was holding the door open for them to leave his private suite, there in the hallway was Perry's former accuser and harsh tormentor standing guard. Coming face to face again with the officer gave Perry cause to wonder if the man would instigate a reprisal for the reprimand of his commanding officer or for unfinished business he might have felt for Perry. But No! Now the tables were turned!

The Bassa proverb "Gedepooh ni zi-kpodo - God never passes on the side of injustice" would apply here. Bassa culture was aware of the justice of God. "My God will see you" was sometimes uttered against someone who had wronged them.[30] Romans 12:19 advises us, *Beloved, never avenge yourselves, but leave it to the wrath of God, for it is written, 'Vengeance is mine, I will repay, says the Lord.'*

After meeting with the Vice President and the timely encounter with the arresting officer, Perry felt relief. The possibility of retaliation from the officer was thwarted by Perry's personal relationship with the Vice President of the country. The tables were turned. Perry was now the esteemed one, the one with powerful acquaintances. Perhaps the merciless accuser quivered in his sandals for several days wondering if Perry had reported his beating to Vice President Moniba.

We realized Perry had his ticket to freedom of heart and mind. The Bassa said, "Nyon-vehnnehn se vonon behin, keh oh dyuo gbaa ka - The Elder is unable to fight, but he has a rich experience of struggles."[31]

We too have a means for freedom of heart and mind. Like the timely appearing of the gracious commanding officer who wiped accusations against Perry from the record book, our Lord and Savior Jesus Christ came at just the right time and completely removed our sin and guilt before God. He washed our records clean with his atoning blood.

When our accuser comes to torment us with relived sins and guilt, we know the one who now sits in the heavenly realms. It is Jesus Christ! He is our deliverer, our redeemer, our friend who opens the door for us to His realm of forgiveness and peace.

If you do not know Jesus as your Lord and Savior, He may be preparing your heart to receive Him by giving you understanding of God's plan for mankind. He sent Jesus to pay the price for your sins! Come to Him and accept his offer for the forgiveness of your sins and guilt. Humbly pray confessing your sins, ask Him to forgive you, and then begin to live your life committed to Him and filled with the Holy Spirit.

31

Christ Alone

Mondamaa Beegar, front row in white blouse and head tie, with some of her congregation in front of her church Note the hanging gas tank on the right, used for a church bell.

Every three years, students of Theological Education by Extension graduated with pomp and circumstance at one of the larger local churches. The second graduation ceremony of Perry's students included Village Health Workers and Traditional Birth Attendants. It was a sight to see the graduates of each program robed in their own color of graduation gowns. They formed a long line and ceremoniously strutted into the hot over-filled church while the choir sang.

After speeches were made, the graduates received their diplomas, and just when the lengthy program seemed to be ending, Pastor Mondamaa Beegar stood up near the front of the church. She congratulated the graduates, expressed how thankful she was for the TEE program, and thanked the instructor, Rev. Perry, for being a great teacher.

She told how she felt privileged to have graduated from the first class a few years back. After receiving her diploma, she handpicked three young men from her church to attend the next session of TEE classes. She announced that since they had studied hard and graduated that day, she was resigning from her position as pastor. She was stepping down to let the graduates become the pastors of her church.

The audience erupted! People started crying and yelling, "No Mommie, No Mommie!" (Mommie was used as a name of endearment.) It was certainly a shock to everyone. I too began to cry witnessing the emotions of the church members. Pastor Beegar was a woman of high position in her denomination. Her resignation would be felt in many capacities. But she persisted.

At the graduation she continued to explain that years earlier God had given her a job to do. He had called her to keep their church going when attendance dropped and there were no men to lead. She gratefully and faithfully carried out God's call on her life but felt the need for further Biblical education.

When she heard pastors in other regions were privileged to attend TEE classes, she gathered pastors from Devil Country together to sign a petition and lobby for a TEE class in their area. Through her efforts Rev. Perry and Mrs. Perry had been sent to live with them and provide classes for church leaders.

As a TEE student she had diligently studied to be a good pastor. In her reading of the Bible and in her TEE classes, she had learned God's plan for His church and that it is only through Christ that we are made right with God, not through works. Specifically, in classes covering the Pastoral Epistles, it had become clear to her that pastors and elders of the church should be the man of one wife. (1 Timothy 3:2)

She reasoned with those at the graduation ceremony that we need to believe Christ alone can save us from our sins and live by the Bible. She was setting an example be obedient to God's call and His Word, even when it directed what she didn't want to hear. Therefore, she had waited until the men from her church were trained and graduated before she publicly stood to hand over the church to them.

Early one Sunday morning we drove the car up and down the road carefully listening above the rain for the sounds of a church service. Perry had been informed by his students that a new community of believers was meeting, and we wanted to worship with them and meet the pastor. Perry intended to invite him to the TEE classes.

As Perry parked the car next to the house they were using for a church, Laura was delighted to see a small monkey someone had as a pet. She asked to go and see it and darted off full of joy in her pretty pink Sunday dress.

The rain had turned the yard into slippery orange clay, and she landed flat in a sticky mud puddle. She came up with a loud scream completely covered in mud, face and all. The village residents felt so bad, and some kind ladies took us behind a house and gave her a bath. They even washed out her dress. Fortunately, I was accustomed to taking extra clothes for the children. They offered to take Laura to the monkey, but somehow the thrill of seeing it had lost its appeal.

On the drive home, our conversation centered on a tricky technique the Bassa used to catch monkeys. A small hole was made in a tin can or a coconut and some peanuts were put inside. The trap was set by securing it to a tree.

When a troop of monkeys happened by, a monkey would stick its hand in the hole to grab a peanut. But surprise! The hole was not large enough for the monkey to get its hand out, since it was making a fist holding the irresistible peanut. The monkeys were stubborn and easily caught since they would not drop the peanut to get their hand out, even when a hunter arrived.

It made us wonder if there were things we held onto which trap us from living whole-heartedly for Christ alone. It was a good object lesson for our children - Let's not be like the monkeys stubbornly holding onto things of this life, only to lose life itself.

The CR mission offered options for study leave, and after eight years of service we accumulated enough time for a three-month sabbatical. In the fall of 1987, we went to Selly Oaks College in Birmingham, England.

I was thrilled to enroll for some Bible courses and found a day care was available. Laura and Michael went there three times a week, and they acquired cute little British accents from their playmates. I started in a class on Genesis but dropped out after a short time. The professor was so liberal he stripped Genesis of any validity. Furthermore, the class was told the Bible contained only mythical stories. I didn't want to waste my time and money listening to garbage like that.

I also took a class covering the Pastoral Epistles at Selly Oaks Seminary, which was led by an excellent theological scholar. It was interesting to study the books through my acquired African viewpoint and the professor was interested to hear about that perspective.

Perry enrolled at the Study Center for New Religious Movements, which was known for its research on African Independent Churches. The churches we worked with fell under this category, so we hoped it would be helpful to learn more about them. One course analyzed Independent Church Movements around the world and another covered different aspects of the AICs.

He also took three courses at the Islamic Study Center: "Understanding Islam", "Contextualization - the Dialog Between Christianity and Islam", and "The 5 Pillars of Islam". At the seminary Perry enrolled for an Old Testament class on Jeremiah, refreshing his skills in Hebrew.

It was striking to learn that Muslims view the Koran as Christians view Jesus - they see the Koran as their salvation. Following and obeying its regulations will fulfill Allah's desires, and there will be an eternal reward. Of course, Christians view Jesus Christ alone as their salvation.

He lived a perfect life, and was crucified as a sacrifice for our sins.

A fellow student in Perry's Muslim class was an Imam from Sudan. He was auditing the class in preparation to teach it the following quarter. After night class the robed Iman and Perry walked home together down a dark alley. Their conversation reached a point where they stopped and just talked. The Imam said to Perry, "I respect you. I don't respect the professor."

He stooped and drew a circle around Perry in the dirt alleyway. Then he drew a separate circle around himself saying, "You are a Christian and will not step outside your circle of beliefs. I am a Muslim and will not step outside my circle of beliefs. You and I as people of our respective faiths can honestly have conversation through inter-faith dialogue. Our professor steps outside of the Christian circle and into the Muslim circle. Perry, I cannot respect a man like that. He has no true religion. You believe Christianity is true, I believe Islam is true; we can dialogue without losing our integrity. So, I respect you, even though one day I may have to kill you." It was a chilling statement to hear alone in a dark alley.

There is a tendency to befriend people of other beliefs and try to meld with them. Some call it "Interfaith Dialogue", saying we are all worshipping the same God. They say no one is wrong in their beliefs, or that dialogue is necessary to understand each other. This is a highly controversial issue, and we don't like to condemn other people, but Scripture teaches in Exodus 43:14, *Do not worship any other god, for the LORD whose name is Jealous, is a jealous God.*

There is no way to Almighty God and the forgiveness of sins, but through the sacrifice of His perfect son, Jesus Christ. Romans 10:9 states, *If you confess with your mouth that Jesus is Lord and believe in your heart that God raised him from the dead, you will be saved.*

Clearly there is a need to acknowledge Jesus as our Savior. When we say that other religions are also valid and that those who adhere to them are accepted by God, we dishonor the righteousness of Christ, and even deny people the opportunity of hearing the truth and coming by faith to Jesus for true repentance and acceptance. It is immensely disappointing that some missionaries and mission agencies feel the belief system of other religions is adequate, without acknowledging Christ.

While studying at Selly Oaks College, Perry was honored by the professors inviting him to pursue a doctoral degree. We seriously considered this opportunity. He was interested in studying under Dr. Harold Turner, who was renowned for his expertise and publications in the study of the independent church movement. Unfortunately, Dr. Turner suddenly announced he was retiring to New Zealand. We were invited to join him there, so Perry could pursue the doctorate focusing on the study of AICs. It would have meant 2-3 years in New Zealand narrowing his scope and future to missiology. Perry's emphasis has always been more on the exegesis of God's Word, so in the end he felt God calling him to turn down the invitation for a doctorate, and to return to Liberia to equip the Bassa church leaders teaching them to correctly exegete the scriptures.

In England our family attended a nearby church. Palm Sunday we listened to a sermon explaining how Jesus' resurrection was scientifically impossible, and anyone who would believe it was a fool! The worship service closed with communion, but our family exited the building without partaking. We felt no cohesiveness with a theology denying the good news of Christ's resurrection . To witness such blatant unbelief preached in a "church" was life changing for us.

Lord, forgive our generation of its unbelief! Pour out your Holy Spirit! Renew the gift of faith to the churches and help us to live for Christ alone!

32

City Living

As we began our fourth term of service in Liberia, we made a pivotal move from living in the bush to finding a rental house in the sprawling city of Buchanan. The CEFL and CEM decided Perry, as the program director, should live there to be more available to the staff and near the hub of our mission work in Bassa County.

This was a difficult move for us since we had loved living in the bush, being part of the local community, and discipling local church leaders. In preparation for the move, a qualified Liberian teacher took over Perry's TEE classes, and Perry devoted himself to administration.

We rented a modern three-bedroom, two-bath ranch-style house made of cement blocks located in the noisy center of the city. The property owners worked at the LAMCO mine in northern Liberia, but they were from Buchanan and would someday retire to their house. Finishing touches on the house was not completed when we rented it, so we hired laborers to finish some details.

Our closest neighbors had a similar cement block house, but many around us lived in traditional mud and stick homes. Out the back door and across the street, was a modest Bassa Church constructed with termite mud and a rusty roof. During worship services we could hear drums playing and Bassa singing, and sometimes the old ladies would dance around the exterior of the church, as was customary.

A dusty gravel road passed by our house which would be a future source of danger for us. On a typical day, taxis and motorcycles constantly scooted by honking for any reason, people passed toting various loads on their heads, and bicycles darted in and out of traffic. Five times a day we heard the Muslim call to prayer broadcast over a city loudspeaker. It became my reminder to voice a prayer as well.

For much of my time in Liberia I lamented being without my mothers or a female Christian mentor. After our move God answered my prayer blessing me with a good Christian friend, Edna. She would become my advisor and a special friend. Her husband Robert was a CEM employee working on the Bible translation team. Their house was just out our back door and when we installed a fence, a gate was put in for easy access to her house and their family.

Michael was three and Laura was five when we moved to the city. Both found good Bassa friends from the neighborhood. Edna and Robert's son, GG was a few years older than Michael, and they became inseparable playmates.

Michael often sat with GG in their outdoor kitchen waiting for Edna to finish cooking and eat with the family. He sampled any number of Liberian dishes, including fried termites, which swarmed at the beginning of rainy season. They were high in protein and quite delicious. The Bassa called them "bug-a-bug". They were fried and pounded into powder to be added later to their soups for protein and flavor.

Our first night in our Buchanan home, Laura expressed fear when going to bed. Indeed, our whole family felt unsettled living in the noisy city. Perry prayed with our children for God's protection and safety while we lived there.

That night we parked our truck very close to the master bedroom window as we did not yet have a secure garage. Even so, in the middle of the night rogues broke a window on the truck and tried to remove gas from it. We jumped out of bed, shined our flashlights, and yelled for them to stop stealing.

Unbeknown to us, Schatzi, our German shepherd was having puppies under the truck, so she took off barking and chased the robbers away. In the morning Laura and Michael were delighted to see two puppies, and they named them Taffy and Jenny.

We had several robberies while we lived in the city. They tried to steal gas out of our vehicle, climbed on the rogue bars securing our windows, and even dismantled our chain link fence. But God kept us safe, and we were thankful for a faithful dog with a big bark.

CRWM recruited volunteer teachers so a school for the children could be held. Children from other missions were welcome to attend, so in all we had around eight to ten students in various grades.

Laura love her teachers – Barb for kindergarten and Connie, who came from Denver, for first grade. Barb's husband Duane completed his Calvin seminary internship by writing and teaching TEE classes. Their son and daughter attended the missionary school.

The school parents converted a rented house into a school. It was close to Perry's office building, so it was convenient for Laura to ride to school with her daddy on his way to work. It changed his schedule some, as he liked to arrive at work by 7:00 before the staff arrived. But on the days he delayed for Laura, I would watch her bounce down the dusty road with her ponytail and pink backpack swinging from side to side and I knew the little girl had a huge smile on her face. Michael later went to preschool for half a year and sometimes rode with on the motorcycle to school as well.

Off to work and school

For our next home-service, we spoke at churches and reacquainted the children with their family members. A few days after we arrived back in Liberia, Laura showed me some new itchy spots and I immediately identified them as chicken pox. It was an alarming discovery since chicken pox in Liberia was rare and could be a public health crisis if it were to spread.

In order to avert a serious situation, I posted a sign on our front door, saying "Please knock, Do Not Enter", and for all practical purposes we quarantined our house. Anne, my housekeeper was given ten days paid vacation and neighborhood children were restricted, too. I didn't want anyone exposed to the virus.

Adults who contract chicken pox can be at a higher risk for complications, including death. I knew it was also important for pregnant women to not be exposed, since the virus is known to cause deformities. We never heard of anyone coming down with chicken pox after Laura had it, so we were very thankful we kept the general population from it.

In the hot humid climate, Laura suffered with a difficult case, and sleepless nights. Anyone to witness her grief would not doubt the blessing of vaccines, which was not yet available for chicken pox. In our present day and age, people have not been exposed to the degree of suffering childhood diseases cause and how potentially dangerous they are for children and the greater population. Those who have experienced them firsthand are not concerned about the minor risks of vaccinating their children.

A new and wonderful phase of our lives began at this point offering relaxation and fun. The city of Buchanan is located on the Atlantic coastline, and just past the CEM office building was a road leading to the mouth of three rivers – the St. John, Mechlin, and Benson Rivers. The town of Edina was there and offered access to the rivers, which Perry had heard were prime fishing areas. He and fellow missionary Joe purchased a ten-foot fiberglass boat with a British Seagull 1.5 horsepower motor and began to explore the sport of saltwater fishing in the mouth of the rivers.

Perry would often come home from work on a hot, sweaty day, and say, "Let's go fishing!" Everyone in the family knew what their job was, so we rushed around getting ready, and within a half-hour would be on the shoreline unloading the boat.

Crossing the river mouth together, Perry would drop the kids and me off on the distant sand bar. We had walkie-talkies for an emergency, and Perry would continue up the river to fish. The kids and I had fun playing in the water and would build a small fire, hoping to cook fresh fish from Perry's catch. We were content on the shore far away from watchful eyes and curious children. There we had complete freedom to relax, and I had no worry of someone seeing me in my bathing suit.

In the mouth of the rivers where the salty ocean water mixed with the fresh water, sea creatures were often lurking. The kids learned to swim there, and sometimes small sting rays would playfully bump us as we floated in the water. They seemed to be playful knocking up against the kids' float toys or air mattresses. We could reach out and touch them as they were quite friendly and fun.

A couple times small, clear, umbrella-shaped jelly fish pulsed through the water wherever we looked, so we stayed on the beach away from their poisonous tentacles. Laura had already suffered a sting from a venomous Portuguese man of war. A wave had carried it to shore and surprised her from behind where she was playing. The gelatinous tubes wrapped around her leg, producing intense burning and leaving a scar which lasted through high school.

Another danger was the threat of sharks moving in from the ocean to feed. The people who lived in the village along the beach told us to not swim across the river mouth, since there were sharks which had attacked and eaten people. I never understood why, but one of our missionaries swam across to the other side anyway.

My parents came for their second visit while we lived in Buchanan. We took them out one day across the river to the sandbar. The men got into some good fishing and stayed out until it was dark. When we heard the boat motor getting close, Mom and I replenished the bonfire to direct them to shore.

Michael and I attract curious children while relaxing on the beach.

As we loaded up the boat it was quite dark with clouds covering any natural lighting in the sky. With everyone and all our gear in the boat the little vessel was weighted down in the water. This was an uncomfortable feeling in the daylight, but in the dark of night it felt precarious. The little motor chugged slowly along, blindly pushing us across the river current to the opposite shore.

When the motor suddenly died, Perry scrambled but couldn't get it started. He tried several things to coax it back to life, and we anxiously waited. We sensed we were drifting with the current downriver towards the ocean. Although it was some distance away, it was possible we could drift into the surf and frightening to think our boat could overturn in the dark of night. Fortunately, it was our rule that everyone must wear a life jacket.

Finally, Perry reached down and found a lot of leaves blocking the water intake. They were cleared away and the motor once again kicked into gear. The boat was turned to face upstream and when we recognized the dim lights of Edina shining on the waterside, we finally knew we would arrive safely on the other side.

Perry and Joe had plans to trailer the boat further upriver and fish their way down to the mouth. This fishing expedition became a reality, and my father had the privilege to go along. He would later say it was one of the most fantastic things he ever did in his life.

We dropped the three men off early Saturday morning some distance upriver at the bridge over the St. John River. They slid the little craft on the grass down the steep ditch, and spent the day fishing their way down the River.

As they passed the indigenous villages along the shores, people ran out waving to greet them. The men stopped to purchase fruit and bananas and to talk to other fishermen along the way. In the late afternoon we picked them up at our usual loading spot, and they were glowing with exciting tales and fresh fish.

Unfortunately, Dad had stepped on a nasty bug while launching the boat. Throughout the fishing trip, his foot continued to swell and it became a huge painful sore, which bothered him the rest of their visit. The culprit was some type of ugly, mud bug with long sword-like jaws, and irritating venom. The other fishermen knew this creepy pest well and said there was nothing to do but keep it clean and let time pass.

We enjoyed many different types of fresh fish from Perry's fishing trips, but our favorite was the white flesh of the barracuda. They were fun to catch because they put up a great fight. We understood it was important to eat the smaller sized 'cuda under four pounds, because the large ones contained the toxin ciguatera from their diet of reef fish. The toxin accumulated in the larger fish, and people who ate too much could get sick with multiple symptoms.[32]

I had a huge barracuda on the line when two families were all crowded together in the boat. Perry told me to throw in a line. I did so and quickly got a powerful bite. In the crowded boat I pointed the fishing pole this way and that trying not to hit anyone as the fish frantically swam under the boat from side to side. I hung on with everything I had while trying to slowly reel it in.

The fish eventually took a breather and I was able to get it close to the boat. When the kids looked over the side, they started screaming and crying because they saw a 5-6 foot barracuda next to them. They knew that fish would be very mean and fighting for its life when we got it in the boat. The men often talked about how aggressive the little barracudas were with their long snout full of razor-sharp teeth. When the 'cudas were brought in the boat, the fish would sometimes take off after them.

Michael and our fishing boat

Perry and Joe got the gaff and the big wooden mallet to control the fish on my line. But then, as the best fishing tales go…the big one got away. Even though I kept tension on the line and the rod tip up, the fish simply did a roll and flipped itself off the hook. What a disappointment for me to lose such a big fish, but also what a great relief. None of us wanted to face the vicious fish, and none of us wanted to eat it or give it to others to eat, since it would be saturated with the dangerous toxin.

Whenever we were in the States, we carefully selected certain lures we knew the barracuda would like. The lures were so valuable to us that we knew each tooth mark in them and the story that went with it. One day Perry unfortunately lost a lure while fishing. It was a big loss, but he did have others.

He had a good Bassa fishing buddy named Joe Freeman. They had met on the river waters, and Freeman had been kind enough to teach Perry a couple local fishing tricks. One day Freeman knocked on our door holding the fishing lure Perry had lost - with a few extra teeth marks in it.

How could Freeman have found it we wondered. He explained he had caught a fish and the lure was attached to its cheek - a double catch that day! And it was his good fortune; because he went on to catch many more fish with that lure, selling them in the market for a profit.

Freeman knocked on our door another time, it was the evening of New Year's Day. In his hand he held a huge fish scale and I screamed with joy, because it meant Freeman had hit the mother-load of fishing. He had caught a huge tarpon, also known as the Silver King. (The Bassa pronounced it tarpoon, instead of tarpon.) We had just put the kids to bed, but we got them up and took them in their jammies to the waterside.

Near the shore we found Freeman's catch of a lifetime with his faithful friends guarding it. We couldn't believe how big it was! We wrapped it in banana leaves to try to keep it cool, loaded it in the Patrol, and drove it to our house. There we covered it with as much ice as we had and kept it over-night in the garage safe from thieves.

A Bassa proverb can be applied here: *A single hand cannot coil a boa constrictor*. This meant when a boa was killed the hunter could not easily carry it into town, because it was a very huge and long snake. More than one hand was needed to coil and carry it, so it was selfish on the part of the hunter to try alone when more than one hand was needed.[33]

The next morning Freeman was at our door bright and early, and Perry drove his fish to the market. It weighed 186 pounds and he sold it for $1 a pound. Freeman walked away with $186 that morning, which was more than the average yearly wage for most people. He kept saying, "God blessed me, God blessed me! It's going to be a good year now."

And indeed, God had blessed him. After that Freeman started going back to church out of gratitude for the New Year's blessing. I asked him how the fish tasted. "I never wasted my money on that fish. I kept all the money in my pocket," was his response.

Later I asked Freeman to tell us his story of how he caught the fish. I pictured him in his little boat, a tipsy round-bottom dugout canoe with no fishing pole. I wondered, "How could he have managed to land such a large fish?"

He told me, "Missy, I caught that fish because you asked me for pineapple in the morning." It wasn't pineapple season, but he thought maybe one of the villages up the river might have one. He paddled his canoe some distance up stream. Then it happened - he saw the "tarpoon" rolling as they do when they are feeding.

That was what an experienced fisherman was always looking for, so he quickly threw his lure out past the "boil", and he was pulling it through when one bit the lure. As he held the line in his bare hands, he immediately knew it was a very strong fish.

He quickly tied a plastic jug to the end of the line, threw it overboard, and it headed upriver attached to the fish. Paddling his canoe as fast as he could, he chased the jug and when the fish slowed down - he caught up to it. Then not having a fishing pole, he began to roll the fishing line around a wide stick to pull the fish in and tire it out. When the fish fought too much and Freeman was afraid the line would break, he threw the jug out again and followed the fish around.

Perry with Freeman and his tarpon

Repeating this process for some time tired the fish, and he finally pulled it up to the canoe, where he got a good look at it. Excited by the size of his catch, he forced the treble hook on another lure into the fish and attached a second jug to the extra line. Now he had two hooks and two plastic jugs attached to his fish.

It still had some fight left in it and was restless, so Freeman threw the jugs out and the fish ran wild for the last time. The extra weight and drag of the second jug tired the tarpon even more, allowing Freeman to once again pull the fish to the side of the boat and finally tie the fishing lines to it. He confessed not only was the fish slowing down, but he was exhausted himself.

Using a rope, he reached under the boat and tied it and the fish together. The fish was still alive when he paddled to the closest village on shore. He called to the people and they brought a big pole to kill it.

Freeman tied a rope through its gill and out the mouth; at this point he finally felt it was secure. He took the fish still tied to the round-bottomed canoe down the river to Little Bassa village where he stored his boat. But he decided he couldn't trust the people there, so he paddled to another village where he knew the people and felt they wouldn't steal his prize fish. They agreed to watch it for him, while he hurried to our house to tell us the news.

Living close to the ocean we watched the chart of tide activity and decided to see what a low-low tide looked like. My sister and her husband, Mary and Loren were visiting at the time, and we took them to Silver Beach to observe the rare phenomena of extra low tide.

People had walked out and were harvesting oysters off large rocks normally unseen and covered by the sea. Perry and Loren ventured out as well and chipped the marine life off the rocks.

Without warning the tide came roaring back with all its might and power. It caught Perry and Loren still at the rocks where they clung for dear life with the returning waves crashing around them to reclaim the beach. Before the next big wave, they ran and thankfully made it safely back to shore. We started a fire on the beach and roasted the oysters in their shells. What a delicious delicacy we enjoyed.

Sometime passed before Perry was startled to notice his wedding band was missing. Apparently, it had been ripped off while clinging to the jagged rocks. We searched the beach until it got dark, but never found the ring. Perry returned home saddened to have lost it, but my sister Mary and I were ever so thankful our husbands were safe.

33

Radio Station

While living in Buchanan, the CEFL added a project to Perry's job description. One of the three goals of the Rev. Dr. Abba Karnga and the CEFL was to establish a Bassa radio station. As a form of communication, a radio station with education and evangelism programs would greatly enhance the life of the Bassa people. Although it seemed a lofty goal, the established TEE school and Bassa Christian High School gave the CEFL confidence anything was possible with God's blessings. Abba and TEE instructor Henry had both worked with ELWA radio station, and they knew the power of radio. It was a goal worth attaining.

Perry became involved in the radio project when Rev. John Innis returned to Liberia. He had been given a CEM scholarship to study at a seminary in the States, and was selected to replace Perry as CEM Director. To ease him into the responsibilities of the CEM directorship, John was to be Perry's assistant for a year and then Perry would assistant him for a year. John was clearly very capable of assuming director's role and only needed Perry's occasional advice, so within a short time CEFL appointed Perry with the task of starting a Bassa radio station.

Seeking to fulfill the wishes of the CEFL, Perry and Ron (a Christian Church missionary) sent letters of inquiry to organizations asking them to underwrite the new radio project. Radio Netherlands replied to one of Ron's letters requesting more information, and the details were quickly provided. That inquiry led to a lengthy application for assistance, which

Perry and Ron completed and returned.

Radio Netherlands' response was to send a representative and engineer, Jim Vastenhood, to Buchanan to explore the feasibility of such a project. He made recommendations for the technical equipment that would be needed. By the time he left he was sold on the project and had spread a desire for a future radio station among the people.

Since Radio Netherland's sole contribution was Vastenhood's analysis and recommendations, he suggested another donor, the ICCO, which was a Dutch protestant inter-church cooperative active in bringing world relief to more than 70 countries.

When the ICCO met to consider the Bassa proposal, we made sure we were in the Netherlands for a vacation. A lot was resting on this meeting and it was important for Perry to be on hand to answer questions in person. Evidently Satan thought so too, because that day Perry came down with a raging headache and other uncomfortable symptoms.

I drove him to the huge Dutch complex and sat in the rental car praying he could survive the meetings. Back at the car, he reported he had endured, but had no idea if the committee was impressed with the idea of helping establish a radio station or not.

Finally, the response came by mail. They would supply $385,000 worth of state-of-the-art equipment! The caveat was the Bassa people needed to provide a building for the radio station, and the stipulations for its construction were rigid. It couldn't be just any building.

Their specifications demanded something they didn't even have in the Netherlands. The radio station needed to be four buildings built only inches away from each other, but all under one roof. Each would have its own foundation, separate walls, and ceiling. This would hamper the sound from traveling from one recording room to another allowing for the purest recordings.

With Liberia's annual per-capita income at $165 the task could have been deemed impossible, but that is not what happened. The CEFL decided to place the matter in God's hands and began to formulate a plan. The Bassa churches worked together and held huge promotional rallies.

Listening clubs were formed and people were asked to pay one dollar to become a member. Missionaries dug deep and gave generously. Little by little money came in.

One day Abba came to our house. While I was serving soft drinks, I overheard him say we needed a visual aid to help people see the progress. Immediately I had an idea and later explained it to Perry.

Using a long piece of cardboard, we drew a huge thermometer and at the top wrote the goal of $80,000. We used red paint to fill in the amount of money we had already acquired. As the contributions accumulated, it would be simple to add more red paint and write on the side the amount of donations given at each meeting. We first brought it to one of the church rallies and it was a big hit, so it became a roving center piece for the fundraisers, accompanied by a can of red paint.

The radio station would be built on the same property that held the CEM offices, and Perry was given the job of radio project manager. All bricks for the station were made by hand on site, foundations were hand dug, and brick walls were laid for the four separate buildings. One of the recording rooms was designed to be large enough to accommodate a church choir, so the beloved Bassa church songs could be recorded and broadcast.

The day the rafters went up there was a huge celebration. The churches were notified, and a crowd assembled. The people roared as the men worked together and heaved each beam into place by shear manpower. The excitement was palpable.

During the lunch break ladies climbed the ladders in their lappa suits and stood above us balancing on the ceiling boards, where they praised God with song, dance, and tears of gratitude. It was an amazing feat and show of solidarity by the Bassa Christians. Here the Bassa proverb is rightly applied, *Red ants bend a nest, only when they are united*.[34]

They were not the only ones in awe of what could be done with God's grace. Many dignitaries from the country were invited to see firsthand what the Christians in Bassaland were building. Indeed, they could certainly be proud of what was nearly accomplished. After all, state of the art equipment would soon be arriving. In fact, Radio Netherlands informed us it was to be the finest radio station in the world - bar none, even better than the Dutch benefactor!

Since the CEFL had secured grants for radio equipment, other organizations took notice. USAID sought Perry down with their black Suburbans to tell him they wanted to know when other projects were pursued. They might be interested in joining a similar project.

Through President Doe and Vice President Moniba, Dr. Karnga and Perry were invited to attend the PAN African Conference for Post and Tele-communications. It was held at Hotel Africa just outside Monrovia, and many African heads of state attended. Dignitaries including even kings and presidents sought Abba and Perry out to gain information regarding aid for such a project in their own countries.

When the radio equipment arrived and Perry had finally gotten it cleared from the port, a large group of people followed the truck parading across town singing and cheering as it neared the radio station. The interior was not completed when the equipment arrived, but several recording rooms could be used, and no time was lost in recording programs in anticipation of actual broadcasts.

The radio staff had been selected some time earlier and trained by government staff at ELBC (Liberia's Broadcasting Corporation) and by missionaries at ELWA. During the training, Perry had the idea to purchase airtime and produce the first remote broadcast ever used in Africa. The news program compared the advantages of swamp rice production over slash and burn farming. It was amazing to think of the potential the radio station held.

Amid the excitement, evil was brewing, and our lives would soon be in danger. Near the end of the huge radio station project, when the antennas were being installed, the political climate in Liberia had become very tense with conflicts in the northern region. Although the radio station came so close to transmitting, no one could have guessed the number of years that would pass before it beamed its first broadcast.

34

Typhoid Fever

When we had been in Liberia nearly ten years, we needed to decide if we should return to the Bassa people for a final term of service. If we completed another three years overseas, Laura and Michael would then be close to middle school age. Our desire was for our children to start living full time in the States when they reached that age.

We had seen too many mal-adjusted missionary children. It seemed as teenagers and adults they were often restless and confined themselves to a narrow sub-culture of people from foreign countries. After living abroad they had difficulty identifying with the country on their passport and preferred other cultures. In addition, it seemed difficult for them to find a mate who shared their international flair. It seemed there were some who wandered the globe searching for contentment.

Observing this, Perry and I had made a pact to provide our children with the opportunity to assimilate and grow in the Stateside culture they would likely adopt, even if God would call them to cross-cultural service.

As we prayed about it, God seemed to be calling us to another term of service by giving us the desire to return. We then began to make plans to go back to the States for six months. During the home service, we would undoubtedly travel extensively speaking to supporting churches. When school began in the fall our children would be enrolled at Calvin Christian elementary school in Sioux Falls and attend classes for at least one semester. We would then return to Liberia for one more term.

During that time the mission programs would be turned over to Bassa Christians, many of whom had studied abroad under our mission's scholarship program. After our return and the last term of service, our family would then move to the States before Laura and Michael attended middle school.

As we neared home service Perry and I were thrilled with the anticipation of welcoming our third child to be born in the States, but all too soon our plans were dashed when I miscarried for the third time. Such were our plans, but God says in Isaiah 5:8, *For my thoughts are not your thoughts, neither are your ways my ways*. And the Bassa said, *Gedeh pau ni ween*, if God agrees.

Perry's brother and his wife, Jay and Kathy, visited us on a summer break from their teaching careers. Laura loved Aunt Kathy and absorbed everything she had to say about the school system in the States. For one of their last meals with us, I served papaya. During the process of preparation, I remember licking my finger and feeling a wave of dread pass through me. Fearing I had exposed myself to some germs, I stopped and recleaned the fruit, utensils, and surfaces with a bleach preparation. It would be only a short time later that symptoms of a disease appeared.

In early August I began to experience frequent episodes of headaches, fever, nausea, and gut-wrenching pain. It was difficult for me to monitor our children, and meal preparation often went unfinished. When it all became intolerable, Perry took me to the LAMCO clinic on our 14th anniversary. Driving across town each bump in the road brought raging abdominal pain.

We had planned to go out for our anniversary dinner at the mining company restaurant, but the diagnosis I received halted all plans, including normal daily living for the next couple months. Called into a dingy doctor's office with paint peeling from the walls, a British doctor locked eyes with me and said, "The lab tests confirm you have the dreaded typhoid fever."

I said, "You can't be serious."

"I assure you, I am deeply serious," was his reply. I asked what treatment I needed and became concerned when he explained that he was a surgeon and didn't have any idea. He told me to return home, take to my bed, and be certain I did not spread it to my family. He asked if I knew what he meant by that and I told him I understood, since I had taken microbiology and pathology in college. I added I had several medical books at our house I could reference. He said, "I think you will find any medical textbooks very helpful."

I then asked if I could return to the States for treatment. "No," he said. "You are weaker than you realize and probably wouldn't survive the trip. You shouldn't travel and risk exposing others. They don't allow international travel with communicable diseases such as typhoid. I will soon be returning to England myself and I'm not coming back to Liberia, so I will not be available for your further treatment." He wrote a prescription for chloramphenicol tablets, and I was dismissed.

I felt numb as I walked out to the waiting room. Perry was working from his briefcase, occupied with writing something important on a yellow legal pad. I gave him time to finish writing his thoughts, and sat in the quiet lull of time, trying to absorb what the diagnosis meant.

When my husband looked up, I simply told him, "We can't go out for our anniversary. I have typhoid fever," and I repeated the conversation I had with the doctor. We sat for a little while in the waiting area stunned, sitting in that span of time between shocking news and the reality of living it out.

Pouring through medical books at home, it became apparent my diet must immediately change to only liquids, and the danger of bowel perforation always loomed over us. Only the night before we had shared a bowl of popcorn - now we realized something so simple could have punctured the intestines and been fatal. God had certainly been watching over me. The medical books said when I began to feel better, I could resume eating soft foods.

Fortunately, we had a spare bedroom, or office, which contained a single-sized bed. I was sequestered there, and we were thankful our rental home had two bathrooms. One of them was then reserved for my use only. We also gave Annie, our house help, time off so she would not be exposed. This only doubled Perry's workload.

They say the treatment for typhoid is worse than the disease itself. I truly remember little of the weeks Perry took off work to attend to myself and our family. The typhoid and treatment left me in a weakened state. It proved to be a very difficult and challenging time, and I spent most of it limp on the bed in our home office.

Strangely, having typhoid was a memorable spiritual experience for me. As I lay on the bed, I prayed simply that God would heal and comfort me. It seemed I was in a deep sleep much of the time, but many times I truly felt the Lord's arms gently surrounding me, comforting me, and sustaining me. It was such a wonderful experience to sense Jesus holding me in his arms, that I thought having typhoid again would be worth it!

Physically as a result of the illness, I experienced general weakness for months and a sharp stabbing pain in my right side whenever I ate. The "stabbing" was due to gall bladder attacks related to the typhoid. Honestly, it was so painful it was difficult to endure. It felt as though someone was stabbing me repeatedly with a dagger.

At the LAMCO clinic an x-ray of the area showed a huge gall bladder that hung well below the hip bone. I asked the technician if that was how large it is supposed to be. In his experience, he recalled seeing only one other gall bladder that large.

One day while recuperating from typhoid on my bed, I was awoken by people screaming frantically. Later a neighbor told me a taxi had stopped nearby and as the people were exiting a swarm of angry killer bees attacked them. A couple people ran away taking refuge in a nearby home, but a mother grabbed her young child and climbed back in the taxi. Unfortunately, too many bees followed them, and they perished.

Six months after the diagnosis of typhoid, the fatigue finally started to disappear and life began to get back to normal, but I still had to deal with considerable stabbing pain in my right side. Since the gall bladder was reacting, it was possible typhoid bacteria were harbored there.

I was frightened of becoming "Typhoid Mary", a case where typhoid bacteria were unknowingly spread by a cook. The typhoid bacillus can be harbored in the gall bladder for long periods of time without the carrier even knowing it.[35]

Sharp gall bladder pains lessened, then continued after almost every meal for five years, after which I was most happy to have it removed.

35

The Demise Begins

The beginning of the end caught us unaware with a chain of events. First the exchange rate began to wildly fluctuate. Liberia had always used the American dollar with a 1:1 exchange rate. American greenbacks were used throughout the country, and some of them were limp and ragged having been in circulation for many years.

The Liberian government did not issue paper money, although it made coins valued at a dollar or less. According to letters written home, in 1982 and again in 1985 a heavy $5 coin was issued. It was hexagon shaped and counterfeits quickly surfaced devaluing the Liberian dollar. The Lebanese shops and the black market began to offer a 3:1 exchange rate for the US dollar. By the time we left Liberia, the unofficial rate had reached 12:1.

One of the materials used for making counterfeits was aluminum, so rogues began to dismantle our fence on a nightly basis. The dog would bark, we'd get up, and yell at the thieves. Then they would quickly unravel a piece of the linked fence before running away. In the end, most of our fence was removed to be melted down for new coins, although the thieves told us they were using it to make pots and pans. Some of the replica coins we saw were obviously fake.

As the CEM director, Perry was responsible for the Liberian staff payroll. With the exchange rate dropping, the national bank was no longer distributing US paper money and began to deal exclusively in Liberian coins.

This meant the payroll became increasingly heavy, so on pay day I would park as close to the bank's front door as possible. The kids and I would wait in the truck for Perry to exit the bank, laden down with a couple of brief cases full of heavy coins. As he loaded the money in the truck, we felt a little like Bonnie and Clyde hurriedly making a get-away from the bank. Perry claimed he was not afraid of getting mugged, because anyone who attempted to grab the heavy briefcases wouldn't be able to run very far.

Suddenly there was disturbing news of a mass killing in the north. The day before Christmas, a large group of Muslims were killed by gunfire while praying in their mosque. They were attacked by a group of approximately 100 dissident Liberians led by Charles Taylor, invading Liberia from neighboring Ivory Coast.[36]

When this first incident occurred, we all believed it would be a short-lived uprising in an isolated area. After all, the national army was mobilized to stop any further disturbances. How very wrong we were.

Born in Liberia to a tribal mother and Americo-Liberian father, Taylor had received a college education in the States. He held an office in the Liberian government under Doe but was removed from position after three years of service for embezzling $1 million.

After fleeing to the USA, he was arrested for extradition, but escaped jail by sawing through window bars. Managing to make his way to Libya, he began guerilla training under Moammar Gaddafi.

Gadhafi hosted this training hoping to establish a radical regime in Liberia and other west African countries.[37] Shortly thereafter, Taylor went to Liberia's neighboring country, Ivory Coast, and began amassing and training discontented Liberians.[38] Arms were shipped from Libya to Taylor's rebels through Burkina Faso, including mortars and small artillery.[39]

After Taylor and his new soldiers crossed the border into Liberia and attacked a mosque on Christmas Eve 1989, we heard his rebels began overtaking whole villages, inscribing men and even boys into service. There were also rumors that they were burying people in mass graves, which were later confirmed. Taylor's group became known as the rebel army, or the National Patriotic Front of Liberia (NPFL). It rapidly gained favor with the Liberian people because of how repressive President Doe's government had become.

In response to the insurgency, two battalions from the Armed Forces of Liberia (AFL) were dispatched to Nimba County. They used brutal tactics trying to crush the rebellion, and indiscriminately killed civilians as well as NPFL rebels. This was followed by relentless waves of violence against those living in Nimba County. They killed unarmed civilians, raped women, and burned villages.

The army was largely made up of men from the Krahn tribe, as was President Doe. They targeted members of the Gio and Mano ethnic groups who lived in the area.[40] The rebels then began to advance in a southward direction toward us, but we mistakenly supposed the AFL would halt the rebel movement.

The Bassa Ministerial Association held a meeting concerning the unrest in the north. Another missionary couple was there, Tom and June, missionaries with United Liberian Inland Church. I had never met them before, but they were renowned for their linguistic gifts and talents having translated much of the Bible into Bassa, Gio and Mano. The Jacksons had lived and ministered in the north for about forty years.[41]

They said they were in Buchanan to gather supplies before returning to their home. They had decided to go back to care for the people in need. They also hoped to have a chance to talk to the rebels who were in the area.

She expressed concern to me since her husband's heart was not strong, and I told her that was all the more reason to not go back. Perry too urged them to not return, citing recent reports of raids, and the US Embassy's advisory for US citizens to evacuate that area. They were however confident of their decision, saying they felt God leading them to go home.

A short time later news was broadcast of the Jacksons' death by the rebel army. We learned they had been abducted by the national army and forced to precede the soldiers as human shields while they moved down the road. The rebels attacked anyway, and tragically the missionaries were killed.[42] What a loss to the people of Liberia and to the work of translating the Bible into several local languages.

For me the effects of typhoid were wearing off, so it was decided to have a nice celebration for Michael's 5th birthday and we talked about party plans with our children. Earlier in the year we had enjoyed a birthday party for Laura with her Bassa and missionary friends, so another birthday party would be fun for the kids to anticipate. We hoped it would be a distraction from the whispers of war they were hearing.

Michael also invited missionary kids and Bassa playmates from the neighborhood. Since it was hot season, the party was held in the morning while it was cooler. They played games together, including an outside obstacle course, and had lunch followed by a traditional birthday cake.

I was just about to take our guests home after lunch when Perry came home unexpectedly. He entered the front door and stood completely stiff, while staring straight through me. Alarmed I asked what was wrong and he slowly let himself down on the terrazzo floor, where he laid with intense pain. "I hurt my back," was all he said. I got what little ice I had and put it on his back, then took Michael's guests home. Later the details came out.

Perry had spent the morning working at the new radio antenna site with a British contractor, who was overseeing the installation of the large antennas. While Perry was carrying a long pipe, he heard "springs" go off in his back, followed by raging pain. He dropped to his knees and crawled to his vehicle. Curious, one of the missionaries asked him what he was doing. "I'm going home for lunch", was all he said.

Now it was Perry's turn to lie on the single bed in the office. The level of pain was difficult to handle. When the kids bumped his bed trying to give him a get-better-kiss, he screamed from the jarring. He couldn't sit up and even moving his arms caused pain, making it necessary to spoon feed him.

We wondered how to proceed. The pain was so intense he refused to get in the car and go to the doctor, fearing the jolting drive. We weren't sure what was wrong and had no idea how long the pain would continue. I prayed hard and often that the Lord would send some relief, since he was suffering so much.

The next day there was a knock on the door. This was a familiar thing, yet strange, since people called out "Bauk, bauk", instead of knocking with the knuckles. It was another surprise to see a tall white man standing on the porch and to find out he was a doctor from the States. He had been told there was a missionary who needed help, so he came to our house to see what he could do. I gladly led him to the office where Perry was.

After a brief examination the doctor said Perry had ripped ligaments in his back. He would have to stay in bed for six weeks and gradually resume movement after that. The mystery doctor gave him a bubble pack of the strongest pain relievers available and left. When the pills were beginning to get low, I considered going to the local pharmacy for more. We could buy almost anything over the counter, if we knew what we wanted.

But then, another doctor from the States showed up at the door just as mysteriously as the first one had. He too examined Perry confirming the diagnosis of torn ligaments, said it would take six weeks to heal, and resupplied him with painkillers before leaving. Both doctors appeared so mysteriously that I often thought of them as angels in disguise come to minister to Perry. As we waited for the six weeks to pass there was much to preoccupy our minds.

We were due for home service in the States and our departure was only a few months away, we foolishly thought we would leave on schedule and the rebellion would lose its fervor while we were gone. We couldn't have been more mistaken.

Practical matters took precedence for me. The owners of our rental home contacted us saying they wanted to move into their house as soon as possible. They had been living in Yekepa and working for LAMCO, but escalated military action was forcing them to leave. The wife was a beautiful Bassa woman and a devoted Christian, who mourned the fact that her husband had bought into the lies of Jehovah Witnesses.

The mining company was not able to function with rebels attacking the rail line and stopping the trains. Hundreds of people were now without jobs and people were moving in mass, wandering the roads and searching for a safe place to stay. We were witnessing the unraveling of a calm and peaceful society.

Since the owners of our rental house wanted us out and home service would soon start, I began to pack all our household belongings into our 55-gallon steel drums. They were normally reservoirs for water when the city water was off, but when we were in the States they kept our belongings secure. I steadily packed, while Perry recuperated in the office.

There was a nearly constant flow of visitors to Perry's bedside. The Bassa CEM staff covered for Perry while he was laid up, likewise they would also manage the mission work while we were on home service. Since they were assuming his duties, they frequently came to our home to talk to him. From his bedside God gave him time to further mentor and train each of the CEM staff.

Friends and co-workers who came to see Perry were kind enough to leave with barrels I was packing and take them to the secure storage room in the radio building. (Our neighbors later told us the barrels were hauled away a week after we left by looting rebels. I wondered why I had wasted my time packing for thieves to easily carry it all away.)

As we waited for Perry's back to heal, we continued to receive news of further atrocities north of us. Things were happening that we could hardly believe. There were rumors of more villages being senselessly burned, mass executions, and open pit graves. The magnitude of the uprising was beginning to sink in.

We were alarmed that the rebel army was slowly and methodically marching towards our city. Traveling mostly by foot, they took village after village, gaining force as they went. National soldiers began to muster at a normally low-key army barrack near our home. From there they were sent out to oppose the rebels, but they were not holding their positions.

At night the soldiers were not only out walking the streets, but sometimes we were alarmed to hear nearby gun fire. We discovered it was also at night that the troop transports brought fresh soldiers into town. These large trucks passed right by our home. I was thankful our children's bedrooms were on the back side of the house and not facing the nighttime danger.

Considering all the army activity and random gunfire at night, it seemed it would be safest to sleep on the floor, rather than lying up on the bed near window height where a stray bullet could reach us. I made soft pallets with bedspreads where our children and I slept on the floor for two weeks, while Perry stayed in the office still unable to get up.

I became exhausted from lack of sleep, caring for my bed ridden husband, anxiety over our security, and the thought of leaving safely. There was no doubt we must leave our brothers and sisters in Christ, our homes, and lives of the past years, but Perry needed to remain on bed rest, since he was literally unable to move and in intense pain. If he had not been laid up, we would have left sooner, but his condition gave us pause, and we closely monitored the actions of the rebels buying time for the torn ligaments to heal.

Troop activity was also a concern during the day. One day Michael and GG came rushing into the house exclaiming a large truck of soldiers had passed by on the road, and the soldiers had pointed their guns at the boys. This seemed like fun soldier games to the boys. They were intrigued by the army trucks and tough soldiers, so it wasn't surprising their new past time was playing war. From that point on the children were restricted to play only behind the house. It would not be the last time our son witnessed the machinery of war.

Adding to our concern, several children in our mission team came down with malaria that was apparently resistant to the weekly anti-malarial pills. After four successive positive malarial smears and ineffective treatments, two boys were hospitalized and put on a quinine drip. The treatment did cure them of malaria, but the boys had suffered frightening hallucinations from it.

Laura was enduring the same symptoms of low-grade fever, nausea, weakness, and lethargy. We had treated her at home with chloroquine, but it seemed it was only partially helpful. Having produced three positive malaria smears after treatment, she was one positive test away from being hospitalized.

We prayed she would not suffer a fourth episode and need to go to the hospital. She was a sensitive child and afraid of imaginary things, like those in CS Lewis' stories. I knew it would be difficult for her to withstand the quinine drip with hallucinations as side effects. With our certain departure, we worried that Laura would face her fourth round of malaria while in transit. Our Lord God would have to be trusted to orchestrate everything, as He normally did.

I talked to Annie, our housekeeper, and told her we would be leaving the country soon. She was a believer and had been a good companion for me in our home. I was glad I had gifted her, some months back, with a beautiful lappa suit made from the best Dutch wax cloth, and I had a matching suit.

With the armies advancing in our direction, we thought it was time for her to decide where she wanted to go for safety. She began to cry and hung onto me saying how frightened she was of fighting in our area. I told her we would give her some money to sustain herself and would continue to pay her son's tuition.

There was no hesitation in Annie's reply - she wanted to go to Camphor mission where her son was in school. Our good friend John, the Methodist Camphor headmaster, assured us Annie could live there temporarily. The mission was already harboring people from the north.

She decided to leave right away and brought her son to the house the next morning. Perry and I tearfully thanked her for her service to us. We were certain dangerous times would soon come, and making sure Annie was safe felt like we were admitting the end was near.

A taxi could have been chartered to take Annie and her son to Camphor, but she was alone in the world, and I wanted to make sure she arrived safely. I drove our vehicle to a supply store to buy a couple 100-pound bags of rice. One bag was a requirement for her son's schooling, and the other was for Annie's survival.

With trepidation I drove the short distance outside of Buchanan to the Camphor mission, knowing we were traveling the road the rebels would one day take into our city. It was a shock to see the already overcrowded mission grounds with people living in makeshift houses. As we drove up, young men readily unloaded the truck and our departing hugs were much too quick. We would not see each other for another 18 years, when she would recount all that happened and how God was with her during the war.

I was fearful as I drove back to Buchanan. On the way there Annie and her son had been with me, but on the way home the empty truck might entice soldiers to ask for a ride. For that very reason Perry had thought I should not make the potentially dangerous trip, but we also wanted to make sure Annie and her son were safe. I prayed and kept my eyes glued straight ahead, not listening if people were calling for a ride.

Two important things happened on Good Friday, 1990. First, Pat radioed me and invited the kids over to their house to make burnt matchstick crosses for Easter. Their home was only a short drive away and I needed a break from ongoing packing, so I accepted the invitation. We figured it would also be a good distraction for Laura and Michael from all that was going on at our house. Not only was their Daddy on bed rest, but I was packing up everything around them. My determination to leave our house almost cost us everything, including our lives.

The easiest route to the mission property where Mark and Pat's family lived was the road past the army barracks. Being naïve and unaccustomed to war, that was the road I took. There was no way to turn around when I noticed the roadblock at the installation and armed soldiers waiting to stop our vehicle. I cautiously approached and rolled my window down. They asked me where we were going. I told them I was going to the mission.

They laughed and ordered me to get out of the truck saying they needed it for transportation up-country. I did not open the locked door and told them, "I'm very sorry, but I can't give you the truck today. We are going some distance and it will be too embarrassing for the children and me to walk in the hot sun." Without giving them a chance to respond, I drove slowly away.

It was a very bold and extremely dangerous thing to say to haughty young men with M16s backing their authority. As I drove away, I realized how stupid I had been. I was certainly endangering the lives of my children. Unconsciously, my shoulders narrowed, and I hunched over in anticipation of a gunshot in the back of my head.

I glanced at my precious children and was going to tell them to lie down so they would not be a target, but I saw their heads did not yet extend beyond the height of the seat. I realized it was only through God's protection that we were allowed to safely proceed, and my body shook in fear as I gripped the steering wheel.

After we arrived at the mission, Pat and I got the kids started on making their crosses. I was extremely nervous and told her I had to talk to her in private - she suggested the guest house. As we walked across the lawn, I grabbed her hand and told her I was so scared. In the guest house I confessed to her the terrible risk I had taken, but we praised God for His protection.

Shedding tears together, we realized we were in our final days in Liberia and worried over what would become of our Bassa friends. What would they have to suffer?

Pat's husband Mark hid my vehicle in a shed at the mission. We left it there until it was time to leave the country. He took us home in an old run-down little station wagon. We traveled down back roads avoiding the army post and finally arrived at our house.

Perry heard us drive up in a different car and very quickly the story came spilling out again. The truck was of no value compared to our lives, he sternly told me, and I agreed. I'm not sure what I was thinking when I refused the soldiers' demand. I just remember being fed up with all the army activity and determined they shouldn't ruin our lives in every way. In God's providence, we now had an escape vehicle safely hidden away.

The second thing that happened on Good Friday was my focus on a section of Scripture. Our family tradition was to read the *Today* devotional guide at mealtime. In preparation for Easter, the *Today* booklet was focusing on the prophetic passages of Christ's sacrifice. On Good Friday the reading was from Isaiah 52:7. *How beautiful upon the mountains are the feet of him who brings good news, who publishes peace, who brings good news of happiness, who publishes salvation, who says to Zion, "Your God reigns."*

That day while I swept the dining room floor after lunch, I sang the song *Our God Reigns,* which comes from that passage. But ringing in my mind was the thought that I should go back and read the rest of the chapter. I continued to sweep, thinking I didn't have time for that. After all, a war was brewing, an army was marching toward our city, I had a house to finish packing, and so many other things to do.

Still the urge to read the remaining verses was unusually strong. I remember literally, and perhaps defiantly, dropping my broom in the middle of the floor. I walked past guests that had come to see Perry and went to the kitchen for the Bible. Verses 11 and 12 were powerful and clear, giving me peace and understanding for the dangerous situation at hand.

Depart, depart, go out from there; touch no unclean thing;
go out from the midst of her; purify yourselves,
you who bear the vessels of the LORD.
For you shall not go out in haste, and you shall not go in flight,
for the LORD will go before you,
and the God of Israel will be your rear guard.

It seemed these verses were saying we would indeed leave, but not in haste. We should not get involved in the unrest of our host country, and the LORD would protect us as we left. He would go before us and provide protection from the rear. I felt an immense sense of relief and shared the verses with Perry and other missionaries when they came to our house.

Perry was Field Director for the Christian Reformed missionaries. It seemed people were coming nonstop to talk about when we should leave, how we should evacuate, where we should go, and who should leave. I prayed God would lead and give wisdom to those making the decisions. It was certainly apparent we would need to leave soon. I wished we could go, since it seemed the rebels were closer every day, but Perry could not travel and was still confined to bed - I couldn't leave him behind.

He told me if we had to run, I should take the kids and just go. I was to leave before the rebel line reached Buchanan and the roads were closed. His plan was to hide out in our house for a while. When his back had healed enough to leave, he would go to the little fishing village where he knew the people. He would wait there for a boat to cross the river. Then he could make his way to the Number 1 area, again people would know him, and would help him get to the airport or Monrovia.

I thought it was a terrible plan, the worst ever. There was no way I could leave him behind, and I was confident our fellow missionaries would not either. Although the end of the six weeks convalescence period would soon be over, we prayed Perry's back would heal before the advancing rebels got too close.

While we were in the process of moving everything out of our home, we began to realize it was necessary to burn all personal documents or letters. Anything that we could not take with us which would reveal our personal information or that of people who had written to us was destroyed. I had saved all correspondence we received through the years. It had been a great resource for us to keep in touch with people, but those letters had to be burned. We did not want the names and addresses of our friends and relatives available to the public. A hot fire was necessary since the letters and envelops were thick with humidity and did not easily ignite.

When my neighbor Edna saw that I was burning our personal affects, she began to cry in her outdoor kitchen just over the fence. I went over and sat with her for a while. Arm in arm we sat in the kitchen wiping tears from our cheeks and telling each other how thankful we were to have had such a special neighbor.

"Everything is changing now", she told me. I told her I was sorry about that and explained we would have to soon leave. Then we prayed together, even though we weren't aware of what the future held. I shuttered to imagine what her family might go through.

About five weeks into Perry's recovery, two black Suburbans with darkly tinted windows came storming up our driveway. Fully armed Marines and US Embassy personnel jumped out of the vehicles and raced up the front steps. Perry had seen them arrive from his bed in the office and struggled to join me at the front door. They seemed to have little doubt they had arrived at the correct house, and they pushed past us entering our living room.

They presented an identification card, saying the soldiers were legitimate US Marines accompanying embassy personnel. It appeared we had no reason to not believe them. A uniformed officer stiffly called out, "Are you Perry Tinklenberg, head of the Christian Reformed Mission?" After Perry acknowledged he was, the marine added, "Sir, you will read and memorize the information on this paper. You will do so now." He stood at attention holding out the paper.

Perry was holding himself up by leaning on the back of a chair. He took the little paper and quickly memorized the information. The marine continued, "Sir, have you memorized the information?" Perry assured him he had. "Sir, you will now destroy this information in my sight." Another Marine in camouflage cracked a smile when he realized Perry thought he'd have to eat the paper. The soldier offered Perry a lighter, which he used to burn it.

We were informed the secret information was to be passed on to a select few in our team, not including myself. It gave designated times and frequencies the embassy would use to transmit information to US citizens. There were also designated passwords which would indicate when we were required to leave Buchanan. The marines told us they would not evacuate us out if we got stuck there and urged us to leave as directed. "We do not want any more American bodies lying on the roads. You cannot stay, you must leave soon." We got the point: the marines would not be coming back to save us, we had to get out soon.

Someone from the embassy added instructions to be very observant and assess our level of danger at the onset of change. We were to assign a number between 1-10 to the current level of danger. This was not to be lowered, unless the situation changed, actually becoming safer. They explained it is human nature to get accustomed to danger and want to decrease the level, when in reality nothing changed. This we found to be true.

They asked if we had any information to give them. I told them my husband couldn't travel yet due to a severe back injury. They nodded their heads, seeming to already know that fact. We also told them the national army was active at night with truckloads of soldiers passing our house on their way to the nearby army post. The embassy entourage left our home as quickly as it had arrived.

A few days later, Perry slowly and carefully left the house for the first time in five weeks to chair the last CEM meeting with other missionaries and national staff. At the meeting missionaries turned over all keys to their Bassa coworkers and encouraged them to find food and other necessities including shelter in our homes. It was an emotional last time together.

The missionaries were encouraged by the Liberians to leave as soon as possible. Since our co-workers felt responsible for us, they could not leave the city and "go hide in the bush" until they were sure we were gone and safe.

On the day Perry left the house to meet with his Bassa coworkers, four Bassa girlfriends came over to visit me before we left. They helped me pack my kitchen and were amazed at the beautiful things I had. How I wish I had given them more than parting gifts. It would have been an easy thing for me to do, and perhaps given them some happiness.

While my friends and I were talking, a large hysterical mob came down the gravel road in front of our house. They were running scared - some were crying, some were screaming. It was alarming, so my friends went to find out what was happening.

They were told the rebels had entered our town of Buchanan. It was terrifying news to receive! I felt physically sick to hear such a report, and I wondered how at such a time Perry could not be home for the first time in five weeks.

My friends were frightened and quickly left for their homes, saying they needed to find their children. As they ran away, I understood I would not see them again.

Speaking calmly, I gathered my children inside and sent their playmates home. Laura and Michael had heard the noise of the mob. They were frightened and began to cry. The neighborhood children had already passed among themselves that the war was coming. I reassured them that God was with us even though the people were afraid. Their daddy would be home soon and then we would figure out what to do.

They watched me close the curtains, double lock the doors, and slide the heavy security bar across the door with shaking hands. But, the hysteria of the mob could not be blocked out. If this news was true, we were in much danger and perhaps Perry would have a difficult time returning home. I wanted to cry but had to remain strong so Laura and Michael would not be afraid.

I called on the mission radio to the other wives - it was strange, but no one answered. Our emergency evacuation bags were ready, I placed them by the door, but I had no car so where would I go with the children? I retreated with them to their bedroom where we prayed together that their daddy would come home safely. The mob passed and with it the fury of emotions died down.

Soon Perry returned home and reported there was a rumor going around that the rebels had entered our town. I told him what the mob passing by our street had said, but he assured me it was not true. He understood there was a man killed in our immediate area by some soldiers, and the gunfire had alarmed the people and created the rumor.

If we were reasonable, we would realize the rebels could not be in Buchanan yet. We knew they had not captured the last villages north of us. Since they had very little mass transportation, they were traveling on foot and could not reach Buchanan for several days.

The missionary school had been dismissed with an undetermined break since the tutor had evacuated a month earlier when the conflict began. With freedom from school, Laura and Michael enjoyed our final days in Liberia playing non-stop with their neighborhood friends. Despite the serious situation, they thoroughly enjoyed themselves and had reached the level of talking almost exclusively in Bassa to their friends and each other.

The last evening at our house, Laura ran past the clothesline, and remembered her ear brushing the wire line. That seemed to be when she lost her earrings, and she wept uncontrollably over their disappearance. The loss was an emotional outlet, while the real issue was knowing we would soon be leaving our home and friends for the unknown. We looked everywhere for the earrings. But in the end, they were just another one of the things left behind in Liberia.

Last night with special friends
Laura and her playmate, Michael and GG
One of my favorite pictures.

36

Departure

At the final CEM meeting the men decided the missionaries would leave the next day, Sunday. They told the Bassa coworkers they would see them at church and say goodbye before leaving.

Since our house was empty, Perry and I decided we would leave and spend our final night safe at the mission guest house. Grabbing our evacuation bags, which contained the only cold weather clothes we had and a couple changes of underwear, we reluctantly but thankfully left our home. Before dark we said goodbye to our beloved neighbors and drove away in the old station wagon. Going down the back streets to avoid the army barrack road, we arrived at the mission guest house.

"Bauk, bauk," Mark announced himself at the door that evening. I let him in and was alarmed by his ashen color - Something was wrong. He asked to speak privately with Perry. In the bedroom behind closed door, he told Perry they had just received a message from the US Embassy. The secret code was used ordering all Americans to immediately evacuate Buchanan.

The broadcast said the national army had deserted their posts. There was no line of defense between our city and the rebel army. It looked like they would take over our city the next day, if not before.

When the evacuation order was announced, the plan was for CR missionaries living in Monrovia to go to work at our travel agency and secure tickets on the next flight. Since it was early evening, that would start the next morning and it would be no small task.

In Buchanan the missionary radio was used to call for an immediate gathering at the guest house. As our beloved colleagues solemnly arrived, the seriousness of the situation was heavy upon us all. There were strong differences of opinion. Perry and I felt it would be extremely dangerous to travel at night as the embassy had ordered. We knew from the nighttime travel patterns past our house that we would have to face multiple troop transports if we left immediately. We had all heard rumors that they often shot anyone who approached them after dark.

In the end everyone agreed we would leave together early Sunday morning and travel by caravan to the airport. We would assemble at a missionary's home on the edge of town and drive out together to the airport. Three missionary families and ours would leave the country, while another family would wait things out with other CR missionaries in the Vai area, west of the capital.

Missionaries from different missions were also contacted and urged to join our caravan. CR missionaries snuck around that night and informed not only other missionaries in town, but also our Bassa coworkers of our plans.

It was final then. We had come to our last night in Liberia. But how would it all end? With the rebel army unopposed we did not know what the situation would be in the morning. Nevertheless, Perry and I slept soundly, confident of the Lord's protection.

Early the next morning our vehicle was taken out of hiding and loaded with our few suitcases. It was April 22, Pat's birthday and one she would never forget. We drove quietly down the road skirting the city, assembling at 6:00AM at a missionary's rented home on the periphery of the city. From there we had easy access to the main road leading to Monrovia and the airport.

Rev. Dr. Abba Karnga was there along with several other Bassa friends and coworkers. We apologized for not staying to worship with them one last time, but they understood. After praying together for God's protection and safety for all, we embraced. When would we see these brothers in Christ again? What might they and their families face in the future? It was too terrible to contemplate.

Before leaving, I was informed the last radio transmission had just been received. There was word from the States that my mother had a large kidney tumor, requiring surgery. One of the nurses informed me it could either be cancer or in rare instances, it could be benign. It was a shock, but there was so much going on that I didn't have time to dwell on the news. It was another uncertainty for the future.

We climbed into the waiting cars and began to drive away. I looked out the window trying to memorize everything. I told our children, "Look at everything. Remember what it looks like because things will change now. There is a war coming and there will be a lot of fighting. We cannot go home again for a very long time." Tears flowed with the knowledge that Liberia and the Bassa people would never be the same again. Inwardly I doubted if we would ever return.

Leaving town, we commented that we understood God's plan for Perry's back injury. His convalescence had given him the final opportunity to train the Bassa men to take over every aspect of the work and equip the churches for God's honor and glory.

We left before doctors had advised Perry to get up, so he felt most comfortable steadying himself by holding the steering wheel. It gave his weak back muscles support, as opposed to bouncing around the roads in the passenger's seat. He felt he would also be needed at the driver's window to talk to the officials at police and military gates. There would certainly be many additional ones during such an unstable time.

We were the last vehicle in the missionary caravan. It was planned that way since Perry was our mission's leader and responsible for us all. He would see to it that no one was detained or left behind at the check points. It was to our advantage that he had traveled a lot over the years. Many official people along the roadside knew and respected him.

When our caravan of cars approached the guarded roadblocks, those in front told the soldiers we were traveling as a group and the mission "bossman" was coming behind. After the missionary vehicles had been individually waved through the gates, they waited along the roadside making sure everyone got safely through.

As Perry drove up to the check points, he told the officials the cars in front of us were loaded with missionary families. He explained that we were trying to leave and go to our homes. When our vehicle was released through the gates, our caravan continued toward the airport.

At each check point the soldiers allowed us to proceed without inspecting our bags or complicating our lives. Passing through the guarded gates, we praised God for safety each step of the way. At the time we did not realize any delay would have put our lives in jeopardy.

It was obvious the situation was very tense with many armed soldiers and vehicles standing ready. The faces of the men in the national army held a variety of emotions from experienced soldiers confidentially holding their automatic rifles, to those who looked inexperienced, unsure, and even afraid. We drove past our former hometown, but no one was in sight and the houses were all shut. Perhaps people had already "ran into the bush" for safety.

As we passed Owens Grove check point, we were greeted by Perry's long-time acquaintances. They were the usual guards assisting additional soldiers at the gate. Perry opened the truck door to shake his friends' hands good-bye, instead the uniformed men snapped to alert and saluted Perry. It was indeed an honor, and he saluted them back before embracing the men. As we drove on, we wiped tears from our eyes knowing we would soon cross the border leaving Bassaland behind.

Our destination was the airport hotel just up the road a half hour or so. We were grateful to get rooms there, where we collapsed in relief and thankfulness for safe passage. Shortly after our arrival Michael and Ryan, another missionary son, stood on our balcony and drew my attention to heavy army tanks and artillery passing by. The boys ran around the room making booming noises, but chills went up my spine when I saw the big guns on the tanks. These armored vehicles were traveling the road we had just been on and were going toward our former city.

It would not be until we were safely out of the country that we would know the grave danger avoided by leaving early Sunday morning. The BBC radio reported the tanks shot up any vehicle they met on the road in keeping with General Doe's earlier order for his troops to shoot on sight anyone they deemed suspicious.[43]

We had arrived at the hotel not more than half an hour before the boys pointed out the convoy. God had certainly been going before us and guarding the rear as He had promised me in Isaiah 52.

Sometime later we learned that our landlord and his family were making their way back to Buchanan that day. Unfortunately, his wife was killed as they traveled the same road we had taken. She was a strong Christian, who would no longer have to struggle with the unbelief of her husband. She and I had sat many times in our home praying about this concern.

Arriving at the hotel did not put an end to our worries that day. The drive had been too much for Perry's partially healed back ligaments and he lay moaning on the floor in pain. He had to be convinced to take heavy pain relievers, being greatly concerned he might need to care for his family or make important decisions.

Laura lay restlessly beside him with a burning fever and recognizable symptoms of malaria. I always carried chloroquine in my purse and gave her the initial dose. I worried it would not be effective, since we suspected this was another outbreak of the resistant malaria. Soon she curled up and slept next to her father on the floor.

I sat nearby attempting to convince myself we were through the worst. All missionaries had safely made it out, Perry was able to travel, and our family was together. All the preparations and packing were over, but the dreaded fear of what would soon happen in Buchanan was upper most on my mind.

With a knock on the door, our colleague, Mark brought information that an international phone line was open in the hotel. He suggested I call home to inform them of our evacuation and find out more about my mother's medical situation. In the lobby the line for the phone was long, and the man standing behind me caught me two times as I slumped over with exhaustion from the past two weeks.

The familiarity of my mother's voice on the phone filled me with emotion and my voice cracked with fear as I informed her that the soldiers were moving to our area. Fighting would certainly happen in Buchanan, so all the missionaries had safely evacuated to the airport hotel. I asked about her condition. All she replied was, "Please talk to your father". The answer chilled me. I was afraid of the worst in Liberia, and apparently the situation at home was equally serious.

My father told me my mother had a tumor the size of a large grapefruit on her kidney and possibly there were other tumors too. It was devastating news to hear. Her surgery would be in a couple of days. I informed him we would be flying out to Europe hopefully the next day and then try to catch a flight to the States soon.

As I walked back to the hotel room, I felt I could collapse with emotion, but decided I should not center my thoughts on my mother's medical condition. Instead, I must concentrate on my immediate responsibilities of getting my family out of the country, while caring for the special needs of Perry and Laura.

We slept one night at the airport hotel and already had tickets to leave the next day. Due to the diligence of our colleague in Monrovia, tickets were secured for us all to leave on the same flight. The next morning in the pouring rain the other missionaries took our luggage and documents along with theirs to the customs office in the airport.

I felt a good deal of anxiety being the only mission family left in the hotel without our passports. Perry and Laura were however in no condition to be standing in lines any longer than necessary. Our teammates kindly got our documents stamped and then came back to pick us up. We ran through a downpour of rain to the car and were able to pass quickly through the airport by showing our completed passports.

A great concern of ours was that seven-year-old Laura would not be allowed to leave the country, since she was quite sick with multiple symptoms. I gave her a cough drop to control her coughing and told her to be very quiet. She was directed to lay her head on my shoulder and face inward while I carried her through the airport. This I hoped would give the allusion that she was sleeping. I carried her through the entire airport and up the stairway to the plane.

Michael was a typical five-year-old and was under strict instructions to hold onto my arm and not touch his daddy for fear it would jar his back. Perry followed behind with an empty carry-on bag. He had worried it would look strange for me to carry Laura and a backpack, and manage Michael, while he did nothing but walk behind us. So, I fluffed up a cloth carryon and he carried it empty.

All passengers were loaded onto a bus, which drove across the tarmac to a waiting KLM plane. Once we found our seats, I noted there was not an empty spot on the plane. The stewards rushed people to get buckled up, saying we would be quickly leaving. I looked around for our beloved coworkers. We were scattered throughout the plane, but I could look back between the seats and Pat was several rows behind us. As the plane taxed away from the terminal, the flight attendants hurriedly gave their instructions. We expected to suddenly take off down the runway, but the pilot abruptly cut the engines.

The ensuing silence within the plane was deafening. No one on the plane moved or said a thing. Even the young children sensed the tension and were silent. No announcement was made, but Perry could see army jeeps circling our plane with 50 caliber machine guns pointed at it.

Air was not circulated and in the middle of hot season the temperature in the fuselage began to rise. What would happen next was anyone's guess. I expected the door would be opened and armed soldiers would rush in. I looked back through the crack in the seats at Pat, and I could tell she was as anxious as I was. She motioned to me with folded hands to pray, indeed.

A long time passed, perhaps an hour, but it seemed longer. No one dared move, not a seat belt clicked with the hope that we would again soon be in motion. From Perry's vantage point he could see the soldiers motioning the plane back to the terminal.

Suddenly the engines started, and the AC blew hot air from the vents, but one jeep was still blocking the runway. Soldiers motioned for the jeep to move to the right side, while the other moved to the left. The plane turned to the left very slowly, and then Perry saw the flaps extend. Perhaps the pilots reacted to the opening between the jeeps and took advantage of it, because suddenly the jets screamed, we lunged to the right, and then were pressed back in our seats with the force of a nearly instant take off.

We always wondered why there was a delay on the runway with the circling jeeps, and had the nervous military shot at us while we were taking off? We have no idea what was going on, and we'll probably never know.

Suddenly, at that moment Liberia, the Bassa people, and our efforts in the name of Jesus our Savior were far behind us. It was hard to comprehend Liberia had become a place we had once lived - a people we would no longer see - a life once lived in the past. As our plane made its steep climb, the clouds were low and necks strained to catch a quick last glimpse, then suddenly Liberia was gone from view.

How strange it felt to leave the conflict so far behind and realize we were completely out of danger. Mixed emotions played in my head. It seemed we were far too privileged with our free tickets out when the going got tough. Our Bassa brothers and sisters in Christ certainly deserved this escape as well.

Uncontrolled weeping could be heard around me. I too wept in fear for those who were left behind and prayed for their safety. I wept in relief to have escaped the dangers of war, for the safe passage God had given, and for the blessing of leaving with my husband and children safe at my side. I wept in thankfulness for the opportunity God had given us to work with the Bassa people, and for how His Spirit had moved men and women to wholeheartedly believe in Him and serve Him.

~~~~~~~~~

By God's grace, Perry and I ministered in Liberia for 10 years with our children. By God's grace the Christian Reformed World Mission's team of seven young couples and one nurse had trained and equipped nearly 1,000 men and women from about 100 different denominations to serve the church of Christ. The pastors could read the books of the Bible translated in their own language and prepare Biblically accurate sermons.
~~~~~~~~~

Bassa missionary men and women in the churches had been trained to meet the needs of the sick, and Christian clinics had been started. Christian midwives were providing safe deliveries, and even the farmers had been introduced to improved farming methods. The completion of the entire Bible translated into Bassa was anticipated, and Bassa men and women had received higher education to equip them for service in God's church.

David Shank, a Mennonite missionary researching missionary endeavors among African Independent Churches, said the Christian Reformed Mission in Liberia was the most successful mission program in modern history.[44] We were humbled by his assessment. Ephesians 2:10, *For we are God's workmanship, created in Christ Jesus to do good works, which God prepared in advance for us to do.*

As we flew away, Perry leaned over and said to me, "It was a 'divine kairos'". I asked what he meant. He explained it is a Greek phrase meaning a privileged window in time. God had given an allotted period of time to minister to fellow Christians and train them while it was still politically possible.

Incredibly, the divine kairos was over. The window of privilege and opportunity God had called us to for ten years had ended, and there was no going back.

37
Readjustment

We arrived at Schiphol Airport in Amsterdam and thought we would say farewell to our fellow missionaries, since we all had free hotel rooms that came with our airline tickets. Other plans were set in motion by Pat's mother in Michigan. She had notified her Dutch sister, saying we were all evacuating Liberia. Aunt Dieneke showed up at the airport with her friends who helped transport everyone and their luggage to her home.

We had visited Cees and Dieneke before in their home along the Amsterdam-Rhine Canal and did not realize it was large enough to accommodate three families. But Pat's aunt found a place for us all to sleep and it was wonderful.

We listened to short wave radios in the attic where reception was the best, trying to keep track of recent developments in Liberia. All news was sobering, including tank movements and shootings on our last traveled road. We learned the rebels had taken our former city of Buchanan only the day after we left and tanks from the national army had shot cars on the road. It was frightening to think we had come that close to danger.

Aunt Dieneke took the children for long walks along the adjacent canal, while the adults stayed behind. Huddled around the warmth of the fireplace we talked, cried, and prayed. Soon we would no longer be together, and it would be a long time before we saw our teammates again.

Our family was the first to leave the Netherlands, since we were concerned about my mother and wanted to get to the States in time for her surgery. Early the next morning, she was wheeled into surgery, and later we were greeted with the wonderful news that her tumor was a very rare form of benign kidney tumors. In fact, the hospital had never removed that type before.

Mentally, I wrestled with the difficult contrast in God's intervention. How was it that He was taking care of our every need, while in Liberia believers in Christ were fighting for their lives? My mother would live and share her life with ours, Laura never got malaria again, and our family was safely home. However, Perry went to the doctor and his health was reason enough for him to be hospitalized, so my mother and husband were in the hospital at the same time. Eventually they both regained their health and strength.

But back in Liberia, we knew from radio transmissions that Liberians were forced to leave their homes and march great distances. We could not imagine the atrocities that were happening, even though we had heard much of it through the grape vine and on the BBC radio. Our hearts ached for them. Liberia was being destroyed, while we were experiencing God's blessing. It seemed all we could do was constantly pray for God's provision for His believers back in Liberia.

Perry's parents were living in Florida at the time, so we took up lodging in their home in Sioux Falls and attended the family's home church. After a couple of Sundays some ladies approached me asking, "Can we help you with anything?" I couldn't really think of anything we needed, so they kindly pointed out that my family had been wearing the same clothes for three weeks. I suddenly realized it was true. Since we were in the States, we no longer had to be in survival/travel mode with minimal necessities. Compared to news on the radio and the devastation going on in Liberia, we had felt we had all we needed.

We had left Liberia in the hottest season and felt rather cold in the stateside spring weather. My children were going to church in coats and sweaters, while the locals were enjoying warmer weather and beginning to wear their summer apparel. We must have looked rather comical to them, but our bodies would soon reacclimate to cooler temperatures. The church ladies organized a food and clothing shower for us, and we suddenly had more than enough - the good old American way.

After Perry and Mom were out of the hospital and everyone in our family had healed, we went to visit Perry's parents in Florida. Later we went to the mission offices in Grand Rapids, where we received a schedule to begin visiting our supporting churches. When we spoke and showed our slide program, we would invite people to pray for the Liberian church.

From the news we knew soldiers were burning villages and forcing the people to march long distances. I was troubled by this, knowing it was rainy season and it would be very difficult for people to be constantly in the rain, especially at night. We asked the Christians in the States to specifically pray that the Bassa sojourners would find shelter from the rain and have nourishment as they were shuffled from place to place. It seemed a tall order, and we weren't sure how God would answer those prayers.

Six months later, Abba Karnga was able to leave his war-torn country and we were blessed to have him stay with us for a while. The war had changed many things. Unfortunately with our displacements and the Liberian war, Abba and Perry were not able to accept their invitations to be keynote speakers at African Independent Churches conference in Durban, South Africa and Malawi.

When Abba heard we had asked supporters to pray God would provide shelter from the rain and supply them with food, he looked shocked. He told us how the soldiers had forced masses of people to leave their towns and walk great distances to other locations. This was to give time for battles to take place.

Abba said it was especially difficult to be moved from one area to another during rainy season. He was always amazed because not once did they have to sleep outside in the rain. It was a true wonder in rainy season, but to hear that American Christians had been praying for exactly that - it was simply a miracle and answer to prayer.

He also told how the mango trees had been over productive and the fruit were especially large. His people had literally survived on mangoes as they walked along. It was truly a joy to realize our prayers had been answered and once again God had allowed us to minister to the Bassa people.

Abba's visit was a personal blessing for me. Six months after our return to the States, I was still emotionally troubled by the aftermath of our evacuation. I often spontaneously wept, coupled with difficulty sleeping at night. Everything in the news was so awful, and we even saw familiar places on TV where people were being executed.

I told Abba I couldn't stop crying for the people of Liberia. He tenderly told me, "Thank you for crying for us, but you should stop now." His permission for me to step out of deep grief and go on with life was freeing. There would still be much sadness and worry while the war continued for fourteen years, but I was given the gift of letting go of the heartfelt agony that had gripped me.

Laura was nearly eight years old and for her the deep-seated grief continued, until we had a visit from our good friend, Rev. John Innis. He told many war stories, things which we had kept from our children. He spoke openly of the death of many people. So many in fact, that when walking from village to village he had seen human bones laying on the side of the path for every step he took. He described how little babies were swept off their mother's backs while crossing swift streams, and how it was not unusual for children to run around screaming since they were separated from their families. In addition, everyone had to be very careful because soldiers shot people for little reason.

Pastor John patiently listened to Laura's sorrows while she cried about the war and the pain of people we had known. She mourned for her life in Liberia, which she called home, and told John she wanted to hear the Bassa language around her and learn more of it.

He finally said to her, "Laura, you should stop crying now. If you keep crying, then the Bassa people will be worried about you. We have so many bad things happening, we don't need any more trouble." It seemed this request made sense to her. She would go on to do her part and not cause any more worries for John or the Bassa people. Still in her heart Laura always called Liberia "home", but she like the rest of the family began to move on with her life, though never forgetting because part of us remained with the Bassa people.

The fighting went on and on, tearing the land and people apart for fourteen years. There were two successive civil wars with a break between them. The first war lasted from 1989-1997, with a cease fire of nine months, and the second war was from 1999-2003. The lives of almost 250,000 people were lost, most of them civilians. Starvation and brutality appeared to have the upper hand. Child soldiers were forced to commit atrocities against their own people. There was a complete breakdown of law and order, causing some 850,000 refugees to flee to neighboring countries.[45]

The city of Buchanan suffered a huge setback when it was left without an electricity source. An ECOMOG (Economic Community of West African States Monitoring Group) Nigerian officer "defending" the area rolled up the power lines from Monrovia to Buchanan and had them shipped to his home city in Nigeria. It was rumored he said, "What is Buchanan? My hometown is much better and has no electricity, so I'll send them power lines." In fact, widespread corruption and looting were so bad, ECOMOG became known as "Every Car or Movable Object Gone".

It was a blessing to discover that during those years God preserved and even strengthened His Bassa church. Abba told us they discovered none of the former TEE students died in the war! It was even more extraordinary that no one in their immediate families lost their lives! That must be a true miracle and answer to prayers of the church of Jesus.

Charles Taylor was successful in overtaking the country and a breakaway fraction from his army brutally killed President Samuel Doe. Taylor was elected as president in a special election and held office for seven years from 1997 until 2003. He resigned after being indicted for crimes against humanity by the United Nations Court for murder, enslavement, and recruitment of child soldiers.

In the neighboring country of Sierra Leone, he was accused of supporting rebel factions and trading arms for "blood diamonds". He fled to Nigeria, was extradited,[46] and in 2012 found guilty in The Hague of eleven charges. Presiding Judge Richard Lussick sentenced him to 50 years in prison saying, "The accused has been found responsible for aiding and abetting, as well as planning some of the most heinous and brutal crimes in human history," which impacted thousands of victims "physically, psychologically, and emotionally" and caused them to suffer "irreparable alienation from their communities."[47]

In 2003 programs for disarmament, demobilization, rehabilitation and reintegration began. Over time more than 100,000 former combatants were disarmed and countless weapons and explosive were destroyed.[48] Training programs for ex-rebel soldiers to learn trades were offered, while the national military and police were revamped, and strategies for a civilian government were put in place. At the time Liberia's population of 3.3 million included 44% under the age of 15, life expectancy was 48 years, and $140 was the annual per capita income. It was obviously an uphill battle for the country to flourish.[49]

Our family lived one year in Perry's hometown of Sioux Falls. After we fulfilled our duties with CRWM by visiting our supporting churches, his home church invited him to be an interim pastor, while they searched for a new pastor. I went back to work as a dental hygienist, and Laura and Michael were enrolled at Sioux Falls Christian School.

Perry and I signed up with CRWM to begin a new mission project in Hungary to again train church pastors. But funding for the additional project was pulled for lack of funds.

Disappointed, we decided to leave missions behind, and Perry put his name on a list for churches looking for a pastor. He received four calls from churches inviting him to be their pastor, but one stood out as the one God was calling Perry to serve. It was New Hope CRC in Spokane, WA., and it was same decisive impetus we had experienced when God called us to go to Liberia. We arrived in Spokane only a few days before school started in 1991 and have enjoyed a long pastorate there.

When we received pictures of the large refugee settlements in our former hometown and saw people wearing thread worn clothes, New Hope Church organized a clothing and supply drive. The church foyer was filled with donations of all sorts, which were shipped to Buchanan for the churches to distribute. Again, we felt the blessing that comes from serving and giving.

In August 2004 Dr. Abba Karnga visited our home in Spokane and spoke at the church. The congregation was inspired by his testimony as a gracious and humble servant of Christ. He and his family had survived the years of civil war and Abba had even recovered from being shot in the head! On another occasion he was brought before a firing squad. The captain of the squad asked him what he would like to say before his death. Abba's gracious manner and eloquent speech won them over - amazingly he left with an escorted bodyguard.

One evening Abba spoke at our church. He told how the Bassa church leaders remained organized and supported each other in many ways. When the war lapsed, the Bassa people were among the first helped by the French Red Cross, since the CEM infra structure was still in place.

A deacon asked him what we could do to help the Bassa people. Abba replied that having a radio station would enhance his people's healing after the war and provide solidarity for them. At that time the CEFL had prepared a house for a radio station and secured a license to broadcast, but a transmitter was needed.

Perry offered the example of his parent's church using a simple radio transmitter. It had cost $4,000 and they used it to broadcast sermons. At our church that evening, an offering was taken on the spot. My shoulders sank, I thought it was too lofty a goal, and people might not be prepared to give.

Then someone privately offered to match every dollar given up to $3,000, and it seemed people got excited. Could they be increasing their donations? With God's mercy nothing is impossible! The deacons announced our humble church had gathered $6,491. "It was a miracle, I tell you." was Abba's comment, and that said it all. Our little church had heard the need, caught the vision, and together made the first radio transmissions possible in Bassaland.

The radio was used for reconstruction after the lengthy war. Transmissions were sent to help lost family members reconnect. Death announcements from years gone-by were relayed, and sermons of hope from God's Word were received. We were so thankful God gave our church the opportunity to bless Abba and his Bassa people. The little transmitter was used for many years and when the time came to repair it, our church again had the honor to help cover those costs.

38

Return to Bassaland

2008 - Eighteen years after our hasty departure, Perry and I accompanied our children and their spouses back to Liberia. What we found thrilled our souls. The Bassa churches were strong and growing. The TEE program was even larger than when we had labored there, and we were blessed to learn the TEE alumni pastors were still meeting for mutual encouragement and to critique each other's sermons. In addition, many of our former Bassa colleagues and friends were hard at work for the gospel's sake.

Although there had been campaigns to get rid of the evidence of combat, there were still bullet holes visible in some buildings. On a positive note, the economy was making great strides to get back on its feet. The refugee camps had been disbanded, people were wearing new clothes, and there was food available. Although they were emotionally dealing with the aftereffects of the wars, the Bassa people showed their resilience and were once again enjoying life.

We knew all the former missionary homes were either destroyed or occupied, so Rev. Dr. Abba and Eileen Karnga graciously invited us to stay in their Buchanan home. They hosted six in our family and three other returning missionaries at the same time, providing everything their guests needed. Their daughter-in-law Rebecca cooked wonderful Bassa meals for us in the open-air traditional kitchen, which were served around a huge dining room table in their home.

The Karnga house is a rambling, spacious affair with many rooms, including three guest bedrooms and two bathrooms on an upper level. Our family stayed in those rooms, accessed by an outside stairway. There were hooks imbedded in the bedroom walls, which we used to tie up our mosquito nets. I had sewn three nets for our trip, and they encircled our beds while we slept. We also took anti-malarial pills and hoped and prayed none of us would get malaria.

It was the month of May when we arrived, which is the end of Liberia's hot/dry season. Coming from the cool spring weather in the States, we all felt the oppression of the hot season's high heat and humidity. Our kids asked us how we could have lived there for ten years! It seemed there was no escape from it. The extreme conditions even made us all feel a bit panicky at times.

Abba attempted to help by running the generator through the night, so we "kwii-poo" could have fans to sleep in the intense heat. That brought some relief but sitting in front of the fan only blew hot air like a furnace vent. Taking a shower brought little relief, since the water was almost warm. The best thing was to wet our skin and let the fan blow on us, but the relief was short lived.

Even with fans running, the nights were hot and restless, and the mosquito nets seemed to impede what good the fans could do. It was necessary to constantly turn to feel the benefit of the fan and keep the body from overheating. We reminisced of how we had always thought Buchanan was hotter than the first area we lived in, and how good it had been to sleep on a cool waterbed. We laughed recalling how the other missionaries quickly followed us in getting one.

Our family often gathered in the bedroom Perry and I shared at Abba's house. It was the largest and had windows on three sides, so the slight breezes at night could be felt there. One night, Perry went down the stairs and saw people were sitting on chairs in the neighbor's yard facing our bedroom. Apparently, they had a view and could watch whatever we were doing. He went over to talk to them and asked if they were watching us. "O yes!" they responded, and culturally there was no felt shame in doing so.

After a week of intense heat, finally one evening a strong wind began to blow forcing the palm branches all back in one direction. It was a unique sight, which had been something I always enjoyed seeing, because it meant the monsoon rains were coming. A cool breeze blew in from the ocean replacing the hot air, and a few drops of rain began to fall, then more and more, until we had a welcomed down pour. We slept under covers that night, as it felt cool, and in the morning, everyone looked refreshed at the breakfast table.

Fortunately, there are beautiful ocean beaches near Buchanan, and we went there each day to cool off in the ocean waves. From a fishing village nearby, we bought fresh fish and lobster for our dinners and our cook appreciated that.

It was sobering to visit Silver Beach where the missionaries beach hut had been. During the war we had seen that place on TV, as it became renowned for executions. Gathered along the high tide line were many shoes, undoubtedly once owned by people who had been executed there or drowned in the ocean. Perry was compelled to take pictures of them, as a tribute to those who had lost their lives.

We inquired of the Karnga family what had happened to their family during the war. In the middle of the night they had been ushered out of their home, leaving all behind to march great distances and sleep without cover. One of the greatest treasures lost were the family pictures.

What a thrill to once again sit with Abba and have the privilege to talk to him. He is a very wise man and many people came to his house to speak with him and gain his wisdom and advice. God truly blessed this gentle man with wisdom and courage, and we are privileged to have known him.

We drove to our long-time former home in the bush at Government Compound Number 1. We were disappointed to find only a handful of children in the village when we arrived, and they were quite shy around so many white people. A young man appeared who remembered us as a child, and grabbing a cutlass said he would take us to the former mission site.

We had heard it was used as command center for the national army during the war. In retreat they had installed land mines in our old driveway, so the compound could not be used again by advancing rebels. For this reason, our guide avoided the driveway steering us clear of any explosives.

Using his cutlass to trim foliage protruding into the path, he led us single file up the back route. We came first to a couple of mold stained walls where the office duplex had stood. The jungle tightly hugged the walls and vines grew across it making it difficult to visualize. Feeling the familiarity of the place, tears sprang to my eyes as I recalled Perry sitting at his desk writing a lesson plan for his TEE class.

We then trudged up the hill on the familiar foot path towards our house. The path was in the same place it had always been, although it was worn somewhat deeper and wider. Jungle growth tightly hugged the path, and we sorely felt the heat and humidity escaping from the soil, making some wonder how far we would have to go. We reminded our family members that Perry and I had both stepped on dangerous snakes, so they'd better watch where they walked.

Perry was enthusiastic taking the lead behind our guide with the cutlass, while I lingered last in line. I found myself reveling to once again hear common sounds and take in sights of the jungle. How wonderful to experience the songs of unique African birds, the call of insects, and the melodic Bassa language as people conversed along the trail. Even the heat and humidity felt like familiar elements of home. The dense jungle foliage and the sound of feet padding along the path brought a contented happiness to me. I noted the sharp contrasts of the brilliant orange dirt with the lush green jungle against the vibrant blue sky, and felt a deep sense of being home.

Unseen people in the village began to call in Bassa to the man escorting us, asking where we were going and had Gardeah and his family really returned? We heard sounds of cheer and excitement, and the promise that old friends were coming from behind to greet us.

The jungle had annoyingly grown back in all its splendor, so that we could no longer envision the beautifully groomed mission lawn with waving palm trees leading to the two white-washed mission houses. The lovely view of rolling hills in the distance was also hidden, so we attempted to paint the picture for our family.

When we suddenly came to the beloved old tree which had graced our front door, Perry gave it a pat and called down the trail to me, "Look Kathy, we're home!" My eyes stung with emotion and my stomach felt homesick for our past lives in the former wonderful setting. I too reached the towering tree and like an old friend there she stood looking pristine as ever. No doubt it had stories to tell after watching the army's command center and listening in on strategic meetings.

As we stepped off the African path, I noted it still passed just off my former kitchen corner. I recalled the frustration of it being so close to our home, but also the intimacy it afforded with our neighbors. All the high-quality roofing and rafters had been stripped from the house, in fact only the walls were standing. They supported a macabre ceiling of large, twisted vines, which raced in every direction, partially concealing the sun's penetrating rays. From experience we were without a doubt that snakes were camouflaged above, but the village children boldly led us in the house, so we carefully followed behind.

We took two steps up and entered the piazza or porch area, which no longer supported screened walls. I reminded Laura and Michael that along the wall there had been a wicker bench and additional chairs. There was also a ledge where people often sat. In the corner a hammock had hung and I could almost see Perry sitting in it, while I served soft drinks to local friends. Many happy hours were spent there talking to guests who had come to see us, and sometimes he had opportune conversations to share the gospel with local dignitaries.

I recalled gently rocking my little babies in the hammock, and we often cuddled with our children there. When they were older, we would swing together and sing songs as we waited for Daddy to drive up the driveway while watching the hummingbirds close by. Scenes flashed in my mind of our children playing with Bassa children on the porch. We had Sunday School there and invited the local children to attend.

The door was gone from the porch to the dining room, but in my mind I heard the twang of the screen door's spring expanding to open and then slamming shut. Fragments of our lives were everywhere replaying in my mind. I recalled wonderful times of fellow missionaries visiting, welcoming special guests, and loved ones visiting from the States.

Standing in the shell of our house, many happy voices mulled into one, and events of days gone by raced before me. It was as if the remaining walls of our house echoed laughter to me from years gone by. In the kitchen I envisioned my younger self cooking endless meals, and the joy of feeling my babies pull on my skirt. I remembered Browne nearby washing dishes, then scooting outside to tend the fire.

I could almost see the large dining room table to accommodate guests. My precious children were perched in their custom-made highchairs eating potato greens and rice at the table with birthday balloons hanging from the wicker light fixture. I envisioned my young husband on a blistering hot day smiling at me as he sat across the table in his usual spot, and from the dining room window I felt the breeze of hot air. I wouldn't have been surprised to look up and see a basket on top of someone's head bobbing past the window on the nearby path.

We advanced forward and in my mind's eye I could see my treadle sewing machine along the living room wall. I recalled after dinner Perry might sit nearby at the desk and shelf unit he had built, calling on his ham radio to the States. Meanwhile, the solar panel light always shone dimly from the ceiling and outside the crickets and frogs would be loudly serenading.

Scenes of sober reality also struck me. A lump swelled in my throat to recall times of alarm with the news of an attempted coup coming over the AM radio. There were also lonely days and nights of isolation, and I recalled weeping and praying on the couch. Yet, God's sweet assurance of His holy presence in our lives was always before us. He had been with us through everything all those years ago, blessing us and molding us with His powerful, sweet Spirit.

We explained where the kids' bedrooms had been and were surprised to see the color of cheap paint still visible in places behind thick mold. Some elements of the bathroom remained, but the master bedroom had been hit by a mortar and the corner walls were blown off. I saw evidence that my wooden closet shelves had finally been depleted by the persistent termites, eventually they had won the long-standing battle.

Out back behind the house, an umbrella tree planted near the bathroom drywell was shockingly huge with twenty years of growth. Only a portion of cement patio we had poured remained. It too had been hit by mortars, and I told our kids of Christmas parties we had hosted there with lighted palm branches decorating the perimeters.

We had lovingly buried our tiny baby in the back yard, and it had been our heartfelt desire to visit the grave. There had been a large flat rock which marked the burial spot, but to our great dismay, we could not locate the gravestone that day. Though Perry searched the area chopping through the jungle with a cutlass, we had to walk away knowing it was covered with twenty years of fallen jungle debris, or possibly hidden by dirt blasted over it when the house was under attack. We contented our hearts to say, "Rest in sweet peace little one of our heart's desire, we will be with you soon at the feet of Jesus."

We sadly walked down the hill and made our way to the village area. Our beloved watchman Old Man Pau and Taa, the grounds keeper, had both died before the war, but many of our local acquaintances had survived. Dabo, the midwife missing a great toe, was amazingly still alive and living in the same town by the road. When she realized we were there, she ran wearing only a ragged work lappa and threw her arms around us crying, "My people, my people". When Dabo realized who Michael was she immediately went to embrace him saying, "My baby! Gamasau, my baby, has become a man like a rock."

Corpu, her son was there with the same grin on his face. He and his family had fled to Firestone during the war. He had always told us Dabo was 100 years old when we lived there, so that day he said she was almost 120. We wondered if it might be true as she did indeed look ancient. The roof of her house proudly displayed one small diagonally cut piece of aluminum roofing from our former house. It was undoubtedly discarded by a demolition crew and lacked any value in shedding rain. Perhaps there was a certain prestige in having even just a bit of aluminum on Dabo's thatched roof.

Everyone looked the same except a few years older and we handed out gifts to all. Clothes, shoes, toiletries, and cash were lovingly distributed to our former neighbors. We also had an array of garden seeds and people were eager to choose what they wanted. Nora a special friend of the other missionary family was given a suitcase and items to sell in the market, and she wondered when her old friends would be coming to see her.

Laura and Michael were of course remembered by all as Jonja and Gamasau, and everyone remarked at what big people they had become. Peéa, the genteel woman who watched Laura as a newborn, caught up to us for a joyous reunion just as we were leaving. How fun to share with her the otherwise unannounced news that Laura was expecting a baby of her own!

We were told the original homes in the village were all burned and broken down by soldiers. The residents were forced to build new ones but could not rebuild on their original spots. When I asked what the reason for that was, they said the soldiers told them it would be a good part of the war for them to get new homes. The people were forced to rebuild the houses themselves, consequently it didn't seem so wonderful to them.

Further up the road, it was a joy to find another friend Teetee, the mother of my steward Browne. She and her family were still living near our former rental home, once owned by an ambassador. I gave her a pretty blouse, but she was especially excited to receive seed packets, commenting she would use them in her garden. A little crowd had gathered to greet us, and they pushed to the forefront the man who had been paralyzed after falling from a palm tree. They pointed, "Look he is still walking", reminding me I had gone to see him, prayed for his healing, and the next day he had walked.

"I praise God - to Him be the glory," I responded in Bassa.

It was simply amazing to watch people get on their cell phones calling each other. While we were gone, they had skipped the land-line era and entered a whole new world of communication with cell phones.

Using a little phone wrapped in her lappa cloth, Teetee made a quick call, and located Browne. She informed us we could catch our former steward at home where he lived a few miles up the road. It seemed he was the same as ever, except for a few gray hairs. He thought we had re-entered his life at the perfect time, since he needed money for "dead body business" and appreciated a cash gift.

We were blessed to find several students from Perry's former TEE class and witness their maturity in Christ as His servants. Wherever we went, we passed out many gifts of seed packets and slowly depleted our personal supply of clothes, shoes, toiletries and even suitcases. Our plan was to leave the country with only the clothes on our backs, knowing our gifts would bless whoever received them.

Later back in Buchanan, what a joy to meet up with David, Perry's first language informant. Our first year in Liberia he had led us aimlessly through the jungle while looking for his relative's village. He had four children and had become a very nice gentleman, which had always been his personality.

Perry's fisherman friend, Joe Freeman met us at Abba's house. Perry was prepared with fishing lures as a gift for him, and we reminisced about the huge tarpon he had caught. He was still attending church and faithfully believing in God.

We visited our last home in Buchanan at the Alfred George field. It had become a training center for youth after the war. Our living room was full of desks with computers, and our former office space was used for practicing keyboard on old typewriters. Laura's bedroom was the beauty school, Michael's bedroom became the staff office, and our master bedroom was the counseling center. The swing set Perry had welded for the kids was still in the back yard, and my outside cooking area was in use. Perry immediately set about linking and connecting ministries, saying the CEM clinic needed copier services, which the training school could provide.

A familiar person appeared, and it was Michael's former playmate GG, also called Bobby. Now young men, they were excited to become reacquainted, and Michael and Jena received an invitation to visit GG's home to meet his wife and baby. He was employed as the driver of large construction equipment and still lived in the same area. His mother had been a close friend of mine, but they had moved to the States years earlier.

We showed our family where Bassa Christian High School was and were treated with some school singing and a small program. Enrollment was down and some of the classrooms needed repair. A short distance away we saw the former mission house and guest house, and then went to the CEM office and radio station sight. We had come so close to completing a state-of-the-art radio station and could not have believed the grand building would never be used for that. Rather, it became the home of squatters from the war and a barn for animals.

Abba told us the building itself came to have another calling. During the war years, it served as a reminder of what the Church of Christ can do together. It gave people hope that one day they would do great things again and perhaps even have their long-anticipated radio station.

Since Perry was visiting, TEE students were invited to a conference in Buchanan and we had a blessed time fellowshipping with them. Perry and Matthew were asked to teach and lecture. Later, Perry and I met with just the TEE teachers in a stifling hot room where we sat packed next to each other. But no one cared since Perry spoke passionately to the instructors of their great privilege and responsibility before the Lord to teach pastors.

Representatives of the CEFL asked to meet with us and presented a many facetted report of their ministries and needs. They appealed us to return to Liberia and opened their invitation to our adult children. Though we shared their heartfelt desires, were impressed with their goals for the future, and felt a true affinity with them as brothers in Christ, we did not experience God moving in our hearts to relocate there and start over.

One of the most memorable visits was with Annie, my former housekeeper. All I had to do was inquire of her, and through the grapevine someone called her on a cell phone. She traveled a great distance and showed up the next day with her grown daughter Rebecca. Their lovely faces were a blessing to see. I often think part of heaven must be getting to spend time with beloved sisters in Christ who are no longer in my life.

Annie was presently living at Number 4, had given birth to three children during the war, and had ten kids total during her life. I asked Annie what had happened to her during the war. She recalled I had dismissed her early from her job and was especially grateful I had given her a lot of money. She said we had also purchased 200 pounds of rice, one for her and the other for her son. Just before the battles started, I had driven her and the rice to the Methodist Camphor mission, where her son was a student. She found safety and food on campus and ended up staying there for a while during the initial invasion of Buchanan.

Camphor mission was a relatively safe place under the protection of the school's headmaster, our friend Pastor John Innis. He negotiated with the national army for the campus to be a haven. Later when rebels stormed the campus suspecting Camphor mission was harboring enemies, God gave him the courage to speak boldly on behalf of the refugees:

"Gentlemen, I would think that the goal of your revolution is to liberate us. But if that is not the case and you would like to get rid of anyone on this campus, I will give my life for that person. Now, go ahead and kill me, but leave these people alone. God has destined this place to be a refuge center, and as long as they have come here, you must let them enjoy their peace and freedom."[50] The rebels responded by leaving the premises and thanking John for his love and care of the refugees.

After a while when food became scarce, Annie had made her way to the interior village of her extended family deep in the jungle. She thought since it was so remote the soldiers wouldn't be there. She reasoned she could make a rice farm and live a secluded life there, but she was wrong.

The soldiers were already there, supposedly to protect the town. They harassed the residents continually. Whenever Annie cooked food, they came just when the preparation was complete, demanding she give the food to them as a thank you for keeping the town safe. When she harvested her rice, they were on the spot taking it from her as a tax for their protection. In the end there was little for her and the family to eat.

Far worse things happened to her there. She was forced to watch as the soldiers executed her brother. He was shot in the head while on his knees pleading for his life. She said he was a good man, there was no reason to kill him. One of her sons was conscripted into the rebel army and the other to the national army, so they had fought against each other. She had not seen nor heard from them since, and feared they were dead. As many women experienced, she was repeatedly raped, while her sons could do nothing to help her.

After some time, she fled her family village in the jungle and walked a great distance through dangerous military areas to the Atlantic shore. There she bought a seat on a crowded tipsy river canoe. Over twenty canoes set out on the ocean and all but four of them capsized in the big waves. Drowning people begged her to give them a hand and save them, but there was nothing she could do. There was no room in the canoe and allowing even one person to hold on the side would capsize it. All they could do was paddle hard to get away. Her canoe made it some distance down the beach, only to reach another area occupied by fighting factions and hardship.

As she reminisced, I grabbed her hands and shed many tears, but Annie was stolid. I told her I was so sorry those terrible things had happened to her, and she replied, "Don't be sorry for me. I learned the most valuable lesson in my life. I learned they could take absolutely everything from me. They could take my food, family, and dignity, but they couldn't take Jesus from my heart! He is the only thing that matters, and nothing they did could ever take Him away."

At this point her daughter Rebecca chimed in, "That's right, they took everything – everything, but we still had Jesus in us!" Then she asked Perry, "Why do American ministers preach so poorly? I listen to them on the radio and they talk to us about improving our marriages and our lives. They speak about how to get blessings, and that God will bless us if we do good. We Liberians think we must be the most sinful people on earth because God must be punishing us with war, destruction, and trouble in our lives. Don't American preachers know that Jesus in your heart is the only thing that matters? It's the only thing that can't be taken from you. If Jesus is the most important, why don't they preach about Jesus? They can take away your house, your family…But they can't take Jesus from your heart. Preach Jesus, Pastor Perry, Preach Jesus!"

Perry reassured her it was the very thing he was eager to do, and it was what he had tried to teach the CEM staff and TEE students all along. "I can't speak for other American preachers. I can only speak for this one - I endeavor to preach Christ from every text."

39

Brush with Death

As we flew home to the States, we were all miserable and blamed it on restaurant food. When we arrived home, Perry's symptoms continued and even worsened with a high fever and vomiting, so I took him to the emergency room. He was sent home with only a minor fluctuation in the readings on his liver, probably due to a virus.

Over the weekend, his condition worsened, and I wished Michael and Jena had not gone out of town for the weekend. I felt Perry needed to return to the ER, but he refused to go. I thought Michael and Jena could have helped me persuade him. When I finally got him to the hospital, he had a raging fever and his liver and kidney functions were quite bad.

He was admitted to the hospital and eventually diagnosed with Typhoid Fever and Hepatitis A. We suspected he also had malaria, but that was never confirmed by lab work. Because his liver was compromised, he was not able to take acetaminophen to lower the fever, so we had to pack him with ice, which was torturous. As a registered nurse, Laura realized how ill her father was and flew from Chicago to be with the family.

People asked, "How could he have gotten these diseases?" In preparation for our return to Liberia, we had all gotten our immunizations updated. Perry and I were so sure he had had hepatitis A, that the nurse didn't give him the injection for it. However, he should have gotten it, because lab work confirmed he was in the hospital with hepatitis A.

I told the doctor that couldn't be right because he had already been sick with hepatitis when we lived there. The infectious disease doctor spent most of the day figuring it all out. He discovered there had been an outbreak of hepatitis E, which started in Egypt and spread to northern Liberia, and new blood work showed Perry had antibodies for hepatitis E, meaning he had had hepatitis E in the past and his body had fought it off!

I was able to fill in the blanks remembering he and a carload of missionaries and Bassa colleagues had driven to northern Liberia for the dedication of a new CEM clinic, which concluded with a feast. Later everyone who had gone to the dedication got terribly sick, including the Liberian men. One of the missionaries who had gotten sick went to the hospital and it was confirmed he had hepatitis. What we didn't know was that they had hepatitis E.

Most Liberians are exposed to hepatitis A in childhood and cannot get it again, but those who went to the clinic opening in northern Liberia had gotten sick, including the Bassa men who normally would have been immune had it been hepatitis A. I also had blood work done and found out that I had contracted Hep A in Liberia, which accounted for the time of illness I had after Michael's birth.

In Spokane, Perry's condition steadily declined, until the doctor told us it couldn't get any worse, or he would die. His liver was 80% compromised and he was the third person on the liver transplant list in Seattle. However, the doctor informed me he would not survive the helicopter trip to the airport.

In the afternoon I was sitting at Perry's bedside and recognized he had entered a new phase of rarely speaking and being semi-responsive at times. As I was talking to him, I recognized that he was giving up. I begged him, "Perry don't give up, fight to live!" He turned, looked at me with sad eyes, and shook his head. I realized he had lost his will to live, and it crushed me!

Michael and Jena were in the room. She rushed over to him, took him by the shoulders saying, "Perry, you fight to live! You hear me, you fight! Don't die!" He just stared at her, so she shook him a little and got in his face, "Perry you listen to me - you can't go now, we need you. You stay here and fight to live!" Without speaking, he tearfully he shook his head agreeing to not let go.

Feeling desperate, I recalled the verse in James 5:14, *Is any one of you sick? He should call the elders of the church to pray over him and anoint him with oil in the name of the Lord. And the prayer offered in faith will make the sick person well; the Lord will raise him up.*

I called an elder in the church, asking him to have anyone who had ever been an elder to come to the hospital and pray for their pastor. Within a short time, they were all there. Wanting to literally follow the verse in James, I had requested someone bring oil to pour on Perry and expected to see a bottle from someone's cooking cupboard. I reasoned the more serious the situation – the more oil needed, but I didn't see any oil.

When we entered Perry's room the elders were startled to see him. His skin and eyes were dark yellow, and he was semi-conscious, not responding to their greetings. Then a retired pastor pulled out a small vial of olive oil and dripped it on Perry's head. "O well" I thought. The amount of oil was not the point, but the prayers offered in faith and the good and perfect will of our Father in Heaven would be the deciding factor.

I urged the elders to lay hands on him and pray. There was some hesitation, and I assumed they might be worried Perry's disease was contagious. I assured them it was safe to touch him. I laid my hands directly over his damaged liver and we began to earnestly pray for our pastor, friend, and husband. We prayed for nearly an hour, pleading with the Lord to bring healing and renew strength.

While we were praying, Perry eerily sat straight up and looked right through us. It was obvious he didn't realize we were there. I told him we were praying for him and he should lie back down. With an elder on both sides, they slowly eased him down.

That night two elders stayed with Perry meeting his needs. I was told to go home for the night, and the hospital would call me if his condition worsened. I was surprised to awaken the next morning without having received a call from the hospital.

Praise God! The first blood draw in the morning revealed improvement. From that time forward, he began to regain his health, his liver regenerated, and months later he eventually returned to his position as pastor.

Perry's brush with death brought me to a new level of trust in God. I came to the point of praying "Not my will, but Thy will." I didn't presume to know the will of our good and perfect heavenly Father, and I could trust Him unequivocally.

The disappointments and tragedies of life can either draw us closer to God or we can turn away and withdraw our trust in Him. The disappointments of life happen not because God has failed us, nor has He abandoned us in our time of need. He is proving his constant care for us with his never-ending presence in our lives to strengthen our faith and equip us for future challenges. When the difficult times come, we have the chance to see our faith in action and realize there is no depth to which we can descend without God proving He is there with us drawing us to himself.

~~~~~~~~~

We spent ten years in Africa, was it worth it?

Without a doubt! It was well worth it in so many ways! We still feel it was a divine kairos, a specific time granted by God to do His will and work of equipping and encouraging His Bassa churches and people.

What a privilege it is to follow where our Savior leads and to serve Him as He sees fit. We give God all the glory for things He did in Liberia, and all we experienced in His constant care. May He continue to spread His Spirit and blessings on the Bassa people to the honor and glory of His Name.

Donations to support ongoing training for Bassa church leaders
may be made through the Christian Education Foundation of Liberia-USA,
a stateside organization for the continuation of CEM.
www.CEFLiberia.org
~~~~~~~~~

The Tinklenberg family in 2018

ENDNOTES

1. Roger Steer, J. Hudson Taylor: *A Man in Christ, Missionary Life Stories* (Carlisle, UK: Authentic, December 1, 1969), 165.
2. Patty Hogan, former missionary to the Philippines, CRWM 125th Anniversary video, 2013, http://www2.crcna.org/pages/crwm_125_videos.cfm
3. Kelly Faye Willard, the Maranatha! Singers, *Make Me a Servant*, Album: Praise Six: Come and Sing Praises, track 2, CCCM Music, Universal Music – Brentwood Benson Music Publishing, Inc. 1982.
4. David B. Barrett, Schism and Renewal in Africa. An analysis of Six Thousand Contemporary Religious Movements (London, Oxford University Press, 1968), 50.
5. Kofi Appian-Kubi, Sergio Torres, *African Theology En Route: Papers from the Pan African Conference of Third World Theologians*, December 17-23, 1977, Accra, Ghana (Maryknoll, NY: Orbis Books, 1979), 117.
6. *Origin of HIV & AIDS*, December 05, 2017, https://www.avert.org/professionals/history-hiv-aids/orgin
7. CDC's HIV Basics, *What are HIV/AIDS*, HIVgov, May, 15, 2017 https://www.hiv.gov/hiv-basics/overview/about-hiv-and-aids/what-are-hiv-and-aids
8. The Carter Center, *Guinea Worm Eradication Program*, https://ww.cartercenter.org/health/guinea_worm/
9. World Health Organization, Media Centre, *Lymphatic Filariasis*, www.who.int/lymphatic_filariasis/epidemiology/en/
10. Lymphatic Filariasis Research Unit, Department of Parasitology, Chulalongdorn University, Bangok, Thailand, *A single dose of doxycycline in combination with Diethylcarbamazine for treatment of bancroftian filariasis*, PubMed.gov, US National Library of Medicine National Institutes of Health, July, 2010, https://www.ncbi.nlm.nih.gov/pubmed/21073054
11. 30 years: *The Mectizan Donation Program*, Merck & Co., 2009, https://Merck.com/about/featured-stories/mecizan.html
12. Mae Azango, *The Costs for Girls: Why I Welcome Leaders' Decisions*, Front Page Africa, March 30, 2012, http://pulitzercenter. org/reporting/costs-girls-why-i-welcome-leaders-decisions
13. Daniele Selby, *FMG Becomes Legal Again in Liberia as Ban Expires*, Global Citizen, January 30,1919, https://www.globalcitizen.org /en/content/liberia-fgm-ban-legal/
14. Azango, The Cost for Girls, Why I Welcome Leaders' Decisions
15. Colonel John H. Thomson, EN, *The Liberian Coup D'etat It's Impact on Economic and Security Assistance*, US Army War College, 30 March, 1988,

http://www.dtic.mil/dtic/tr/fulltext/u2/a195745.pdf, 16.

16. Thomson, Liberian Coup D'etat, 20.
17. Ibid., 34.
18. Ibid., 45.
19. Gregory Jaynes, *Liberia's Young Sergeant Still Learning How to Rule*, The New York Times, January 20, 1981, www.nytimes.com/ 1981/01/20/world/liberia-s-young-sereant-still-learning-how-to-rule.html
20. Perry Tinklenberg, *The Indigenization Principle in the Christian Reformed Church*, Calvin College Library, 1981, p 64, 70.
21. John P Cunha, DO FACOEP, Medical Director, *Aralen Side Effects, Aralen Consumer Information*, February 13, 2017, www.rxlist.com/aralen-side-effects-drug-center.htm#overview
22. Melissa Conrad Stoppler, MD, *Scabies*, April 27, 2017, https://www.medicinenet.com/scabies/article.htm#scabies_facts
23. Abba Karnga, *Bassa Proverbs for Preaching and Teaching*, 1.6.1 (a), Asempa Publishers, Christian Council of Ghana, Box 919 Accra, 1996, www.liberianforum.com/docs/bassaintro.rtf
24. Arnold Lieber, MD, *Postpartum Depression (PPD)*, Psycom, Feb 14, 2018, https://www.psycom.net/depression.central.post-partum.html
25. "K" attributed to George Keith (1787) or R. Keen (1787), tune adeste fideles, *How Firm a Foundation*, Great Hymns of the Faith, 1968 by Singspiration, Inc, Zondervan Publishing House, p 268.
26. John E. Pike, Military, November 7, 2011, Liberia – *Election and Coup Attempt* – 1985, https://www.globalsecurity.org/military/ world/war/liberia-1985.htm
27. Earth Networks, *3 Things You Should Know About Indirect Lightning Strikes*, July 13, 2017, https://www.earthnetworkscom/ blog/indirect-lightning-strikes/
28. Karnga, Bassa Proverbs for Preaching and Teaching, 1.6.6 (a).
29. *Ebola Virus Disease*, World Health Organization, 12 February, 2018, www.who.int/news-room/fact-sheets/detail/ebola-virus-disease
30. Karnga, Bassa Proverbs for Preaching and Teaching, 1.6.16 (a).
31. Ibid., 1.6.1 (b).
32. Charles Patrick Davis, MD, PhD, *Ciguatera Fish Poisoning (Ciguatera Toxin)*, https://www.emedicinehealth.com/ wilderness_ciguatera_toxin/article_em.htm
33. Karnga, Bassa Proverbs for Preaching and Teaching, 1.6.3 (b).
34. Ibid., 1.6.3 (a).
35. Filio Marineli, Gregory Tsoucala, and George Androutsos, *Mary Mallon and the History of Typhoid Fever*, Annals of Gastroenterology: Quarterly Publication of the Hellenic Society of Gastroenterology, Nov. 19, 2012, https://www.ncbi.nlm.nih.gov/pmc/articles/PMC3959940/
36. Sean MacFate, *Building Better Armies: An Insider's Account of Liberia*, Strategic

Studies Institute and US Army War College Press, November 2013, https://ssi.armywarcollege.edu/pdffiles/pub1181.pdf, 31.

37. Douglas Farah, An 'Axis' Connected to Gaddafi, The Washington Post, , November 2, 2001, http://www.washingtonpost. com/archive/politics/ 2001/11/02/an-axis-connected-Gaddafi/a7580f63-b23e-4a66-869b-0ea7a5973282/?noredirect=on&utm_term=.4b1398707886
38. Dr. Fred van der Kraaij, *President Charles Ghankay Taylor,* www.liberiapastandpresent.org/charles_taylor.htm
39. Argus Leader, Sioux Falls, SD, November 6, 1992.
40. Liberia – *First Civil War – 1989-1996,* https://www.globalsecurity.org/military/world/war/Liberia-1989.htm
41. *American Missionary, Wife Slain in Liberian Fighting,* March 29, 1990, https://www.washington post.com/archive/politics/1990/03/29/American-missionary-wife-slain-in-liberian-fighting/06d9c0ca-d101-4ed7-900d-502793090e1f/?utm_term=.55efe7fab020
42. Complied by Miriam Gautier, *In the Hollow of His Hand, the Life and Letters of Tom Jackson,* theaqilareport.com/wp-content/ uploads/2014/10/life-letters-of-Tom-Jackson-small-file.pdf, 4.
43. *Liberia: Flight from Terror,* Africa Watch Report, May 1990, Human Rights Watch, https://www.hrw.org/reports/1009/liberia2/
44. David A. Shank, An Approach to Understanding 'Mission' to 'Independent Christianity'.
45. *United Nations Mission in Liberia, UNMIL Background,* https://unmil.unmissions.org/background
46. CNN Library, *Charles Taylor Fast Facts,* https://www.cnn.com/ 2013/04/26/world/africa/charles-taylor-fast-facts/index.html, (December 27, 2017).
47. *Human Right Watch, Sierra Leone: 50-Year Sentence for Charles Taylor,* https://www.hrw.org/news/2012/05/30/sierra-leone-50-year-sentence-charles-taylor, (May30, 2012).
48. *World Bank, Liberia Country Program Evaluation 2004-2011: Evaluation of the World Bank Group Program, World Bank Publication,* Inweb90.worldbank.org/oed/oeddoclib.nsf/ 24cc3bb1f94ae11c85256808006a0046/191c8de3458e6c3285257aa3006e5fa6/$FILE/Liberia_cpe.pdf, page 7, (February 1, 2013).
49. *United Nations Mission in Liberia, Mission Brief,* https://www.slideshare.net/mobile/datacenters/unmil-mission-brief, slides 51-52.
50. John G. Innis, *By the Goodness of God,* Autobiography of John G. Innis, Abingdon Press, books.google.com, page 124.

APPENDIX A

It's just for Thank You (Oh mohn zuo-je)
Rev. Dr. Abba Grogro Karnga
Unpublished Message at the 150th Year Celebration of the CRC in North America", 6-7-07

The primitive cultural condition of the indigenous people in which the pioneer missionaries met them, looked very savage and barbaric. They thought that to civilize the barbarous before Christianizing them, was the priority. Before the new civilization of the missionaries could be effective, every new convert must deny and reject their cultural identity. [If they did not, they] were rejected and judgment was passed on them as "unbelievers, pagans or nominal Christians."

In the 1950's some of the National Christian leaders with the missionary-planted Church felt the call of God to take the risk and cater to their brothers and sisters being stopped from the membership of the Church. A very few of them took the risk and became break-away independent Churches of the missionary Churches for the indigenous people. Yet, the decision made by the indigenous church leaders was frowned upon and rejected by their former missionaries with the following judgments to wit:

1. The Mid-Liberian Baptist church in 1981, "terminated mission efforts in Bassaland, saying that they had given the Bassa people over to satan for [a] time."
2. The Sudan Interior Mission, commonly known as ELWA, in 1985, "gave their TEE program to the Bassa leaders, saying that they may as well let them have the program because they were not serious about Church."
3. The Southern Baptist Church in 1989, "Increased their ministry in Bassaland working exclusively with Southern Baptist Churches, calling "anyone who worked with the small pagan, Bassa Churches, crazy."
4. The Liberian Inland Missions in 1989, described the Bassa Church leaders as "false teachers who twisted the Scriptures."
5. The German Pentecostal healer, Evangelist Eric Cowley, in 1990 said that "he would shake the dust off his feet in Bassaland." (See

African Independent Church: 1991, p. 3 edited by Houtent L. Van, Grand Rapids, Michigan.

Note Well: Cecil Northcott was right when he observed that, "making judgment from little knowledge is perilous." Christianity in Africa: North cott, 1963, p. 16

Although the rejected converts with their break-away Church leaders had no theological knowledge, [they] organized Churches and became leaders and members of their own Churches, being described as "Churches with pagan elements."

When the former missionaries of Liberia felt that the Bassa people had frustrated them because they refused to be deculturated, they were "given over to Satan". Moreover, "calling anyone who worked with the Bassa pagan Churches, crazy." Such a pronouncement put great fear in the leaders of the Bassa Churches, and placed their hope in despair, because the indigenous Church leaders have had a strong belief that "the white man is next to God." But missionaries of the CRWM disproved that kind of a belief, and they encouraged us.

...The missionaries of the Christian Reformed World Missions emulated the Lord Jesus and desired God's best for the condemned Churches, and prayed for God's blessings upon the worried and fearful Bassa Churches. Indeed, we were blessed by God to see a group of White American Missionaries, coming down to the level of the already rejected Black Church leaders, and to truly call us their Christian brothers and sisters, co-workers in Christ, and partners in progress.

The former missionaries' strategy to exclude the Bassa Church leaders from the Christian ministry failed. It was killed by the Christian love of another group of missionaries. We are very happy to know that God did not exclude those who truly believed and are saved by grace through faith. We are very glad to know also that God's ways are not men's ways, neither are His thoughts men's thoughts (Isaiah 55:8).

...The theological impact made on the Bassa churches by the CRWM missionaries is an example of God wanting nothing from mankind. Their working relationship with the sixty independent indigenous Church denominations was very cordial and sincere. It was demonstrated by Christian love. Each of the 60 independent denominations has the average of 25 local Churches or congregations, and each local Church has the average of 100 baptized members. In other words, the average of 25 local

Churches for each of the 60 denominations is equal to 1,500 local...members, named as nominal Christians groping for light in the dark world of Satan.

...We greatly appreciate the successful ten years of theological impact you have made on our Christian lives, and on the little knowledge that we have had of the Christian Bible, we believe it to be like "The First Touch" upon our "zero knowledge" of the gospel and of the Christian Education as a whole. Of course, our forefathers knew about the God Almighty, that He was not their peer so as to talk to Him, but worshipped Him through their ancestors. Such a worship became a tradition from generation to generation with the belief that our ancestors are mediators between us and God the Almighty, not knowing that Jesus is the only mediator between God and man.

Appendix B

The Indigenization Principle in the Christian Reformed Church
Perry Tinklenberg, Calvin Seminary,
December 3, 1981
Major Research Paper Prize
Calvin College Library

Pages 42-44

The program in Liberia began as a response to a letter from a Liberian pastor requesting aid for his church. Rev. Peter Kyne became acquainted with the CRC through the Back to God Hour which was broadcast from the Sudan Interior Mission's radio station ELWA (Eternal Love Winning Africa) in Monrovia, Liberia. Apparently impressed with the Back to God Hour, Rev. Kyne wrote to them requesting aid for his church. The Back to God Hour referred the letter to Christian Reformed World Missions (CRWM). The CRWM then asked Peter Ipema, a CRWM missionary on loan to the Islam in Africa program, who was stationed in Liberia, to contact Rev. Kyne and study his request for aid. Ipema saw a need that should be pursued and set up a meeting between Rev. Kyne and Dr. Eugene Rubingh (Executive Secretary of CRWM).

Dr. Rubingh in turn asked Larry and Ann, a Christian Reformed couple serving as volunteers with the Christian Service Corps in Liberia, to meet with Peter Kyne and himself in May 1973. As a result of this and subsequent meetings, a survey was taken assessing the need for mission work in Liberia and reported to CRWM by December 1974. The following are some key points from the survey. (Larry Vanderaa, Challenge in Africa, unpublished report to CRWM, January 1975)

1. Focus on the Bassa people.
2. The Bassa have a unique phenomenon of many independent churches functioning in their society.
3. Edward Pentecost, Reaching the Unreached, quotes a MARC survey listing the Bassa as an unreached people.
4. 60% are members in embryonic independent churches.
5. 2-3% are active committed Christians
6. 27% are totally unchurched
7. The need for teaching is great.

a. Recommends Bassa Bible School.
b. External conditions necessitate an extension school.
c. Linguistics and translation and literacy are needed.

8. Two doors.
   a. CRCL – foreign backing for independent churches.
   b. CRCL – independent church

In 1975 [the CRC] Synod adopted the Liberian field as a new area of outreach under the following grounds:

1. The unique nature of the time in Liberia. The gospel was confined to the Americo-Liberians (10% of the population). The indigenous people are undergoing a cultural change, so now is the time to challenge them with the gospel.
2. There is a receptivity to the gospel. Embryonic churches are springing up.
3. We could have a distinct approach. Current mission work among the Bassa is conducted in English.
4. Proximity to Nigeria. Allow for the possible use of staff and resources.

The strategy for the mission was uncertain at this time, yet it seemed to be leaning toward a church planting program along the order of the work in Nigeria. However, this emphasis changed when Larry Vanderaa came in contact with Abba Karnga and the Christian Education Foundation of Liberia (CEFL), a visionary, committed group of Bassa Church leaders dedicated to the evangelization and education of their tribe. The CEFL was already in the process of developing a Christian High School and a college and they were planning to eventually establish a program for the training of Church leaders. The CEFL also confirmed Vanderaa's conviction that the independent churches were to be taken seriously. In 1979 Synod responded to this contact between Vanderaa and the CEFL by authorizing the development of a well-rounded program of witness and education to the untrained leaders and laity of the Bassa Churches. (Acts of Synod. 1979, p. 202)

The phenomenon of the independent churches, the contact with the CEFL and the vision of Larry Vanderaa characterize the work in Bassa County today. The Christian Reformed Mission is developing Christian

Extension Ministries (CEM) for the CEFL. Extension classes are being taught in the areas of Bible and theology, health and nutrition. Within the next two years classes will be developed in literacy, community development and agriculture and thus provide a well integrated program functioning under the direction and vision of the Bassa leaders through the CEFL. The CEFL body functions as a Board of Directors of which the Christian Reformed Mission in Liberia (CRML) is a member. In addition to their participation on the Board as members of the CEFL, the CRML serves as faculty with Liberian nationals of the Christian Extension Ministries. As faculty personnel the CRML staff have been given freedom by the CEFL to develop both the program and the curriculum within the program of CEM. The CRML also offers assistance and advice to the CEFL in their vision to develop Liberia Christian High School and Liberia Christian College, which in spite of their small enrollment are rapidly becoming quality Christian Institutions.

Page 52-57

...The program among the Bassa emphasizes teaching and it also emphasizes the utmost respect for the Bassa community and culture...

There are an estimated 400-500 indigenous churches in Bassaland representing many different denominations. (Christian Reformed Mission in Liberia, Mandate and field Strategy, 1981, p. 12) These groups range from "Church" to "non-Church". In other words some of these groups are Christian and some are not. In general, these churches are characterized as schismatic, syncretistic or independent churches. Admittedly these adjectives convey a negative overtone and so we apologize to many of these churches who should be called Christian and nothing less.

...These churches came into existence through a variety of means. It appears to this outsider that many churches were started early in the contact between the Americo-Liberians [A-L] and the native Liberians that was opened up by the building of roads into the interior of Liberia after WWII. Some of the new churches were imposed on the nationals as a means of displaying civilization. Others were started by the natives for basically the same reason (although not imposed upon them); they saw churches as a distinct element from the A-L culture which could easily be adopted. Still other churches were started as genuine segments of the Body of Christ through A-L outreach.

Although neither theory has been sufficiently tested in Liberia, it also appears that churches were started through the ministry of prophet Harris and through the reaction to oppression as described by Shank. Furthermore, at the same time as the development of the A-L churches, the Harrist churches and the "liberation" churches there was the development of mission churches. These four factors seem to have had the most significant influence in the development of Bassa churches. It is from this nucleus that other churches started to evolve. To get a better feeling for this whole phenomenon let us discuss some common elements that are found in many of these churches.

...Probably the most controversial both in its expression within the churches and in the eyes of western observers... is the area of prophecy. Many of the Bassa churches contain element of prophetic expression. This expression ranges from various forms of use to abuse...[This] is a verbatim of my Field Journal recording an experience that I witnessed in Liberia.

Friday night, June 12 [1981], Daniel Garsuah asked me to go to a prayer meeting with him. A family down the road had lost a child and some people were getting together to pray with the family. This sounded like an interesting experience for me so I told him I would go. I had been impressed with Daniel just a few days before when Kathy and I were at Josephine's house expressing our sympathy to her son-in-law Daniel over the sudden death of his son, Junior. While we were there talking to Daniel, Daniel G. came over and said his "never minds" and then he started to talk about Job and the suffering that he went through and how he had lost his children, too. He was encouraging Daniel to take heart and trust the Lord in this whole matter, so we should not feel bad over the death of Junior. We should trust that it was his appointed time to die so he "went back". So as a result of this encounter at Josephine's I was starting to wonder where Daniel G was at and he seemed to have a genuine commitment to the Lord.

Anyway, back to Friday night. A boy child of the old man had died. The report was that he died of smallpox, although malaria is more probable. There were several other children there who were sick as well and I began to wonder if the baby didn't die of smallpox or cholera as they said Daniel's baby died of. There were so many sick children at that meeting that I was frightened. It was very clear that some of them were on the verge of death. There were mothers trying to get the children to nurse and one baby in particular could not hold his head up anymore. I wanted to get the car and run the whole lot to the hospital, and I might have if I hadn't felt it was already too late.

The people said that there was an evil spirit there and he was making all of the children sick and so they wanted to have this prayer service. The agenda was fourfold: (1) Pray for the old man and his wife in their time of sorrow so they might be comforted. (2) Pray for the sick children so they might be healed. (3) Pray for the Holy Spirit so they could grow in their faith and so they could discern if there was an evil spirit present. (4) Pray over the water to purify it and then bathe the children in the water.

About 30 people met on the open porch of the home of the old man. There were chairs lined around the room. At one end of the room there was a small table with three chairs behind it. I was asked to take the one on the left as we faced the people. The center one was for Daniel and the remaining one for the old man. There were two candles, some incense sticks and a pail of water on the table in front of me. Then the service was ready to begin. The people had started to fill the room and they were sitting on the chairs and on the floor.

The service started with singing. The people sang several songs and each one seemed to be building in tempo. As the singing progressed some of the women got up and started to dance and soon nearly all the women were dancing to the beat of the songs they were singing. After a few songs with everyone dancing they made a few announcements that were followed by a time of prayer…

…A mother brought a sick child forward (the one I expected to die any second). Daniel held the child, looked at the child, said a prayer and gave him back to his mother. Then the mother blew in each ear, each nostril and the mouth. After she finished this Daniel took a candle off the pail and touched the tip of each index finger to the flame. Then Daniel took the candle and held it over each child, said a prayer and went back to the first child. He laid his hands on the child and prayed as the people sang a song.

The prayer service was followed by the first scripture lesson…The second lesson was a sermon proper which was a topical discussion on Jesus Christ as the only way to the Father. The basic thrust of Daniel's message was that the only way to the Father the God of Abraham and the God of Elijah (PT note: Elijah is a figure of some importance to the Bassa

Churches.) is through Jesus Christ His Son who came to die. We are separated from God and Jesus wants to bring us back into fellowship with Him. One curious thing is that the restored fellowship was a coming together again through Jesus Christ in two ways. First, Jesus is a bridge over our sin and second, Jesus is a tunnel that busts through the evil spirits and the evil realm. The whole coming together with God is a very violent action-packed thing. Through Jesus Christ we bust through the evil realm and are then united with the Father, the God of Abraham and Elijah. There didn't seem to be any end in sight. I went home.

The next morning, I asked Daniel about the prior evening. He said:

1. He had to prophesy to get the evil out.
2. There was an evil spirit under the house.
   -one woman had learned how to control it
   -she kept it in a small jar and used it as medicine.
3. The spirit was used against one woman and her baby died.
4. The spirit was used against another woman and she was kept barren.
5. As an indirect result of the spirit being loosed several other children were sick and dying.
6. Through prophecy he learned where the jar was and he had the people get it. They took it into the bush and burned it.

They returned to the town and prayed over the babies and the water was sprinkled all over the house and the babies to drive the evil out. I was still trying to feel Daniel out on this whole matter and I asked him how he was able to prophesy. He said God had given him the gift (my June 16 entry is the "Call of Daniel G".) I asked him how he could discern the evil spirits and how he could drive them out. He replied that through prayer and the fullness of the Spirit of God he could discern the evil and then cast the evil out in Jesus' name because Jesus had the most power...When the evil spirits are told to leave in Jesus' name they don't have any choice; they have to leave. "So, then you cast the spirits out in Jesus' name?"

"Of course, how else can you do it? I said He had the power."

For a change of pace I asked Daniel what they should do with the sick people and he said they should be taken to the hospital bit for the people in the bush it was not always possible to go to the hospital so those who are Christians pray to God and if He will bless them then their children will get well. I also asked if this type of prophecy was only found in his church. He said, No, they do it in all of Liberia. You can find it in different-different [sic., Liberian English] denominations." I then asked him if this prophecy was only found in the church. He said that all the true prophecy was found in connection with some church because God used the prophecy to make His church grow, but most of the time he uses visions and dreams and not prophets.

This account gives us some exposure to the "prophecy" found within the Bassa church. I cannot testify to the accuracy of the supernatural utterance or knowledge that Daniel had that Friday night, but I do know that he proclaimed God's word as a faithful prophet. His theology was correct for the most part and he presented Jesus Christ as the only way to God the Father and Creator. I can also testify to seeing those same sick children the next day and noticing recovery instead of death. The children were not cured immediately but in the span of no more than three days they were as healthy as could be. It seems to me that the only fitting response is to Praise the Lord!

However not all prophecy sessions were of this nature nor is the outcome always so pleasant. There are many so-called prophets who hold meetings called Tarry worship. In these services the prophet leads a service for a fee of about $10.00. The nature of the service depends on the cause of need for the prophet's services. The prophets in these services also prophesy and heal in the name of the Holy Spirit when actually "they have modified the witch doctors' acts and incorporated them into a form of church service and are using church instruments, church songs and even the Bible for their familiar spirit. They attract many followers who will give them more money, more praises, and more women. How do we discern the difference between the true and false? Did I observe a session where the gospel was proclaimed as I thought or was Daniel conducting a Tarry worship and thereby fooling me? The solution is to recognize that these prophets are not to be taken lightly nor are the prophetic meetings. Christ is presented in these meetings either purely or out of selfish motive; nonetheless Christ is proclaimed. Second, we should realize that these people are open to discussion and teaching from or on the Bible which must be seen as a work of the Holy Spirit and we must see to it that these people are taught the true Biblical doctrine out of love for them and not for self. Third, I think we have to take these people at face value and affirm that the

Christ awareness is something upon which we must build. We leave the judgment to God and to strong committed Bassa leaders who will be able to discern if the commitment behind the talk is true or not, whereas an outsider may not be able to see through the charade.
Page 61-63:

...The Bassa like most Africans believe in a creator God. At one time He was very close but now He has withdrawn Himself from man. Most of the people I questioned on God's withdrawal from man say that God withdrew because man did things that offended God. Two of the most common myths that I heard were: first, the story that God was walking around in heaven and the man's wife starting a fire to make some food for her husband and the smoke from the fire got in God's eyes and so He became vexed and decided that He would go live someplace far from man. Second, there is the story that God was walking over to see what man was doing but the woman hit Him in the stomach with her mortar as she was beating the rice and so God broke the link that was keeping earth and heaven close and He went off by Himself. It is interesting that in both accounts the woman is simply going about her daily task, but God happens to get in the way, He becomes offended and leaves. Therefore salvation or restoration is seen as trying to win God's favor, doing things that please him and things that will make God want to be close to man again. Because God is distant, it is hard to communicate with him. The Bassa by and large believe that God speaks to them through dreams and visions (as do many Africans). I asked my class the following question on one of the exams: "What is the main way God speaks to us today?"

a. through our pastors
b. through dreams and visions
c. through the Bible
d. through creation

I was not concerned with a right or wrong answer; I simply wanted to get a feel for where the class was at. Over 90% answered "B". The tape they were listening to clearly stressed "C"...Furthermore, nearly every pastor or leader in my class said that they received their call to be a church leader through a vision.

Larry ..., a colleague in Liberia, has a theory that there are at least six things that missions tend to assume as true that the Bassa do not assume.

The first column is Vanderaa's list and the second are some alternatives that I suggest as functionaries in the Bassa culture:

1. Sin offends God
2. God cares about man
3. Salvation is for the individual
4. Jesus = salvation
5. Everyone wants to be a friend of God
6. Assume man is born in sin

1. Sin destroys the community or brings shame upon the community
2. God is distant, He has pulled away from man
3. Salvation is corporate. Important issue is not the relationship with the Messiah, it is the relationship in the Messianic community
4. Salvation (traditionally) = status quo of community, harmony
5. Those who isolate themselves have no friends
6. Man is basically good, subtle, prideful

If indeed these items prove to be true after further testing in the Bassa culture, they could change some of the ways the gospel is presented in Liberia. Most emphasis will have to be put on the community, a case will have to be carefully worked out that presents God as one who does care about his creation, his creatures and especially man. The gospel itself will not need to undergo any changes or compromise but the initial emphasis may have to be a different "hook" than the gospel has traditionally been hung on in Bassaland. This calls for more cultural sensitivity and for the input of Bassa Christians and Bassa Church leaders.

APPENDIX C

Recipes for Liberian Dishes
Kathy Tinklenberg

*Collard Greens

3 bunches Collard greens
Carefully inspect leaves, discard spoiled portions,
Wash a couple times. Chop in food processor.
Fry in 1/3 cup oil, stirring occasionally.
Add 1 cup water to steam.

Chop 1 Onion. Add to "Soup"
Fry soup, stirring frequently, till greens cook down and are tender.
Add more water as necessary, so it doesn't burn.

Meanwhile:
2 lbs white fleshed fish - de-bone and dice
Fry in oil with salt.
Add to "Soup" in Crock Pot. Serve over Prepared Rice.

Honey-Baked Chicken

Prepared for our last dinner with missionaries when we left Liberia after the first year.

Preheat oven to 350.
Arrange 1 3-lb. Fryer, cut up in shallow baking pan, skin-side up.
Combine: 1/3 cup butter, 1/3 cup honey, 2 TB prepared mustard,
1 tsp salt, 1 tsp curry powder and
Pour over chicken, bake 1 ¼ hour, basting every 15 minutes
Bake until chicken is tender and nicely browned.
Serve with rice.

* Recipes were used for church dinner preparation
at our supporting churches and serve 50 people.
The "soups" or sauces are to be served over white or brown rice. Provide

optional hot pepper.

Mango (Peach) Cream Pie - Perry's Grandma Hattie's recipe

Unbaked 9" pie crust
3 cups fresh slices mango, place on pie crust
Mix together and spoon over peaches:
1 cup sugar
1/3 cup flour, more if juicy
1/8 teas. Salt
2 beaten eggs
½ cup sour cream

Topping – Mix together with a fork:
½ cup sugar
½ cup flour
¼ cup butter
Sprinkle evenly over pie, Bake 350° F – 1 hour

***Okra Soup -** A favorite of my children

3 bags frozen sliced Okra – brown single layers in vegetable oil
Be patient, it takes time for it to get brown, but it is necessary or it will be slimy.
Use plenty of oil, and the pan needs to be scraped clean between panfuls.

Brown ground Beef in a separate pan.
Add chopped onion to taste. May add a little salt, but No black Pepper

Combine:
Browned Okra, Ground Beef, 2-pint size traditional Spaghetti Sauce.
Place in Crock Pot to keep warm. Serve over prepared rice.

***Palm Butter**

ice 2 Chicken Breasts (for each 28 oz. can of palm nut pulp)
Dice 1 large onion, cook with chicken
Cook in 1/2 cup water for about 10 minutes.
Salt to season, No black Pepper

Stir together Palm Butter and 1 Can of Hot Water for each can of Palm Butter. Add chicken, allow to simmer uncovered for 40-50 minutes, stir occasionally.

Place in Crock Pot to keep hot. Serve over Prepared Rice.

*Pumpkin Soup

2 lbs white fleshed fish, de-bone and cube
Dice 1 onion. Sauté, add fish, cook until just until soft.
Fry in light oil, with salt. No Black Pepper.
Remove fish and onion from pan.

Meanwhile:
Peel and dice orange fleshed butternut squash
(called pumpkin in Liberia).
Fry "pumpkin" in 1/3 cup oil slightly browning it
Add 1 cup water to simmer.
Cover and stir frequently, squash is cooked down to applesauce consistency.
It will be necessary to add more water and some oil as it cooks.

Add fish to "Soup", stir gently
Place in Crock Pot, serve over Prepared Rice.

*Sweet Potato Greens

(Use Spinach in the U.S.)
It is necessary to prepare or "burn" the Palm Oil outside, it'll smoke a lot.
Heat raw Palm Oil in a heavy kettle, let it smoke. Keep checking oil with a metal spoon, until the oil has burned clear. Remove from heat, set aside.

This dish requires two types of meat: Beef and Chicken.
Slice meat in thin stripes and cube. Fry lightly in prepared palm oil with salt. Add 1 onion - chopped when meat is nearly cooked.

4 bunches fresh spinach leaves - Carefully inspect discard unhealthy portions.
Wash a couple times, then Chop in food processor
Fry in prepared Palm oil. Then add 1 cup water to steam
"Fry", stirring frequently, till greens cook down and are tender
Add more water as necessary, so it doesn't burn.
Keep "Soup" warm in Crock Pot, serve over Prepared Rice

Appendix D

Historical Roots of the Bassa People
Part 1, Chapter 1, Emphasis of Bassa Proverbs
Bassa Proverbs for Preaching and Teaching
Rev. Dr. Abba Karnga
Asempa Publishers, 1996, Online: Liberianforum.com

The story of the roots of the Bassa is preserved in their ancient proverbs. One of those proverbs says: *Sodoa soa nyon dabain die kon.* (on the old mat is woven the new.) This proverb was passed on to me by Elder Geah-Kwui Deputy Sarwah. The Elder looked back to the time of the ancestors and narrated a legend from which the "Old Mat" proverb was taken. The word for "legend" in the Bassa language is "dyuaun-kadyu".

No Bassa Elder would speak a sentence or two without citing a proverb. In this respect, Elder Sarwah is eminent among the Bassa Elders. While Elder Sarwah was searching for information about the origin of the "Old Mat" proverb, he discovered that the "old Mat" was a seat of authority used solely by the Bassa king. Nobody could weave its replacement or one like it, unless he wove it on the "Old Mat". Traditionally, it is "on the old mat that we weave the new."

The roots of the Bassa were traced by knowing the origin of the "Old Mat" proverb. The Bassa people, according to the legend, were led by their King on the Lone "Old Mat" when they migrated from Ethiopia in the 16th century to this part of West Africa, the then "Grain Pepper Coast," known as "Liberia" today. The story continues that the people escaped from the destruction of the 16th century war which broke out between Ethiopia and Egypt. The migration was led by their King, called Suah Vehnehn, a name meaning "Great ape." Later, Suahn Vehnehn was changed to Fannah Boeh Behnehn, meaning "great man of wisdom."

The King and his people were identified as people from the direction of the sunrise. They travelled from Abyssinia (Ethiopia) and passed through six countries: Sudan, Chad, Cameroon, Slave Coast (Nigeria), Gold Coast (Ghana), and the Ivory Coast (Cote d'Ivorire) before reaching the Grain Pepper Coast. Finally, their "Hook of Leadership" (a "Hook of Leadership" is a supernatural guide for a traditional leader) got stuck in the soil of the Grain Pepper Coast, and suddenly, they stopped by the decree of the King. The "Old Mat" was spread on the ground and the King ordered each family to build a home.

This Bassa legend based on the "Old Mat" proverb is worth accepting to be converted into a written history of the Bassa people of Liberia who have had no previous written history up to this time. That legend is based on factual events and real people can be authenticated and substantiated by the following three pieces of circumstantial evidence.

1. *Traditional Name:* The original name of the Bassa people was Gor-Nyon Be, meaning, people of the East or people from the direction of the sunrise. The country of Ethiopia mentioned in the legend, is also located in the East.

2. *Historical Evidence:* The traditional legend narrates the event of the war which broke out between Ethiopia and Egypt in the 16th century. World history confirms that in the 16th century, Ethiopia and Egypt fought, and Ethiopia was conquered by Egypt. That was the cause of the migration of the Ethiopian Bassa to the Grain Pepper Coast. The Book, Liberia – History of the First African Republic, 1970, by Dr. C. Abayomi Cassell, confirms the 16th century migration of the Bassa from the East, including the Grebo, Bassa, Kru and the Krahn. Cassell concluded that "Those who settled in the Montserrado and Bassa areas became the Bassa Tribe and that a portion of them formed what is known today as the Krahn Tribe. Those who reached the Cavalla River eventually became the Grebo Tribe."

3. *Religious Evidence:* The people of Ethiopia are a very religious people. So also are the Bassa people of Liberia; they are involved in Christian activities more than any other ethnic group in Liberia. Grand Bassa, their Country, is rightly described as "Church County."

In further conversations with Rev. Dr. Abba Karnga, he explained that tracing their history from Ethiopia gave reason to believe there was a real chance the Ethiopian Eunuch was from the original Bassa ancestors. In Acts 8:26-40, he was in a chariot, converted by Philip and baptized along the side of the road. One fact that draws this conclusion is that the Bassa people love to serve others as the Ethiopian Eunuch himself was doing being in the service of Candace, queen of the Ethiopians.

Through interviews with Bassa elders, Dr. David Shank learned that the Bassa actually traced their history back to Noah's ark. The verbal historians included the explanation that for some reason God was so angry with people that he directed Noah to build an ark so he could destroy most of them. Ever since that time God's anger has been against people.

What a thrill it was for us to go to Liberia and tell the Bassa that God's anger was appeased through the sacrificial death of his unblemished and sinless Son. No longer is the human race outcast from God. There is no need to make the sacrifices under the trees or bury young girls alive with the ancestors. God's perfect sacrifice has put an end to all that and if we believe in Him and acknowledge that He has saved us from our sins in this way, God will forgive us and prepare a place in eternity for us.

Appendix E

Our Humble Role in Liberia
Andrew Kyvenhoven
February 7, 1983
Article from The Banner (CRC denominational magazine)

During my only Sunday in Liberia I sat in church for five hours and enjoyed every minute of it. I was in Buchanan, an old town on the ocean. In the morning I worshiped at the Open Bible Church. There were two preachers; both were loud and evangelical. The congregation and its two choirs did some vigorous singing. I conveyed your greetings. The service was conducted in English and in Bassa, the language of the people among whom our mission efforts are concentrated.

Should you ask why I did not attend a Christian Reformed worship service, you would be showing your ignorance. The mandate for our mission in Liberia says: "We shall promote the growth of Independent Churches which presently exist, rather than forming a new denomination in Bassaland." There is no Christian Reformed church in Liberia and we do not intend to establish one.

The Bassa tribe is still predominately pagan. Yet there are about 500 churches divided over 100 denominations. This phenomenon is still being studied by some of our missionaries (ask Larry.... or Perry Tinklenberg). "Having a church" is a respectable thing for any hamlet in Grand Bassa County. Besides, these people have always believed in the unknown God. There are no atheists in Africa. And a church is a way to reach God.

But "having a church" and "being Christian" are not the same. A church is welcomed, but life-shaping power is still wielded by two ancient institutions: witchcraft and the Society. The latter is a name for the secret organization that, through initiation rites, sets its stamp on every member of the clan during his or her most formative years. And the Society sets the rules for funeral feasts, which are more elaborate among the Bassa people than among most other African peoples.

The leaders in these independent churches are Liberians who have been in contact with the Americo-Liberian mission churches. They know the name of Jesus, they have some understanding of the significance of his death, and they preach in African/Pentecostal fashion. Most leaders are illiterate or semiliterate. Their services rely heavily on the performances of the choirs.

And these people can sing! At 2:00 PM on Sunday a large crowd, representing about thirty denominations, came together in the Apostolic Faith Church. This was graduation day for Bible students and midwives who had followed the courses sponsored by our mission. I will never forget the procession of graduates and choir members. In their long robes they shuffled and swayed into the building, repeating in ever stronger chanted responses (in the Bassa language): Come, let us go / This is great joy / For the Lord himself is there.

Eleven men had successfully completed a three-year course in Theological Education by Extension (TEE). And eight women had fulfilled the requirements of the Health Program for Traditional Midwives, a course taught by our Canadian nurse, Margaret….

TEE is a course for church leaders. It is taught by means of cassettes and recorders carried into the bush. Our missionaries aid in the preparation and teaching of these lessons. The lessons are a mere retelling of biblical history.

The service was impressive. The main speech was given by Dr. David …., a son of our church. At present he is a pediatrician in the John F. Kennedy Hospital in Monrovia. His gospel message and his straight-from the shoulder legal application were clear to all.

Dr. David Van Reken made the Word of God concrete for the Bassa.

Van Reken's Seven Rules:

1. The best advertisement for Christ is a healthy family.
2. Don't cheat or steal. Those who steal 5 cents will steal $5.
3. Christians must have all members of their family immunized.
4. Build latrines. People who don't use latrines don't love their neighbors.
5. Whether you bring 3 or 30 children into the world, you are responsible for them. You are Christians!
6. You must not be envious of each other. If one of the clan gets ahead of the rest, you must learn to rejoice.
7. The law of God prevents sickness. In my years of medical practice, I have never found venereal disease among people who honor the seventh commandment.

Contrary to the experience of most African nations, Liberia has never been a colony. The country was a land of liberty for freed slaves who came from the United States and began to settle there 150 years ago. Today Liberia has a population of fewer than 2 million. The Americo-Liberians, descendants of the freed slaves, constitute less than 10 percent. This minority had the political power in Liberia until 1980.**

In 1979 Liberia hosted the Organization for African Unity-a prestigious event it could not afford. A hardtop road was constructed from Roberts Airfield to a brand-new conference center, built in the swamps near Monrovia. Since 1979 this beautiful white elephant has been sitting there. A town of luxurious villas was especially constructed to house the heads of the African states. Today nobody lives in the villas. Neither does anybody know what to do with the Grand Hotel that was erected for the occasion.

In April 1980 Sergeant Samuel Doe and his People's Redemption Party took over. President Tolbert and his ministers were executed on the beach. Today [1983] the country is still under martial law. But according to Lou…, the CRWRC Africa director in Monrovia, no political prisoners are being held.

Appendix F

Michael's Baptism
Worship Service Liturgy and Sermon Notes
May 19, 1985
Soniwiohn Mission Station, Liberia
Rev. Perry Tinklenberg

The Spirit of God has made me:
The breath of the Almighty gives me life. Job 33:4

Call to Worship, Psalm 68: 32-35
Song 366, "Alleluia! Sing to Jesus"
Sentence Prayers
Song 408, *Great is Thy Faithfulness*
Meditation, Acts 2:14-39
Song 419, *Thus Saith the Mercy of the Lord*, 1-3, 5
Form of Baptism of Infants #3
Song, *Jesus Loves Me* – Small Children
Baptism
Song, *Welcome to the Family* – Joe and Mary
Closing Prayer
Doxology

Intro: Celebrate the Ascension & Celebrate the sign and seal of Michael
as a member of the covenant community

In an attempt to lead in this celebration, I would like to share a few thoughts from Peter's Pentecost message and especially highlight the prominent place of the ascension for the Christian Church.
Acts 2:14-41

Peter's Outline (if you will)

I. Introduction vv. 14-16
Scripture lesson from the prophets, "I will pour out my Spirit."

II. Peter preaches Jesus - The sermon proper vv. 22ff
not the Jesus of myth or Jesus the prophet
- A. The Jesus of Nazareth v. 22
  1. An historical person, one who can be dated and placed among men
  2. Accredited by God or witnessed to men by God himself through miracles, wonders and signs
- B. The Jesus who was handed over by God to men who killed him, v 23. - no further explanation, just a two-fold fact. God handed him over via his purpose and you put him to death.
- C. The Jesus God raised from the dead, vv 24-32.
  1. As was prophesied
  2. No resurrection for David. (Messiah figure)
  3. A fact of which the Apostles were witnesses
- D. The Jesus whom God exalted to his right hand, vv 33-36
  1. No ascension for David yet he knew that one of his line would reign supreme
  2. Right hand of God = power base of universe
- E. The Jesus who from his ruling place poured out the promised spirit, whose coming they had seen and heard, v. 33.

Permit me to interject – Jesus has ascended!
  1. We do not have to wait for heaven or for God's kingdom with bare hope. We possess it already in our head – our hope is sure!
  2. We have a constant advocate and intercessor!
  3. Christ daily transfuses us with power to live our new lives and to work sanctification within us.
- F. Peter concludes his sermon – "The spirit is poured out, the prophecy is fulfilled and the bottom line is this: Jesus is both Lord and Christ."
  1. The Jesus you killed is Lord and Christ.
  2. In this statement Peter uses the Greek equivalents for the Hebrew words Yahweh and Messiah.

3. To get the full impact we must place ourselves in the mindset of a Hebrew looking daily for the Messiah, the one to come in Yahweh's name and liberate them. Now, Peter says, his Jesus is both Yahweh and Messiah.

III. The people respond.

A. What do we do? V 37
B. Repent – change your attitude about Jesus and embrace him
C. Be baptized in the name of Jesus (the one they had publicly denounced)
D. Then they would be forgiven, and they too would receive the Holy Spirit and become new people and a part of the new order; and that not an exclusive club. For the promise (or gift), that is to say, the Spirit is open to them and their children and even to the Gentiles – whoever the Lord our God will call.

IV. Today

Baptism is a public testimony of our allegiance to the risen ascended Lord and his community and we take him at his word and call upon him to seal the promise for our children. We know that God does act in baptism and Michael too, is an accepted member of the covenant community and heir to the Kingdom of God through the washing of Jesus' blood.

APPENDIX G

Conference on African Independent Churches
July, 1986
Abidjan, Ivory Coast
Seminar presented by Perry Tinklenberg

I always enjoy taking new visitors to Liberia for a short ride early in their stay, be it parents, mission board members or visiting missionaries. On a typical four-mile spin I like to ask them how many churches and towns we've passed. The answer is usually two of each. Then on the way home I begin to point out the eight churches we've zoomed by and the few little towns they may have missed. Except in the most densely populated Christian areas eight churches in one four mile stretch of road is a striking observation; one that characterizes much of the area in which Christian Reformed World Missions is at work with the Bassa people. One such visitor, known to all of us at this conference, was also struck by the quantity of Bassa churches. In his January 1985 Missiology[1] article, Dr. David Shank recalls counting sixty church buildings in one fifty mile stretch of road, the same road to which I have just referred. It is too bad statistically speaking that we as a mission cannot take credit for the planting of these congregations. However most of them preceded us and they are today classified as African Independent Churches (AICs).

Let me say at this point that we have come to this conference to benefit and learn from all of you and from your efforts at ministry with AICs. But we have been led to understand that "takers only" are not allowed so we will share a description of our efforts with the Bassa AICs and that will constitute the bulk of this presentation. Yet I would like to try to set the context for our efforts by looking briefly at the Bassa church in its general structure and its worship.

In terms of organization the Bassa churches have a hierarchical structure. There is general uniformity on the local level but there are denominational differences on the top level. Locally, every church has a choir which is essential to the worship life of the congregation. The choir is not directly related to the official hierarchy but it does function as a proving ground for future leaders and in any given service the choir leader, who maybe either male or female, may add as much to the worship experience as all the officers combined. Above the choir we have a chain of male dominated officers (there are exceptions on every level) from the church secretary, exhorter, local preacher, assistant pastor, and pastor. Also, on the local level in a standing on many respects equal to the pastor, we find the deacon who is almost always an old man in charge of the church property. In general he is the controlling authority of the area that has given land to the church. He is often one of the founders of the local congregation and he may also be a man of some status in the tribal secret society. The organizational opposite of the deacon is the head missionary. The missionaries of the Bassa church are women whose foremost function is to pray for the church members, especially in cases of physical illness or spiritual malaise. Functionally they do a great deal of pastoral care on the local level. On many nights we see and hear the missionaries called to the church a few hundred yards from our house for the purpose of praying for some special concern.

On the denominational level, all the local congregations are organized into groups or districts. Some churches have district pastors who are responsible for several congregations, others do not. All denominations have the office of elder which is above that of the pastor (or district pastor). Some assign an elder to each congregation but in most cases the elder is the spiritual leader in charge of several congregations or districts. It is usually the elders' responsibility to administer the sacraments. Above the elder we find a mixture of officers; some have district superintendents and bishops, others have district leaders and church boards. But most have one administrative officer and some type of governing board or council of elders.

Even with this elaborate structure, the real functioning authority for the majority of Bassa churches is the pastor. Therefore, the churches tend to be "one man shows" or to depend upon the charismatic drive of one single leader who is sometimes an assigned officer but more often the leaders are self-proclaimed. Let me illustrate. One of my friends, Mondamaa Beegar, is a fiery old gal who started out as a missionary in a small Methodist church. Later, around 1950, after she had witnessed numerous miraculous events, healings, and people dropping out of the tribal society and seeking a church, she had a vision in which she saw herself as the pastor of her small growing church. She shared her vision with her missionary colleagues and friends and was proclaimed pastor against the desire of the District Superintendent. After seeing her function for a time the church unanimously elected her pastor, then her denomination acquiesced and assigned her as pastor of the St. Paul United Methodist Church in Kpor Town, Liberia. In terms of functional authority the life and future of this church rests in her hands and leadership.

Let us now turn our attention to a typical Bassa worship service. We enter the church, either a concrete block building or a mud and stick affair with a thatch roof, from the rear. The choir and congregations are already singing even though there are only seven people present. We take our seat, the women on the left and the men on the right of the center aisle, on benches made of three ten foot pieces of three inch bamboo lashed together. We are trying to remain inconspicuous but our white skin had invited us to join the officers on the platform area in front of the church. We are not only promoted to a place of honor but we are also given wicker chairs. They are one chair short so amid some confusion a young man races out to the town and returns with an additional chair or two.

As we sit behind the low railing separating us from the laity watching the people trickle in, we begin to feel the steady booming of the bass drum and the rat-a-tat-tat of the second drum moving our soul. We begin to clap along with the worshippers and we listen to the choir leader's ballad welcoming the Lord or telling us that God is calling us so we should come. We hear the choir members respond in their appropriate antiphonal response and we the congregation answer repeatedly through the entire song, "The Lord calls us, the Lord calls us". There are about thirty people present now and someone has picked up the gourd shaker and another is keeping the beat with a homemade tambourine. The pastor rises to call us to worship but we already feel that the songs have prepared us and we are worshipping in our hearts. He also makes a few announcements; Elder Zogar will give the first scripture lesson, Teetee the missionary will pray and one of us will give the message.

We sing another song, "There is a good thing in my love". The elder stands at the lectern to read a verse or two from the New Testament in faltering self-taught Bassa. Around us we sense the pride the people feel in having the N.T. in their tongue and in the old man's ability to read. He had a young school boy get him started and now he reads out loud daily in his kitchen or palaver hut slowly improving and sharing his skill with all who would learn from him. The choir breaks into song again and the taut deer hide on the square frame resonates with the steady booming beat of the drum. Today is an exceptional day, there is a guest minstrel present and he leads us in a ballad of god's saving activity from Noah to David. "There is none mightier than He." We cannot remain seated any longer. We and our neighbors spring to our feet and we smile as the old grandmothers dance at the front of the church. We smile still more as we think of their dance before God at the center of the church. The laity face them from one side, we on the platform are opposite them and the deacon and a few men sit opposite the choir completing the circle.

After the song we remain standing for the recitation in unison of Psalm 23 and another song, then the windows and doors are closed and many turn to kneel, the choir sings softly and bedlam breaks out as every man, woman, and child pray out loud at the same time. We are confused and self-conscious but soon we pray too. The choir resumes their chorus and Teetee prays forcefully and loudly. The prayer is frequently punctuated by other acclaiming cries from the congregation. She quiets down and leads us in the Lord's Prayer in unison. The windows are opened and our eyes blink to the flash of light. The steward announces 53 souls present that day. "The Lord makes 54", the Pastor says and 54 is entered into the ledger. The penny collection begins with the women, each one sharing a testimony or praising God as she places her gift at the table in the center of the church. We all take our turn and some pause to make change and move back to their seats. The choir leads us in another song as I step to the pulpit to deliver the message. Our hearts have been prepared in song and prayer and two times during the sermon someone burst into song followed by the choir and the congregation. After the final "Amen" we have a closing song and the parting blessing. In this church, the Mt. Sinai Bethlehem Healing Temple, all the people turn and face the door as Pastor Gaaseen gives the blessing and challenges us to live for Jesus outside the church as well as within.[2]

We had a good experience that day, Gaaseen is a committed leader, he and his wives love Jesus even though they actually know very little about him. Gaaseen has studied with me for four years and we think we are seeing fruits in his ministry. But not all experiences are so happy. We still occasionally get the feeling that someone is playing charades or we find out that the pastor himself is unable to read 10 words of Bassa or worse still that he only attends services one Sunday in six for various reasons. Yet even in those cases the old missionary or someone like her comes to us and says, "God bless you for coming," and she means it with all her precious redeemed heart that hurts deeply for a viable expression of the Church in her town.

Let us now round out the context with a brief comment about normal lifestyle. The Bassa are primarily subsistence farmers using farming practices that have remained unchanged since the early 1800s.[3] Traditional medical practices are also the norm in Bassaland. The entire county only has three hospitals, an ill supplied one belonging to the government and two concession hospitals primarily for company use, with a total of 350 beds for the 300,000 people.[4] Traditional Bassa communities have changed over the years. Early sources mention typical Bassa towns with 20 to 100 or even 200 houses.[5] Yet today a town of 20 houses would be considered quite large. Theories abound re the breakdown of the Bassa towns but no conclusive studies are available.

In summary then, we see that the Bassa people are still firmly grounded in their traditional form and manner, yet they are churched. In fact today as a result 1950 phenomenon we have an estimated 100 denominations and some 500-700 congregations among 300,000 Bassa people. Even within the many churches however, we could only hope to find 60% of the population who would regard themselves as "church members" and perhaps only half of them would be Christians holding to a poorly understood scaffold of the gospel. Many of the church leaders are totally untrained and illiterate. It was the strategy of CRWM to join forces with an organization of the Bassa Church leaders called the Christian Education Foundation of Liberia (CEFL) to develop Christian Extension Ministries (CEM). The ministry of CEM recognizes the independent church as exhibiting or having the potential to exhibit, as the case may be, an indigenous expression of faith and to promote their growth and mission.[6]

A final thing we should note here about the Bassa is that they recognize much of their Biblical inadequacy and are crying out for teaching and for Christian literature that they can use to increase both their reading skills and their understanding of the new life that is embryonic within them.

TARGET GROUPS

Let us now turn to a fuller description of the educational ministry involved. It should seem obvious from the introduction that our first and primary target group is the indigenous Bassa Church. All of our efforts are focused on the Church and it is one criterion in each of our training programs that participants be members of a local church. We believe that the best way for us to communicate to the broader unreached population is to develop, strengthen and motivate the local churches in their witness to their communities. However, this does not excuse any of us from daily modeling the gospel or being prepared to share the news of the Kingdom of God with people we meet.

A more specific target group that has in varying ways taken a primary roll has been the church leaders or officers. The officers by the very nature of their leadership roles are crucial targets for our efforts in developing the independent churches. We are not involved in the selection of leaders, rather we recognize those already in office as the charismatic force within the church. These people are either leading their congregations closer to Christ or farther from Him. They are the crucial focal point for church renewal or reformation. It is our goal that the present level church officers; pastors, elders, deacons, missionaries, et al will take the Word of God more seriously as they relate the impinging Kingdom of God to the present day Bassa life.

I mentioned above that the traditional forms are still the general rule of the day for most Bassa life. In that light we are also involved in the so called development projects. Here too our target group is the existing Bassa Church. We are not involved in development as some naïve helping of our fellow man or humanisticly helping one to help himself. We are concerned about making the signs of the Kingdom appear through the Bassa Church. Against that backdrop (or baggage) we are involved in educational ministries of agriculture, community development, and rural health.

In agriculture our main concentration is toward practicing Christian farmers. It is our goal that these farmers will be challenged to consider and practice improved farming methods so they can (1) grow more food, (2) reflect that we are all stewards of God's creation and concerned about its just use and that these trained farmers will be catalysts for continued change and improvement within their church and their communities.

As regards Community Development, we are concerned with the development of the church in its communal setting and its unique communal witness as the body of Christ. It has been our practice to focus on specific geographical areas and to encourage the churches within a given radius to send representatives to form a joint committee for diagnosing and meeting church and community needs and for the supervision of CEM programs within the region.

In rural health we have two foci. We are exercising our concern for primary health care among the Bassa people through Christian Village Health Workers (VHWs) and Traditional Birth Attendants (TBAs). Again our primary target group is within the Church. The local churches recommend individuals for training as VHWs to demonstrate the healing power of Christ through nutrition, sanitation, prevention and cure. The local church also recommends practicing midwives for TBA training in Christian health care, pre-natal care, and safe and sanitary deliveries.

From this information we have seen that the primary target group of our ministry is the existing Bassa Church. With that Church we focus on the officers and a selection of practicing farmers, practicing midwives and concerned individuals; all of who ideally are "leaders" or respected people in their church and community so they will be good agents for the sake of change. Just for the record, I would like to mention that CEM has a ministry in formal education where applicants are sent for training in Bible, agriculture, health, literacy, etc. We also have a literacy program that has played a supportive role in the efforts of the Bassa people to teach themselves to read and write; we supply reading material through a bookstore and the reprinting of Old Testament scripture portions. Finally, we have people working in Bible translation so that the Bassa people may soon have the whole Bible in their language.

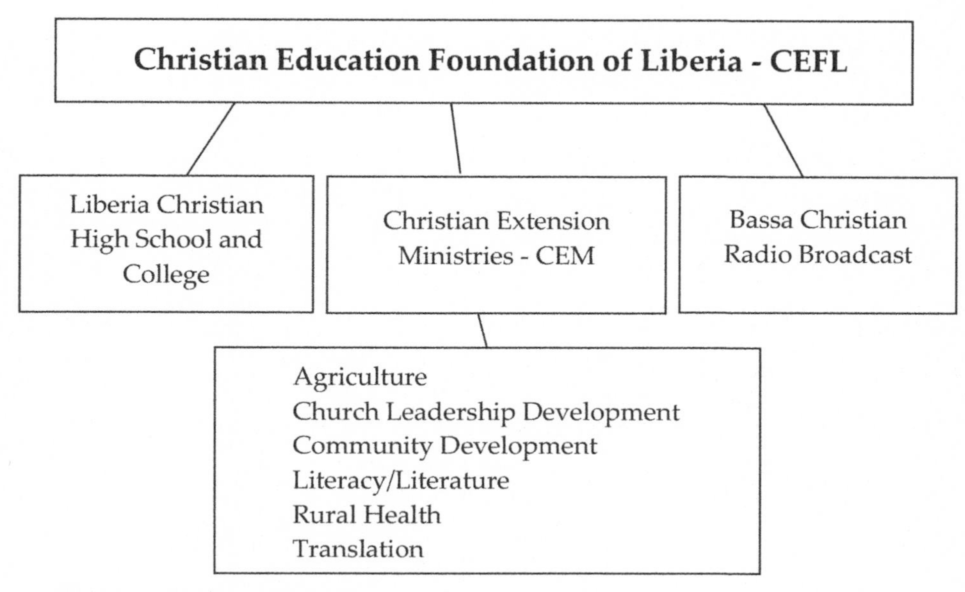

Member Churches of CEFL

1. African Gospel League
2. Bible Healing Church
3. Bassa Ministers Association
4. Christian Reformed Mission in Liberia
5. Liberia Christian Mission (at the time, pending approval)
6. Pentecostal Churches of the Apostolic Faith
7. St. Mark African Methodist Episcopal
8. United Methodist Church – St. John River District
9. World-Wide Mission church of Liberia

Footnotes

1. David Shank, "Mission Relations with the Independent Churches of Africa", Missiology (January 1985) P. 29.

2. P. Tinklenberg, Worship Service at Mt. Sinai Bethlehem Healing Temple, Kardakpubli, Liberia, June 1, 1986

3. cf. Rebecca Medberry, Memoir of William G. Crocker: Late Missionary in West Africa Among the Bassa, Including a history of the Bassa Mission (Boston: Gould, Kendall, and Lincoln, 1848) passim.

4. Abba Karnga, "A Christian's Mandate on Health" address to CHAL Board, Monrovia, Liberia, January 24, 1986. p. 13

5. Medberry Ibid.

6. cf. Appendix A.

Made in the USA
Coppell, TX
30 January 2021